GLOBALIZING MIGRATION REGIMES

Research in Migration and Ethnic Relations Series

Series Editor:
Maykel Verkuyten, ERCOMER
Utrecht University

The Research in Migration and Ethnic Relations series has been at the forefront of research in the field for ten years. The series has built an international reputation for cutting edge theoretical work, for comparative research especially on Europe and for nationally-based studies with broader relevance to international issues. Published in association with the European Research Centre on Migration and Ethnic Relations (ERCOMER), Utrecht University, it draws contributions from the best international scholars in the field, offering an interdisciplinary perspective on some of the key issues of the contemporary world.

Other titles in the series

East to West Migration: Russian Migrants in Western Europe
Helen Kopnina
ISBN 0 7546 4170 8

Migration and its Enemies: Global Capital, Migrant Labour and the Nation-State
Robin Cohen
ISBN 0 7546 4658 0 (Pbk)/0 7546 4657 2 (Hbk)

Migration, Regional Integration and Human Security: The Formation and Maintenance of Transnational Spaces
Edited by Harald Kleinschmidt
ISBN 0 7546 4646 7

**EUROPEAN RESEARCH CENTRE
ON MIGRATION & ETHNIC RELATIONS**

Globalizing Migration Regimes
New Challenges to Transnational Cooperation

Edited by

KRISTOF TAMAS and JOAKIM PALME
Institute for Futures Studies, Sweden

CABRINI COLLEGE LIBRARY
610 KING OF PRUSSIA ROAD
RADNOR, PA 19087

ASHGATE

JV
6011
.S76
2006

63702875

© Kristof Tamas and Joakim Palme 2006

All rights reserved. No part of this publication may be reproduced, stored in a retrieval system, or transmitted in any form or by any means, electronic, mechanical, photocopying, recording or otherwise without the prior permission of the publisher.

Kristof Tamas and Joakim Palme have asserted their right under the Copyright, Designs and Patents Act, 1988, to be identified as the editors of this work.

Published by
Ashgate Publishing Limited
Gower House
Croft Road
Aldershot
Hants GU11 3HR
England

Ashgate Publishing Company
Suite 420
101 Cherry Street
Burlington, VT 05401-4405
USA

Ashgate website: http://www.ashgate.com

British Library Cataloguing in Publication Data
Stockholm Workshop on Global Migration Regimes (2nd : 2004
  : Stockholm, Sweden)
   Globalizing migration regimes : new challenges to
   transnational cooperation. - (Research in migration and
   ethnic relations series)
   1.Emigration and immigration - Congresses 2.Emigration and
   immigration - Government policy - Congresses 3.Emigration
   and immigration - International cooperation - Congresses
   I.Title II.Palme, Joakim III.Tamas, Kristof
   304.8'2

Library of Congress Control Number: 2006921291

ISBN 0 7546 4692 0

Printed and bound by Athenaeum Press, Ltd.,
Gateshead, Tyne & Wear.

Contents

List of Figures and Tables

Figures

Tables

Notes on Contributors

Sabina Alkire is an economist, working on multidimensional poverty, the measurement of freedom, human security, and Sen's capability approach. She holds a Masters in economics of development and a DPhil in economics from Oxford, and is a research associate at the Global Equity Initiative, Oxford.

Robert L. Bach is Senior Fellow at the Inter-American Dialogue in Washington, DC. He served as Executive Associate Commissioner for Policy, Programs, and Planning at the Immigration and Naturalization Service, US Department of Justice between 1994 and 2000. He is author of numerous publications on migration, security, and development and recently served as an Advisor to the United Nations Development Programme's 2004 Human Development Report.

Rainer Bauböck is a political scientist focusing on political theory and comparative studies of migration, citizenship, nationalism and minority claims. He holds a PhD from Vienna University and is currently a senior researcher at the Austrian Academy of Sciences' Institute for European Integration Research and the Commission on Migration and Integration Research. He is author and editor of several books, including *Transnational Citizenship* (1994), *The Challenge of Diversity* (1996) and *Blurred Boundaries* (1998).

Lincoln Chen founded the Global Equity Initiative at Harvard in 2002 after serving as executive vice president for strategy at the Rockefeller Foundation. Dr. Chen has been Professor of International Health and Chair of the Department of Population and International Health at Harvard and Director of the Harvard Center for Population and Development Studies. He has also represented the Ford Foundation in India and Bangladesh. He is chair of the board of directors of CARE/USA. He is member of the Institute of Medicine, the American Academy of Arts and Sciences, the World Academy of Arts and Sciences, the Global Advisory Board to the UN Fund for International Partnerships and the Task Force on Human Security of the Globalization and Democracy Initiative.

Delanyo Dovlo is a Ghanaian public health physician and a health human resources specialist with interests in health worker migration. He trained as a doctor at the University of Ghana Medical School and holds an MPH from the University of Leeds, UK. He is a member of the West Africa College of Physicians and fellow of the Ghana College of Physicians and Surgeons. He currently heads a technical assistance project of the Population Council Inc., in Accra, Ghana.

Luca Einaudi is an Italian economist and an economic historian. He holds an undergraduate degree in economics from the University of Rome and a PhD in economic history from the University of Cambridge. His main fields of work are money and immigration. He is a research associate of the Centre for History and Economics, Cambridge.

Robert Holzmann is Sector Director of the Social Protection Unit in the Human Development Network of the World Bank. Prior to this he was Managing Director of the European Institute and Full Professor for International Economics and European Economy, both at the University of Saarbrucken (Germany) as well as Professor of Economics at the University of Vienna and Senior Economist at the IMF and OECD. He has also been Visiting Professor at various universities in Japan, Chile, and Austria. Since 1992, he has served as editor of *Empirica* and since 1985 as Research Director of the Ludwig Boltzmann Institute for Economic Analysis in Vienna. He has also frequently acted as consultant to the World Bank, the IMF, the EU Commission, ILO, German Technical Cooperation Agency (GTZ), and the Council of Europe. In this capacity he was involved in the reform of pensions and other social programs in Eastern Europe and Latin America. He has published 23 books and over 100 articles on social, fiscal and financial policy issues.

Rey Koslowski is Associate Professor of Political Science at Rutgers University, Newark. He has held fellowships at the Woodrow Wilson International Center for Scholars, Princeton University and Georgetown University. He is the author of *Migrants and Citizens: Demographic Change in the European States System* (2000) and editor of *International Migration and the Globalization of Domestic Politics* (2005).

Melissa Lane is a political philosopher and historian of ideas. She holds a PhD in Philosophy from Cambridge University, where she is now University Lecturer in History and a Fellow of King's College. She works on topics ranging from Greek philosophy and its modern reception, to global health, democracy, and public policy; her most recent book is *Plato's Progeny* (2001). She is Associate Director of the Centre for History and Economics, King's College, Cambridge, and involved in convening the Common Security Forum.

Peggy Levitt is Associate Professor of Sociology at Wellesley College and a Research Fellow at the Hauser Center for Nonprofit Organizations at Harvard University. She is currently directing a comparative, historical study of transnational migration and religion that is funded by the Ford Foundation. She is also co-director of the Emerging Transnational Dynamics Initiative at the Hauser Center and co-principal investigator on an NSF-funded project on the localization of global discourses about women's rights. She has written *The Transnational Villagers* (2001) and co-edited with Mary Waters *The Changing Face of Home: The Transnational Lives of the Second Generation* (2002).

Torbjörn Lundqvist is docent (associate professor) in economic history at Uppsala university. Since 2000 he is a researcher at the Institute for Futures Studies, Stockholm. He has studied several policy areas and different aspects of the Swedish Model, including labour migration.

Bo Malmberg is Professor of Geography, Stockholm University, and Research Associate at the Institute for Futures Studies, Stockholm. His speciality is demographically based, long-term forecasts of social and economic change. His publications include (with Thomas Lindh) 'Age Structure Effects and Growth in the OECD', *Journal of Population Economics* (1999) and (with Lena Sommestad) 'The Hidden Pulse of History', *Scandinavian Journal of History* (2000).

Rainer Münz is Senior Fellow at the Hamburg Institute of International Economics and Head of Research at Erste Bank. He is member of several advisory boards, among them IOM, COMPAS at Oxford University, International Metropolis Project and Association of German Pension Insurers. His most recent books are (with Robert Holzmann) *Challenges and Opportunities of International Migration for the EU, Its Member States, Neighboring Countries and Regions* (2004) and (with Rainer Ohliger) *Diasporas and Ethnic Migrants: Germany, Israel and Post-Soviet Successor States in Comparative Perspective* (2003).

John O. Oucho is a Professor of Population Studies at the University of Botswana in southern Africa and a seasoned scholar of migration. He holds a PhD in Population Geography from the University of Nairobi and was a post-doctoral fellow in Demography at the University of North Carolina at Chapel Hill, USA in 1982–1983. He has researched and published extensively on different types of International migration in Africa. He is a member of several editorial/advisory boards of reputable international journals. In 2002, he was nominated a Fellow of the World Academy of Art and Science.

Joakim Palme is Director of the Institute for Futures Studies and Professor (adjunct) at the Swedish Institute for Social Research, Stockholm University. His research has focused on social rights; pensions; social protection and policy reform; the welfare state and equality; social class, gender and social insurance; the welfare state crisis and European social policy. He has recently co-edited a book (with Olli Kangas) *Social Policy and Economic Development in the Nordic Countries* (Palgrave, 2005). In 1999–2001 he was chairman of the *Welfare Commission* appointed by the Swedish Government. The final report from this work was also published in 'A Welfare Balance Sheet for the 1990s', *Scandinavian Journal of Public Health, Supplement 63* (2003).

Bhargavi Ramamurthy is a doctoral student in economics at the New School University, New York. Her research interests and experience are in employment and private sector development issues in transition economies. On behalf of SIDA, Sweden she has published *International Labour Migrants: Unsung Heroes of Globalization* (2003).

J.P. Sevilla is Assistant Professor of International Health Economics at the Harvard School of Public Health. He is a citizen of the Philippines and received his PhD in Economics at Harvard University in 1999. Some recent research includes the impact of population age structure changes on child labour, child schooling and women's fertility; the relationship between economic growth and gender equality in well-being; the relationship between education and AIDS mortality; the measurement of health-related quality of life; and ethical issues in life saving.

Ninna Nyberg Sørensen is an international migration and development scholar. She holds an MA in Cultural Sociology and a PhD in Social Anthropology, both from the University of Copenhagen. Her main field of work is around migrants' transnational practices. She is currently the Head of the Globalization Department at the Danish Institute of International Studies.

Kristof Tamas is a political scientist and has been a researcher at the Centre for Research in International Migration and Ethnic Relations (CEIFO) at Stockholm University and Deputy Director in the Department for Migration and Asylum Policy in the Swedish Ministry for Foreign Affairs. He has co-edited (with Tomas Hammar, Grete Brochmann and Thomas Faist) *International Migration, Immobility and Development* (1997). He is currently a Research Consultant at the Institute for Futures Studies in Stockholm focusing on the links between migration, development and labour markets.

Patcharawalai Wongboonsin is Associate Director of the Institute of Asian Studies, Chulalongkorn University, Thailand. Besides extensive research on Asian migration and human security, she has served as consultant to regional and multilateral forums dealing with the issues. Among others, they include ASEAN Inter-Parliamentary Organization National Group Commission on Human Resources Development, APEC, WHO, UN ESCAP Population and Rural and Urban Development Division, and the Japanese Ministry of Education's 21st Century Center of Excellence Program.

Preface

The contributions to this volume were originally prepared for the *2nd Stockholm Workshop on Global Migration Regimes* in June 2004. The workshop was organized by the Institute for Futures Studies in Stockholm together with the Centre for History and Economics, Kings College (Cambridge University) and the Global Equity Initiative of Harvard University, under the general auspices of the Common Security Forum. The workshop brought together scholars and experts in the field of international migration, in order to identify options for progress in transnational cooperation and improvements in existing national policies as well as regional and global migration regimes. An important objective was to contribute to the development of a policy-oriented research-agenda for advancing the security of people on the move and those in source and destination communities. Here, the workshop attempted to make an input to the work of the independent Global Commission on International Migration (GCIM). Both the Commission's co-chair Jan O. Karlsson and its research coordinator Jeff Crisp took part in the workshop.

Lincoln Chen, Emma Rothschild and Carl Tham had initiated the *1st Stockholm Workshop on Global Migration Regimes* in 2003. They shared the view that the lack of an adequate global mobility regime continued to be a threat to human security. This was also identified in the final report of the UN-sponsored Human Security Commission (2003), where a need to develop an international migration framework of norms, processes and institutional arrangements to ensure the orderly and safe movement of people was emphasized. The 1st Workshop was organized to encourage the formation of a new Commission that should have a specific focus on global migration. The ground for such a Commission had also been prepared by an internal report presented to the UN Senior Management Group in early 2003. Migration was identified as a key global issue, with salient gaps in the current migration regimes regarding norms, institutions and leadership. The report suggested the setting up of a global Commission.

Subsequent to having received the UN Secretary-General's support and a first proposal in mid-2003, the GCIM was launched on the 1 January 2004. The initial draft of the Commission mandate was developed by the Swedish and Swiss governments together with Brazil, Morocco and the Philippines. This circle was later expanded by several other states into a Core Group. This group of 32 states from all world regions as well as the EC/EU acted as an informal consultative body for the GCIM.

After the 1st Stockholm Workshop the Institute for Futures Studies conducted a mapping study on research and cooperation in international migration, which was handed over to the GCIM Secretariat when it started its work in January 2004 (see Tamas, 2004a).

The GCIM overall objective was 1) to place the issue of international migration on the global policy agenda, 2) to analyze gaps in current approaches to migration, 3) to examine the interlinkages between migration and other global issues, and 4) to suggest appropriate recommendations to the Secretary-General and other stakeholders. Although the Commission has been independent, it reveals the growing interest of the UN system, and especially the Secretary-General Kofi Annan's personal interest, in international migration. In his 2002 report on *Strengthening of the United Nations: An Agenda for Further Change*, the Secretary-General expressed his growing concern, arguing for a comprehensive examination of the causes of population movements and their impact on development.

GCIM handed over its final report on migration to the General-Secretary in early October 2005. The report is the basis of a High Level Dialogue on migration and development under the auspices of the United Nations during the autumn in 2006.

What impact the GCIM report may have on actual national migration polices or international cooperation is of course yet to be seen. What is evident, though, is that the regional hearings organized by the Commission showed a large interest in international cooperation and the sharing of best practice in the field of migration management. We welcome the proposal in the 2005 GCIM report to establish an Inter-agency Global Migration Facility. Such a flexible institutional arrangement could be set up quickly, and at low cost. In a medium-term it could pave the way for improved coordination, coherence and efficiency among existing international organizations and regional arrangements. It could also pool analytical, policy and capacity-building resources at a global level. In the long-term, however, the issue of more far-reaching institutional reforms needs to be addressed in order to adapt the post-war migration related organizations to the more complex transnational migration patterns of the twenty-first century. In any case, existing regional processes on migration management need to be reinforced and exchange of information and best practice could be undertaken more regularly also across regions. The GCIM report points out that there is in fact a large body of international law on migrants' rights and the international management of migration. States need to take this body of international law seriously and simply achieve a better implementation. States are also urged to fill some of the legal gaps that still exist, for example in terms of the rights of domestic workers, family reunion, dual citizenship or the conduct of recruitment agencies.

A fundamental observation in this context is that the interests of migrants, states and international organizations converge around the need to regulate the status of all international migrants. This is a basic requirement for the fulfilment of many parallel concerns, including human rights, human security, state security and sovereignty, labour markets and economic development, demography and social cohesion. If the GCIM has set a process in motion that could further these objectives and inspire closer transnational cooperation towards the globalization of regional migration regimes, it has indeed been a valuable undertaking. This volume is an attempt to contribute to that process. The value of promoting a research-based agenda lies, in our view, in the important potential for social science to reveal some of the myths about migration and development, as well as their consequences.

The Editors

Acknowledgements

This book is the result of efforts on the behalf of many individuals to whom we wish to extend our sincere gratitude. First of all we wish to thank the authors of the various chapters for not only agreeing to contribute to the book, but also for being very cooperative in the process of limiting their manuscript in order to make room for this large number of chapters. This has been very important for making possible such a wide and comprehensive coverage of themes.

The discussions during the *2nd Stockholm Workshop on Global Migration Regimes* were very lively and fruitful. This was a result of excellent work of the appointed chairs and commentators as well as of interventions from other participant. We would thus like to thank the chairs Joaquin Arango, Jeff Crisp, Jan O. Karlsson, Marco Martinello, Carin Nordberg, Emma Rothschild and Carl Tham. We would also like to thank the commentators and panelists for their oral as well as written contributions: Martin Baldwin-Edwards, Frans Bouwen, Graeme Hugo, Christoph Kurowski, Gallya Lahav, Kathleen Newland, Judith Oulton, Ron Skeldon, Barbara Stilwell (and posthumously) Jonas Widgren. These comments have been of great value for us in editing the book and they are in themselves also thought-provoking contributions to both the scholarly and policy discussions. The written comments have therefore been published in electronic form at http://www.framtidsstudier.se/.

No doubt the presence of GCIM in the persons of Jan O. Karlsson and Jeff Crisp added to the energy and importance of the workshop in different ways, especially in focusing on GCIM's key themes. Here we would especially like to mention the very active contributions of the late Jonas Widgren who inspired us not only with his great passion for international cooperation as a way of securing the situation for migrants, but also by his longstanding commitment about linking migration to development issues. Also, the organization of the Workshop was carried out by Märta Carlsson and Eva Brömsegård in a very professional way, which contributed to the atmosphere in an excellent way. In the final editing of the manuscript, we have received very useful comments and assistance by Pat FitzGerald and Ingrid Rydell.

List of Abbreviations

ACP	Asian, Caribbean and Pacific countries
ADHA	Additional Duty Hours Allowance (in Ghana)
APC	Asia-Pacific Consultations Process
CBP	Bureau of Customs and Border Protection
DHS	US Department of Homeland Security
ECN	European Convention on Nationality
EMP	Euro-Mediterranean Partnership
FDI	Foreign Direct Investment
GAMMS	General Agreement on Migration, Mobility and Security
GATS	General Agreement on Trade in Services
GCIM	Global Commission on International Migration
HTAs	Home Town Associations
ICCPR	International Covenant on Civil and Political Rights
ICPD	International Conference on Population and Development
ICT	Information and communication technology
IDB	Inter-America Development Bank
ILO	International Labour Organization
IMF	International Monetary Fund
IOM	International Organization for Migration
JHA	Justice and Home Affairs
JLI	Joint Learning Initiative
LMMC	Labour Migration Ministerial Consultations for Countries of Origins in Asia
LO	Swedish Trade Union Confederation
MDGs	Millennium Development Goals
MIDA	Migration for Development in Africa
MOU	Memorandum of Understanding
NEPAD	New Partnership for Africa's Development
ODA	Overseas Development Assistance
OECD	Organization for Economic Development and Cooperation
RFID	Radio frequency identification
RQAN	Return of Qualified African Nationals
SAARC	South Asian Association for Regional Cooperation
SAF	Swedish Employers' Confederation
TEU	Treaty on European Union
TFR	Total fertility rate

TNCs   Trans-National Corporations
TOKTEN   Transfer of Knowledge Through Expatriate Nationals
UDHR   Universal Declaration of Human Rights
UNHCR   United Nations High Commissioner for Refugees
WTO   World Trade Organization

INTRODUCTION

Chapter 1

Transnational Approaches to Reforming Migration Regimes

Kristof Tamas and Joakim Palme

The Objectives

The estimated 185 million international migrants in 2005 make up just below 3 per cent of the global population (see Tables 1.1 and 1.2). Yet international migrants set in motion a long range of significant transnational interactions. Migrants connect countries. Long-lasting and deep migrant networks often result from initially limited flows of migration. Such migration can be of benefit both to source and destination countries.[1] Migrant savings or remittances, the return of migrants with novel work experience or training acquired abroad, or the establishment of investment and trade links are all part of the positive inducements benefiting the development of source countries. Destination countries may gain to a great extent from additional human capital that is taking on jobs shunned by nationals, or where the national workforce is inadequate in meeting the demands of the labour market.

At the same time, migration often gives rise to heated sentiments among the majority population in the destination countries. Many individuals feel that cohabiting with people representing another culture than their own conflicts with their collective national identity. Fears of competition in the labour market can also be strong. There are obviously expectations of downside pressures on wages and social welfare benefits as newcomers offer their work at lower prices and as more people must share the community's waning welfare resources. Employers may exploit migrants to cut wages. Migration becomes politicized in ways which may have negative repercussions also for settled immigrants, their children and grandchildren. As governments in the favoured destination countries are increasingly under pressure from their constituencies to manage and regulate the inflows, control policies tend to become harsher and more restrictive. In the process, migrants take ever larger risks if they travel clandestinely to circumvent the control measures protecting the narrowing legal doors of asylum and immigration. By using ruthless traffickers who may be part of international organized crime syndicates, many migrants jeopardize their savings, their health and even their lives.

A growing number of migrants are thus victimized and their rights, welfare and security are under severe threats. Source countries, frequently in the developing South,

Table 1.1   International migrants, 1965–2005

Year	International migrants[a] *Millions*	World population *Billions*	International migrants as share of world population *Percentage*
1965	75	3.3	2.3
1975	85	4.1	2.1
1985	105	4.8	2.2
1990[a]	120	5.3	2.3
1995[b]	164	5.7	2.9
2000	175	6.0	2.9
2005[c]	185	6.5	2.9

a   Standard UN criteria define international migrants as persons residing outside their country of birth or citizenship for 12 months or more. However, the UN Population Division has to rely on national data sources and some countries define migrants according to other criteria.

b   Some of the 1985–1995 increase in the number of migrants reflects people who did not actually move but became international migrants through the breakup of their countries (for example, the former countries of Czechoslovakia, Soviet Union, and Yugoslavia).

c   The value for 2005 is based on the assumption that the number of international migrants during the period 2000–2004 grew at the same pace as during the period 1995–2000; see Münz (2004). According to IOM's extrapolation of past trends there would be 185–192 million international migrants in 2005 (IOM, 2005).

Sources: United Nations (2002b); Martin (2003); Münz (2004); Holzmann and Münz (2004).

attempt to protect the interests of their nationals abroad, but are often unable to do so short of a regulatory framework. Some source countries' governments that have themselves caused forced migration flows are eager to gain from the remittances, but are unwilling to admit back their own citizens who may be illegally present in destination countries. The fact that migration policy is moving up the political agendas of many destination countries in the North also indicates that the challenges of regulating and integrating migrants are overwhelming for individual states. At the same time, common and widely accepted norms of conduct are still lacking but may be increasingly needed if more developed countries start turning to orderly labour immigration with a view to defuse the disparaging labour market effects of aging populations.[2]

Notwithstanding the apparent need for intensified international cooperation and some attempts in recent years, there is presently no functioning international regime[3] for the mobility of economic migrants in any way close to the refugee regime dating back

Table 1.2   **Evolution of the number of international migrants in the world and major areas 1970–2000**

	Number of international migrants (millions)			
	1970	**1980**	**1990**	**2000**
World	81.5	99.8	154.0	174.9
Developed countries	38.3	47.7	89.7	110.3
Developed countries excluding USSR	35.2	44.5	59.3	80.8
Developing countries	43.2	52.1	64.3	64.6
Africa	9.9	14.1	16.2	16.3
Asia[a]	28.1	32.3	41.8	43.8
Latin America and the Caribbean	5.8	6.1	7.0	5.9
Northern America	13.0	18.1	27.6	40.8
Oceania	3.0	3.8	4.8	5.8
Europe[b]	18.7	22.2	26.3	32.8
USSR (former)	3.1	3.3	30.3	29.5

a   Excluding Armenia, Azerbaijan, Georgia, Kazakhstan, Kyrgyzstan, Tajikistan, Turkmenistan and Uzbekistan.
b   Excluding Belarus, Estonia, Latvia, Lithuania, the Republic of Moldova, the Russian Federation and Ukraine.

Source: United Nations (2003b).

more than 50 years and pivoting around the 1951 Geneva Refugee Convention. While cracks have appeared on the surface of the refugee regime, a few attempts to dismantle it have been resisted by the bulk of influential states. They are still eager to preserve the refugee regime although the Cold War context in which it originally emerged, has been replaced by a globalized and more complex world where mixed flows of voluntary and forced, economic and political migrants have become commonplace.

This book addresses some of these issues by posing the following three sets of questions:

•   How can the security and well-being of international migrants be enhanced, while at the same time the manifold interests of states which migrants leave, pass through and arrive in are met?
•   What can be learnt from past examples of national policies and regional migration regime cooperation and applied at the global level for the sake of reforming current transnational cooperation on international migration?
•   How can a framework of basic norms be arrived at that simultaneously 1) augment migration's developmental effects for the source countries, 2) meet the security

and rights interests of both states and migrants, and 3) improve the prospects of integration of migrants in the destination countries?

Finding a golden path to fulfil all these objectives appears to be very challenging. It is also often at a very abstract level that policy-makers lately have deliberated on the likelihood of a win-win scenario, whereby it will be clear for all concerned parties that they in fact may benefit from international migration. While such an ideal world may be beyond reach in the foreseeable future, in the medium-term perspective it is crucial from an analytical point of view, as well as from a policy perspective, to identify the various and often conflicting interests involved in the process of international migration. These contradictory interests have contributed to a deficit in terms of international cooperation, and suboptimal and irrational outcomes for both migrants, states and the international system, or rather what we prefer to call the international society.[4] What we will argue in the following is that the answers, moreover, will depend on the perspective applied – whether the migrant, the state or the international society is at the core of the analysis.

Outline

Following this introductory chapter, Part 1 of the book includes chapters on the concept of transnational migration by Peggy Levitt and on global population changes by Bo Malmberg. This is setting the stage for the other parts of the book, which take different starting points for deliberations on global migration. Part 2 deals with different perspectives of the source countries. It contains chapters on brain drain by J.P. Sevilla; remittances by Bhargavi Ramamurthy; and migration, development and conflict by Ninna Nyberg Sørensen. The special case of medical worker migration is covered by Sabine Alkire and Lincoln Chen and regarding the situation in Ghana, with a chapter by Delanyo Dovlo.

Part 3 of the book gives different perspectives of the destination countries. It contains matters of principle in both Melissa Lane's chapter on ethical and historical perspectives and citizenship by Rainer Bauböck; and practical case studies of labour migration covered by Luca Einaudi's study of Italy and France and Torbjörn Lundqvist's study of Sweden. Part 4 addresses various aspects of transnational cooperation, primarily from the perspective of regional migration processes. In this part are to be found regional studies on Asia by Patcharawalai Wongboonsin; on Africa by John Oucho; on Europe by Robert Holzmann and Rainer Münz; and on the Western Hemisphere by Robert Bach. Finally, Rey Koslowski looks into possible steps towards an international regime for mobility and security.

Transnational Perspectives on Global Migration

We argue in the following that the concept of transnationalism is not only relevant but also potentially appealing to policy-makers. Through the theoretical, conceptual and empirical work that has been undertaken by a number of anthropologists, sociologists, political scientists and economists, transnationalism as a field of enquiry has shed new light on the interlinkages between various actors and stakeholders; the migrants and those that remain at home, the source countries and destination countries; various international organizations and nongovernmental organizations. Many migrants conduct parallel lives in both their host country and their country of origin. Through such simultaneity they live their lives in *transnational social spaces*. Peggy Levitt argues convincingly in her chapter for this change of the nation-state based scientific approach to an approach involving equally both source country and destination country in the study of migration patterns.

In addition to a transnational approach to the study and management of future migration, we argue that it is important to have an idea about the nature of future migration. Here we take Bo Malmberg's long-term demographic forecast as a point of departure. In the next 20–30 years, the changes in the population structure in many countries suggest that there will be large net migration flows. However, the migration hump is followed by a migration slump. By 2020, the number of countries with population structures likely to generate a high level of emigration will be drastically reduced, almost by half. Also the number of countries receiving high levels of immigration will shrink almost to the same extent. Income growth in many of the current emigration countries is also likely to slow down emigration rates in the future. Moreover, if population aging in developed countries leads to slower growth rates, developing countries might be able to reduce the income gap quicker and this will also reduce pressure for emigration. Even though global population growth thus may decrease after 2020, in the years up till then the main challenge for policy-makers will be to make vital decisions on whether to expand labour migration, and to improve migration management especially in terms of integration in destination countries. There are no doubt other factors that can be referred to as the root causes of international migration, and which are likely to contribute to variation in future migration flows. They are, however, more difficult to project than migration induced by changes in the population structure.

A transnational approach calls for an alternative focal point for the analysis of how international cooperation can be advanced. A state-centred approach is simply not enough when looking at various currents of globalization, for example the role of non-state actors as pressure groups or international terrorism. In summarizing and considering the chapters in this book therefore, we outline three alternative perspectives or points of departure for the analysis of cooperation on international migration – states, migrants and the international society. These are partly inspired by Rainer Bauböck's chapter in this book, which introduces a discussion of the interests of different stakeholders. The concept of transnational cooperation and regimes here is used rather than international cooperation and regimes in order to indicate an approach whereby the interests of all three stakeholders are to be addressed. Moreover, since states can be divided into source, transit and destination countries (although all states are all three at once), the term transnational also refers to an approach whereby the often-conflicting interests of these various actors are taken into account. The basic concepts of *rights*, *integration*, *norms*, *development*, *security* and *international cooperation*, introduced in question 3 above, have different meanings and priorities depending on whether our point of departure is the individual, the state or the international society.

The first perspective is to start the analysis from the point of view of the *individual migrant*. The individual is encircled by a web of factors influencing the causes, effects and conditions of the act of migration (as suggested in question 3 above). This bottom-up approach suggests that migrants, in common with everyone else, need security of life and livelihood and this can be protected by a set of fundamental human rights. The interests of migrants are primarily to maintain protection of these rights such as security of residence, access to employment, living together with family members, the right to return to the country of origin as well as rights of property and inheritance there. Gender differences need to be taken into account as the interests, needs and vulnerability of men and women might differ. The migrants' desire to find employment or political asylum in other countries, often conflicts with the interests of the potential destination countries, whose interests are to control the volume and type of immigration. For migrants who settle permanently, integration in host countries are perhaps more important than development in the countries of origin, but the relationship may be the reverse when migration is short term and cyclic. Norms and international cooperation on migration issues are of the least immediate interest to migrants, although in the longer-term, it may have important positive effects on the lives of individual migrants through the establishment of bi- or multilateral agreements and more elaborate legal frameworks for the protection of migrant's rights.

The second (intermediate) perspective is the currently prevailing one where *state interests* shape the essential framework for policies. Bauböck recalls that from a realist perspective in international relations, the primary interest of states is to maximize their sovereignty. International norms that can prevent other states from interfering with their sovereignty constitute a secondary interest. In order to protect their sovereignty, states exercise their right in accordance with international law to regulate and control the type and volume of immigration. It is thus the security interests of states and state norms that set the parameters also for the discourse on international migration, although migration has only more recently been associated with what is traditionally referred to as state security issues. In addition, states have interests in developing policies of integration of immigrants in order to maintain stability and security at the domestic level. It can be argued that this is necessary for 'societal security' in order to avoid migration issues from becoming politicized on an agenda set by the Extreme Right or populist parties in destination countries.[5] This also relates to the desirability of protecting other vulnerable groups in the destination countries from potentially negative effects of migration. States also seek to avoid migration causing conflicts in the host countries over welfare and community issues and governments have the role of mediator among the various stakeholders and interest groups at the sub-state level. For source countries, security interests mainly concern the protection of their own citizens abroad, or in some instances to get rid of people who (by undemocratic governments) are regarded as a threat to the ruling regime. Moreover, development in countries of origin is a growing focus of attention for receiving countries as a way to prevent or reduce migration pressures. Development is thus an issue-area where the interests of source and destination countries can partly meet. As the record of international cooperation on migration issues is relatively meagre compared to security and economic issues, it can be argued, however, that this is paradoxically a less prioritized issue-area for states. Destination and source countries, moreover, have mainly different interests to protect which makes agreement on common norms more challenging.

Finally, the top-down perspective takes the *international society* as its starting point for regime change or enhanced cooperation on migration issues. The main interest of the international society as reflected by the structure of international law is to establish a legal order and international organizations that help to maintain peaceful and friendly relations among states. Bauböck argues in his chapter that since the end of the Second World War human rights have become a secondary interest and normative foundation of this order. In the case of migration, the United Nations system as the broadest possible forum for international cooperation could be an adequate choice as the starting point to encourage and help organize a reformed global migration regime.[6] The question of which organization should take on a leading role in the field of international migration is however a sensitive one, as competition is rather fierce among mainly IOM, UNHCR and the ILO. As the delineation of the mandates of each of these organizations have become somewhat blurred, it is increasingly obvious that there should be an improvement in the division of responsibilities and coordinating arrangements. For the international society or state system itself, international organization of migration issues could be regarded as a necessary priority in order to meet the growing security and rights concerns of both states and migrants. A starting point could be the formulation of a set of common norms to guide national migration policies. These norms could be based on a common understanding of migrant's rights and responsibilities as well as state's rights and responsibilities. They could be based on the need to promote development in both source countries and destination countries. The integration of migrants in host societies is a secondary priority of the international society as it is mainly an issue for the state level. Nevertheless, the international society, or the UN itself could play an important role also in this regard by developing norms or best practice to be implemented by states.

Some common points appear from these three perspectives. The first is that security surfaces as the first priority and rights as second priority for both migrants and states. Security is however regarded from fundamentally different angles by states and migrants. While migrants want to reduce risks, costs and harassment related to mobility, states aspire to regulate and control migration across their borders through methods ranging from laissez-faire to outright repressive. In the same way, migrants and states operate within different sets of rights. States exercise their sovereignty right to reduce and control migrants' access to their territory and welfare rights independently of the pressures or demand for entry. Migrants have a right to leave their country of birth or citizenship, and they attempt to seek out the country of destination that can best fulfil their needs and interests, while exercising the rights offered to them by international and national legislative frameworks. Such a conflict of interests gives rise to a struggle between states that constantly invent new and tighter regulations and controls, and the migrants who driven by fervent needs unremittingly circumvent those control mechanisms. There are however shared interests, including the need to avoid exploitation of migrants by traffickers and smugglers. This is also the field in which the most successful international cooperation has recently taken place (through the negotiation and ratification of the UN Convention against Transnational Organized Crime and its Protocols on Trafficking and Smuggling of Migrants that entered into force in 2003 and 2004 respectively). The interests of states and migrants to develop migrants' rights coincide to a certain extent, but diverge where the rights become favourable towards migrants rather than towards the states (for example illustrated by the fact that only very few states have ratified the 1990 UN Migrant Workers Convention).

A Framework for Deliberations

Rights and Integration

With the help of Melissa Lane's chapter we can identify the historical and ethical foundation of migration control policies and the contrasting of migrants' versus states' rights. She holds Michael Walzer's famous assertion that admission and exclusion are at the core of communal independence to be an argument for state control of migration. Lane is however critical towards Walzer's implied controllability of migration, as well as of David Miller's similar line of reasoning based on ethical claims of national identity. Miller's argument is derived from current international law, according to which everyone has a right to emigrate, while no one enjoys a coinciding right to immigrate to a country of ones own choice. This, according to Miller, is a sound basis of states' claims to control and limit immigration. Based on the interests of the welfare of its existing citizens, the right of states can overrun the rights and interests of immigrants. Nevertheless, Miller contends, states should balance their own interests against the interest of the would-be immigrants and controls should not be 'morally irrelevant' or 'insulting'. In her critique of the arguments of both these philosophers, Lane's position is that powerful forces drive people to migrate and states will therefore never be able to succeed in attempts of totally controlling migration. Thus, there is a perpetual conflict between migrants' interests and states' interests, and about notions of their respective rights.

Rainer Bauböck contends that some traditional elements of state sovereignty have been eroded through the processes of economic globalization. While migration control policies have become harsher, legally settled immigrants have increasingly found it easier to gain political rights and citizenship. There is also a tendency to blur the distinctions between citizens and permanent residents, which have effects on integration prospects. Some of the migration source countries in their turn, for example Turkey and Mexico, have changed policies in order to encourage their emigrants to acquire dual citizenship – keeping their original citizenship in the source country as well as naturalize in the host country. Through dual citizenship it may be possible to avoid unwanted or uncontrolled massive return flows of irregular migrants and to ensure continued return of remittances from well-integrated migrants.

Bauböck suggests some principles for more consistent and inclusive citizenship policies that also take into account state interests regarding self-determination over their own nationals. Restrictive and uncoordinated citizenship polices, he argues, could also lead to additional irregular migration flows and more permanent rather than temporary migration that augments brain drain. If immigrants are denied access to citizenship in the destination country, migrants are likely to become marginalized and will have less chances of integrating socially and economically as well. One option would be to introduce a stakeholder citizenship norm. Birth or long-term residence in a state would thus suffice to establish the necessary social ties for a migrant to qualify as a stakeholder in that community. Similarly close family ties or life plans including a return, would be adequate for a migrant to keep his or her stake in the country of origin and thus to retain citizenship and other rights there.

For this volume, Sweden, Italy and France have been selected as the main examples of the different types of policy frameworks found in Southern and Northern European countries (cf. Hammar and Brochmann, 1999; Geddes, 2003). The chapters by Luca Einaudi and Torbjörn Lundqvist covering these cases can be read through the lenses of Melissa Lanes ethical and historical framework for the study of rights and control policies. While a very strict regulation of labour immigration since the early 1970s has mainly been based on influential trade unions and the employer organizations in the case of Sweden, in Italy and France more open labour migration policies have to a much larger extent depended on populist outcries as well as stronger labour market needs. An important difference has also been the use of recurrent regularizations of clandestine migrants in Southern Europe, while such policies have hardly ever been used in Sweden and other Northern European countries.

While reviewing the history of migration control in Italy and France, Luca Einaudi argues that Italy in the last decades has improved enforcement of regulations, and successively opened up new channels for labour immigration in response to migration pressures. While applying a labour immigration quota system and recurrent regularizations, control policies have been made more rigorous. The Italian case is illustrative of the dilemmas faced by governments as much of such policy measures are the result of immigration becoming highly politicized. Einaudi shows that when Italy in 1997 increased penalties for traffickers and smugglers, their ships dropped clandestine migrants further away from the Italian shores, or they left migrants on boats without a crew (cf. Massey et al., 2002). Human, social, political and economic costs as well as the security risks for both states and migrants are thus enhanced by the very same policies that are set up to eradicate such iniquity.

Simply offering wider legal doors to labour migrants is not necessarily a sufficient method to gain control of clandestine migration. In resemblance to Einaudi's conclusions, Lundqvist points to the various labour immigration systems tested in Sweden since the 1950s, which have all proved the limits of government regulation. Lundqvist argues that both the unions and the employers had ideologically consistent and rational arguments based on their own interests. Both sides were also concerned that political control alone would not solve all problems of migration. A thoroughly regulated recruiting system in the 1950s became overly expensive for the government and this was subsequently replaced by a scheme more adapted to the market mechanisms. This gave however rise to unexpected social costs. While these European case studies are certainly specific and contextual, the conclusions about the limits to regulation and control as well as the importance of taking into account national interest groups, may be valid for most countries that receive migrants.

Norms and Development

Remittances and brain drain are two of the most important factors that link migration with development. Chapters by J.P. Sevilla (brain drain) and Bhargavi Ramamurthy (remittances) were contributed to shed more light on norms and development as fundamental parts in an improved transnational migration regime. Sevilla notes that the loss incurred by brain drain to developing countries, may be compensated by changes in redistribution policies in the migration source countries. He points to the poor empirical evidence of the magnitude of the brain drain loss in developing countries (with the exception of the medical professions). Estimates are susceptible due to excessive unemployment among the highly skilled in developing countries. The investments in education are in any case lost when skilled people who stay at home remain outside the productive labour markets. However, he argues from a normative redistribution perspective, that citizens of developing countries should not be required to subsidize human capital losses. Therefore, the system of educational subsidies should partly be replaced by a conditional loans system. Although Sevilla does not fully answer the ensuing questions about equality in access to educational opportunities (as a loans system tends to disfavour the poor), he claims that the incentive of employers to fund education of their (potential staff) would increase with such a system.

The related chapter by Ramamurthy explores the recent literature and data on migrant remittances and surveys the world regions regarding their effects. Main points among her arguments include that remittances have a lifecycle – they tend to decrease over time the longer the migrant stays abroad. Remittances tend mainly to favour families, households and local communities, while data only indicate a weak link between remittances and macro-economic growth. She argues therefore that developing countries should not rely too much on remittances as there is no predictability in flows. This is in contrast to Dilip Ratha (2003), who has recently shown that remittances are a more stable source of development finance than other flows such as foreign direct investment, aid or portfolio investments. Ramamurthy argues that most remittances are spent on short-term consumer goods (including housing and the repayment of loans), and much less is spent on community investments in infrastructure, health and sanitation, or private entrepreneurial projects.

The migration of medical professionals epitomizes the challenges faced by the South in terms of brain drain, but also the spread of diseases like HIV/AIDS and SARS are affected by the lack of doctors and nurses and adequate medication. The epidemic proportion of HIV/AIDS in Sub-Saharan Africa is alarming and is getting worse by the day. This is why Sabina Alkire and Lincoln Chen argue in their chapter that migration of medical professionals should be treated differently from a policy perspective than other forms of migration. They also suggest a large-scale re-investment fund that should be financed by the countries in the North. It should be used to compensate poorer countries in the South that loose their human capital and investments in public education and that suffer from the consequences of the lack of health workers.

This ethical dilemma is important when designing policy initiatives to steer or prevent migration flows. While emigration in this case is to the detriment of the source country and its population, it would also mean an infringement of the human rights of individual doctors and nurses to curtail their right to leave a poor country if they have found employment elsewhere. Rather, it should be a question of creating incentives to stay or to return, by investing in improved remuneration and working conditions. It could also be argued that the labour importing countries have a rational self-interest in averting brain drain. The brain drain of medical professionals in the longer term could trigger off other unwanted flows of economic migration and even refugees as the general living conditions in the source countries worsen. The emigration of health workers is often also just symptomatic of the deteriorating conditions in a developing country which struggles with rigid bureaucracy, corruption, unemployment, ethnic conflicts and civic strife, over-urbanization and environmental pollution, lack of democracy and good governance. Alkire and Chen contend that these latter countries should introduce retention strategies through better compensation and working environments as well as higher output of trained people in the medical professions. But without cooperation on behalf of destination countries conditions in the source countries are hardly sustainable.

The case made by Alkire and Chen is also supported by an empirical survey targeting health worker emigration in Ghana carried out by Delanyo Dovlo. Based on a number of interviews with Ghanaian doctors and nurses on their intentions to emigrate, he draws the conclusion that health workers are deeply frustrated with their working conditions, their remuneration, the lack of medical equipment, the lack of efficiency in human resource management and leadership in the health services, and the career opportunities in Ghana. Dovlo therefore argues for the need of internal dialogue in Ghana to kick-start strategies to solve these problems and to implement consistent policies. Such policies should appreciate the health workers' contribution to national development and reorganize poor human resource management structures in order to enhance the morale and self-respect of health professionals.

Ninna Nyberg Sørensen's work is based on a case study in Somalia and transnational networks of Somalis. The chapter focuses on the nexus between migration, development and conflict. Sørensen argues that international migration is both driven and eased by the process of globalization. Reasons behind growing international migration flows, are the obvious and widening gaps in 'livelihood possibilities and human security' between various parts of the world. Poverty and human rights abuses are often interlinked so that migration flows are triggered from countries where there are both economic hardships and ethnic or social conflicts. Sørensen argues that a transnational approach needs to be employed whereby international mobility is regarded as an essential prerequisite for economic and social development. She shows how the choice between integration and repatriation can be replaced by a combination of the two in 'durable transnational, transregional and translocal strategies'. Indicative of such strategies is the type of 'staggered return' by which returning refugees from Somalia have chosen to develop a transnational livelihood utilizing their rights and resources in several countries. Sørensen points to several studies indicating that return after a short stay abroad often is associated with failure and hardships, while migrants who return after a long period of stay, who have been well integrated in the host country and been able to save money while abroad, are more likely to play a role in development in their countries of origin.

Security and International Cooperation

The chapters on regional cooperation experiences start off with the burgeoning cooperation in Asia. Patcharawalai Wongboonsin shows that cooperative arrangements on migration in the region have been relatively limited. Attempts so far have mainly focused on identifying a common comprehensive and balanced approach through information exchange, and only partly on the promotion of legislative change and thorough implementation. She suggests that nongovernmental stakeholders need to be more involved, that there is a need for more coordination and synergies among the several regional and subregional arrangements, and that collaboration needs to be more focused on human development and human security. While these regional arrangements so far have been very state centric, only limited attention has been devoted to the migrant and his or her intentions, rights and interests (one rare exemption being the recognition of the needs of victims of trafficking). A change in focus might enhance the migrants' contribution to social and economic development, and thus also further the state interests. While differences in state interests and limited resources have hampered a deepening in cooperation, at least the actors in the region are now becoming aware of that no single state can adequately manage migration, and that intensified cooperation therefore is essential.

John Oucho's contribution about Africa reminds of the historical, colonial, cultural, and migration ties which link it to the North and which also influence patterns of current cooperation. He reviews policies regarding international trade and the control of international migration from the South, arguing that the North has imposed restrictions on both migration and goods from Africa. This contributes to the continents' maintained dependency on the North. While some bilateral cooperation, such as the French co-development arrangements, seems to have benefited African countries there are also many failures and drawbacks associated with cooperation programmes, especially those focused at return migration and brain drain. An internal African initiative on these issues within the framework of the New Partnership for Africa's Development (NEPAD) needs to put more efforts into basic analysis of the characteristics of the African brain drain, its size, diversity and geographical pattern. The General Agreement in Trade in Services (GATS) would need to be based on trust among equal trading partners, but it is not and according to Oucho, it will serve as an impediment to smooth and growing trade in services. On good grounds, Oucho also maintains that African countries need to renegotiate their human resource and trade relations with the North.

The regional study on Europe by Robert Holzmann and Rainer Münz is a broad policy-oriented review of the key demographic, economic and migratory challenges and opportunities to Europe and its neighbouring regions. The authors argue that Europe needs to develop a proactive policy in order, on the one hand, to recruit the skilled workforce it needs and manage unwanted migration and, on the other, to assist developing countries to become politically stable and economically stronger. They suggest a number of mutually benefiting strategies to be developed through a permanent dialogue between source and destination countries. Applying such strategies, migration could partially solve some of the problems associated with source countries' surplus labour supply as well as the aging and shrinking workforces in Europe. One way would be for European countries to focus on skills development via support to educational systems in migrant source countries. Another way would be to improve transferability of social insurance and benefits to migrants. Such measures have the potential to improve both the integration of transnational migrant communities in host countries, and facilitate their reintegration in home countries for those who chose to return.

Robert Bach analyses cooperation within the Western Hemisphere, arguing that several lessons can be learnt from this region in what he calls 'an age of terrorism'. Measures against terrorism will continue to interfere with and shape policies towards migration, trade and development. Security considerations are likely to function as a barrier to further regional integration. The answer to address economic inequality in the region cannot be migration alone considering the security concerns. However, as one of the root causes of migration is inequality, there needs to be more attention to the question how migration is influenced by different kinds of mobility strategies. Democracy reform is a prerequisite of further economic development and social stability. Bilateral or regional migration cooperation also requires democratic governments that respect human rights and take decisive measures against widespread corruption. The security agenda has also brought about an opportunity to create a joint regional objective through the shared common values against terrorism and for open societies based on democratic principles.

Finally, concluding this Part, Rey Koslowski's chapter explores the recent attempts at transatlantic cooperation on migration and security. With a reference to the GATT and GATS models, his aim is to find a sufficient basis for an international regime for mobility and security, and he proposes a General Agreement on Migration, Mobility and Security (GAMMS). Koslowski adeptly illustrates how the events of 11 September 2001 triggered a far-reaching overhaul of US security and migration policies and how cooperation with especially the European Union was intensified. As several of the terrorists entered the US as tourists, Koslowski emphasizes that a new migration regime needs to cover all forms of mobility, which also naturally magnifies the challenges ahead. His review of transatlantic cooperation illustrates how the outcome of collaboration tend to be more restrictive and repressive policies, rather than more liberal as predicted by international relations theory. The setting up of a viable global, transnational regime with a legal framework allowing more labour mobility, would require a major shift in attitudes, strategies and security arrangements.

Cooperation as a Path Towards a Functioning Global Migration Regime

Demographic change with aging populations and shrinking labour markets in developed countries will inevitably place the question of labour migration even higher on political agendas in the next decades to come. Labour migrants can become key players in this regard, contributing to economic development in both source and destination countries. A transnational approach to migration policies has the potential to address the challenges from several perspectives at once. The likelihood of arriving at strengthened transnational cooperation depends on a willingness to re-evaluate interests and to involve more stakeholders. Migrants, states, regions as well as the international society can be the starting point of cooperative efforts. At both ends of the migration chain, stakeholders include governments, municipalities and local authorities, political parties, migrant organizations, NGOs, international organizations, employers, unions, banks and remittance transfer companies. Bilateral and regional multilateral efforts need to be simultaneously reinforced before any viable global regime can be formed.

There is a lack of widely accepted global norms to govern the management of labour migration and to incorporate both the need for integration in destination countries and the development needs of source countries. The most comprehensive international treaty protecting migrants' rights, the 1990 UN Convention on Migrant Workers' Rights, which entered into force in 2003, has only been ratified by about 30 states, all being migrant source countries. A recent study has identified four types of obstacles concerning the contents of the Convention as well as administrative, financial and political aspects. The political obstacles dominate and the study highlights a very controversial part of the Convention, which is its coverage of undocumented migrants. As granting rights to these migrants is regarded as a threat to state's sovereignty, it is necessary, argues the study, to find a balance between protecting migrant's fundamental rights and states rights (Pécoud and de Guchteneire, 2004).

In this context, it would probably help to regard international migration as a process rather than a flow. As the migration process has been set off, it will contribute to build links between source, transit and destination countries. Such links can be shaped to strengthen cooperation and development. States undermine their legitimacy and sovereignty in the field of migration control by an overly unilateral and defensive stance. One-sided restrictive control measures can become counter-productive, as evidenced by the simultaneous rapid growth in both border control costs and migrant smuggling in the last decade. Migration policies must be proactive, comprehensive, coherent, consistent and collaborative. This is a prerequisite in order for the general public as well as for migrants to regard policies as legitimate and efficient.

Migrants link states together and migrants' interests can benefit both source and destination countries. Migration can lead to human capital development in source countries that counteracts the drain of talents and resources. Remittances can contribute to development if they are facilitated through legitimate and efficient channels. Enabling legal labour migration can benefit both source and destination countries and can counteract irregular migration, smuggling and trafficking. Intensified exchange of best practice and codes of conduct among all stakeholders would be an important building block for the establishment of a transnational legal framework for labour mobility.

A major challenge for governments in destination countries is the integration of migrants and the degree of public acceptance of newcomers in the receiving communities. There needs to be a clear and transparent distinction between civic rights and economic welfare entitlements based on whether migration is temporary or permanent. Citizenship rights need to be strengthened and dual citizenship may also bring source and destination countries' interests closer. One part of such relations concerns the portability of social welfare rights. There is also a need to firmly address the insecurities felt among people in destination countries who regard migrants as threats to culture as well as competitors for scarce employment opportunities and shrinking welfare entitlements. The rights and obligations of residents as well as the adequate management of heterogeneous societies, must be the focus of a continuous public debate and policy adaptation in order for the populations in both source and destination countries to be able to prepare for the increased globalization that is so closely linked to the process of international migration.

As noted in the foreword the contributions to this volume were presented at the *2nd Stockholm Workshop on Global Migration Regimes* in June 2004. The workshop was among other things an attempt to provide an input to the work of the independent Global Commission on International Migration (GCIM). The regional hearings organized by the Commission showed that there is in fact a large interest in international cooperation and the sharing of best practice in the field of migration management. We welcome the proposal in the 2005 GCIM report to establish an Inter-agency Global Migration Facility. Such an institutional arrangement could be set up quickly, and at low cost. In a medium-term it could pave the way for improved coordination, coherence and efficiency among existing international organizations and regional arrangements. It could also pool analytical, policy and capacity-building resources at a global level. In the long term, however, the issue of more far-reaching institutional reforms needs to be addressed in order to adapt the post-war migration related organizations to the more complex transnational migration patterns of the twenty-first century. If the GCIM has set a process in motion that could further these objectives and inspire closer transnational cooperation towards the globalization of regional migration regimes, we hope that this volume can contribute to that process.

In the process of improving migration policies there is a vital role to be played by research in addressing some of the prevailing myths in the area. We therefore emphasize that the improvement of rights does not necessarily imply more migration. On the contrary, the extension of rights might reduce migration pressures. Wages are not necessarily pressed down by immigration. On the contrary, as many migrants fill gaps where there is labour shortage or take up jobs which are rejected by nationals, they often contribute to economic growth. Linking different policy areas to enhance coherence, for example trade and development, has the potential to break up old stalemates. By placing international migration within a broader context, it is possible to address many of the structural, long-term causes of migration that cannot be solved merely by stricter, defensive control policies.

We should also recognize that there are important knowledge gaps about global migration and the links between migration and development. Alkire and Chen provide us with an important list in the case of migration of medical professionals, but it can be generalized. More needs to be done regarding: 1) data and analyses; 2) policy effectiveness; 3) migration and trade; 4) the political economy of diasporas; 5) ethical issues; and 6) the role and functioning of international institutions. Research needs to be stimulated especially in developing and net emigration countries where these issues are insufficiently covered by academics and institutions due to the general lack of resources.

We would argue that what this boils down to is the necessity to improve our knowledge about the effects of policy regimes at various levels. Such a priority coupled with political will is a requirement in order to utilize the potentials in migration for enhancing the welfare of citizens in all countries both in terms of resources and agency (cf. Sen, 1985). The fact that there are conflicting interests in this context between countries of different kinds and individuals with different relations to migration, should not prohibit us from exploring ways of mediating these different interests. What is important to understand here is that international migration entails a number of paradoxes. Recognizing migrants' rights may actually embody a potential of reducing conflicts of interests and create positive-sum solutions. In any case, increased transnational cooperation is the way forward if we want to avoid the various prisoners' dilemmas that are threatening the security of individuals and, in a different way, nations. Any global approach needs to rely on national and regional experiences as the first steps that could lead on to more progress towards globalizing migration regimes.

Notes

1   All countries are source, transit or destination countries of migration. For the sake of clarity and distinction however, the terms source and destination country are consistently used in this volume in order to relate and contrast net emigration and net immigration countries. Following the UN recommendations, we refer to international migrants as persons who reside for at least 12 months in a country other than the country of their birth or habitual residence.

2   The concepts of South and North are somewhat misleading as many mid-range developing countries are economically stratified with parallel and mixed rich and poor populations within their borders.

3   Regime in this context is defined very loosely as patterned transnational cooperation in a given issue-area. The term as used here does therefore not entirely correspond to the so called 'consensus-definition' in Krasner (1983) (cf. Koslowski in this volume).

4   International society as a term has its roots in the so called English School and captures the institutionalization of common interests among states, including shared norms, rules and institutions and is partly related to regime theory (see Buzan, 2004).

5   Although we do not entirely agree with its use and connotations, the concept of societal security as introduced by Waever et al. (1993), can be useful in this specific context.

6   As Koslowski points out in his chapter, the attempt by IOM in the late 1990s to sponsor a project led by Bimal Ghosh on the establishment of a *New International Regime for Orderly Movement of People* (NIROMP) by setting up guiding principles did not succeed as many states feared it to be a top-down approach. Subsequent attempts have not been favoured by for example the US as it prefers bilateral over multilateral cooperation.

PART 1
TRANSNATIONAL TRENDS OF MIGRATION AND POPULATION

PART I
TRANSNATIONAL RESIDENTIAL
MIGRATION AND POPULATION

Chapter 2

Transnational Migration: Conceptual and Policy Challenges

Peggy Levitt

The transnational village created by migration between the Dominican Republic and Boston, Massachusetts is emblematic of changes in contemporary migration patterns. Migration to Boston from the Dominican village of Miraflores began in the late 1960s. By the early 1990s, almost two-thirds of the nearly 550 households in Miraflores had relatives in the Boston area, most around the neighbourhood of Jamaica Plain. Community members, wherever they are, maintain such strong ties to each other that the life of this community occurs almost simultaneously in two places. When someone is ill, cheating on their spouse, or finally granted a visa, the news spreads as fast on the streets of Jamaica Plain as it does in Miraflores (Levitt, 2001a). This paper proposes a conceptual framework for understanding these transnational connections and explores their implications for policy-makers.

Mirafloreños started to migrate because it became too hard to make a living at farming. As more and more people left the fields of the Dominican Republic for the factories of Boston, Miraflores' economic situation initially weakened. But as a growing number of families began to receive economic remittances from the United States, their standard of living improved. Most households can now afford the food, clothing, and medicine that previous generations struggled for. Their homes are filled with the TVs, VCRs, and other appliances their migrant relatives bring them. Many have been able to renovate their houses, install indoor plumbing, or even afford air conditioning. With money donated in Boston and labour donated in Miraflores, the community built an aqueduct and baseball stadium and renovated the local school and health clinic. In short, most families live better since migration began, but they depend on money earned in the United States to do so.

Many of the Mirafloreños in Boston continue living near one another and working with one another, often at factories and office-cleaning companies where speaking Spanish is the norm. Consequently, they live within the small Miraflores community, nested within the broader Dominican and Latino communities. They participate in the neighbourhood organizations of Boston, but feel a greater commitment toward community development in Miraflores. They are starting to pay attention to elections in the United States, but it is still Dominican politics that inspires their greatest passion. When they take stock of their life's accomplishments, it is the Dominican yardstick that matters most.

The transnational character of Mirafloreños' lives is reinforced by connections between the Dominican Republic and the United States. The Catholic Church in Boston and the Church on the island cooperate because each feels responsible for migrant care. All three principle Dominican political parties campaign in the United States because migrants make large contributions and also influence how relatives back home vote. No one can run for president in the Dominican Republic, most Mirafloreños agree, without campaigning in New York. Conversely, mayoral and gubernatorial candidates in the north-eastern United States now make obligatory pilgrimages to Santo Domingo. Since remittances are one of the most important sources of the foreign currency in the country, the Dominican government instituted policies to encourage migrants' long-term participation without residence. During Dominican President Leonel Fernández's first administration (1996–2000), he ordered that all government housing projects set aside a quarter of the new units for returnees. When emigrants come back to visit, regardless of their current passport, they go through the customs line for Dominican nationals at the airport and are not required to pay a tourist entry fee.

Many people feel that pursuing American and home-country dreams at the same time is a recipe for disaster. In his recent book, *Who Are We?*, the political scientist Samuel Huntington (2004) argued that the United States is headed toward its own internal 'clash of civilizations' because Latinos do not assimilate Anglo-Protestant values and they remain behind linguistic and political walls. Don't countries need newcomers to subscribe to a core set of shared values to continue to survive and thrive? If people stay active in their homelands, how will they contribute to the countries where they settle? Aren't dual loyalties suspect, particularly after 11 September?

The experiences of Mirafloreños and others like them suggest that the answer is a resounding 'no'. The assumption that people will live their lives in one place, according to one set of national and cultural norms, in countries with impermeable national borders no longer holds. Rather, in the twenty-first century, more and more people will belong to two or more societies at the same time. They will work, pray, and express their political interests in several contexts rather than in a single nation state. Some will put down roots in a host country, maintain strong homeland ties, and belong to religious and political movements that span the globe. These allegiances are not antithetical to one another. Instead, as increasing numbers live parts of their social and economic lives across national boundaries, the challenge is to figure out what can be done to ensure that they are protected, represented, and that they contribute something in return.

When migrants live their lives across national boundaries, they challenge many long-held assumptions about membership, development, and equity. Understanding this reality requires new methodological and conceptual tools. It also requires new policy responses. The next section of this chapter outlines a conceptual approach to transnational migration. The section that follows outlines selective policy responses in the Latin American context. The concluding section raises questions that should be taken into account by future policy- and grant-makers.

Analytical and Conceptual Shifts[1]

Using a transnational lens to understand migration requires letting go of methodological nationalism. According to Wimmer and Glick Schiller (2003), most social scientific inquiries start from the assumption that the nation state is the logical, natural container within which social life takes place. Because the social sciences emerged at the same time that the contemporary nation state system was consolidated, many social scientific categories are embedded with a national bias that impairs our capacity to grasp transnational forms and processes. Analyses of the emergence of twentieth century corporations are usually comparative. They overemphasize the role of the nation-state and nation-state system rather than seeing firms and markets as parts of transnational systems of investment, production, distribution, and exchange. Studies of religion and politics have been similarly hampered, despite abundant evidence that movements as diverse as evangelical Protestantism, Roman Catholicism, freemasonry, trade unionism, and political progressivism crossed territorial borders and cultural boundaries to create powerful transnational communities and identities.

Abandoning methodological nationalism for a transnational perspective requires asking a different set of questions and taking into consideration a different set of factors than those that migration scholars normally take into account. The first important shift is to locate the study of migrants and their religious practices within the *transnational social fields* in which they may or may not be embedded. Levitt and Glick Schiller (2004) have defined social fields as a set of multiple interlocking networks of social relationships through which ideas, practices, and resources are unequally exchanged, organized, and transformed. Social fields are multi-dimensional, encompassing interactions of differing forms, depth, and breadth, such as organizations, institutions, and movements. The boundaries of social fields do not necessarily overlap with those of nations. National social fields are those that stay within national boundaries while transnational social fields connect actors, through direct and indirect relations, across borders.

Conceptualizing the migration experience as taking place within social fields is important for several reasons. First, it moves the analysis beyond those who actually migrate to those who do not actually move but are connected to migrants through the networks of social relations they sustain across borders. One does not have to move to engage in transnational practices. Because people who stay behind are connected to migrants' social networks, they are exposed to a constant flow of economic and social remittances (or ideas, practices, and identities that migrants import) on a regular basis (Levitt, 1999). Even individuals who have barely left their home villages adapt values and beliefs from afar and belong to organizations that now operate transnationally.

A social field perspective also reveals the difference between *ways of being* in a social field and *ways of belonging* (Glick Schiller, 2003; 2004). *Ways of being* refers to the actual social relations and practices that individuals engage in rather than to the identities associated with their actions. Social fields contain institutions, organizations, and experiences, within their various levels, that generate categories of identity that are ascribed to or chosen by individuals or groups. Individuals can be embedded in a social field but not identify with any label or cultural politics associated with that field. They have the potential to act or identify at a particular time because they live within the social field but not all choose to do so (Levitt and Glick Schiller, 2004).

In contrast, *ways of belonging* refers to practices that signal or enact identities that demonstrate a conscious connection to a particular group. An individual may invest, vote, or belong to a religious community that links them to their country of origin but not identify at all as belonging to a transnational group. They are engaging in transnational *ways of being* but not transnational *ways of belonging*. In contrast, individuals who engage in transnational *ways of being and ways of belonging* take part in transnational practices but also actively identify with groups that span space. Ways of belonging combine action and an awareness of the kind of identity that action signifies.

A social field perspective not only brings to the fore the multiple sites that constitute transnational social fields but their multiple layers as well. If, for example, I want to understand the Brazilian immigrants' religious experience in Boston, I need to map the connections between local congregations in Boston and Brazil and their ties to the national denominations between and across each context (for example ties to the national Brazilian denomination, ties that the immigrant congregation develops with its US denominational counterpart, and ties that emerge between the US and Brazilian denominations at the regional and national level in response). It is not enough, therefore, to look only at the local-to-local connections but at how these are integrated into vertical and horizontal systems of connection which cross borders as well. Rather than privileging one level over another, a transnational perspective holds these sites equally and simultaneously in conversation with each other and to grapple with the tension between them (Khagram and Levitt, 2004).

Finally, locating migrants within transnational social fields makes clear that incorporation in a new state and enduring transnational attachments are not binary opposites. Instead, it is more useful to think of the migrant experience as a kind of gauge, that while anchored, pivots between a new land and a transnational orientation. Movement and attachment is not linear or sequential but capable of rotating back and forth and changing direction over time. The median point on this gauge is not full incorporation but rather simultaneity of connection. Persons change and swing one way or the other depending on the context. Rather than expecting full assimilation or full transnational connection as the ultimate goal, we expect some combination of the two. In fact, it is more likely that migrants will engage in selective transnational practices on a periodic basis (Portes et al., 2002; Guarnizo et al., 2003; Levitt, 2001b). The analytical task is to explain why migrants manage the pivot in the way that they do and to specify how host country incorporation and homeland ties mutually influence each other (Levitt and Glick Schiller, 2004; Morawska, 2003).

A transnational lens, then, is both a perspective and a variable. It departs from a different set of assumptions about social organization. Rather than expecting migrants to move back and forth between two impermeable nation states, and exchanging one national identity for another, it locates migrants within social fields that combine several national territories. It is not enough for studies of the South Asian experience in the United States to look only at the immigrant experience in America. Rather, the American experience is as much a product of what goes on in India as it is of what goes on in the United Kingdom and in South Africa. The analysis begins by asking what kinds of origin, source, and other country factors are at play and then empirically examines their character and impact. In some cases, source country factors will not be important. The key, however, is that the inquiry begins from a transnational, rather than national, standpoint and then analyzes each case.

Clearly, not all migrants are transnational migrants, and not all who take part in transnational practices do so all the time. Studies by Alejandro Portes and his colleagues reveal that only 5 to 10 per cent of the Dominican, Salvadoran, and Columbian migrants they surveyed regularly participated in transnational economic and political activities; even occasional involvement is not universal (Portes et al., 2003; Guarnizo et al., 2003). Most migrants are occasional transnational activists. At some stages in their lives, they are more focused on their countries of origin while at others they are more involved in their countries of reception. Similarly, they climb two different social ladders, moving up, remaining steady, or experiencing downward mobility in various combinations with respect to two contexts.

Furthermore, transnational migration is not new (Foner, 2000; Glick Schiller, 1999). In the early part of the 1900s, European immigrants also returned to live in their home countries or remained active in the political and economic affairs of their homelands from their post in America. Some things are new, however, including ease of transportation and communication, the mode in which migrants are inserted into the labour market, source countries' increasing dependence on remittances and the policies they put in place to encourage migrants' enduring long-distance nationalism.

But if few migrants engage in transnational activities on a regular basis, does this really merit serious attention? The answer is yes for several reasons. The regular activities of a few combined with those who participate periodically add up. Together, they can transform the economy, culture, and everyday life of whole source-country regions. They challenge notions about gender relations, democracy, and what states should and should not do. For example, migration completely changed life in Miraflores. Young women no longer want to marry men who have never migrated because they want husbands who will share in the housework and take care of the children the way men who have been to the United States do. Other community members argued that Dominican politicians should be called on the carpet just as Bill Clinton was when he made questionable real estate deals and had his infamous affair with Monica Lewinsky. The source and destination countries become not separate social and political spheres but part of the same social system within which ideas about morality, equality, and democracy are renegotiated. Economic status, health, education, and community development are not nationally but transnationally determined. Looking only at Dominican activities in the United States misses the fact that what takes place there is also a product of activities in Spain and Venezuela.

Religious pluralism in the United States is as much, if not more, about what happens outside this country as about what takes place inside it.

Migration and Development Revisited

A transnational perspective challenges conventional notions about migration and development in fundamental ways. Yet the current policy-making apparatus and standard repertoire of policy tools does not adequately address this reality. I began this chapter laying out some of the economic impacts of transnational migration at the local level. Mirafloreños live better but they are almost completely dependent on remittances from the United States to be able to do so. Both households and the community at large have grown dependent on migrant contributions to meet their daily needs, to build the infrastructure, and to provide basic health and educational services.

This scenario is replicated throughout Latin America, in the villages of El Salvador to the mountains of Peru producing a national-level equivalent. For one thing, remittances far exceed the funds received for official development assistance or foreign portfolio investment in many less-developed countries, not just those in Latin America (Naim, 2002). According to the Inter-American Development Bank (IDB), remittances to Latin America increased from 2001 by 18 per cent to \$32 billion in 2002 (*Migration News*, 2003). That constituted 2 per cent of the region's GDP (Sørenson, 2004). Some states use the promise of future remittances as collateral to secure international loans (Guarnizo et al., 2003). The economies of countries such as Albania, El Salvador, Tonga, and Lebanon would collapse if remittance flows dried up (Becker, 2004).

Furthermore, some source country governments recognize the role that migrants can play in advocating for their foreign policy interests. Migrants, especially those paying the bills for family members back home, strongly influence how non-migrants vote. They also represent a potential lobby that, if well organized, could work in favour of source country interests.

In response, source countries throughout the region have put into place policies designed to encourage emigrants' long-term, long-distance nationalism. In 2000, ten countries in Latin America had passed some form of dual nationality or citizenship, including Brazil, Colombia, Costa Rica, the Dominican Republic, Ecuador, El Salvador, Mexico, Panama, Peru, and Uruguay. Only four countries had such provisions prior to 1991 (Jones-Correa, 2001). Other countries recognize dual membership selectively, with specific signatories. Guatemala has an agreement with other Central American Countries and several countries have such agreements with Spain. At least ten Caribbean basin countries including Antigua, Barbados, Belize, Dominica, Grenada, Jamaica, St Kitts, St Lucia, St Vincent, and the Grenadines, and Trinidad and Tobago also recognize dual nationality.

Countries such as Brazil, the Dominican Republic and Mexico also allow the expatriate vote. Again, the Dominican case illustrates the interdependence between source and target country political outcomes. Each of the three principal Dominican political parties has offices in the United States. The Partido de la Liberación (PLD), in particular, has encouraged Dominicans to become US citizens so that they will enjoy a more secure position in the United States and they will be in a better position to advocate for Dominican national interests.

Finally, some countries even grant political rights to emigrants while they are abroad. Colombia allows the expatriate community to elect representatives to the Colombian legislature (Escobar, 2004). In the Dominican Republic, several people have been known to run for office from their home communities although it is common knowledge that their primary residence is in the United States. They officially represent their island-based constituency but they are unofficial representatives of the immigrant community as well (Itzigsohn, 2000).

Granting rights and representation is just one strategy for maintaining migrants' loyalties. Latin American governments have also instituted several different packages of initiatives (Levitt and de la Dehesa, 2003). They reformed ministerial and consular services to be more responsive to emigrant needs. They put into place investment policies designed to attract and channel economic remittances. They extended state protections or services to nationals living abroad that went beyond traditional consular services. Finally, they implemented symbolic policies designed to reinforce emigrants' sense of enduring membership (Andrade-Eekhoff and Silva-Avalos, 2003).

These policy-initiatives raise several red flags. First, there is the age-old question about migration and development. On a macroeconomic level, Orozco (2003b) argues that the development impact of migration can be captured by '5 Ts' – remittance Transfers, Transport, Tourism, Telecommunication, and Trade. Migrants increase demand in each of these sectors in economically beneficial ways. Migrants also contribute financially to home country development by generating demand for and purchasing power with which to buy local goods and services (Guarnizo, 2003). But what is the effect of remittances on household level dynamics? Are remittances spent productively, on investments and improvements, or are they merely used for consumption (see Sørenson, 2004)? While much research focuses on the appliances, home renovations, and clothing purchased with remittances, several recent studies found that remittances are being used to fund education expenses or to offset retirement expenses by functioning like quasi-pensions. They also found that a higher percentage of income was being allocated toward health care and toward making improvements in agriculture (Andrade-Eekhoff and Silva-Avalos, 2003). In fact, because remittances seem to have increasingly productive potential, policy-makers are focusing their efforts on lowering the cost of remittance transfers to increase cost effectiveness (Orozco, 2002). A Salvadoran federation of cooperatives, promotes remittance productiveness by providing financial services to migrants and their families in both the migrant destination and source countries (FOCAL, 2004).

The second and third red flag concern the role of collective resources. Many immigrant communities organize in the US to promote infrastructure and social service programs in their home communities. They may organize Home Town Associations (HTAs) in cooperation with a counterpart group that already exists in their community or they may be the impetus for such a group's formation. Orozco (2003a) estimates that in Mexico alone these groups contribute up to $60 million a year for public works projects above and beyond what they are already sending to their families. Several governments, including Mexico, El Salvador and Guatemala have worked actively to promote HTA growth and cooperation (Goldring, 2002; Popkin, 2003). The Mexican government, for example, instituted a 3X1 program whereby migrant-generated funds are matched by funds contributed at the local, state, and federal government level. The Salvadoran government has a similar program entitled, *Programa Unidos Por La Solidaridad* whereby associations, municipalities, and groups of Salvadorans living outside the country can compete for government funding to support public works and social development projects (MREES, 2003).

HTAs are at once touted as the powerful development engines and criticized as disproportionately burdening migrants with the task of economic growth. In one of the most comprehensive reports to date on HTAs in Mexico, Manuel Orozco concluded that these groups are 'small philanthropic players with capacities to promote development, particularly when working in partnership with other players' (2003: 42). He found, however, that most groups had limited ability to manage and oversee projects and emphasized the importance of providing technical assistance before more challenging and ambitious activities are undertaken. He suggested that donors focus on providing technical assistance in project identification, bolstering governance and democratic capabilities, and encouraging partnerships in social and infrastructural projects. In addition, he also stressed the potential role of government incentives to attract private sector involvement and to carry out investment feasibility analyses.

HTAs are just one manifestation of collective remittance use. Migrant source country governments have also tried to develop a market within the migrant community for home country goods and to stimulate migrant investment in private sector initiatives in the home country. One such effort initiated by the Guatemalan government (1996–1999) worked as follows. To avoid unproductive individual remittances and to capitalize on the large numbers of Guatemalans affiliated with migrant organizations, the Guatemalan Embassy in Washington initiated a program called *Chapines Sin Fronteras* (Guatemalans without Borders) which encouraged collective migrant direct investment in business ventures in target migrant source communities. Working with several government ministries and a number of large private sector organizations, the program tried to generate financing from migrant organizations for a package of agricultural development proposals. In the words of Popkin (2003: 361):

> Migrant organizations were encouraged to invest in a BANRURAL account established for the project of their choice. Migrant organizations would invest directly in BANRURAL certificates of deposit and receive 7.5 per cent interest on their investments. In turn, BANRURAL, through its 160 branches throughout Guatemala, would offer loans at 10 per cent interest rate to local producers to implement the projects in the prioritized communities.

The products were then marketed to the immigrant community in the United States through small companies run by immigrants. To start these companies, immigrant organizations sold stock to members of specific communities. Government ministries assisted with labelling, shipping, marketing, and product development. Although successfully implemented, the project stonewalled when there was a change of government in 1999. Particularly difficult was the complexity of coordinating between so many actors and organizations. Others questioned the volume and quantity of goods produced in Guatemala.

Policy Challenges

The previous section outlined some examples of policies designed to systematically harness the benefits of transnational migration. In this concluding section, I highlight some of the challenges and contradictions that future policy-makers should keep in mind.

Social Categories like Class and Race May Not Be What We Think

Those who live transnationally define their class, race, and gender according to two cultural yardsticks. Where do people fall on the poverty line when they receive US government vouchers to assist with housing costs while they are building a home in their home country? What about individuals who cannot afford their rent in the United States because they are too busy sending remittances to support those at home? To what extent does wage labour 'liberate' migrant women who now have to maintain households at home and abroad? These questions bring to light the need for broader frames of reference that can capture the multi-sitedness of migrants' economic and social experiences. The problems facing individuals, households, and communities, and the resources they have for solving them, need to take into account the context of the transnational social field in which they are embedded.

Who is the Target Population?

Transnational migration creates at least three distinct categories of experience – those who actually migrate, those who stay behind but receive support from those who migrate, and those who do not migrate and have no sources of outside support. Clearly, those who have no outside support are the most needy. Not only do they lack access to the additional resources generated by migration but they now live within a cultural context where it is the norm to consume goods that are beyond their reach. Households and communities become accustomed to a lifestyle that is unsustainable with their own resources. Incentives to undertake economic reforms weaken with the arrival of each remittance transfer. This is an important point, often forgotten by policy-makers, who have been caught up by recent craze to use remittances as a development tool.

The unequal distribution of migration's rewards also creates a disjuncture between the needs of the individual and the collective. Migration might endow individuals with more money to go to school or get health care but it does not always bring about concomitant improvements to the educational or health care system. This disconnect between the better-off individual and the perpetually needy collective also creates a challenge for targeting programmatic resources.

Conflicts between Migrant and Nonmigrant Interests

Over time, migrants' and nonmigrants' interests tend to diverge. Many migrants want their homeland to stay the way it was before they left. They want a place that is comfortable to visit or retire to. Who should speak for the village or the nation? How can migrant concerns be taken into account without discounting the priorities of those who remain behind? Should source countries devote resources toward emigrants that could help those at home?

Another way of putting this is whose voice is and should be heard? Since migrants foot the bill for many development activities, their priorities often come to the fore. Luin Goldring (2003) found that hometown associations were better platforms for men than for women. Similarly, governments and political parties, interested in courting migrants, have been found to pander to their interests at the expense of those who stay behind (Popkin, 2003).

Development, but at Whose Expense?

Migrants make major contributions to community development. Some argue, however, that despite improved living conditions and infrastructure, such projects disproportionately burden migrants and make them responsible for functions that rightfully belong to states. One way out of this conundrum is to build capacity, strengthen organizations, and increase skills so that migrants can protect their interests more effectively. Another strategy is to foster cooperation between grassroots groups so that communities work cooperatively and no one community is disproportionately burdened.

The Possibility of Simultaneity

A transnational perspective reveals that host-country and enduring homeland ties are not incompatible. All too often, these two loyalties are seen in opposition, if not antagonistic to one another. The challenge is to use the resources and skills migrants acquire in one context to address issues in the other. For example, transnational entrepreneurs are more likely to be US citizens, suggesting that full membership in the new land enables them to run more successful businesses in their countries of origin (Portes et al., 2002). Similarly, Latino activists sometimes use the same groups to promote political participation in the United States as they do to mobilize migrants around homeland political concerns. Some of the associations created to promote Dominican businesses in New York, for instance, also played a major role in securing the approval of dual citizenship on the island. Likewise, Escobar (2004) argues that Columbian transnational organizations have contributed positively to political engagement in the United States. Exploring mutually reinforcing type activities and the kinds of institutional arrangements that allow them to emerge is important.

Social Remittances: A Potential Resource?

Social remittances are the ideas, behaviours, identities, and social capital that migrants export to their home communities. They include ideas about democracy, health, and community organization. They differ from global cultural flows in that it is possible to identify the channels through which they are disseminated and the determinants of their impact. Social remittances are both positive and negative. While some saw migrants as a force for greater democratization and accountability in the Dominican Republic, others held them responsible for rising materialism and individualism (Levitt, 2001a).

How can social remittances be purposefully harnessed to improve socioeconomic indicators in both source and destination countries? How can certain types of information be disseminated to particular target audiences? These purposeful transfers should by no means go one way. Information about health care practices and educational outcomes could also be strategically channelled to providers in for example the United States.

What are the Rights and Responsibilities of Transnational Membership?

Along with the benefits of dual membership come responsibilities. But the rights and responsibilities of dual belonging are not clear. For one thing, it is not readily obvious which state is ultimately responsible for which aspects of transnational migrants' lives. Where should those who live across borders get health care, pay taxes or serve in the army? Which state assumes the primary responsibility for migrants' protection and representation? What should states expect in return? The Paraguayan government recently tried to intercede on behalf of a dual national sentenced to death in the United States, arguing that capital punishment is illegal in Paraguay even though it is legal in the United States. The Mexican government recently invented a special consular ID card, issued to all Mexican emigrants, including those living without formal authorization in the United States. More than 100 cities, 900 police departments, 100 financial institutions and 13 states in the US accept the card as proof of identity for obtaining a drivers' licence or opening a bank account. These examples illustrate the ways in which countries of origin assume partial responsibility for emigrants and act on their behalf. While gaining in acceptance, they are by no means permanent.

The Second Generation

A transnational approach to migration remains controversial. While some admit that transnational activism may be important for the first generation, they predict that these ties will disappear among their children. It is unlikely that the children of immigrants will be involved in their ancestral homes in the same ways and with the same intensity as their parents. However, since many of these children have been raised in households saturated by homeland influences, even those who express little interest in their roots have the knowledge and skills with which to activate these values and identities if and when they decide to do so. The children of Mexican immigrants who travel to Mexico and return are better able to understand the meaning of Mexicanness in New York. They are exercising their membership in a transnational social field. The children of Gujaratis who go back to India to find marriage partners, or the second generation Pakistanis who begin to study Islam and Pakistani values when they have children, are doing so as well. Many Dominicans born in the United States and Puerto Rico frequently visit their parents' country and keep in touch with their relatives there. At critical stages in their lives, these individuals may activate the potential contacts and identities available to them and become transnational activists. Transnational strategies need to take this potential pool of participants into account.

The Possibilities for Pan-ethnicity

One reason why new immigrants' interests are seldom taken into account in their host country is that they do not naturalize, vote, or make campaign contributions at the same rates as the native-born. Strong minority coalitions are difficult to come by. The relationship between transnational involvements and pan-ethnic mobilization across different national groups, such as among Latinos or Asians in the United States needs further attention. If immigrant political advancement and participation in homeland politics sometimes compete with one another, then transnational loyalties are likely to pose an even greater challenge to the creation of viable pan-ethnic and/or minority coalitions.

The Issue of Trust

The vast majority of migrants distrust government. The word 'corruption' is the first thing on their lips when they describe politicians at home. They wonder why the government is interested in them now, when it never was when they were at home. They prefer to give directly to a needy individual than to any group, particularly one associated with the state. For any state-driven efforts to be successful, migrants need to learn to trust government. Moreover, they need a good reason to do so. This is a particularly high barrier to making transnational policies work.

Note

[1] This section draws heavily on Levitt and Glick Schiller (2004).

Chapter 3

The Boom and Bust of Net Migration?
A 40-year Forecast

Bo Malmberg

Introduction

There is no such thing as a net migrant (Rogers, 1990). Migration instead takes the form of gross migration flows – people moving from one place to another looking for new opportunities. Indeed, one of the fundamental laws of migration is that migration flows are bidirectional: '[e]ach main current of migration produces a compensating counter-current' (Ravenstein, 1889). Nonetheless, neoclassical economic theories of migration generally focus on net migration as if migration streams were unidirectional. Net migration, the difference between immigration and emigration, is assumed to respond to differences in wages between regions and countries. Net migration is assumed to have effects on wage levels and per capita income. The neoclassical theory of migration should be treated with caution. It is based on an assumption of homogenous labour for which the attraction of a specific labour market is captured by the market wage. With homogenous labour, migration flows will only go one way. For what would be the reason for someone to move from a labour market with a high wage to a labour market with lower wages?

The simultaneous existence of migration flows in both directions shows that this assumption of homogenous labour is false. If one person finds region A more attractive than region B whereas another person prefers B over A this indicates, of course, that there must be heterogeneity and an exchange of flows. When it comes to policies these different assumptions about migration are of fundamental importance. With heterogeneous labour, the full benefit of an increasing global division of labour will not be realized if people cannot move to those places of production where their specific skills are valued the most. If labour is homogenous, the effects of restricting movement are most pronounced on the distribution of income. It will keep wages low in surplus countries and high in countries with a low supply of labour.

In this chapter, I will argue that international net migration is a phenomenon that will be drastically reduced in the twenty-first century. The global movement of people will continue but for most countries inflows and outflows of migrants will be more balanced. If my argument is correct, international agreements on how to manage migration flows should not focus only on situations where the flows are unbalanced. Of equal importance is to prepare for a situation where the difference between inflows and outflows becomes smaller.

The end of global net migration also has an important implication for policy-makers in the rich and aging countries. It is that relying on immigration from countries with high birth rates cannot indefinitely solve the problems associated with a rapid increase in the share of old people because of low domestic birth rates. Instead, a long-term balance between the working and non-working population requires both birth rates not too much below the replacement level as well as an effective retirement age that increases alongside substantial gains in life expectancy.

However, during a transitory period of 20–30 years there is a great potential for large net migration flows. And during this period, both sending and receiving countries can benefit from having well-managed mechanisms that allow individuals from countries with oversized cohorts in migrant ages to seek employment and a future in countries with undersized cohorts in the corresponding age.

The Demographic Transition

The prediction that international net migration may be drastically reduced in 20–30 years is based on the theory of the demographic transition. What we now call the demographic transition was discovered in the second quarter of the twentieth century by demographers observing the variation of death rates and birth rates across countries and over time. The finding was that:

> in the Western cultural area there has been a general process of change from the relative population stability at high levels of mortality and fertility to the slowing growth or actual decline of population numbers at low levels of mortality and fertility that characterized the interwar period. The initial effect was a decrease in mortality, leaving largely intact the large family pattern. For reasons that are not entirely clear a small family pattern became not only an ideal but also a goal realized by increasing proportions of the population. Birth rates fell rapidly, at first in cities, later in the surrounding rural areas. (Taeuber, 1945)

The prerequisite for this observation was increasing efforts to assemble demographic data from the nineteenth century and onwards that had made available time-series stretching over multiple decades or longer. Researchers in the inter-war era, thus, could base their analysis of population trends on a comparatively rich empirical material. However, the concept of demographic transition was not only used as a name for an empirical pattern. Instead the researchers who introduced the term saw these trends in mortality and fertility as the expression of an underlying social transformation process. Moreover, their conclusion from observing similar demographic trends in different countries was that the process of demographic transition would not be restricted to Europe but would spread also to other parts of the world. In fact, Irene B. Taeuber's original formulation of the transition idea appears in a paper that analyses the population development of Southern and Eastern Asia.

In 1945 the idea that the world would witness demographic transitions throughout Asia, Africa and America was basically a scientific hypothesis yet to be verified or falsified. The key assumption behind this hypothesis was essentially a belief that the technologies giving rise to lower mortality would continue to spread to those parts of the world that still suffered from high mortality levels. Developments after 1945 have demonstrated that this assumption was well-founded, although even proponents of the transition hypothesis soon became surprised by the amazing decline of mortality in underdeveloped areas (Davis, 1956).

Today, almost 60 years later we can conclude that the demographic transition hypothesis has proved to be correct. First, the mortality decline observed in the Western world and in parts of Asia before 1945 has indeed spread to practically all parts of the world. Before 1945 the life expectancy at birth in many non-Western populations was appreciably below 40 years. In India 1941–1950 for example, the expectation of life at birth has been estimated to be only 32 years (Stolnitz, 1965). Similarly, the Bantu population of South Africa had an estimated life expectancy at birth of 34 years in 1936–1946 (Walle and Page, 1969). Life expectancy in China was lower still: data on the Chinese farmer population in 1929–1931 indicate values of 28 years in North China and 24 years in South China (Barclay, Coale et al., 1976). In other parts of the world the picture was somewhat brighter with male life expectancy at birth at 41 years in Chile (1940) and Taiwan (1936–1941) (Toppozada, 1968), and 47 years in Japan (1935–1936) (Stolnitz, 1965).

Since the Second World War life expectancy in these countries has risen dramatically. The most impressive gains have been made in China. In 1999 the World Bank estimated a life expectancy at birth of 70 years. That is a gain of 44 years compared with the life expectancy for the Chinese farmer population around 1930. Japan, Taiwan and Chile have gains in life expectancy around 35 year. The gains in India are around 30 years. In South Africa there was a 23 years gain in life expectancy up to 1980 but nine years of this gain has been lost between 1980 and 1999 primarily because of AIDS related deaths. Of the large world regions only Sub-Saharan Africa now, despite a substantial increase, has a life-expectancy at birth below 50 years. In the rest of the world life expectancy is above 60 years.

Also the second prediction of the demographic transition hypothesis – that birth rates for an extended period will stay high when the death rates have begun to decline – has proved correct. Using UN data (UN, 2001b) this process can be most easily traced in African countries like Kenya, Ethiopia and Nigeria where falling death rates and relatively stable birth rates lead to accelerated population growth during the 1950–1970 period. However, the starting point of the UN data is 1950–1954, which means that this data set does not capture the dramatic decline in death rates in the first few years after 1945. According to a study by Kingsley Davis, the total decline in the crude death rate between 1935 and the 1950–1954 period can be estimated to 58 per cent, with the largest part of the decline after 1945. The UN data gives us a picture of what is happening to the population directly after a sharp mortality reduction. If Kingsley Davis' estimate is correct – and assuming stable birth rates – the population growth rate in the less developed countries (UN, 2001a definition) would have accelerated from 0.3 per cent annually in 1935 to 2.1 per cent in 1950-54. This growth rate was the result of a crude birth rate of almost 45 per cent and a crude death rate coming down from around 41 per cent to 24 per cent. Declining death rates, thus, led to accelerated population growth exactly as the Princeton demographers had predicted.

Towards the end of the 1960s the death rate of the less developed countries had declined a further nine points but the birth rate had only declined by half as much. Population growth in the less developed countries, thus, had accelerated further and now stood at 2.5 per cent annually. The end of the 1960s, then, was a time when the transition hypothesis did not seem to be correct. Had not the hypothesis assumed that declining death rates would be followed by lower birth rates? And, what would happen if birth rates remained high? This, thus, was also a good time for dooms-day predictions concerning the future of the earth and its population (Ehrlich, 1968; Ehrlich and Ehrlich, 1970). Not everyone lost their nerves, though. The UN forecasters continued to base their projections on the assumption of a slow but continuing fertility decline that would bring down the population growth rate. And – as it turned out – the UN forecasters were right.

Between 1965–1969 and 1970–1974 there came an important shift in the population trend as growth rates in Eastern Asia and Southeastern Asia started to decline. This had happened in Korea and in Latin America already some years earlier but it was with the Asian turn-around that the shifting trend became globally significant. Later in the 1970s population growth rates started to decline in Southern Africa and in the mid 1980s, population growth began to slow also in North Africa, Western and South Central Asia. In the early 1990s, it happened in Western Africa and in Eastern Africa too, although in the latter case this slowdown was partly due to an increase in the death rates. And at the end of the 1990s, Middle Africa also seems to have passed its peak in the population growth rate.

A more detailed view of factors behind the downward trend in population growth comes from a look at how the *Total Fertility Rates* (TFR) have developed after 1950. In Figure 3.1, the most important patterns of fertility change in the world between 1950 and 2000 are outlined. Countries with a similar pattern of fertility change have been grouped together and for each year the mean fertility rate in each group has been calculated. Figure 3.1 shows clearly that fertility rates differ much across the world and that there are different patterns of fertility change. However, there are also strong common trends. In all groups, except two, fertility has gone down since 1950 although at different rates.

Only two groups have a record of no significant decline in mortality. In these groups we find a number of very poor countries many of which have experienced strong social disruption: Afghanistan, Angola, Burundi, Ethiopia, Liberia, Mali, Somalia, Uganda, and Yemen all belong to the group where the TFR still is close to 7 children per woman. Also for Cameroon, Congo, Gambia, Lao, Mozambique, Namibia, and Pakistan there has been very little change in the TFR, almost constant around 6 children per woman.

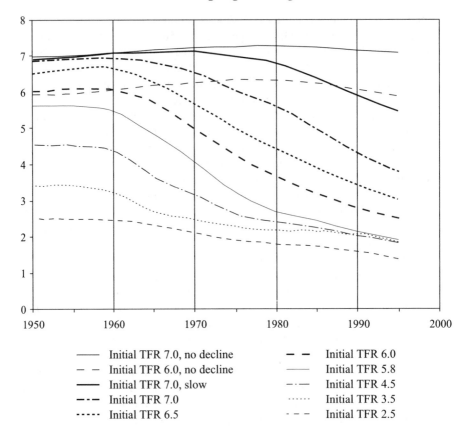

Figure 3.1   Fertility rates and outcomes (five-year periods)

Note: TFR = total fertility rate. Mean fertility rates are calculated in groups from 2.5 to 7.

Another group for which the fertility rate in 1995-2000 was still very high, around 5.4, is inter alia made up of several West African countries, Eritrea, Guatemala, Iraq, Jordan, Rwanda, Saudi Arabia, Sudan, Tanzania, Zambia, and Zimbabwe. For this group starting with a TFR of 7 in 1950, there has, however, been an appreciable reduction in the fertility rate, especially since 1980. A trend which, if we are to judge from the development of other groups, can be expected to continue.

The group consisting inter alia of Bangladesh, Botswana, Egypt, Honduras, Iran, Mongolia, Morocco, Nicaragua, Philippines and Tajikistan in 1950 also had an average TFR of 7 but by the end of the 1990s the average rate had been reduced to 3.8, a very considerable reduction. Three groups including Costa Rica, the Dominican Republic, El Salvador, India, Malaysia, Mexico, South Africa, Tunisia, Turkey, Uzbekistan, and Viet Nam starting at a TFR of 6.5, followed by Albania, Brazil, Indonesia and Thailand starting at TFR at 6.0, and finally Chile, China, the Republic of Korea, and

Sri Lanka also starting at a TFR of 6.0, have essentially tracked one another with respect to the fertility decline and arrived at mean TFR rates of 3.0, 2.5, and around 2.0 respectively in the late 1990s.

What we can see in Figure 3.1, then, is a quite impressive corroboration of the demographic transition hypothesis. To be sure, some countries have yet to enter the phase of fertility decline and others have a long way to go before they reach replacement fertility, that is, a level of TFR slightly above 2 that in the long run keeps a population constant. But the patterns of fertility change during the last 50 years strongly suggest that a continuing fertility decline in today's high fertility countries is to be expected. The Princeton hypothesis of a demographic transition affecting countries all over the world, thus, has turned out to be one of the most successful predictions made by social scientists in the twentieth century.

The Age Transition

In the 1990s some scholars have pointed out that population growth will not be evenly distributed across the different age groups during the demographic transition (Chesnais, 1990, 1992). On the contrary, as the demographic transition unfolds the growth rate of different age groups will follow an uneven pattern (Malmberg and Sommestad, 2000b). In some periods during the transition, population growth will be concentrated to the youngest part of the population. In other periods the young adult, middle aged, or old age population segments are increasing most rapidly. This implies that population growth will give coherent effects on per capita income only if it is correct that the economic effects of population growth are the same irrespective of whether it is children, young adults, middle aged adults, or old age adults that are increasing in numbers (Bloom et al., 2003). Even as a scientific simplification that seems to be a rather far-fetched hypothesis.

How Does Age Structure Change during a Demographic Transition?

This question can be answered both empirically and through the use of demographic models. As it turns out, both methods give very similar results, at least over long periods with moderate levels of immigration and emigration. The typical pattern of a mortality decline followed – after a lag – by declining fertility will generate a very distinct pattern of age structure change. This pattern can be observed in most countries affected by a demographic transition. One way to summarize is to distinguish four different phases of population growth during the demographic transition.

The first phase following the onset of mortality decline is characterized by an increase in the number of children. The primary reason for this is that in high mortality regimes it is among newborns, infants and young children that the death toll is especially high. So when mortality comes down it is to a large extent the lives of the very youngest that are spared. In time, this increase in the number of children will also increase the young adult fertile population and – as long as fertility rates are unchanged – this will, by inducing more births, further accelerate the increase in the number of children. This first child-rich phase of what can be called the age transition will continue as long as the fertility rate remains high. The fertility decline eventually slows down the increase of the child population.

The second phase is characterized by an expansion of the young adult population. The mechanism behind this expansion is simply that with declining mortality, and later an increase in the number of births, the number of surviving individuals in each cohort will increase. As these ever larger cohorts reach adult ages the young adult population will start to expand. Because it takes time for newborns to reach adult age the young adult phase will start 15–20 years later than the child-rich phase and it will continue 15–20 years after the expansion of the child population has stopped.

The third phase is characterized by an expansion of the middle-aged population. This phase starts when the cohorts enlarged by mortality decline and increases in the number of births reach the middle ages. Depending on how one defines 'middle age' this expansion is initiated 20–30 years after the young adult phase starts. It thus takes four to five decades or more before the mortality decline of a demographic transition produces an appreciable increase in the number of middle aged.

The fourth phase, finally, follows when the enlarged cohorts reach retirement and is characterized by an expansion of the old age population. Often, this expansion starts after the fertility rates have dropped to a low level and this means that the old age phase, and also at least part of the middle age phase, lies outside the time span that we normally consider when we talk about the demographic transition. In Sweden, for example, the classic transition was complete in the 1930s when the TFR had come down to, or even below, the replacement level. The middle age phase of the age transition however did not end until about 1970 and the old age phase continued for another two decades.

Two things should be noted about the age transition. First, as pointed out above, the age transition as a phenomenon extends for a considerably longer period than the classical transition. This implies that the demographic transition, because of population momentum, will have social and economic effects also when there are no longer any current changes in the vital rates. Secondly, it is important to remember that, to some extent, the phases of the age transition will overlap. Depending on for how long later cohorts keep getting larger than earlier cohorts, this time of overlap may be short or long.

The fact that countries with large differences in terms of historical traditions, climate, and geography have gone through demographic transitions that in terms of changing mortality and birth rates have been similar, is certainly a challenge to social science. In this study, where the purpose is not to explain why demographic transitions have occurred but to utilize the effect the transitions have on income growth, the existence of numerous instances of demographic transitions in very different contexts is, however, a great advantage creating variation and correlations that can be exploited to forecast income.

Forecasting Net Migration

Long-term forecasting of social phenomena is a contentious business. In his essay 'The Poverty of Historicism', Karl Popper has, for example, argued that social trends cannot be predicted (Popper, 1960). The basis for his argument is that social processes are influenced by the development of new knowledge. Since, by definition, we cannot know what new discoveries will be made in the future we do not have access to the information we would need to make correct forecasts. And, therefore, historical predictions such as Marx's about the necessity of socialism are not valid.

Popper, however, does leave a door open for conditional forecasts. That is, forecast that are dependent on the realization of given premises. Such premises could be, for example, the continued validity of certain empirical laws or the continued stability of certain empirical trends. As it turns out, migration research of the last 100 years has in fact provided us with some empirical laws that may be used for conditional forecasts. Most important here is the strong correlation between age and migration propensity. Over and over again, from the early twentieth century and onwards, it has been shown that an overwhelming proportion of all migrants are young adults in the ages between 15 and 35 years, with people in their early 20s being the most active group. This pattern is not restricted to developed countries and the postwar period but can be found across cultures and in different temporal and geographical settings. Thus, if this empirical law is not broken, young adults will dominate migration flows also in the twenty-first century.

Theoretically, the high migration propensity of young adults can be explained by the theory of human capital. In this perspective migration is seen as an investment. You move from one place to another in order to increase the valuation of your human capital. But it is costly to move, especially over large distances. You have to pay a passage, perhaps learn a new language and it becomes difficult and expensive to maintain contact with old friends and relatives. For young people this cost can be balanced by many years in a more rewarding employment. For older individuals, however, the net benefit will be much smaller or even negative.

High migration propensity among young adults implies that rates of out-migration will be higher in countries where young adults are numerous relative to other age groups, then in countries with relatively few young adults. If countries with the same population size have the same probability of being chosen as destination country, this would imply then that net migration rates will tend to be negative in countries with many young adults and positive in countries where young adults are few.

This association between high population shares of young adults and negative net migration will be further strengthened by economic factors. Countries where large cohorts are entering working age will experience a rapid increase in labour supply. This might lead to a downward pressure on wages and to unemployment problems creating a push effect on migration. Moreover, countries where the cohorts that reach working age grow from year to year tend to be countries that have had high fertility rates and, therefore, high child dependency rates and low per capita income. Countries where cohort sizes are constant or falling have low fertility rates, low rates of child dependency and high per capita income.

Demographic factors, thus, can play a key role in influencing net migration rates. This can be the case directly, by determining the size and growth rate of the highly mobile, young adult population, and indirectly, via age structure effects on per capita income. The importance of demographic factors is good news for our abilities to forecast net migration. The reason is that population change, especially age structure change, is relatively easy to forecast. The procedure is, first, to use historical data to estimate a model where net migration is related to demographic structure. Then, this model can be combined with data from population forecasts to produce predictions of future net migration.

The Model

The model used here to estimate how demographic factors influence net migration is based on Hatton and Williamson (1994, 2003). In order to capture the effect of cohort growth on migration Hatton and Williamson use the rate of natural population growth 20 years earlier. That is, the births minus deaths in relation to the total population. As long as infant mortality is high this measure gives a relatively good approximation to the cohort growth rates. However, in ageing populations with low infant mortality most deaths occur at high ages and then the Hatton and Williamson formulae will not produce a good measure of cohort growth. In the estimates presented below the measure of cohort growth is, instead, based on an approximation of the number of survivors in each cohort at five years of age.

This model also uses a different specification of the dependent variable. Hatton and Williamson use the number of gross emigrants as their dependent variable. However, due to lack of good data on gross migration flows for many countries this variable cannot be used to estimate demographic effects on migration in a larger world sample. In the population data made available by the UN Population Division, only estimated net migration rates are available. These rates can be inferred by comparing the result from different censuses and do not depend on any registration of gross migration flows.

A problem is however that net migration rates can be both positive and negative. This rules out the use of a logarithm specification that, for other reasons, would be preferable to a linear specification. Instead of using net migration rates, the dependent variable used in this estimation will, therefore, be the number of survivors in a birth cohort up to age five. This figure is adjusted for the number of net migrants estimated for the period when the cohort reaches between 20–24 years of age.

The dependent variable used in this estimation is therefore constructed by adding the number of net migrants (a negative number if net migration is negative) during a five-year period to the estimated number of survivors at age five for the cohort that reaches the age 20–24 in the period. If all net migrants would come from the 20–24 age group this sum would represent the current size of the cohort. This is generally not the case. However, by dividing this hypothetical current cohort size with the size of the birth cohort adjusted for survival we do get a measure with some desired properties. This ratio – which will be designated net migration index – will be equal to one if there is no net migration. The net migration index will be below one if net migration is negative and above one if net migration is positive. As long as total net migration is less than the size of the birth cohort minus deaths before five years of age, the net migration index will be positive. And hence, the log of the net migration index can be used as the dependent variable in the regression.

Trends in the Net Migration Index

A consequence of using the size of the birth cohort adjusted for 0-5 survival is that using UN data, the net migration index can only be computed for 1970 and onwards. Thus, the analysis of net migration trends has to be restricted to the post 1970 period. The results of such an analysis are presented in Figures 3.2a and 3.2b. Here the development of the net migration index for eight different country-groups is illustrated. The countries have been grouped both according to the level of the net migration index and in response to changes in the index. The sample here is the 187 countries for which the UN Population division provides data minus 27 small countries that sometime during the 1950–2000 period have experienced a negative net migration index – that is, migration losses larger than the size of an entire cohort.

As illustrated in the figures the data can be conveniently grouped into immigrant and emigrant countries. In the late 1990s, about a third of the countries could be classified as immigrant countries. Of these, however, about half have become immigrant countries during the period of study and another ten, including China, Germany, Greece, Italy, Japan, Slovenia and Switzerland, have experienced large increases in their net migration index. Countries with relatively constant net migration indexes during this period include Australia, Canada, Denmark, France, Netherlands, Sweden, United Kingdom, and the United States. On average in these countries, total net migration is about 20–30 per cent the size of a birth cohort.

An interesting feature in the data is that a large group of emigrant countries have experienced declining net migration rates. This group includes Chile, Dominican Republic, Gambia, India, Indonesia, Malaysia, Mexico, Morocco, South Africa, Sri Lanka, Tunisia, Turkey and Viet Nam. In the early 1970s total net migration from these countries could be as high as 40 per cent the size of a birth cohort. In the late 1990s this figure has declined to around 10 per cent. A majority of the emigrant countries, however, are still experiencing high rates of out migration, although there is a tendency towards a decline, especially in the last, 1995–2000 period.

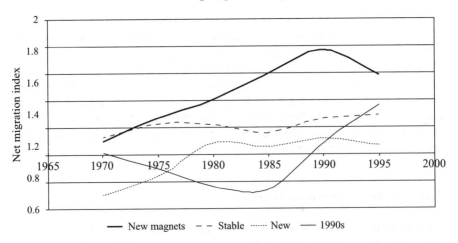

Figure 3.2a   Trends in net migration, immigration countries (five-year periods)

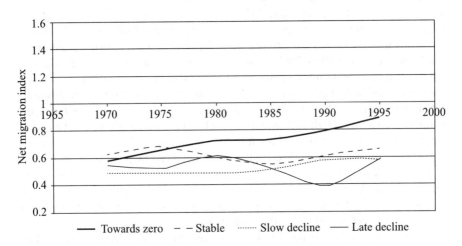

Figure 3.2b   Trends in net migration, emigration countries (five-year periods)

Determinants of Net Migration

The rate of net migration experienced by a specific country during a certain time-period is influenced by a long range of factors, including war, social unrest, religious conflicts, political repression, educational opportunities, labour market conditions at home and abroad. In order to fully explain historical patterns in net migration it would, therefore, be necessary to study each migration flow as an almost unique event.

However, such an idiosyncratic approach to net migration is difficult to use as a basis for forecasting. The approach taken here is instead to analyse to what extent a factor that one can predict – population change – has an influence on net migration. This is not to say that only demographic factors matter. But if net migration is influenced by demographic factors in a systematic way, and if the effect of demographic change on net migration in the future will be similar to what we have seen historically, then an understanding of demographic influences on migration can help us to predict future trends in net migration.

Thus, the model estimated below will be very simple. The dependent variable is, as stated above, the log of the net migration index. And following Hatton and Williamson the cohort growth rate twenty years earlier is included among the regressors, cohort growth. The hypothesis here is that large increases in cohort size will be associated with high net migration. Unlike Hatton and Williamson it has not, however, been possible to include data on relative wages in the model. Instead we use purchasing power adjusted GDP per capita as a measure of income (in logs), *ln initial*, the hypothesis being that a high level of income will attract migrants whereas low per capita income will stimulate emigration. Data on this variable is available in the Penn World tables. The third explanatory variable is the population size of the largest city in the country (in logs), *ln maxpop*. The argument for including this variable is that population-driven migrations tend to go from rural areas towards larger urban centers (Berry, 1993). Therefore, in countries endowed with large cities, significant shares of the migrant population will end up not in large cities abroad but in the metropolitan areas of their home country. Furthermore, since large metropolitan areas are attractive also for foreign-born migrations we should expect city-rich countries to have a high net migration index (UN, 2000).

The number of countries that can be included in the regression depends on which regressors are used. Data on the dependent variable are, as stated above, available for 187 countries (160 excluding outliers). This is the case also for the cohort growth variable since this variable is from the data set. Note though, that the first observation for cohort growth is from 1950–1955 to 1955–1960. Since this variable will be used with a 20-year lag the first observation of the dependent variable in the regression will be the net migration index for the 1975–1980 period. The Penn data set contains 116 countries with data from 1975. Of these only 113 are parts of the UN data sets. Another restriction on the sample is necessary in order to include the city size variable. The UN only reports the size of cities if they during the 1950–2000 period at one time have had more than 750,000 inhabitants. The largest cities of 115 countries meet this criterion but of these ten have been excluded as net migration outliers. The effective sample size for a regression with cohort growth and largest city size as explanatory variables is thus 105 countries (times 5 periods). And for only 80 of these 105 does the Penn data set provide information on per capita income.

There are indications that net migration reacts somewhat differently to cohort growth in these samples. More specifically, the effect of cohort growth on migration tends to be weaker for countries lacking large cities and even weaker still for countries that were not included in the Penn data set in the 1970s and 1980s. That net migration in non-Penn countries is less influenced by cohort effects could be explained by the fact that these countries tend to be non-market economies. It could be argued that the experience of these countries could be less interesting for forecasting purposes, if it is believed that the late twentieth century diffusion of the market model will continue in the twenty-first. In the estimates presented below we therefore use two samples. First, the 104 country sample for which there is both income and migration data, excluding migration index outliers. Second, the 80-country sample that in addition to income and migration data also has information on the size of the largest city.

Estimation Results

The estimation results for the migration model are presented in Table 3.1. The table shows as expected that cohort growth has a significant negative effect on net migration. That is, strong growth in cohort size leads to negative net migration whereas declining cohort size will stimulate positive net migration. The effect is particularly strong when per capita income is not controlled for. With initial income included, the effect is reduced but it is still strong and significant. Varying the sample and controlling for urban size, however, has negligible effects.

Initial income is also, as should be expected, a strong determinant of net migration. In accordance with theory high-income countries receive net inflows of migrants whereas low-income countries have net outflows. With respect to urban structure the hypothesis that countries with large cities are less affected by migration outflows is born out by the data. Taken together, cohort growth, per capita income and urban structure account for about 60 per cent of the variation in the migration index. This implies that a forecast model based on these variables could help us to predict migration trends in the twenty-first century.

The Effects of the Age Transition on Net Migration

In the model estimated above it was demonstrated that trends in net migration are closely associated with cohort growth, per capita income and urban development. Given that these explanatory variables can be forecasted it would, then, be possible to forecast the future trends in net migration. A projection for the cohort growth variable is easily calculated from the UN population forecasts. And for projection of future trends in per capita income it is possible to rely on earlier work in this area that recently has been presented at a symposium on global income growth organized by the Institute for Futures Studies. These projections are based on the stable correlations that exist between per capita income on the one hand, and age structure, life expectancy and urban structure, on the other (Lindh and Malmberg, 2004). The same report also contains a projection of the size of the largest city for the countries that were used in the regression above.

Table 3.1   Cohort growth, income, and urban structure effects on net migration

	(1) 80 countries	(2) 104 countries	(3) 80 countries	(4) 80 countries	(5) 104 countries	(6) 80 countries
Intercept	−0.038	−0.072	−0.84567	−2.561	−2.475	−2.918
	(0.023)	(0.020)	(0.132)	(0.141)	(0.123)	(0.157)
Cohort growth	−2.238	−2.167	−2.033	−0.520	−0.530	−0.483
	(0.167)	(0.149)	(0.163)	(0.157)	(0.141)	(0.153)
ln initial				0.282	0.271	0.268
				(0.016)	(0.014)	(0.016)
ln maxpop			0.103			0.062
			(0.017)			(0.013)
R square	0.312	0.290	0.372	0.620	0.592	0.641
Adj. R square	0.310	0.288	0.369	0.618	0.590	0.638
Obs	400	520	400	400	520	400

Notes: (log migration index). Regression analysis with estimation results for six different models.
Standard error in parentheses.
ln initial = purchasing power adjusted GDP/capita.
ln maxpop = population of largest city.

Source: United Nations, 2001a; United Nations, 2002a

Thus, with access to the UN-based projections of cohort growth, changes in per capita income, growth in the size of the largest cities, and an estimated model for how these variables influence net migration, prediction becomes relatively straight-forward. For the prediction we use the model presented in the last column of Table 3.1 with one modification. Instead of using the log of per capita income for each country, the mean value of logs per capita income across countries for every period is subtracted from each observation. The reason for this is that differences in per capita income rather than levels should be what influences net migration. This change has only marginal effects on the estimates. Most pronounced is that the numeric value of the cohort growth parameter increases slightly, from −0.48 to −0.55.

Results

The main results of the projection are shown in Figure 3.3. The curves depicted here represent the frequency distribution of the migration index in three different years for the countries for which we have data on all the explanatory variables. The first curve is based on the observed values for 1980. The second curve shows the projected frequency distribution for 2020. And the third curve represents the projected frequency for year 2040. Looking first at the distribution for 1980 we can see a situation characterized by strong polarization. A large group of countries – half the 80-country sample – in 1980 had very low values on the net migration index, around 0.6 or less. This implies that in these countries population losses through net migration amounted to about 40 per cent or more of an entire cohort. Simultaneously, a fairly large group of 12 countries experienced large net migration gains – around 40 per cent or more in gain compared to the size of a cohort. Only five countries had less then 10 per cent gain or loss from net migration.

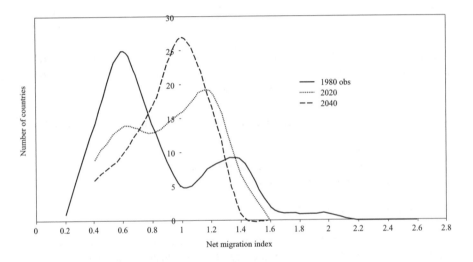

Figure 3.3   Frequency distribution of the net migration index, 1980, 2020 and 2040

Note: The index represents the ratio when dividing a hypothetical current cohort size with the size of the birth cohort adjusted for survival. As long as total net migration is less than the size of the birth cohort minus deaths before five years of age, the net migration index will be positive.

In 2020 this situation is projected to have changed substantially. Most pronounced is the reduction of high emigration countries (migration index below 30 per cent). The number of countries in this group has been almost halved from 40 to 23. There has also been a decline in the number of high immigration countries, from 12 to seven. However, the number of countries with moderately high immigration has risen from eight to 19. That is, in 2020 we should still expect substantial global net migration flows. The major sending countries will however not necessarily be the same. Also, since there will be an increase in the number of immigrant countries, we can expect that there will be increased competition between receiving countries for talented immigrants.

Looking another 20 years ahead, there is an even more pronounced shift in net migration patterns. According to the projection the number of high emigration and high immigration countries will be further reduced between 2020 and 2040. Compared to 1980 the share of high emigration and high immigration countries has fallen from 66 per cent to 20 per cent. The most important group in 2040 is instead the low net migration group, that is countries where net migration as a share of cohort size is less than 10 per cent. Every third country will be in this group by 2040 compared to one in 16 in 1980. In 2040 the low to moderate net migration group constitutes 80 per cent of the sample.

Our forecast thus predicts very substantial changes in the patterns of net migration during the next four decades. The forecast certainly does not predict that there will be no international net migration in 2040. However, if mass migration is defined as net migration flows that are very large in relation to the size of the native-born cohorts that arrive on the labour markets, then the forecast presented here does indicate a substantial reduction in global mass migration. As was pointed out in the beginning, gross flows may still be substantial, but it will not necessarily be the case that many countries make big population losses from migration whereas others make large gains.

The most important factor behind the decrease in the number of high emigrant countries is the reduction in cohort growth rates. The median cohort growth rate, for example, is projected to decline from 2.5 per cent annually in the early 1980s to practically zero in 2040. In addition, the UN also predicts that the declining cohort size that has affected a group of countries during the end of the twentieth century will slow down after 2020. And according to the estimated model this will decrease the demand for immigration. Income growth in many of today's developing countries may also help to slow down net migration. The reduction in birth rates in former high fertility countries will bring about a more advantageous age structure with drastically improved prospects for economic growth. At the same time there is a risk that population ageing in today's developed countries will lower their rates of economic growth. As a consequence, many of today's developing countries may be able to catch up with the richer countries and this will reduce their demand for emigration.

Policy Implications

Sharply reduced fertility in most developing countries will in a few decades drastically alter the demographic determinants of net migration. Much of today's high migration pressure is likely to decline. There are also strong indications that some of the late twentieth century's emigrant countries will become immigrant countries in the twenty-first century. An important trend is also that net migration in relation to cohort size will become much smaller for a large group of countries. As discussed in the beginning of this chapter, low levels of net migration need not imply low levels of gross migration. However, in a situation where net migration pressures are reduced the demands on a global mobility regime may change drastically. There will no longer be a strong need for measures that regulate large population transfers. Instead more emphasis can be put on removing obstacles to educational and professional mobility.

Another policy implication can be drawn if the current strong net migration pressures are transitory. Ageing countries that would like to profit from an inflow of working age adults must not be too slow to move towards a more open policy. If such a country fails to find ways of taking advantage of the present demand for immigration, an important opportunity to compensate for low fertility rates may be lost. Finally, the cohort growth perspective on international net migration also points to an issue of global justice. Individuals who happen to belong to cohorts that are much larger than before have been struck by a demographic event that has been beyond their own control. If they due to this event have difficulties in finding a livelihood in their country of birth, this is not something that they themselves can be blamed for. Neither is the fact of rapid cohort growth among people in their 20s something that can be solved by bringing down current fertility rates. Instead, one could argue that all nations have a responsibility to help to accommodate the present situation. It is not a problem that will go on forever. But finding ways to relieve the strains put on societies that experience a very rapid expansion of young adults could have important and positive long-run effects.

PART 2
GAINS AND DRAINS OF SOURCE COUNTRIES

Chapter 4

An Economic View on Brain Drain[1]

J.P. Sevilla

Introduction

This chapter focuses on the consequences for developing countries of skilled migration. Thus, I ignore consequences for developed countries, and those related to low-skilled migration. I wish to argue four points. First, the forces that create pressures for the global migration of workers are likely to remain strong at least over the next half century. Governments must accommodate themselves to this fundamental likelihood, and focus on managing it and mitigating its negative consequences rather than reversing it. Secondly, global migration is a powerful engine for the betterment of individuals and societies by making the global allocation of labour more efficient, and by allowing people to free themselves from the contingencies of their birth and join societies whose prosperity, sociocultural values, institutions, and way of life they find more attractive.

Thirdly, the negative consequences of the brain drain include the loss of positive externalities, the interaction between migration and educational subsidies, the adverse impact on developing country consumers of goods and services, such as health care, produced by migrants and the strains of familial separation. Of these four effects, the first is difficult to measure, but likely to be small and more than compensated for by remittances. The second is best solved by changing the rationale of public financing of higher education from subsidy to eliminating credit constraints. The third is the central distributional challenge of migration, and perhaps the most valid concern about its negative consequences. The fourth can be partly mitigated by government policy, but must be considered substantially a matter of private personal choice.

Finally, traditional economic arguments imply that the migration of skilled workers is a potential but not actual Pareto improvement. That is, the magnitude of its gains is larger than the magnitude of its losses. But the gains are unevenly distributed so that migration makes some of the people left behind worse off. In such situations, traditional economic theory argues for a two-pronged policy: implement policies that facilitate the production of the gains, and then implement redistributive policies to spread these gains more widely.

Pressures for Migration will Remain Strong at Least over the Next Half Century

Migration is driven primarily by differences between countries and the desire of people to take advantage of these differences to improve their lives. The most important of these are differences in income, technology, and age structure. As Pritchett (2003) states, in the early nineteenth century, the world was almost uniformly poor, and material well-being did not much vary across political boundaries, but today these variations are vast:

> Bourguignon and Morrison (2002) estimate that in 1820 only about ten percent of the differences in incomes among all individuals in the world was due to differences in average incomes across countries. This has shown a steady increase and today over 60 percent of the inequality in the world today is because of differences in incomes across countries. (Pritchett, 2003: 6)

In addition, the wage gaps that gave rise to the era of great migration from Europe to the lands of recent settlement in the late nineteenth century seem small relative to the wage gaps that currently exist between migration partners:

> The wage ratios between Japan and Vietnam (9.1) or the UK and Kenya (7.2) or the USA and Guatemala (6.1) are substantially larger today than the historical ratios between the mass senders and the USA (Ireland, 2.3, Sweden 4.1). (Pritchett, 2003: 7)

The traditional theory of economic growth (Solow, 1956) predicted convergence, that is, that poor countries will tend to grow faster than rich countries and catch up with them. This would reduce the wage and income gaps and therefore migration pressures. Yet this has not occurred. Rather, Pritchett (1997) argues that convergence only occurs among the developed countries, and that divergence is at least as good an explanation of the differences in economic performance between developed and developing countries, and within the developing countries themselves. The persistence of wage and income gaps implies that economic incentives for migration are likely to remain high.

The second important difference is technological. Developed country workforces are more educated and have higher human capital than those of developing countries, reflecting the greater role of human capital in their technologies. Such workforces have little incentive to perform low-skilled work such as housekeeping or cleaning services, the harvesting of agricultural crops, low-skilled services such as security or taxi driving, or even teaching at public schools. These goods and services have two additional characteristics. They are non-tradable (that is they have to be produced locally because you cannot import a clean bathroom) and possibilities for substitution of inputs in their production is low (there are limits to replacing low-skilled service workers with, say, machines). Developed country demand for low-skilled migrant workers exists because some goods and services consumed by developed country populations have these three characteristics: intensiveness in the use of low-skilled workers, non-tradability, and difficulty of substitution.

A final difference is demographic. We are coming to understand that there is an intimate relationship between the age structure of a population and its migration flows. Two mechanisms are important (Hatton and Williamson, 2002). First, migration propensities are especially high among young adults. Second, populations with a large share of elderly require the inflow of adult migrants to prevent rising dependency ratios and support pay-as-you-go welfare systems. Labour immigration of particular occupational categories such as nurses, doctors, and caregivers, also satisfies the growing health services needs of aging populations. Because the demographic transition occurred first among the developed countries, and only afterwards among the developing countries, the elderly-rich phase of the former is coinciding with the adult-rich phase of the latter. The pull from the developed countries is coinciding with the push from the developing countries. While we might expect age structures across countries to converge over the course of the twenty-first century, reducing the demographic pressures for migration (Malmberg, 2004), these demographic disparities are likely to exist for at least a few decades more.

Between 1975 and 2000, the number of international migrants, defined by the UN as persons living outside their country of birth or citizenship, doubled to 175 million (Martin, 2004). It is not easy to predict what the future of migration will be. Some trends, including job outsourcing, trade liberalization, and age structure convergence across countries, might reduce migration pressures. Yet, on the whole, the disparities in income, technology, and age structure are likely to remain with us for at least the next few decades, and technological and cost barriers to movement are likely to continue to decline, so it is likely that pressures for migration will remain high, at least over the next half century. Thus the medium-term future of the world will probably be characterized by freer population movements, especially among the highly skilled. National governments and international agencies must appreciate the strength of these pressures and design migration policies compatible with them. This would surely rule out as futile and counterproductive any attempts to reverse these flows or significantly reduce their magnitude. It should limit policy-makers to the more modest task of managing these flows, maximizing their benefits, sharing the benefits as widely as possible, and mitigating their negative consequences.

Global Migration, Global Efficiency and Individual Betterment

Clearly, rich and poor countries are different. For economists, two of the most important differences are that poor countries tend to have a relative abundance of labour, and relatively low *total factor productivity*, or TFP. For simplicity, one can interpret TFP as an economy's ability to transform a particular fixed bundle of inputs, say a particular quantity of workers and capital, into output. So if countries A and B are given the same fixed quantities of inputs, and A is able to produce more output out of them than

B, we say that A has higher TFP. Both characteristics make labour less productive in developing countries: the first implies that production tends to be labour intensive, and when large quantities of labour work with scarce quantities of capital, the productivity of each particular worker is low; the second implies that labour productivity is low because inputs are in general less productive, even if there were no relative labour abundance. As economists put it, a given worker with given abilities and skills has a lower marginal product in developing countries than in developed countries.

A caveat in the interpretation of this claim is in order. It might be tempting to interpret this lower productivity as somehow reflecting an implicit belief that the goods and services produced in developing countries have intrinsically lesser value. For example, people might be tempted to infer that if economists claim that public school teachers or nurses are less productive in developing countries than in developed countries, this is because somehow the analyst has implicitly assumed that the education and health of developing country populations is essentially less valuable than that of developed country populations. This is an erroneous interpretation of the economic argument. The economic argument does not depend on the social valuations of the outcomes produced. It only says that for a fixed quantity of the outcome, labour abundance and low TFP imply that developing country workers will be less productive in the making of that outcome.

Since the migration of workers from developing to developed countries is a flow of labour from low labour productivity areas to high labour productivity areas, it raises the global average of labour productivity, and therefore the global efficiency of labour allocation. This is accompanied by an increase in the average global earnings of labour. According to standard theory, the magnitude of the global efficiency gain is proportional to the square of the wage gap between developing and developed countries. Since these wage gaps are quite large, the efficiency gains are likewise large.

Another way of understanding the economic benefits of migration is through the concept of comparative advantage. Although developed to explain the gains from the trade of goods and services among nations, it sheds light on the effects of population movements as well. An understanding of comparative advantage, in turn, is facilitated by an understanding of an even more fundamental economic concept, exchange. Exchange is the central economic activity in modern economies, and the most powerful social engine for the creation of material well-being that the world has ever come up with. The idea of how it promotes well-being is simple, yet far reaching. Imagine that each of us, as individuals trying to achieve material well-being, has access to different opportunities, endowments, and technologies. For example, I might have a herd of sheep while you have a vegetable garden. If exchange were not possible, we would each be restricted to making a living only using those resources to which we each have access. I would have lamb chops everyday, and you would have salads. However, exchange allows us to have access to each other's opportunities since we can swap goods that reflect these respective opportunities. We might trade meat for vegetables and both live on more varied diets. Note that the benefits of exchange do not presume anything about you and me having different preferences or diets, just that each of us has different opportunities. Exchange allows each of us to benefit from opportunities that we ourselves do not have but others do. The benefit is that we are able to enjoy goods that our particular opportunities are not conducive to producing.

These benefits of exchange exist whether the actors involved are individuals or countries. At the level of countries, the formalization of the idea of the gains from trade is precisely the theory of comparative advantage. This theory says, in brief, that even when different countries have the capacity to produce the exact same set of goods, they will usually have different relative competencies in producing these goods. These relative competencies are measured by the concept of opportunity costs (the opportunity cost of producing a particular good, say a TV set, is the number of other goods that need to be foregone in order to produce this one). The theory says that when the menu of opportunity costs of producing goods varies across countries, then each country should specialize in the production of the goods for which its opportunity costs are lower than other countries'. These are the goods in which the country has a comparative advantage and ought to specialize. It should produce more of these goods than it requires domestically, and less of other goods than it requires domestically. It should export the former, and use export revenues to pay for imports of the latter. Since each country specializes in goods in which its opportunity costs are lower than those of other countries, trade results in the global minimization of opportunity costs: at a global level, each good is produced using up the least amount of other goods. This maximizes global efficiency and global material wealth. This remarkable logic holds even when some country is able to produce all goods more cheaply than any other country, since opportunity costs are equal to the ratio rather than the level of costs.

According to the traditional example of comparative advantage, developing countries are relatively labour abundant and capital scarce. Their opportunity costs for producing labour intensive goods tends to be low, so they should specialize in the production and export of labour intensive products, while developed countries should specialize in capital-intensive products. The theory of comparative advantage is relevant to the issue of the migration of skilled workers and especially health care professionals since some developing countries may have a comparative advantage in their production. To a large extent, this is simply due to the fact that education is a labour intensive activity, so that the migration of health care professionals becomes an extension of the export of labour intensive goods.

What are the gains from this process for the developing countries? The migrants themselves enjoy the largest gains in terms of increased labour productivity and therefore incomes. Households and the macro economy benefit from remittance flows which finance consumption and the accumulation of human and physical capital. The possibility of skilled migration raises the demand for education and stimulates investments in the educational sector. Domestic labour allocations become more efficient as labour surpluses are reduced and people are redeployed from low productivity occupations – ranging from economic inactivity, unemployment, underemployment, to low productivity work – to higher ones. This raises domestic labour productivity and incomes.

Some may find my analogy between skilled migrants and labour intensive exports an unacceptable objectification of people. Some may also believe that population movements from developing to developed countries are unjust or exploitive just because they are the results of economic pressures affecting the decisions of the global poor. To the first concern, I respond by saying that the economic argument I put forward does not imply or assume anything like a normative view that people have the same moral status as tradable goods. I only make the empirical claim that socioeconomic forces, just like the forces of nature, exert their influence on people and objects alike. The fact that both people and objects are affected by gravity does not imply that they have equivalent moral status, and neither does the fact that both people and traded goods are affected by market forces. To the second concern, I believe that the claim that economically motivated migration is unjust or exploitive must be framed as a hypothesis that empirical study can demonstrate to be true or false, rather than something that is logically or by definition true. It is hard to think of a reasonable theory of justice that would judge a process such as economically motivated migration unjust merely because it is economically motivated. It must also be shown, as a separate and non-definitional matter, that economically motivated migrations have demonstrable bad consequences.

The Losses from Migration

While the migration of skilled workers is a powerful force for the production of material wealth, and while I believe that its impact on the well-being of the average person in the world is significantly positive, it has negative consequences as well. It is important for both our understanding of this phenomenon, and the design of policy, to come to a proper appreciation of its dangers along with its opportunities, and the nature of the relationship between them. The term 'brain drain' is used to represent the collection of these negative consequences. In general, fear of brain drain comes from the reasonable worry that the development process is already quite fragile, and that the loss of human capital can jeopardize this process even further. This outflow has the potential of turning into a vicious cycle whereby brain drain feeds socioeconomic disparities between nations, which in turn provokes even more brain drain, and so on. Of more specific concern than the loss of skilled labour in general, is the loss of health care professionals in particular. According to Pang et al. (2002), around 23,000 qualified academic professionals emigrate annually out of Africa, a third to a half of South African medical school graduates emigrate, and there are more than 150,000 Filipino and 18,000 Zimbabwean nurses worldwide. The outward flows of health care professionals have the potential to deprive developing country health systems of much needed human resources, jeopardize the health of poor populations and feed global health inequities.

The hypothesized negative consequences particularly associated with skilled migration can be analytically grouped into three: the loss of externalities from higher education; the regressive implicit subsidy to migrants arising from publicly financed higher education; and the regressive effect on consumers of goods and services embodying migrant labour, including the effect in particular of poor consumers of publicly financed health services and education. I argue that no good estimates of educational externalities exist in developing countries, but that labour surpluses make it likely that they will be small, and that at any rate, externality losses are probably well-compensated for by remittance income. I argue that the second is not primarily a problem of migration and is best solved by transforming public subsidies of higher education into loans, potentially forgivable – and therefore turning into a subsidy – if one does not migrate. Such a transformation is more pro-poor as it should not reduce education below socially efficient levels, and as it ensures that skilled migration is not a drain on public resources. It also makes externality concerns even less urgent. Since migration is no longer a drain on public resources, it would not hinder government efforts to subsidize the education of non-migrants for externality reasons, if it chose to. The third seems to capture accurately the central distributional challenge posed by skilled migration, though the empirical magnitude of these consequences is probably overstated by simple counts of quantities of say, migrant nurses and public school teachers. It is imperative to measure the empirical magnitude of this effect, and to think about the policy mechanisms that would redistribute the gains from migration to compensate those who suffer these adverse distributional consequences.

Externalities and Efficiency

The argument that the brain drain is a threat to economic development presumes the existence of an externality, that is, a gap between the value of a person's contribution to society (what an economist calls the social marginal product of skilled labour) and that person's wage. It is this gap that measures society's net loss from migration: society loses the social marginal product, but then it saves the income it paid to the worker. How large are these externalities? We know remarkably little about them, and all rigorous measurements come from the developed countries. Consider some excerpts from the literature:

> the evidence on social returns to education is very limited. The large macro-growth literature that looks at aggregate returns to human capital in a cross-country setting yields rather inconclusive findings ... A number of studies fail to find a significant effect of human capital on aggregate output while others find very large social returns – well in excess of private returns found in micro-data ... As argued persuasively by Krueger and Lindahl (2000), this may well be due to problems of measurement error and reverse causality. (Besley, 2000: 19)

> From the micro-evidence, it is unclear whether social returns to schooling exceeds the private return, although available evidence suggests that positive externalities in the

form of reduced crime and reduced welfare participation are more likely to be reaped from investments in disadvantaged than advantaged groups (Heckman and Klenow, 1997). The macroeconomic evidence of externalities in terms of technological progress from investments in higher education seems to us more fragile, resulting from imposing constant-coefficient and linearity restrictions that are rejected by the data. (Krueger and Lindahl, 2000: 43)

[we estimate] private returns to education of about seven percent, and small social returns, typically less than one percent, that are not significantly different from zero. (Acemoglu and Angrist, 2000: n.p.)

a percentage point increase in the supply of college graduates raises high-school drop-outs wages by 1.9%, high-school graduate wages by 1.6% and college graduates wages by 0.4%. (Moretti, 2004: 1175)

Among careful microeconomic studies that measure externalities, only Moretti (2004) finds them, and he finds them in the US. All other studies either find no effect, or find effects but suffer from methodological shortcomings. We have little if any evidence on whether externalities exist, and if so how large they are, in the developing countries.

There are also two reasons, both related to the labour market, that lead one to be less concerned about loss of externalities in developing countries. First, many developing countries remain labour surplus economies in which existing stocks of human capital are under-utilized. This is reflected in economic participation and employment rates among college graduates that are relatively low compared to those of developed countries. For example, in the Philippines, a country with very high rates of skilled migration, only 62 per cent of college degree holders were employed in the late 1990s (Alburo and Abella, 2002). Thus as far as stocks of workers with tertiary levels of education go, there is little sense in which they are depleted by migration.

Second, the language of brain drain arguments seems to imply that a country has a relatively fixed supply of human capital so that there is a one for one relationship between migration and reductions in domestic human capital. However this is only true in the very short run. In the long run, a country's supply of education and human capital is variable and potentially infinitely elastic, rising as much as necessary in order to meet both domestic and international demand. As long as the education sector is sufficiently flexible to accommodate larger volumes of students, the supply of educated workers can grow to meet demand.

Of course, educational attainment is only one part of human capital. Work experience is another, and there is a legitimate concern that while human capital in the form of education is probably available or replenishable, human capital in terms of experience is more scarce and difficult to replace. In fact, anecdotal evidence about migration usually emphasizes that it is the loss of the most experienced workers, say nurses or school teachers, which is most painful. This argument must be taken seriously, and an important first step towards doing so is measuring experience-specific rates of employment, unemployment, and migration. As far as I can tell, such data do not exist. This prevents us from knowing the magnitude of this concern. Also, the empirical work that measures the existence and size of externalities has focused exclusively on the impact of increased supplies of education, not experience. Thus it would seem that we are quite far from having measures of any of the relevant magnitudes here.

Finally, as I argued at the outset of this section, the loss to society from the migration of an individual is given by the externality effect, or more generally, the gap between that individual's social marginal product and his or her wage. However, in return society receives the remittances of that migrant. Thus society loses economically from the migration decision only if the externality is larger in value than the migrant's remittances. If we believe that the value of remittances, say as a share of GDP is larger than the value of externalities, also as a share of GDP, then we might reasonably believe that on average, society enjoys a net benefit from migration. Again, using a Philippine example, remittances to the Philippines are about 9 per cent of GDP. This means that remittances fully compensate the Philippines for the brain drain as long as the value of externalities does not exceed 9 per cent of GDP, and this is almost surely the case.

In sum, the absence of good evidence on the magnitude of externalities, prior reasons to believe that they are small and probably compensated for by remittances lead me to believe it is imprudent to design policies that presume these externalities are large.

Migration and Public Financing of Education

A second negative consequence of migration arises when it interacts with public financing of higher education. In many countries, higher education that includes college and the professional training of nurses and health care professionals is subsidized by the state. This is often rationalized for four reasons: for social equity, to eliminate cost barriers to education, for the production of educational externalities, and to ensure an adequate domestic supply of certain critical human resources like health care workers. With respect to the latter two objectives, the subsidy is in effect the first part of a social contract: the state invests in a person's education, and in return, that person will be a productive member of society and confer benefits on others. Migration frustrates the latter half of this social contract, and creates the potential for a regressive distribution of resources. If the average tax payer who bears the costs of the subsidy is less well-off than the average highly-skilled potential migrant, then a combination of the subsidy and the migration decision implies that resources are taken away from the average tax payer to subsidize the wage gains of the already better off migrant. It also subsidizes developed country populations who get to enjoy the externalities of that migrant's work.

We believe that the first two objectives, while extremely important, are not well-served by subsidies. With respect to the first aim of promoting social equity and redistributing resources to the less well-off, the government would be better served by improving access to and the quality of goods that the less well-off, particularly in rural areas, consume more of: primary and secondary schooling, primary health care, crime reduction, environmental protections, basic social and physical infrastructure, etc. Many individuals who receive higher education in developing countries are still from the relative upper reaches of the income distribution, and are not the most obvious targets of resource redistributions. The second aim is eliminating cost barriers to schooling so that everyone with the ability to benefit from higher education has access to it, regardless of socioeconomic background. Achieving this aim only rationalizes the use of educational loans, which frees individuals from paying educational costs up front and allows them to amortizing educational costs over a work life. Loans accomplish this without imposing a net financial burden on the public sector. The third aim, that of creating a supply of well-educated citizens who can be a source of externalities, has already been discussed in the previous section. The weakness of the evidence for general externalities does not support the use of subsidies for these purposes.

The fourth objective is to subsidize the education of individuals who enter into occupations whose values to society are particularly poorly reflected in their wages. Thus, society may value the services of nurses, who are willing to work in the public sector, or lawyers who work in public interest law, or educators who are willing to teach in far flung public schools, and yet are unable to compensate them through wages for these occupations which are usually low. Thus subsidizing their education is one way to provide alternative compensation, and to increase individuals' incentives to consider these career choices. These reasons for subsidy are legitimate, but they provide reasons not for a general subsidy but for conditional ones, that is, conditional on choosing the occupations that satisfy the characteristics just described.

The possibility of migration both strengthens the argument against a general subsidy and the argument for a conditional one. A general subsidy, already potentially regressive in the absence of migration, becomes even more regressive if the beneficiary migrates. A conditional subsidy, conditional, that is, on residing locally and choosing certain domestic professions, creates incentives only for those occupational choices that yield benefits for the local population.

Adverse Distribution

The third concern regarding migration of skilled workers is perhaps the most serious. When migration pressures from a particular occupational category are high, for example as it is for nurses in some countries, this threatens domestic stocks of human capital in that category. As I have stated previously, the more serious aspect of this threat is to a slighter degree the loss of people with educational qualifications than it is the loss of experienced workers. One of two things will have to happen in response to these pressures. Either domestic wages or working conditions will have to rise in order to reduce workers' incentives to migrate, or if these fail to rise, domestic supplies of these human resources will fall. Consumers of the goods and services produced by these workers will therefore face scarcities, lower product quality, higher prices, or a combination of all these. Thus there is very strong concern that when nurses who work in the public sector migrate, public sector nurse wages are unable to change in response. And the quality and quantity of publicly provided health services falls since workloads must be spread over fewer nurses. To the extent that migrants produce goods and services consumed particularly by the domestic poor, as public sector employees do, this decline in quantity and quality, and increase in price, has a regressive effect on social welfare.

Yet traditional economic theory also implies that the mechanisms described in the previous paragraph, while real, overstate the adverse consequences of human resource loss. Let us take the example of the migration of nurses and the potential effect on population health. The ultimate social objective is the promotion of health, not the provision of health services. Economists view population health as produced using a health production function in which the output, society's health, can be thought of as a function of the various inputs, or population-level determinants, of that health. Examples of inputs are utilization of health services, nutrition, environmental quality, education and knowledge, or exercise and risk behaviours. In any actual society, therefore, there are multiple levers that governments and individuals can use to promote health, and we can expect that the relative use of inputs should reflect their relative prices. That is, if one input becomes expensive or scarce, then we can substitute away from this input towards more intensive use of the other inputs. If health services become more expensive or scarce, society can partially, though not fully, offset its adverse effect on population health by more intensively using the other inputs such as improving nutrition or environmental quality, or reducing risk behaviours.

Even particular health services, say treatment for cardiovascular disease, have their production functions. And in these production functions, there will always be a degree of substitutability among inputs. When one input such as experienced nurses becomes scarce, an optimal response is to adopt a 'technique' that relies less on the scarce input, and more on more abundantly available inputs. Such input substitution is readily observable in many developing country settings. The scarcity of doctors and nurses in rural settings have led to innovative programs of community-based primary care provision in which the main health care provider is a community health worker often with little more than a high school diploma and a few weeks or months of special training. The scarcity of a particular input does not only provoke input substitution, it also over the longer run provokes technological innovation that makes production less dependent on the scarce input. This general paradigm of constraint leading to innovation is profoundly broad, and has been used to explain not just innovations in health services, but in agriculture (Boserup, 1981; 1965), and even the basic structure of society (Marx). Examples relevant to the provision of health services include information technology in the form of computers, electronic medical record systems, treatment protocols loaded onto handheld computer devices. The point here is not that the loss of experienced nurses has no adverse consequences. The point rather is that possibilities for 'input substitution' imply that a mere accounting of the number of experienced nurses lost overstates the social losses.

Despite these caveats, it is the loss of experienced human capital in particular, socially valuable occupations, and the regressive impact this has on the well-being of the less well-off consumers of the goods and services they produce, that constitutes the main adverse economic consequence of migration. Thus while I argue in section two that migration produces many gains for the domestic economy, it is only a potential rather than actual Pareto improvement. Migration produces losers, and one of the central challenges of policy is to look after the well-being of the losers.

Efficiency and Redistribution

Another traditional economic argument is relevant here. In situations where a particular policy choice open to governments produces greater efficiency and therefore benefits to the average person, but losses for others, governments should consider a two-pronged policy in which one prong promotes the realization of efficiency gains while the other redistributes these gains to compensate the losers. The primary gainers are migrants and the developed country populations to which they migrate, while the primary losers are poor consumers of publicly financed health and educational services. How might redistribution from the former to the latter be effected?

First, my recommendation that general subsidies to higher education be transformed into conditional loans should free up considerable resources that could be used to effect these redistributions. In the case of skilled migrants, such a transformation would shift the burden from the general tax paying public to the migrant and any developed world employer wishing to hire the migrant. The employer effectively bears some of the burden of the migrant's education because the employer will either have to explicitly help the migrant pre-pay the loan, or provide the migrant an income high enough to allow the continued financing of the loan.

In general, however, redistribution from gainers to losers will require some form of explicit or implicit taxation. And there are theoretical reasons why taxation of migrant human capital has a good mix of efficiency and equity characteristics. The economic theory of taxation tells us that from an efficiency point of view, it is best to tax inelastic decisions, that is, decisions that tend not to change in response to the size of the tax. And from an equity point of view, it is clearly best to tax the better off. Taxing highly skilled migrants has a rare confluence of attractive efficiency and equity properties. Since the wage gain from migration is so large, the decision to migrate is probably relatively unresponsive to marginal variations in the degree of taxation. And since the migrants experience large improvements in material well-being, taxing them to redistribute to the poor has good equity characteristics as well.

And yet, these attractive theoretical properties of taxing international flows of human capital must also cope with significant practical obstacles to doing so, well summarized by Desai et al. (2002). It is well beyond my scope here to discuss how these practical obstacles can be resolved. My point is not that we know how to tax the human capital of migrants. Rather, it is that economic theory points us in a direction where we can target our efforts at fiscal innovation.

Conclusion

As stated initially, my aim in this chapter has been to make four points. First, pressures for migration will remain strong for many decades. Secondly, that it is a powerful force for improving the well-being of societies and individuals. Thirdly, that the gains from migration are unevenly distributed and that some, particularly poor consumers of publicly financed health services, can suffer. And fourthly, that the central challenge migration poses is that of redistributing its gains to those who suffer from it. What I hope my arguments also make clear is that an understanding of migration, its causes and consequences, its promise and its peril, requires a considerable amount of theoretical as well as empirical work, so much of which remains to be done.

Notes

[1] I would like to thank Bo Malmberg for valuable exchange of ideas about brain drain.

Chapter 5

Remittances and Labour Source Countries[1]

Bhargavi Ramamurthy

Historically, the major motives for emigration stand out as employment, study/skill improvement and refugee/asylum-seeking. Huge disparities in earning potential between advanced and developing countries, especially in the twentieth century, have prompted a large number of migrants to move toward the former countries. Globalization is increasing the volume of migrants across the world but, as the net migration statistics in the 1990–1995 period show, the volume of net settlers is not great (Ramamurthy, 2003). Research on the impact of emigration of labour source countries addresses three main issues – brain drain, remittances and the labour markets in the source countries (Ramamurthy, 2003).[2] This chapter addresses the impact of remittances on the labour source countries. A general theoretical treatment precedes an empirical overview and a continent-wise literature review on remittance flows.

Remittances are financial flows from the migrants to their home countries. They are central to the debates about the costs and benefits of emigration. If labour is considered an exportable commodity, then remittances are that part of the payment for labour exports that returns to the exporting country. Given the nature of remittances, their impact can be studied at three levels: at the micro (household) level, community level and macro (national) level. The flow of money goes mainly from the workers abroad to their families. Hence, the direct impact of remittances would be on the household income level. However, when remittances are of significant amounts their impact is felt in national balance of payments, foreign exchange reserves and current accounts of the balance of payments. Also, remittances are sometimes intended for community or social purposes and sent to organizations instead of households, in which case the impact is felt on community development.

Remittances may also be invested in source country government bonds. Further, remittances are not always in cash and can be in the form of consumer goods, capital goods or skilled services. They may be sent by an individual migrant or groups of migrants (for example the 'hometown associations' where emigrants join together and send money to Mexico and Central America for public fiestas, public works projects and other activities). The channels by which remittances are sent may be formal or informal: bank transfers, postal money orders, money transfer organizations or cash/in kind through family, friends or money couriers. It is obvious that it is very difficult to capture the magnitude of remittances. Officially recorded remittances can access only flows made through formal organizational transfers, and then only a portion of them. Official data on remittances, therefore, understate the actual flows across international borders.

The most widely used official data on remittances are IMF estimates, which classify three kinds of remittance flows: *workers' remittances* sent by workers who lived abroad for more than a year; *compensation of employees* (previously called labour income), which are remittances sent by migrants who have lived abroad for less than one year; and *migrant transfers*, which are the net worth of people who move from one country to another. For most practical purposes, total remittances ignore the last category and are calculated as the sum of workers' remittances and compensation of employees. Even these data suffer from inconsistencies arising from the different ways individual countries define, collect and report on remittances. For instance, postal money orders sent do not document whether the sender (migrant) has been abroad for less than a year or more than a year. These amounts therefore slip out of the official statistics or are included arbitrarily in one or the other categories.

Furthermore, there are two types of leakage in these statistics: 'personal imports' of migrant workers (that is goods imported by return migrants under the duty free allowance facility or brought along with them under personal baggage/gift facilities) and the savings brought home on return (in the form of cash or traveller's cheques) subsequently converted into local currency at domestic banks (Puri and Ritzema, 1994). Despite these problems, the IMF statistics offer the most comparable numbers and are thus widely used in research on remittances.

Remittances have a positive impact on their recipient countries as they ease foreign exchange constraints and improve balance of payments; they permit imports of capital goods and raw materials for industrial development; they are potential sources of savings and investment capital for development; they help to cushion the effects of external shocks (that is oil price increases); they are a net addition to resources; they raise the recipients' immediate standard of living; and they improve income distribution (when the poorer and less skilled migrate) (Russell et al., 1990: 23).

Counter-arguments include the unpredictability of transfers; that they are used mainly to buy consumer goods and thus fuel unproductive consumption, inflationary pressures and artificial increases in wage levels as well as increased imports and balance of payments problems; that they constitute little or no investment in productive capital; that they lead to increased personal investments in real estate; that they encourage dependence on the remittance as a source of income and erode good work habits; that they heighten potential effects of return migration; and, finally, that they stir up envy, resentment and induce consumption spending by non-migrant households.

Much of the research relating to remittances has focused on the uses, determinants and volume of remittances, and their impact on senders and recipients. Studies on the use of remittances serve as evidence to support or negate the above-mentioned impacts. Depending on national circumstances and the nature of the remittances, remitters and the receiving households, the evidence may qualify either side of the debate.

Russell (1986) offers a useful framework for analyzing the determinants of remittances and their impact on decisions regarding the amount, how to remit and how to spend or invest it. The determinants of remittances include the number of workers abroad; wage rates; economic activity in the destination and labour source countries; exchange rates; relative interest rates between labour source and destination countries; political risk factors in the source country; facility of transferring funds; ratio of females to males in destination countries; years since out-migration; household income level; employment status of other household members; marital status; level of education; and the occupational level of migrants.

Another major area of research on remittance flows is the characteristics of the remitter and recipient household. The aim here is largely to understand the propensity to remit among migrants at an aggregate level and also to identify regional or specific cultural patterns and nuances in determining remittance flows. As mentioned earlier, migrants tend to belong to the younger age groups, so remitters are also more likely to fall in that category. As a corollary, recipient households are mainly skewed towards the older and very young categories. A gender perspective of remitters has been highlighted in other studies and these have found that female migrants have a greater propensity to remit, and over a longer period of time, than male migrants.

The use of remittances is also a common theme of research. As the discussion earlier illustrated, the impact and nature of uses are diverse. A broad distinction is drawn between productive and consumptive uses of remittances. Since most remittances are aimed at easing the financial constraints of the households back home, it is hardly surprising that consumption tends to dominate remittance uses. The more immediate needs of the families are usually food, housing, health care and purchase of consumer durables. It can be argued that these are important 'investments' in human capital terms. Potential problems, however, arise in very poor countries that have to import the most common consumer durables in order to meet this increased demand since it will have adverse impact on the balance of payments.

Empirical Data on Remittance Patterns

The IMF *World Economic Outlook* 2005 reports of total worker remittances to developing countries as close to $100 billion. Remittances to developing countries have increased steadfastly since 30 years and for many of them, remittances make up the most important source of foreign exchange, exceeding export revenues, foreign direct investment, and other private capital inflows (IMF, 2005). The latest available data according to the IMF *Balance of Payments Statistics Yearbook 2004* indicate that total workers' remittances in 2003 were recorded at $90.8 billion. The share of remittances to developing countries was $79.5 billion. In addition, compensation of employees amounted to $58.4 billion, of which $21.3 billion went to developing countries (Reinke and Patterson, 2005).

Since this chapter is an extract from Ramamurthy (2003), the remainder of the data used here covers the period 1994–2000. Total remittances (workers remittances plus compensation of employees) registered a 38 per cent increase in 1994–2000 (Table

5.1), rising from US$ 74.6 billion to US$ 103 billion. Developing country shares of total remittance credits ranged from 57 per cent in 1994 to 64 per cent in 2000, with increases in each year. The growth in the share of developing countries is reflected in larger shares of most regions of the developing world except for the Middle East (Table 5.1). In the 1990s, the relative shares of developing regions did not display wide fluctuations: Africa accounted for about 6 per cent, Asia for about 22 per cent, Europe around 7.5 per cent and Latin America for about 15 per cent.

Table 5.1   Total remittances, 1994–2000 (US$ billions)

	1994	1995	1996	1997	1998	1999	2000
Total	74.62	85.06	88.27	103.19	99.81	103.58	103.10
Industrial	31.77	35.32	34.12	39.02	39.75	38.99	37.25
countries	(42.6)	(41.5)	(38.7)	(37.8)	(39.8)	(37.7)	(36.1)
Developing	42.85	49.74	54.15	64.17	60.06	64.58	65.85
countries	(57.4)	(58.5)	(61.3)	(62.2)	(60.2)	(62.4)	(63.9)
Africa	4.43	5.35	5.57	6.33	6.35	6.02	6.65
	(5.9)	(6.3)	(6.3)	(6.1)	(6.4)	(5.8)	(6.4)
Asia	16.50	19.56	22.92	29.87	22.99	27.25	25.46
	(22.1)	(23.0)	(26.0)	(28.9)	(23.0)	(26.3)	(24.7)
Europe	4.61	5.92	6.62	7.44	9.19	8.17	8.82
	(6.2)	(7.0)	(7.5)	(7.2)	(9.2)	(7.9)	(8.6)
Middle East	6.53	6.11	6.29	6.97	6.50	6.51	6.12
	(8.8)	(7.2)	(7.1)	(6.8)	(6.5)	(6.3)	(5.9)
Western	10.78	12.80	12.74	13.56	15.02	16.64	18.81
Hemisphere	(14.5)	(15.1)	(14.4)	(13.1)	(15.1)	(16.1)	(18.2)

Notes: Figures in parentheses refer to percentage of total remittances. Western Hemisphere includes Latin America and the Caribbean

Source: IMF Balance of Payments Statistics Yearbook (2001).

Putting these figures in perspective, total remittances accounted for around 0.3 per cent of world GDP between 1995 and 2000. Another commonly used benchmark of the extent of remittances is to express them as a percentage of merchandise exports. For developing countries, the share of remittances in merchandise exports ranges from 25 to 50 per cent. Individual countries display wide variations around this. For example, in 1989 remittances were 94 per cent of exports in Egypt, 153 per cent of exports for Yemen and 1.159 per cent of exports in Lesotho (Russell and Teitelbaum, 1992). As a percentage of GDP, the average fluctuations were smaller, varying from 2 per cent to 8 per cent.

These figures are officially recorded flows. As has been repeatedly emphasized, unofficial flows may add 50 per cent or more to these numbers (Stalker, 1994: 122). As Table 5.2 illustrates, the percentage of unrecorded remittances to total remittances ranges from 8 per cent in Korea to 85 per cent in Sudan. This percentage depends on the extent of foreign exchange controls in the economies. The more open the economy, the greater the incentive to use formal remittance channels. For example, in 1986, a study in Thailand found that 94 per cent of workers were using banks (Tingsabadh, 1989: 317).

Table 5.2   Unrecorded remittances as a percentage of total remittances

	Source	**Estimation period**	**Estimate***
Bangladesh	Mahmud (1989)	1981–86	20
Korea	Hyun (1989)	1980–85	8
India**	ESCAP (1987)	1983	40
Egypt	Adams (1991)	1985-86	33
Philippines	Alburo, Abella (1992)		
	Tan and Canlas (1989)	1990, 1982	50
Pakistan	ILO-ARTEP (1987)	1986	43
Sri Lanka	Rodrigo and Jayatissa (1989)	1980–1985	13
Sudan	Choucri (1984)	1984	85
Thailand	Tingsabadh (1989)	1977–86	18
Tonga	Brown and Connell (1993)	1992–93	43
Western Samoa	Brown and Walker (1994)	1992–93	42

Notes

*   Derived as ((TR − RB)/TR)*100, where TR = total estimated remittances and RB = remittances through banking channels.
**   Estimate represents remittance behaviour of migrant workers from Kerala only.

Source: Puri and Ritzema (1994: Table 4).

Top Remitter Countries

The top ten countries sending and receiving remittances are shown in Tables 5.3 and 5.4. The US has taken over from Saudi Arabia as the top remitting country since 1996 (Table 5.3). Net remittances[3] were on average US$ 20 billion per year in 1996–2000. Saudi Arabia was not far behind, with an annual average of US$ 16 billion. Combined OPEC outflows among the top ten matched US outflows every year in the period

1994–2000. The volume of OPEC outflows declined gradually between 1994 and 1999 from US$ 21 billion to US$ 15 billion but picked up in 2000 to US$ 18.5 billion. The other top remitters are industrial countries in Europe. Apart from the financial side, this pattern highlights the extent of dependence of the developing world, on the economies of the First World. Any changes in the labour markets and/or immigration policies are thereby bound to affect the remittance receivers in a significant way.

Table 5.3   **Ranking by net remittances of source countries (US$ billions)**

1994		1997		2000	
Saudi Arabia	−18.1	USA	−19	USA	−24.2
USA	−15.3	Saudi Arabia	−15	Saudi Arabia	−15.4
Switzerland	−7.1	Switzerland	−6.3	Switzerland	−5.7
Germany	−4.4	Germany	−5.2	Germany	−4
Kuwait	−1.3	Japan	−2.5	Israel	−3
Oman	−1.3	Israel	−2.2	Luxembourg	−2.1
Israel	−0.7	Malaysia	−1.8	Japan	−1.7
Japan	−0.7	Luxembourg	−1.5	Kuwait	−1.6
Netherlands	−0.6	Oman	−1.4	Oman	−1.4

Source: IMF Balance of Payments Statistics Yearbook 2001.

Table 5.4   **Ranking by net remittances of recipient countries (US$ billions)**

1994		1997		2000	
India	5.5	India	10.1	India	9.1
Mexico	4.1	Philippines	6.7	Mexico	7.5
Portugal	3.4	France	5.7	Philippines	6.1
Egypt	3.4	Mexico	5.5	France	4.8
Philippines	3.3	Chinese PR	4.3	Turkey	4.5
Greece	2.6	Turkey	4.1	Portugal	2.9
Turkey	2.6	Portugal	3.3	Egypt	2.8
Morocco	1.8	Egypt	3.3	Morocco	2.1
Spain	1.7	Greece	2.7	Spain	2
Pakistan	1.7	Spain	2	Bangladesh	1.9

Source: IMF Balance of Payments Statistics Yearbook 2001.

Top Receiving Countries

On the receiving end, the list is dominated by the developing countries in Asia (Table 5.4). Mexico, Morocco and Egypt in Africa, and Portugal, Spain and Turkey in Europe comprise the other major receivers. The only entry from the developed world is France, which has had net remittance inflows of around US$ 5 billion since 1997. India has topped the list for maximum net remittances during the 1990s, with around US$ 10 billion per year in the latter part of the decade.

The data in Tables 5.3 and 5.4 only show net inflows and outflows; it is not possible to match the recipient and source countries. Also, the importance of remittances to national economies is not completely captured by this ranking in absolute terms. The percentage of net remittances to GDP would give a better idea of the reliance of national economies on remittances. For India, the largest recipient, net remittances amounted to less than 2 per cent of GDP in 1994–2000, whereas for some Pacific Island nations like Kiribati, the Cook Islands and Tuvalu, their significance is so high that they have been christened the MIRAB states where *M*igration, *R*emittances and *A*id and the resultant largely urban *B*ureaucracy are central to the socioeconomic system (Connell and Brown, 1995).

For the list of countries in Tables 5.3 and 5.4, calculations of net remittances as a percentage of GDP yield familiar results. For Saudi Arabia, Oman and Luxembourg, net remittances ranged from 9–15 per cent in 1994–1998. Saudi Arabia had the highest proportion, though it declined from 15 per cent in 1994 to 10 per cent in 1998. Kuwait's share of remittances as a percentage of GDP for the same period ranged 4–6 per cent. On the recipients' side, remittances contributed even less to GDP. The highest shares were in the Philippines (5–8 per cent), Egypt (4–6 per cent) and Morocco (6 per cent). The rest of the source and recipient country shares of net remittances as percentages of GDP were in the 0.1–2 per cent ranges.

Continent-wise Review on Remittance Flows

Remittance Flows in Africa[4]

Data on remittances in Sub-Saharan Africa are not very comparable due to the differences in the methods used to report remittances, the extensive use of informal channels and the non-distinction between internal and international sources of remittances. Russell et al. (1990) note that the Sudanese in the Gulf tend to hand-carry gold jewellery back home, both in the interests of a safe investment and of personally compensating women for managing the household in the absence of men. In 1983, it was estimated that almost 90 per cent of remittances did not pass through the banking system (Russell and Jacobsen, 1988: 55).

Where few currency restrictions exist, as in Francophone Africa, it is harder to trace the extent of remittances. Sahelian migrants to France are said to send more than one-third of their remittances by hand and almost an equal amount by post office transfer. Lengthy delays by post offices, banks and other official channels in actually crediting the remittances have prompted more creative ways of sending money. In the Maghreb[5] countries, emigrants avoid exchange control restrictions by buying goods for 'clients' in the home country who in turn credit the emigrants' accounts with the money in local currency at a black market rate (Garson, 1993).

The studies also show the close links that remittances form between migrants and their families. Condé et al. (1986: 108) found that 84 per cent of Senegal River migrants to France send money home regularly, at least once a quarter. The importance of remittance income to the household is most pronounced in Lesotho, where 42 per cent of households report income from mine labourers as their principal source of subsistence. Studies of Sudan (Choucri, 1985; Galaleldin, 1979; al-Ghul, 1982 cited in Russell et al., 1990: 29) conclude that the principal uses of remittances in Sudan (from Yemen) are for consumption, land acquisition, housing construction and establishment of small businesses. They also show that agriculture, although not high on the list, features in the uses of remittances, while there is little evidence of lavish expenditure on weddings and luxury items. An interesting use of remittance income, noted by Condé et al. (1986) (about 10 per cent) is for tax payments (which was the third major expense item, after food and clothing, for the households of Sahelian migrants to France). Other uses in the region are for healthcare, school fees, wages for seasonal workers, improvements to housing and religious observances. In Sudan, remittances have been used to finance business investments (purchase of pickup trucks, agricultural land acquisition and modern farming equipment and seed) (Young, 1987: 212).

Evidence from Botswana, Malawi, Mozambique, Swaziland, the Sahel and Zambia suggest that remittances have been positively associated with improvements in rural areas: cattle; housing; education; agriculture; grinding mills; tools and equipment; wells; transport vehicles; and establishment of enterprises. In Botswana, remittance incomes have been used for cattle purchases, especially in female-managed households with male emigrants, though there is a tendency for a long-term decline in holdings. Russell et al. (1990) maintain that remittances in the region have contributed to increasing social and income inequality. The distinctive feature of Sub-Saharan Africa would be the greater use of remittances for education and small enterprises and relatively less on land acquisition. Households with remittance incomes had a higher savings rate and the investments were most often in real estate.

Remittance Flows in Asia

Remittances in the 1980s and 1990s were substantial in Asian economies, particularly in South and Southeast Asia. The major beneficiaries of remittances were India, Egypt, Bangladesh, Pakistan and the Philippines. There is scant data on the profile of remitters and the use of remittances in the region. Reflecting the major movements in the 1980s, the impact of remittances from the Middle East has been studied extensively, more from the point of view of the macro and regional impact than at household level (for example Amjad, 1989).

For the Philippines (Jurado, 1997: 5), the monetary impact of remittances has been estimated for households. An average of US$ 3,000 was remitted to the households of temporary labour migrants (working in Hong Kong, Singapore and the Middle East) per year between 1992 and 1996. This is higher than the minimum wage in Philippines measured on a monthly basis. Much was spent on such consumer durables as television sets, washing machines and other home appliances. Delays in bank transactions and the presence of black market rates translated into a preference by migrants to carry cash back home or use 'money couriers', who took hard currency from the migrants overseas and gave the equivalent in local currency to the migrant's family in the home country. A survey of 600 overseas Filipino workers shows that only 40 per cent of transfers passed through formal banking channels, with the rest brought during home visits (15 per cent), money couriers (22 per cent) and in kind (23 per cent) (Tiglao, 1991). In the Philippines, a 1988 household survey found that around 15 per cent of all families received income from abroad, contributing around 30 per cent of their total income (Abella, 1991: 7).

There is also evidence that households receiving remittance income have a higher propensity to save, and this rate is not insignificant. Surveys in Bangladesh (Amjad, 1989: 15) have shown that 50 per cent of remittance income in rural migrant households and 40 per cent in urban areas is saved. In contrast, 'control' households that received no remittances with comparable incomes save only 1.8 to 4.2 per cent of their incomes.

Data for Pakistan, the Philippines, Sri Lanka and Thailand in a study by Tan (1987) compared savings and investment uses of remittance income in these four countries in the 1980s. The percentage of remittance income going into savings/investment was highest in Thailand (58 per cent), followed by Sri Lanka (44.5 per cent), Pakistan (41.5 per cent) and lowest in Philippines (15.1 per cent). Investments took the form of land, housing and real estate acquisition and investments in transport, trade and services. Financial savings/deposits accounted for about 10 per cent of the remittance incomes in the four countries. The surveys also showed that return migrants saved a portion of their incomes abroad which they bring back with them on their final return. These savings, when added to the migrant's household savings, increased the savings rate from 10 per cent to 15 per cent. Remittances from the Middle East took the form of cash, bank transfers as well as consumer durables. Stalker (1994: 125) notes that planes from the Middle East were often filled not just with migrant workers but also with television sets, video recorders and other electronic goods. The amounts of remittances were highest among temporary workers certain of returning home after a short stay abroad (Mahmud, 1989: 82).

Use of remittances for housing is more prevalent in Asia than in Africa. Data for Bangladesh for 1986 suggest that around 60 per cent of the gross volume of remittances is saved (Amjad, 1989: 15). On the use of remittance incomes, Mahmud (1989) showed the percentage distribution of remittance use as follows: current consumption (36 per cent), housing (22 per cent), land purchase (21 per cent), investment in business and bank deposits (6 per cent each), loan repayment (5 per cent), farm equipment (3 per cent) and gifts (2 per cent). The results of a similar exercise for Thailand by Tingsabadh (1989) were: housing (34 per cent), loan repayment (21 per cent), current consumption (18 per cent), bank deposits (13 per cent), farming (6 per cent), vehicles (5 per cent) and personal loans (2 per cent). For Thai migrant workers in South and Southeast Asia, remittances were sent back mainly to parents. The remittances were used mainly to repay debts, for household expenses and for buying land and house construction (Chantavanich, 2001).

In villages close to Rawalpindi, Pakistan, between 1974 and 1984, the price of bricks increased three times faster than the general price index and land prices doubled as a result of a spurt of construction by returned migrants (Burki, 1991: 104). A study by Nair (1989) indicated the impact of remittances from the Gulf in the state of Kerala, India. The evidence showed that districts with higher incidence of migration experienced greater expansion of their tertiary sector. Apart from this impact, the weak linkages between remittances and the state economy are said to have dampened the impact of remittances. However, another study holds that the first wave of Kerala migrants' remittances went into a construction boom. But now the second generation migrants' remittances are being used more for daily consumption expenses and the reliance of the Keralite regional economy on Gulf remittances has grown stronger (Venier, 2001).

There are some important Asian country studies of the remittances impact on the macro-economy. Mahmud (1989) in the Bangladesh case study draws attention to the multiplier effects that arise out of migrant households' expenditure as opposed to the direct use of remittance income on investments. He finds evidence of a shift in emphasis in the domestic economy from production of import substitutes to non-tradables such as construction and services that are compatible with the labour-intensive economy. This has created benefits in the form of higher current income and employment growth, mainly in labour source regions. Hyun (1989) reports the impact of remittances on stimulating domestic demand through increases in private consumption and fixed investment. He found that in Korea in the 1970s a 10 per cent increase in remittances resulted in a 0.3 per cent increase in private consumption, a 0.5 per cent increase in fixed investment and a 0.2 per cent increase in GDP. He argued that the more immediate effects of remittances were decreased exports due to increased prices and wages, but the net effect in the long run would be positive.

For Sri Lanka, Rodrigo and Jaytissa (1989) show the effects of expenditures from remittances as higher employment and output as a percentage of GDP between 1980–1986. In Pakistan, the study by Burney (1989) concludes there was no systematic relationship between remittances and the national capital stock. The only obvious benefit was an increase in house ownership. India, the largest beneficiary of remittance flows, yields surprising results. Remittance variables are still small in relation to macro variables, though are not insignificant. According to Nayyar (1989), they were equal to 1.5 per cent of GDP, 2 per cent of final consumer expenditure, a little more than 6 per cent of gross domestic savings.

Findings on the impact of remittances on poverty alleviation and income distribution are pretty inconclusive. It has to be noted that most migrants do not belong to the poorest strata of the population. In this sense, the impact will be seen more in the deterioration of income distribution than in the lifting of households over the poverty line. Asian cases bear witness to this trend. Although Pakistan's poverty estimates showed decreasing poverty during the mass exodus to the Middle East, it is difficult to separate the effects of remittances from the general growth in agriculture and manufacturing that occurred during the same period. Only in the case of Sri Lanka (with one migrant per 47 households) is there evidence to prove that remittances lifted many migrant households over the poverty line. Some upward mobility in the size and distribution of income was also noticed in Korea. Income distribution was calculated as having worsened in Pakistan, Korea and Sri Lanka.

With a slowdown in outflows to the Middle East, the Asian financial crisis and the bursting of the IT bubble in the West, a new issue facing Asian economies (in particular) is the impact of return migration. With the safety valve of migration no longer available, the pressures for creating employment are higher as the economy will have to generate jobs to absorb both population increases and increased return migration. Another important issue emanating from the above analysis is that the majority of remittances seem to be sent by semi-skilled or unskilled workers working for indefinite periods of time abroad, and aimed at changing the financial position of the households back home as well as preparing for life on return. Little is known about the remittance behaviour of more permanent settlers, or among the highly educated and skilled. Scattered evidence points to the fact that this latter category remits more for financial investments and other income-producing assets in the remitting countries.

Remittance Flows in Latin America and the Caribbean (LAC)

Much of the literature on remittances in the region is on Latin America. There is very little data on remittances, and their uses, for Caribbean countries. The major source country for LAC inflows is the US. According to the US national census in 2000, about 14.5 million people of LAC origin lived in the US. The only other major country for LAC migrants is Spain, which hosts about 250,000 Ecuadoreans.

The major beneficiaries of remittances in the 1990s were Mexico, Dominican Republic, El Salvador, Brazil, Ecuador, Peru, Colombia, Jamaica, Guatemala and Honduras. Net remittances to Mexico increased from US$ 4 billion to US$ 6.6 billion in 1994-2000. Brazil actually saw a slight dip, from US$ 1.6 billion to US$ 1.1 billion. In terms of net remittances as a percentage of GDP, the figure for Mexico was between 1 per cent and 1.5 per cent in 1994-1998. For Brazil, it was less than 1 per cent. In six countries, remittances exceeded 10 per cent of GDP: Haiti (17 per cent), Nicaragua (14.4), El Salvador (12.6), Jamaica (11.7), the Dominican Republic (10) and Ecuador (10). Salvadorean workers sent home nearly seven times the country's FDI. Remittances to the Dominican Republic were three times agricultural exports, while those to Colombia were the equivalent of half its coffee exports.

The average Latin American worker in the US earns US$ 26,000 a year, with the average worker from Mexico and Central America earning about US$ 21,000. Most of these transfers are from poor people in the US to very poor people in Latin America. Orozco (2001) conducted a comprehensive review of the market for remittances in Latin America and concluded it had widened and deepened due to the proliferation of companies facilitating transfers, a gradual decline in transfer costs due to competition, expansion of services for money transfer as well as commodity transfers, better access to rural areas in Latin America and the growing participation of banking institutions in money transfers. Transaction costs for remitting money from the US equate 15–20 per cent of the funds remitted but have declined in the last few years. Three Salvadorian banks set up branches in the US to facilitate easy remittances. Banco de Mexico estimated that in 1995 almost 40 per cent of remittances were made via money orders, 27 per cent by electronic transfer and almost one-quarter via telegraph. Eight per cent were pocket and in-kind remittances and less than one per cent were personal cheques (Lozano-Ascencio, 1996 cited in Meyers, 1998).

The importance of electronic transfers increased in the 1990s, while that of money orders declined. Of the US$ 7.3 billion remitted to Mexico in 2001, it is estimated that money transfer fees accounted for US$ 1.5 billion and money transfer profits (from e.g. exchange rate speculation) for US$ 168 million (*Migration News*, November 2002 9:11). The dominant mode of transfers for El Salvadorians was via money courier. Dominicans sending remittances rarely use international services, instead sending more than two-thirds of their remittances through their own industry of *remesadores* (Dominican-based money transmitters), who offer better prices and better service (Meyers, 1998). These remesadores are licensed to operate under the Money Transfer Code and have created their own association (Boly, 1996; Despradel, 1997 cited in Meyers, 1998).

Evidence from El Salvador shows that remittances are higher in the initial years of migration and then taper off. But remittances in the first year of a stay abroad are minimal as time is spent looking for work. It is estimated that one-third of all households in El Salvador have remittance incomes. Two studies of Mexicao have shown that the length of time spent in the Meyers was negatively associated with the amount remitted (Massey et al., 1990, Cornelius, 1990).

Stalker (1994: 128) notes two contrary effects of emigration on agricultural production. On the one hand, emigrants may feel it is not worthwhile for their families to work on the land. On the other, emigration may lead to increased investment in agriculture. Families of migrants have access to 'migradollars' to invest in increased productivity and output. On the use of remittances, Meyers (1998) gives a good overview of the situation in Latin America. While many households receive money from more than one relative abroad, it is generally the female, who as the head of the household decides the use patterns. For instance, in El Salvador, 47.5 per cent of families receiving remittances are female-headed. In the Dominican Republic and El Salvador, researchers have found that remittances are spent on basic household expenses, with the remainder used to improve the standard of living through better housing, education, additional consumption, and loan repayment (Georges, 1990; Pessar and Grasmuck, 1991; Siri and Delgado, 1995; Boly, 1996). In Mexico 76 per cent of Mexican migrants surveyed spent remittances on consumption, 14 per cent on housing, and 10 per cent spent some money 'productively' (Durand et al., 1996).

While critics point to the 'unproductive' uses of remittances and the short-term focus on consumption needs, others refer to the rational allocation decisions made by recipient families. Given the limited market for investment activity, except in small businesses, households tend to allocate remittance monies into safer bets like housing, cattle herds and the like. Meyers (1998) also finds that remittance income is not spent any differently from other sources. This was confirmed in the case of El Salvador and Guatemala, where the majority was spent on consumption. Statistical analysis finds that each US$ 1 remitted to Mexico produces an increase of US$ 2.90 in GDP and an increase of US$ 3.20 in economic output, which leads to an increase in national income and generates billions of dollars each year (Durand et al., 1996).

Research on Latin America finds that remittances have had positive and negative effects providing discretionary income, middle-class consumption, investments in land and cattle, increased local commerce and contributions to the balance of payments and job creation. They also have led to a disparity between recipients and non-recipients, to decreased food supplies because of reduced agricultural production, to rising prices, and to a vulnerable economy (Meyers, 1998). In El Salvador, remittances are said to have eased unemployment by decreasing labour participation rates among migrant households. One report estimated that up to 55 per cent of Salvadorian families were affected by remittances of between US$ 100–150 a month, which is substantially higher than any other source of income. Remittances are said to have affected living standards, attitudes towards work, consumption habits and broadened the social composition of the elite. They have become the means to upward social mobility in El Salvador.

In Mexico, remittances have had mixed effects (Meyers, 1998). They are used for 'non-essential' consumption, inflate prices for land, housing and food, and lead to income inequality and little productive investment. Moreover, dependence on remittances often accounts for a large percentage of family income. Nevertheless, they also reduce poverty, reduce internal migration, increase employment and investment (above what it otherwise might have been) and create local demand for goods and services such as livestock, seed, cattle, transportation and education. Further, the money spent by rural recipients tends to produce larger income multipliers because rural recipients tend to consume more domestically-produced goods than urban households.

Remittance Flows in the Pacific Islands

The economies of a number of Pacific island countries have become increasingly dependent on remittances of migrants (Brown et al., 1995). Most of these islands have limited resources and the most probable and viable development strategy to meet people's aspirations for higher living standards is often perceived to be reliance on migration and remittances (Faeamani, 1995). The most common destinations are New Zealand, America and Australia. Some of the greatest concentrations of Pacific islanders are said to be in cities like Auckland, Honolulu and Los Angeles rather than in the South Pacific. Data on the amount of remittances for the region are scant. According to IMF estimates, Fiji received remittances (compensation of employees) of US$ 30 million in 1994. The flow peaked at US$ 35 million in 1997 and by 1999 had fallen to US$ 23 million. Vanuatu had about US$ 18 million in 1997 and US$ 21 million in 1998. Kiribati received about US$ 3 million in 1994 as workers remittances. The most important beneficiary in the region seems to be Samoa, with total remittances in the range of US$ 37 million in 1994 to US$ 47 million in 1998. With few outflows, net remittances were about US$ 40 million, about 18 per cent of GDP in 1998.

On the whole, the benefits of remittances have been considerable in the Pacific Islands. Remittances have gone beyond merely supporting subsistence and consumption levels to enabling a more balanced structure of development. Cross-sectional data from these studies prove that remittance levels do not appear to decline with the migrant's length of absence from his/her home country, and a significant motivating factor for migrants to remit is the accumulation of assets and investment in the home country (Brown et al., 1995).

Conclusion

The discussion on remittances opens up many issues. First, remittances are determined by a host of factors in source and recipient countries, many of them at the level of the individual remitting household's circumstances. As such, they exhibit two patterns. At the individual level, remittances are higher in the initial years of migration. The greater the number of years spent abroad, the smaller the flows of remittances tend to be (except in the case of the Pacific Island countries, where this remittance-decay hypothesis does not seem to hold). There are two reasons for this. First, families reunite and the majority of recipients' needs in the home country can be met by the migrants within a few years. Second, the flows, although consistent at an aggregate level, are erratic at an individual level. As mentioned earlier, the economic situation in the labour source and recipient countries determines the amount and frequency of remittances so that there is no predictability in the nature of flows. This uncertainty becomes a problem only when dependence on remittances becomes high.

Unless there is an initial big push for the economies which will then take off and begin to rely less on these flows in the longer run, economic policies cannot rely on remittances over the long run. The analysis of regions in this chapter shows that weak linkages between remittance flows and the productive capacity of the nations often prevent this Big Push from happening. The benefits are more at individual, family and community level than at the macro level.

Remittances, we have seen, are determined by a host of factors in the source and recipient countries and the personal circumstances of the migrant household.

Remittances have been most significant in the island economies of the Pacific. Although the volume of remittances is high, net remittances as a percentage of GDP are still very low. Total remittances (workers remittances plus compensation of employees) registered a 21 per cent increase between 1995–2000, from US$ 85 billion to US$ 103 billion. Developing country shares of total remittance credits ranged from 57 per cent in 1994 to 64 per cent in 2000, with increases every year. Official data on remittances understate the volume of remittances, since a large proportion of them are sent through informal channels or brought as cash or in kind.

Analysis of the nature of remittances across continents shows some common patterns relating to the use of remittances. Remittances tend to be used mainly for immediate consumption needs, repayment of debts, housing and other asset building, purchase of transport equipment and consumer durables. They are used, to a lesser extent, to finance small enterprises and agricultural investment. On the micro level, the household seems to be the most important beneficiary. Without exception, remittances have raised the living standards of migrant households. However, they have not made much difference to the macro-economy, only occasionally fuelling temporary price rises, especially in the construction industry. The potential role for remittances in any planning and policy exercise has to take into account the fact that remittances seem to have a lifecycle. They are not consistent and reliable over the whole lifetime of the migrant staying abroad; they indeed exhibit an inverse relationship to the number of years the migrant lives abroad.

Remittances exhibit two distinctive features: individual household flows are inconsistent and peter out with time; but at the national level have been consistent and rising in the 1990s. The second feature that the studies bring out is that their impact is felt much more intensely at the household level than the macro economic level. On the distributional side, however, studies in the Pacific Islands show that emigration has indeed increased income and wealth inequalities among the remittance receiving communities. With the bias toward skills and education among the migrants, this has led to the increasing divide between the haves and the have-nots in the source countries.

As far as the source of remittances are concerned, undoubtedly the US has been the top remitting country in the 1990s. Combined OPEC outflows match the US in every year in the period 1994–2000. This pattern only underscores the extent of dependence of the developing world on the US economy. The highly porous borders in our globalizing world encourage movement across borders, along with apathy from source countries. Often, the only interest shown by governments is in remittance money. Policy measures relating to remittances should therefore take a broader view in the areas of migration and human resource planning.

Notes

1   This paper is based on Ramamurthy (2003).

2   For a comprehensive study including brain drain and labour market impact see Ramamurthy (2003).
3   Calculated as the difference between remittance credits and debits.
4   This section is based on Russell et al. (1990) which is a comprehensive review of literature up until the late 1980s concerning migration flows in Sub-Saharan Africa only.
5   Comprising Algeria, Tunisia, Morocco, Libya and Mauritania.

Chapter 6

Migration, Development and Conflict

Ninna Nyberg Sørensen

Introduction

Against the background of increased human mobility over the last three decades, resurgent interest in the migration-development nexus has stimulated novel lines of academic inquiry and pushed policy considerations in new directions. This chapter outlines current discussions around the links between migration, development and conflict. It also considers the complex nature of 'mixed flows', the difficulties in distinguishing between forced/political and voluntary/economic migration, and the links to development from these often overlapping types of flows.

Of the estimated 175 million global migrants (UN Population Division, 2002) some are persons with legal status in the countries of settlement. Others are in an irregular situation and try by various means to regularize their status. A relatively small proportion has been granted refugee status (Van Kessel, 2002). It is generally acknowledged that increased mobility has led to a growing complexity of migratory movements. This complexity manifests itself in a substitution of 'old' migration destinations with new ones, a growing class diversification and informalization of migration, a feminization of particular streams, and the phenomenon of 'mixed flows'. In the tension between transnational flows of people and states, new control mechanisms and policies are emerging as the scope and constituency for policy interventions into the migration-development nexus are broadened. Any informed discussion of how to make migration work for development and related policy options can only be achieved by considering such complexities.

International migration has been both prompted and facilitated by globalization. Apart from the growing disparity in livelihood possibilities and human security to be found in different parts of the world, other factors have contributed to the current magnitude, density, velocity, and diversity of human population movements. These include improved transportation, communication and information technology; the expansion of transnational social networks and diaspora formations; and the emergence of a commercial (sometimes criminal) industry devoted to facilitating human movement across international borders. However, while the cornerstone of globalization has been an increase in the international flow of trade, capital, information and services, the right to freedom of movement – especially poor migrants, refugees and asylum seekers – has been severely curtailed. Migrant workers and people in flight, although mobile by definition, are actually among those excluded from the freedom and benefits of borderless globalization (Jordão, 2001). The increasing number of migrants, as well as the containment of others, therefore reflects the limitations of globalization (Martin, 2001a).

Together with poverty, human rights abuses associated with poor governance have become among the key factors impelling much current migration, and it is no coincidence that conflict-ridden countries are often those with severe economic difficulties. In many parts of the world, people are forced to abandon their homes due to severe breakdown of economic and social conditions. In addition, environmental devastation beyond restoration and lack of access to natural resources increasingly propel people to migrate. Others find that the growing inequalities in wealth between and within countries make migration the only viable option in order to secure better economic prospects and upward social mobility.

Well into the twentieth century, many nation states regarded emigration as a serious loss of its human resources. Increasingly however, migrant source countries recognize that although many migrants are unlikely to return, they can still advance state consolidation and national development from abroad (Levitt, 2001). Not only do migrants send remittances, they also have the potential to be organized into strong lobbies that advocate for source country interests. In response, source countries may endow migrants with special extraterritorial rights, protections and recognitions, in the hope of ensuring their long term support (Basch et al., 1994; Smith, 1998; Goldring, 2001).

A similar awareness about the role that migration can play in development processes is increasing at the international level. Besides an increasing commitment by the European Commission in this field, individual member states are currently experimenting with different approaches to policies linking migration and development. Most of these attempts have taken their point of departure in *either* migration *or* development concerns (for example reallocation of development aid to migrant producing countries conditioned on such countries' willingness to limit emigration and the return of their nationals as compared to making migration a tool for development, see Sørensen et al., 2003a).

Contrary to discussions linking migration and development, international refugee policy has increasingly been characterized by attempts to contain refugees (and other migrants) in the countries or regions of origin. The attempts at creating 'safe havens' within areas of conflict, the discussions raised regarding 'the right to stay', and the progressive institutionalization of the field of internally displaced persons have been interpreted as a kind of 'internalization' of the refugee problem. The latest developments in the EU point in the same direction, in particular the attempts at developing an 'external dimension' of Justice and Home Affairs since 1999, and the British, Dutch, and Danish proposals for new approaches to asylum policies and protection (Stepputat, 2004).

The following discussion uses migration from Somalia/Somaliland as the main example.[1] This case – like the cases of most other source countries – is of course specific. Still, lessons can be drawn that are useful in other contexts, and may provide a basis for constructive discussions of 'mixed flows', migration as a development resource and possible opportunities in the current migration and international cooperation regimes.

'Mixed Flows' and the Problem of Distinction

In 2003 the European Commission noted that the 'abuse of asylum procedures is on the rise, as are *mixed migratory flows*, often maintained by smuggling practices involving both people with a legitimate need for international protection and migrants using asylum procedures to gain access to the Member States to improve their living conditions' (2003b). Entangling the issues of asylum and economic migration easily leads to the accusation that asylum seekers more often than not are economic migrants abusing the system, an accusation further confounded with the issue of human smuggling and trafficking.

In reality, few source countries produce only asylum seekers or economic migrants. In many cases, migrants from one source country comprise economic migrants who have used the asylum route, asylum seekers who have used the migration route, and individuals who have used other routes, including both legal and illegal. In other cases, the reasons for migrating may have changed over time. What maybe began as economic migration may due to changes in local circumstances come to include internal displacement or international refugee movements, and conversely, what was originally refugee movements may transmute into migration for economic improvement. Statuses also change over time in ways that differ according to the policies of destination countries (Martin, 2001a). In both cases, transnational families or households may consist of individuals who migrated for different reasons. When migrants reach their destinations, refugees may live alongside co-nationals who are not necessarily refugees but rather part of broader communities of newcomers (Crisp, 1999). Moreover, as has been the case of Somalis, asylum seekers and refugees may also enter prior currents of labour. Finally, variation in migration regimes in countries of destination may lead to situations in which dispersed family members – who may have migrated for the same economic or political reasons – hold different statuses.

The dispersal of the Somali diaspora – in peace as well as during protracted periods of armed conflict – is emblematic of such complexities and provides a good illustration of the problem of 'mixed flows' as well as the difficulties in distinguishing between different, overlapping, and shifting flows.

Somali Mobility

Throughout the years, substantial numbers of Somalis have migrated. The total number of Somalis living outside Somalia has been estimated at one million (Nair and Abdulla, 1998; UNDP, 2001). This figure presumably includes those who have naturalized in their countries of residence. In addition, Somalis are currently one of the most widely dispersed diasporas in the world. In the late 1990s, asylum applications by Somali nationals were recorded in more than 60 countries. The African neighbour states remain the main countries of asylum.

One explanation of this dispersal can be found in Somali nomadic livelihoods, which is often said to be at the heart of Somali culture. For example, Lewis (1961) describes the livelihoods of the Somali pastoralist as characterized by strategies of mobility and dispersal in order to survive in an extremely harsh climate. Likewise, Marshal (1996) points to the centrality of migration in Somali culture, which he distinguishes by its subsistence economy, trade to procure necessities not domestically produced, and mobility to adapt to cycles of climate in search of pastures. Among pastoralists in Somalia, social relationships established between extended family members reflect not only the production of a livelihood but also this livelihood's continued reproduction (Besteman, 1999).

Apart from the well-established traditions of nomadic movement within Somalia and across the border to neighbouring countries (Ethiopia and Kenya), Somalis have a long tradition of migration outside the region. During British colonialism, an early Somali diaspora emerged as seamen from colonial British Somaliland working in the Merchant Navy began settling in the port cities of London, Bristol, Cardiff, Liverpool and Hull. The Somali community in the United Kingdom grew further with the expansion of the steel industry in the 1950s and 1960s (Simkin, 2002). Other seamen went to America, Russia or Arab countries to work in the maritime trade (Cassanelli, 1982). Today, after sailing for almost a century, several retired seamen have settled in cities like Cardiff and Copenhagen, while others have returned to the Somali-inhabited area of the Horn of Africa (Hansen, 2004).

After independence in 1960, many disappointed supporters of the ruling Somali Youth League, especially those stemming from the northwestern Isaaq clan, migrated abroad as they had lost their assets and were denied access to new resources. From the early 1970s, Somalia became a major labour exporter to the oil producing Arab countries. It is estimated that between 150,000 and 200,000 Somalis migrated to the Gulf during the 1970s. By 1987, their numbers had doubled to an estimated 375,000. These migrants were relatively well educated, travelling abroad for better employment and higher earnings than they could find in Somalia (Gundel, 2003). Another group of Somalis began migrating for higher education to North America, Europe and the Soviet Union during the same period. Due to new entry restrictions (and the high cost of education in the West), educational flows have today been redirected towards India and Pakistan (Hansen, 2004).

The largest number of Somalis to leave the Horn of Africa has done so because of civil war and political unrest. Hundreds of thousands of Somalis were sent into exile in the late 1980s and early 1990s. The outbreak of civil war in 1988 and the inter-clan fighting after the fall of Siad Barre in 1991 displaced hundreds of thousands of Somalis within the country (UNDP, 2001). It drove many others to leave to seek refuge in Ethiopia, Kenya, Yemen and other neighbouring countries, as well as to seek asylum further afield in the UK, Italy, the Netherlands, Scandinavia, Canada, the US and other Western states (UNHCR, 2002). Some were able to follow paths and networks already established by 'economic' migrants.

At present the UK and Italy host the largest long-distance Somali diaspora communities, based on historical and colonial ties. These long-established communities have been supplemented by more recent inflows of asylum seekers. In 2000, the UK received nearly half the asylum applications by Somalis in European countries, nearly 4,800 out of 10,900. Most Somali refugees in London originate in the by now self-declared Republic of Somaliland (Ahmed, 2000). The Netherlands and Scandinavian countries have been the next most 'popular' destinations for asylum seekers. These countries, together with Germany, to which asylum applications in recent years have been minimal, have substantial Somali populations, mainly based on asylum migration. Italy has become one of the major destinations for irregular labour migration, including Somalis. Today Somali women compete with Philippine, Romanian and Ukrainian housekeepers, babysitters and care workers to take up jobs for millions of Italian families. Integrated Regional Information Networks (IRIN) (2003) reports that agents in Mogadishu can charge double the price for smuggling Somali girls into Italy (US\$ 7,000 as compared to US\$ 3,500 to other European countries) because the girls get jobs as housekeepers and can start sending money home immediately. Outside Europe, North America has been the major attraction: some 19,000 Somalis applied for asylum in Canada and 8,000 in the US during 1990–1998 (Frushone, 2001).

Many Somali families have separated along the way, and the paths of those who managed to flee armed conflicts to the wider diaspora were seldom straightforward but involved years in refugee camps or convoluted journeys via countries where they could get temporary visas (McGown, 1999: 14). Deteriorating conditions in certain asylum countries have provoked some Somalis to move on. This has for instance been the case for a smaller group of Somalis who have gained citizenship in Denmark but subsequently have moved to England, a country they perceive as being less xenophobic and more open to Somalis than Denmark.[2]

This brief overview of Somali migration patterns gives evidence of the growing complexity of migratory flows. Throughout the years new migration destinations have been added to old ones, class diversification seem to be congruent with distance (the better off, the longer distance travelled), and certain out-going flows – for example to Italy – have become feminized. As has hopefully become clear, the Somali diaspora does not fit neatly into either the 'forced' or the 'voluntary' category. Not because the bulk of Somali asylum seekers in general have been 'economic migrants' using the asylum procedure to circumvent established migration controls, but rather because different historical periods have provoked different forms of movement. Differing migration regimes in different host countries have further added to a situation in which Somalis – who may have left Somalia at the same time and for the same reasons – hold different statuses. Access to financial means and social networks (including access to diaspora links established prior to the conflict as well as access to 'carriers' or 'human smugglers') to a large degree explains why Somali refugees ended up in different destinations – were internally displaced, fled to neighbouring countries, or were able to find refuge in the wider diaspora.

It may well be that the muddling of the metaphors of 'fleeing poverty' and 'fleeing to escape persecution' has been seriously damaging to those genuinely in need of shelter (Nicholson, 2002). It has also provided fuel to the current dysfunctional asylum and migration regime (Crisp, 2002). With the difficulties in maintaining a clear distinction between forced and voluntary migration in mind, it is still relevant to ask if the relationship between different types of migration and development are of the same nature and to what extent refugees and migrants have the same interests in and potentials for contributing to local development?

Migration as a Development Resource

As migration has steadily climbed up the list of public and policy concerns, it has become increasingly recognized that migration can be affected – intentionally or not – by interventions in the kindred areas of development policy and humanitarian assistance, as well as by the wider policies and practices in the foreign and domestic spheres. Underlying much international thinking on development and migration has been the effectiveness of reducing migration and refugee flows by generating local development, preventing and resolving local conflicts, and retaining refugees in neighbouring or first countries of asylum, an approach commonly referred to as 'combating the root causes of migration'.

The idea that development should be fostered to stop – or at least reduce – migration pressures can be found in various documents of the European Commission throughout the 1990s. During the late 1990s, however, this approach demonstrated its structural limits. Academic analysis (within sociology and anthropology, but also within economics and political science) presented evidence that economic and social development does indeed affect mobility, but not in the rather instrumental way suggested by the 'root cause' approach. On the contrary, a simultaneous increase in economic productivity may increase mobility, at least in the short term (Pastore, 2003). The 'root cause' approach therefore gained competition from what became known as the 'migration hump' approach, the paradox that the same economic policies that can reduce migration in the long term, can increase it in the short term (Martin, 2004).

During the Danish EU presidency, the former Centre for Development Research in Copenhagen introduced a third 'transnational' approach to the policy arena (Sørensen et al., 2003b).[3] This approach sees internal, regional and international mobility as an intrinsic dimension of development and understands mobility as an essential condition for economic and social development. The arguments forwarded in this chapter build on this approach and are elaborated in relation to three particular areas, namely remittances, return and repatriation, and diaspora support.

Remittances

Policy discussions on migrants as a development resource have primarily focused on remittances. Evidence suggests that the financial flow from migrants and refugees are likely to be considerably larger than the size of development aid and as least as well targeted at the poor in both conflict-ridden and stable developing countries (Sørensen, 2004). The World Bank estimated that in 2002 the global flow of migrants' official remittances amounted to US$ 80 billion, with over 60 per cent going to developing countries. To further underline the development dimension of migrant transfers, remittances seem to be more stable than private capital flows and to be less volatile to changing economic cycles (Ratha, 2003: 160). In many less developed countries remittances amount on average to 13 per cent of GDP (IOM, 2003), and often account for a much higher share as, for instance, in Somalia, where an estimated 25–40 per cent of all families receive remittances from abroad (UNDP and ECSU, 2003).

Compared to other regions in the world, African remittance data are generally scarce or confronted with a lack of reliability. According to a recent World Bank study, this may in part be explained by the relatively low share of migrant remittances flowing to the African continent. Contrary to remittances to Latin America and Asia, remittances to Africa have grown only little and, as a result, have declined in relative share (Sander and Maimbo, 2003). Remittances seem to be even more important if informal remittances are taken into account. Evidence from Sudan and Egypt suggest that the informal remittances double, and in some cases even triple the total amount of migrants' financial transfers. Given that the banking systems in many African countries still is inadequately developed, it is safe to assume that informal remittances are very important in Africa (IOM, 2003: 227).

Because of the collapse of the Somali state and commercial banking system, formal financial institutions still do not function. Remittances are therefore sent through private remittance companies known as *xawilaad*. As in other post-conflict countries, where little or no formal financial infrastructure exists, informal remittance systems may help maintain entire payment systems and channel external funds for reconstruction from the diaspora (DfID, 2003). It is likely that remittances are unevenly distributed, since poorer households do not have the resources needed to send members to places where earnings or welfare provisions are sufficient to allow sending money home.

To Somalia as a whole, remittance estimates range from 120 million a year (Montclos and Kagwanja, 2000) to US$ 1 billion in 2000 (UNDP and ECSU, 2003). To Somaliland alone, estimates range from US$ 1–500 million annually. A 1997 study conducted by the Ministry of Planning in Somaliland estimated that US$ 93 million were being transferred that year (Ahmed, 2000). Members of the Somali Diaspora remit money to support the livelihood of their remaining family members. These remittances typically stand at US$ 50–200 per month, and are primarily spent on consumption, education and health. During interviews in urban resettlement areas of

Hargeisa in 2002, a *Dahabshiil* substation manager told that relatively few repatriated camp refugees receive remittances as compared to those living in central Hargeisa with links to the wider diaspora. Those who do, receive a monthly money order of US$ 100 from Europe, North America and the Arab states (in that order). This money is distributed among extended family members, including people still living in rural areas. Interviews in rural areas have confirmed this pattern.

The limited evidence available on refugees' remittances suggests that these transfers are used in ways similar to those sent by other migrants: for daily subsistence, health care, housing, and education. Paying off debt may also be prominent, especially when there have been substantial outlays to send asylum migrants abroad, or when assets have been destroyed, sold off, or lost during conflict. Expatriates may also fund the migration of other family members, either in the form of monetary transfers back home, payments for tickets, documents, and accommodation and migration agents. Expatriates may also meet other costs incurred during and after travel (Van Hear, 2003).

As previously mentioned, Somaliland is seen by many in the diaspora as a country of opportunity where commercial regulations are minimal and the scope for entrepreneurship is wide open. As the 2001 UNDP report points out, the civil war achieved what the structural adjustment programmes of the 1980s did not, that is, economic deregulation that enabled the expansion of the private sector. One should not forget, however, that the conditions that provide an environment conducive for the activities of the diaspora and other businesspeople are those that spell poor conditions for the population at large.

Somalilanders from the wider diaspora are currently engaged in opening small scale businesses – restaurants, beauty salons, transport companies, supermarkets and kiosks – often through the investment of savings made while abroad. Compared to starting a business abroad, the capital needed to open up in Somaliland is quite modest. Partly because of the absence of a functioning state, with its financial, economic and social institutions, the private sector has grown tremendously, and traditional government services like the provision of education, health care and electricity has largely been taken over by private companies, or in practice been privatized. Apart from small-scale business investments, remittances are also invested in land and housing. Finally remittances flow in the form of collective donations made by organizations created in the diaspora (Hansen, 2003; King, 2003).

Return and Repatriation

Return and repatriation are generally seen as the natural 'end product' of the migration cycle and a prerequisite for migrants' and refugees' continued engagement with local development. Ideally, migrants are expected to have saved capital and acquired skills abroad that can be productively invested in the source country (Sørensen et al., 2003a). Of the three 'durable' solutions to refugee crises – integration in the first country of asylum, resettlement in a third country or return to the homeland – the latter is seen as the best and most 'natural' option. Yet, inadequate attention has been given to selectivity in terms of returnees' personal characteristics, duration of stay abroad, level of incorporation into host countries, and the motivations underlying different types of return.

Several studies suggest that return after a relatively short period abroad, especially among low skilled migrants and if caused by an inability to adapt to the host country or unforeseen and adverse family circumstances, is less likely to contribute to development. Return after a longer stay abroad, when the migrants have saved money to meet specific development purposes back home, has far better development prospects (ibid.). Whether return/repatriation will benefit local development will vary and is primarily determined by two factors: the aptitude and preparation of the returnees, and whether or not the country of origin provides a propitious social, economic and institutional environment for the returnees to use their economic and human capital productively (Ghosh, 2000a). In the case of refugee repatriation, a political climate facilitating former adversaries to begin to work together is an additional factor. Evidence nevertheless suggests that states with a history of violent conflict or civil war may be more eager to capture the resources of refugees abroad than to encourage their return and competition over resources in the post-conflict nation-state building process.

In the case of Somalia, repatriation has picked up in recent years, primarily to the relatively peaceful self-declared Republic of Somaliland. From February 1997 to October 2001, UNHCR officially assisted the voluntary repatriation of an estimated 170,000 refugees back to Somaliland (Frushone, 2001). UNHCR estimates that 456,700 refugees returned to Somalia (mainly Somaliland) under their protection (UNHCR Somalia, 2002). Others highlight that most repatriation has been 'spontaneous' and 'self-organized' as opposed to organized by UNHCR. Instead of relying on international institutions, refugees and returnees have relied on social networks, mobility and diversified investments to overcome the endemic insecurity of the region. Social networks were mobilized both at the time of flight (the vast majority of refugees settled in their clan areas across the border) and of return (reliance on charity from relatives once the repatriation package was exhausted) (Ambroso, 2002).

In addition to repatriated refugees from neighbouring countries, substantial numbers of Somalilanders from the wider diaspora have been coming back over the last few years to see if they can live in Somaliland again. These have taken up roles in government, aid agencies, non-governmental organizations, health care, education, and in business. They are putting energy and resources into reconstruction. During my short field visit to Somaliland in 2002, I found that several research and higher education institutions were headed and staffed by returnees. Founders and teachers at several primary and secondary schools were returnees (and funds were usually raised in the diaspora). Several businesses were run by returnees (telecommunication companies, Internet service providers, insurance companies and private health clinics), and NGOs as well as government institutions were staffed by migrants returning from the wider diaspora. Interestingly, most of the returned female professionals worked for international agencies and NGOs whereas male professionals were found to concentrate in state institutions and private businesses.

Return from the wider diaspora often took the form of 'staggered repatriation' in which one family member, often the family father, had gone back while the rest of the family stayed in the country of asylum or residence. The acquisition of a high status citizenship (European or North American) usually precedes such staggered returns (Fink-Nielsen et al., 2002). Together, the acquisition of citizenship and the dividing of family members secure both continued access to diaspora resources and security should a new conflict break out. However, even the most dedicated and patriotic Somalilanders who have returned to Somaliland to engage in processes of reconstruction may not return in the sense of settling permanently in the country. Many may become 'revolving returnees' who after an intended 'permanent' return go back to Europe or North America, either because they have been unable to renew their contracts within the 'development industry', have failed in their business efforts, or have been unable to convince their families in the wider diaspora to join them (Hansen, 2003; Ambroso, 2002).

Nicholas Van Hear has convincingly argued that when people flee conflict or persecution, a common pattern is for most to seek safety in other parts of their own country, for a substantial number to look for refuge in neighbouring countries, and for a smaller number to seek asylum in countries further a field. If displacement persists and people consolidate themselves in their territories of refuge, complex relations will develop among these different domains of the refugee diaspora. He goes on to suggest that each of these domains to some extent correspond to the three locations associated with the three durable solutions that the UNHCR is charged with pursuing for refugees. Looking at some of the shortcomings of the notion of 'durable solutions', Van Hear suggests that diaspora and the sustaining of transnational relations might represent the most enduring, if not durable, solution to many current situations of displacement (Van Hear, 2003). The case of Somalis/Somalilanders seems to lend itself to this suggestion. Massive repatriation and return, on the other hand, may have negative consequences for local development not least due to a diminution of remittances which – in the worst case scenario – may lead to renewed instability, socioeconomic or political upheaval, and the resumption or provocation of conflict.

Diaspora Support

Several studies have indicated that migrants are important not only as a source of family remittances and investors in the local economies, but also as potential lobbyists or 'ambassadors' of national interests abroad. Homeland engagement can take a variety of forms, including exile groups organizing themselves for return, groups lobbying on behalf of a homeland abroad, external offices of political parties, or opposition groups campaigning or planning actions to effect political change in the homeland

(Østergaard-Nielsen, 2001). Apart from beneficial homeland political allegiances, diaspora support may also involve buying-in to dubious regimes and overseas support for insurgency and terrorism.

The valuable contribution of diasporas to home country development is increasingly acknowledged. Efforts to create closer relationships between state institutions and a given state's migrant communities abroad has included forming and/or consolidating migrant associations abroad, often in the form of Home Town Associations (HTAs). HTAs have served as platforms for matching funds schemes that pool remittances with government funds and expertise, potentially resulting in improvements in local health, education and employment conditions, benefiting migrant and non-migrant households alike (Smith, 2001). Towns and villages that are connected to home town associations abroad tend to be better off in terms of infrastructure and access to services than those who have no such connections (Landolt, 2001). However, the cooptation of migrant resources into development projects – 'designed by the state but financed by migrants' – may be contested by migrants if they experience 'the state as diverting their energies from true civil society and local development initiatives across borders' (Smith, 2003: 467).

The existence of Somali diaspora groups is a consequence of traditional mobile livelihood patterns, colonialism, labour migration and the humanitarian disasters in the late 1980s and early 1990s. Unwilling to accept a life in exiled silence the groups have continued to perform an active role through remittances that in turn has given entitlement to a strong and vocal political participation, facilitated by new technology (IRIN, 2001).

The most assertive Somaliland diaspora group is the Somaliland Forum, which started as a discussion group on the internet and only later developed into an association involved in Somaliland through collective remittances for development projects and politically motivated activities in Somaliland, Europe and North America. The Forum describes itself as an association working with Somalilanders around the world, its main premise being that the most important asset for the future development of Somaliland is the human resources scattered in the diaspora. Its activities include the sponsoring of public programmes benefiting a wide range of needs, for example education, health and infrastructure (Hansen, 2004). The Forum has run a relentless campaign for Somaliland independence, concentrating primarily on direct petitioning of politicians and international organizations, as well as monitoring media output. This leads IRIN (2001) to characterize the Forum as a diaspora constituency that may be as much a political liability as an asset, over which the Somaliland leadership exercises no control.

Somali peace and equality activists constitute another group worth mentioning. These activists have consistently argued that it is Somali women who bear the brunt of the problems facing Somalia/Somaliland. They use the argument that local women are the mothers, sisters and wives who have had to care for the family after the men were killed and that the majority of Somali families are supported by their daughters, nieces and sisters who send remittances from abroad. They have lobbied internationally for the recognition of women in a country ruled by clan structures denying women any voice (PeaceWomen, 2003).

As the examples above have shown, diasporas can potentially strengthen the peace and development processes by bringing together the human resources in the diaspora with a view to stimulating reconciliation, reconstruction efforts, and a combination of traditional and modern forms of government. In addition, the diaspora may also participate in the development of the educational system; the supply of professionally trained health workers with both formal and cultural competences; help establish occupational projects in the business sector, agriculture, animal husbandry and the fishing industry; and, in the case of Somaliland, strengthen local opposition to excessive qat chewing and female circumcision. It should be stressed, however, that diaspora activities do not necessarily benefit society at large. As seen from the three quotes below, the potential contribution of the Somaliland diaspora is evaluated in different ways by different stakeholders:

> The Somaliland educated and viable strata – at home and within the diaspora – must strive to cooperate through the formation of professional organizations, trusts and NGOs … The diaspora should be urged to organize to promote the welfare and development of their peoples. They should … pay particular attention to visits by their children so as to strengthen their knowledge of their language, religion and culture.[4]

> We need those with skills to return, the professionals. If the returnees have no resources when they come here they are not welcome … [Such returnees] put more pressure on society and create more unemployment. They have to return with something … [We] do not want them to come with empty pockets.[5]

> Regarding the idea of diaspora involvement, I am sceptical. It would be very difficult unless they are well organized from abroad. They need to define clearly which objectives to achieve – but I have never seen that. Those who return have a leg abroad and only try to make money here. Somalis are all individualists.[6]

Development Opportunities

Recognition of the shifting geopolitical context has promoted diverse forms of migratory movements, and in particular has demanded a rethinking of the hitherto largely separated policy fields of migration and development. Acknowledgement of the difficulties of making and maintaining a clear distinction between voluntary and forced migration has emerged, and awareness of the complexity of diaspora formation has grown.

The habitual separation between refugees and migrants is to a large extent a reflection of categories which have been developed in (and between) state institutions for the administrative and political control of mobility. But while distinct approaches to asylum and migration makes sense from a humanitarian as well as from an immigration policy perspective, working with mutually exclusive categories may be less helpful in facilitating migration-development links from a development policy angle. Attempting to 'undo' the determining link between status categories and development impact, I suggest bringing refugee and migrant diasporas together and to juxtapose and illuminate the under-explored development potentials in 'transnational', 'transregional' and 'translocal' mobility.[7]

From their often precarious position in Western as well as neighbouring countries, migrants provide dependants back home with remittances for their daily survival, and several states on the margins of the global economy encourage and receive vital funding from their diasporas. However such contributions may be double-edged: at times the diaspora may be involved in development and/or post-conflict reconstruction, while in other cases such funds are channelled into prolongation of local inequalities or even the financing of violent conflicts. Hence, the recent interest on behalf of some international agencies in policing such diasporas.

The use of remittances as a resource for development requires better answers to some fundamental questions such as: how can governments best estimate the actual flows of financial as well as social remittances; are there better ways to estimate more precisely how remittances are transferred and used, and what alternative ways can be envisioned; to what extent can the multiplier effect of remittances be increased by initiatives to encourage productive and work creating investments; what can be done to lower transfer costs in order to maximize the level of remittances reaching family members, local communities and ultimately states; and how can governments and international development organizations assist organized groups, such as HTAs and home villages to make the most effective use of collective remittances for development without impeding local initiatives?

The development potential of remittances can obviously be improved by increasing the total flow of remittances, lowering the transfer costs, reducing the risks involved in transfers and offering more attractive investment alternatives. In addition to monetary remittances' potential for improving economic activities, social remittances may gradually spread to political, cultural and social activities and create transnational communities (Levitt, 2001). Such developments should be encouraged by international development agencies.

In conflict-ridden countries such as Somalia, the securing of open transfer channels seems crucial. An initial challenge facing development efforts linked to remittances is to ensure that existing 'informal' remittance sectors are not automatically closed down because of accusations of being linked to international terrorism. To counter the possibility of such charges being made, the international community should engage in dialogue with *xawilaad*, *hundi* and other traditional transfer systems with a view to increasing the level of accountability and formality of such systems.

As remittances make their way home and contribute to family survival and economic development, it is worth underlining that the demand may pose a substantial drain on those who send them. Family and kinship links, while providing network support, are also a source of perhaps never ending obligations. Diaspora attitudes to the family back home may therefore be highly ambivalent. Sending remittances back home can be a large drain on the resources of those who have employment in the West, and even more so for those who do not. Such demands may work against the diaspora's social mobility in the host country and also make accumulating capital for return or broader investments back home very difficult. On a similar note, Susan Martin (2001b) has asked if the remittances come at a cost to those settling abroad. What trade offs are migrants making to save sufficient resources to remit? Are they unable to make investments in education and skills upgrading in order to send all this money home? Are remittance expectations another form of dept bondage that takes over as soon as other migration costs are paid off? Development agencies should make sure that their renewed focus on diasporas and remittances as a source of development finance does not place additional stress on already vulnerable groups.

In relation to return and repatriation, policy-makers should be aware that repatriation or tight restrictions on entry might have far-reaching consequences for the migration-development link. If the resolution of conflict is accompanied by large-scale repatriation, the source of remittances will obviously diminish, raising potential for renewed instability and further conflict. Moreover, the trend towards containment in countries or regions of origin will mean that those remaining in such places may have less in the way of earning and therefore less remittance power than those in more prosperous migration countries (Sørensen et al., 2003b).

As recently argued by Beryl Nicholson, many returnees return to developing countries ravaged by conflict. Since the benefits labour migrants bring when they return are also those needed in the home countries of refugees, he advocates that refugees should be allowed to work and to obtain capital, skills and ideas for their return. He further argues that refugees should perhaps be given continuous permission to work abroad during an initial rebuilding phase, allowing them to contribute remittances to families who are otherwise dependent on international aid (Nicholson, 2002). This line of thought seems worth pursuing.

Some return programmes have demanded returning families to stay, undivided and permanently, in the places of return. However, people who are living at the edge of the global economy may be unable to establish sustainable livelihoods without incorporating highly mobile strategies for gaining access to work, education and markets (Stepputat and Sørensen, 2001). This pattern is repeated when we look at conventional repatriation policies. As the Somali case has shown, if return becomes a possibility, returnees may choose a 'staggered return' that allows them to develop a transnational livelihood, drawing on rights and resources from several places, including the country of origin and the countries of refuge.

So-called durable solutions are not bound to be either integration or repatriation but could well combine the two in durable transnational, transregional or translocal strategies in which dispersed social networks are acknowledged as important factors of political and economic development. 'Go-and-see' programmes for potentially repatriating refugees are a sign of an emerging awareness of the importance of transnational networks within humanitarian agencies. Other concrete measures to increase the development impact of migration could include maintaining flexible asylum and resettlement policies that relieve pressure on poor first countries of asylum hosting refugees (burden sharing), and introducing flexible residence and citizenship rights to allow migrants to return home without prejudicing their right to stay in host countries. This measure seems particularly important in relation to migrants/refugees from countries evolving from violent conflict.

If class background, educational background, access to financial means and social networks, and gender determine destination, and destination in turn determines the development potential of a given diaspora, will diaspora networks and transnational transfers inevitably lead to greater socio-economic differentiation? Are there ways to link up those who started out better endowed in terms of resources and networks, who may return better educated, with better networks and resources they can call upon, with the poor who remain excluded from such networks? In other words, are there means of linking the poor with the better endowed in productive ways?

In subtle ways, state regulation in host societies – through immigration policy, citizenship, integration, labour market regulations, social welfare policies, and so forth – are related to the more implicit, micro-political forms of exclusion and inclusion in the everyday lives that shape the standing and status of the different, and hierarchically ordered, groups of transnational and regional diasporas and local populations. It should remain the prime objective of development policy to reduce poverty and make globalization work for all. From this point of departure, attempts to align migration and development policies should focus on establishing fairer and effective migration and asylum approaches that do not, by definition, exclude the poor and unskilled from developing countries from access to regular migration opportunities and those in need of protection to be granted it.

Notes

[1]   I build on a two-week field visit to Somaliland in September 2002 as well as secondary data from the literature concerned with the Somali nomadic culture, the diaspora, the refugee crisis, and return and repatriation. My analysis has benefited from a study of livelihood and reintegration dynamics in Somaliland that I undertook jointly with Nicholas Van Hear for the Danish Refugee Council (Sørensen and Van Hear 2003), as well as from numerous discussions with Nauja Kleist, Peter Hansen and Joachim Gundel, all conducting their PhD research at DIIS.

[2]   In January 2002, following a heated media debate on female circumcision, a group of Somali refugees living in Denmark were asking UNHCR to be transferred to another and less xenophobic country.

[3]   The European Commission adopted large parts of this approach in its preliminary Communication on Migration and Development (COM 2002/703 final).

[4]   Recommendations from the 1st conference on reconstruction strategies and challenges beyond rehabilitation, Hargeisa, 1998.

[5]   I owe this interview extract to Peter Hansen, who interviewed the Somaliland Minister of RRR in Hargeisa in 2003.

6   Personal interview with the Deputy Programme Manager of the Danish Refugee Council, himself a returnee from the wider diaspora, Hargeisa, 2002.

7   I take these three domains to correspond to the wider diaspora, migrants in neighbouring countries and intra-national migrants/IDPs.

Chapter 7

'Medical Exceptionalism' in International Migration: Should Doctors and Nurses Be Treated Differently?

Sabina Alkire and Lincoln Chen

Introduction

In February 2004, the South African Medical Association organized a public protest complaining about working conditions that sparked the emigration abroad of 4,000 doctors over the past four years. 'The most depressing thing is that, without exception, all the good people you train leave. All the friends from the old days are in private practice or abroad' (Kapp, 2004).

At the May 2004 World Health Assembly, the 'brain drain' of medical professionals was debated. Issues included the human resource crises in low-income countries, unethical recruitment by importing countries, the chronic dependency of richer countries on human resources of poorer countries, and the consequent deepening of global health inequity.

In July 2004, The *New York Times* featured an article by Celia Dugger on the brain drain of nurses from Sub-Saharan Africa. At the epicentre of the HIV/AIDS epidemic, Malawi's largest 1,000-bed hospital has only 30 nurses remaining, 26 of whom have expressed the intention to migrate. The NHS in the UK, meanwhile, has ambitious plans to expand care through continuing importation of nurses from abroad.

These cases are illustrative of growing controversy surrounding the international movement of medical professionals. The debate has recently intensified, partly because the capacity of many of the world's poorest countries to address health crises is severely crippled by acute shortages of workers exacerbated by out-migration of medical professionals (Narasimhan et al., 2004). The double crises of escalating disease and personnel shortages have refocused attention on medical migration. The fact that these medical labour movements are considered part of the globalization process fuels the controversial social effects of accelerating transnational flows.

At one extreme are those who defend the basic human right of professionals to move, irrespective of occupation. They also cite the potential benefits of open international labour markets, including economic and efficiency gains, diaspora remittances (now twice the size of official overseas development assistance), and 'brain circulation' including the return flow of new ideas, entrepreneurship, technology, and contacts.

Joining these labour market proponents are those who seek freer movement of labour for equitable globalization. They argue that restriction on labour movements accentuates global economic inequities. Rather than less migration, these proponents argue for more and freer movement.

At the other extreme are those who charge Northern countries with exploitative predatory behaviour towards Southern countries. They argue that poaching the best and brightest of human resources exacerbates global health inequities. A normative lens is cast on unethical recruitment practices and the self-serving Northern policy of selective immigration that captures public educational subsidies from Southern source countries. As health conditions worsen in some Southern countries, the depletion of skilled health workers has rapidly reached crisis proportions. In many source countries, the concerns of ministries of health are in conflict with the labour export policies of ministries of finance and planning.

In the midst of these debates, two questions naturally arise. First, what is the knowledge base? Although the debate generates much passion, what are the facts? What are the causes and consequences, and what can be done? A second question relates to public policy. Are the social consequences sufficiently alarming to warrant policy intervention? If so, should migration of doctors and nurses be treated differently than other highly skilled professionals? In other words, should 'medical exceptionalism' prevail – and if so, how?

These questions are addressed in this chapter. Through a literature review, the chapter focuses on the longer-term migration of medical professionals from source countries in the South to destination countries in the North. It is recognized that intra-national migration (especially rural-to-urban movement) and intra-regional migration (among neighbouring countries) are important; indeed, there is a continuum and circularity of migration from local to national to global levels. But our focus is on the most politically controversial of these flows, South-to-North transfer of highly skilled medical professionals.

Health Workers, Health and the Millennium Development Goals

The well-being of the world's 100 million health workers is of intrinsic value. Their human rights must be protected; their skills must be cultivated; they need the freedom to follow their professional and personal aspirations. At the same time, health workers are instrumental to the health-related aspects of others' well-being. The Joint Learning Initiative (JLI) on health and human resources notes that the current stock of health professionals varies greatly from less than 70 health workers per 100,000 in the population to over 1,820 per 100,000 (Figure 7.1).

Furthermore, empirical studies have found that health worker density is correlated with better health outcomes such as, for example, lower mortality rates for the under-5s and higher immunization rates. The JLI estimates that to meet the Millennium Development Goals (MDGs) of reducing child and maternal mortality, an estimated

250 health workers per 100,000 would be needed. Thus just to reach the MDGs, the stock of health workers in over 15 African countries would need to triple.

Against this backdrop of health worker scarcity, the accelerating out-migration trends of health workers are examined as an issue of some urgency.

Data and Information

Statistics on international migration are weak, fragmentary, and incomplete (Bach, 2002; UN Population Division, 2002; ILO, 2001; UN Statistical Commission and UN ECE, 2001). For doctors and nurses, administrative necessity for professional certification, licensing, or registration generates supplemental information. An incomplete picture of global medical migration, therefore, can be pieced together from three primary sources:

First are educational and certification data in sending or source countries. In some source countries, data are available on pertinent matters such as application for permission to leave, sample surveys of intention to leave, or the proportion of school graduates who have emigrated abroad. But accuracy and consistency are variable. Source country data from, for example, South Africa severely underestimate migration recorded in destination countries for South African migrants. Similarly, although data are weak, Ghana's medical service estimated that 1,200 physicians were in the US in 2002, whereas the American Medical Association had licensed only 478 to practice as physicians (Action Plan, 2004; Hagopian et al., 2004).

Second are administrative or immigration data on stocks of foreign-trained health workers in receiving or destination countries. These offer snapshots of foreign-trained health workers in rich countries. Definitions can be quite complicated, as illustrated in Anglophone destination countries (Australia, Canada, Ireland, UK and US). While Ireland and the UK have one single point of entry, Australia has multiple entry points. In the United States, each state licenses professionals independently, and some professionals are licensed in more than one state (Buchan, 2002).

Thirdly, the World Health Organization compiles data on national stocks of doctors, nurses, midwives, dentists, and pharmacists (WHO, 2004b). Although silent about migration and various categories of workers, these data count the pool of medical personnel in source and destination countries.

Demography of International Migration

Who are Medical Migrants?

Medical migrants consist of professionals who enjoy equivalency certification in source and destination countries. Nurses and doctors, including highly-skilled specialists, are especially sought, but also in demand are dentists, pharmacists, and technicians.

Excluded in this analysis are low-skilled migrants who perform cleaning and other low-paying menial tasks in the health sector. These workers may find medically-related work in destination countries but their migration was not determined by their education or skills.

In the year 2000, the world had about 8.5 million doctors and 15.2 million nurses and midwives, giving an average world density of 1.4 doctors and 2.6 nurses per 1,000 population (ibid.). There were 1.8 nurses for every doctor. Figure 7.1 shows severe regional maldistribution. Although Europe and North America have only 21 per cent of the world's population, these two wealthy continents commanded 45 per cent of the world's doctors and 61 per cent of its nurses. In contrast, Africa which contains about 13 per cent of world population has only 3 and 5 per cent, respectively, of doctors and nurses. Sub-Saharan Africa averages only one of these skilled workers per 1,000 in comparison to Europe's density of 10.4.

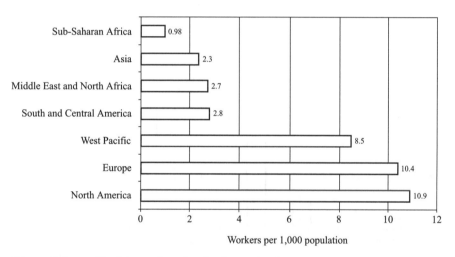

Figure 7.1 Workers per 1,000 population

Figure 7.1   Health worker density by region*

*   Includes only physicians, nurses, and midwives. Global weighted average density is 4.0/1,000 population. There is disparity between the WHO data and those of the OECD and the Council on Graduate Medical Education (see http://www.cogme.gov/16.pdf).

Source: WHO (2004).

What is the Net Redistribution?

Net movement of workers is distorting these imbalances even further. The pool of graduates departing from source countries and the stock of foreign-trained health workers in destination countries reflect these shifts. The proportion of foreign-trained health workers is particularly high in Anglophone countries, reflecting several decades of net accumulation. Figure 7.2 shows that 23–34 per cent of physicians in New Zealand, the UK, Canada, the US, and Australia are foreign-trained. Not all immigrants come from developing countries, of course. There is, for example, considerable within-OECD circulation from the UK and Canada into the United States. About a quarter of US medical practitioners are foreign-trained. Of these, 20 per cent have become US citizens; 33 per cent are green card holders (permanent residents); 7 per cent have business (H1-B) visas, and 30 per cent hold non-renewable temporary work (J1) visas (Buchan and Dovlo, 2004). While the percentage of foreign-trained nurses may be lower than doctors in the workforce, the absolute numbers are higher. In 2002, the UK National Health Service reported more than 30,000 nurses of foreign origin (8.4 per cent) out of a total of 356,500 (Wolf, 2004).

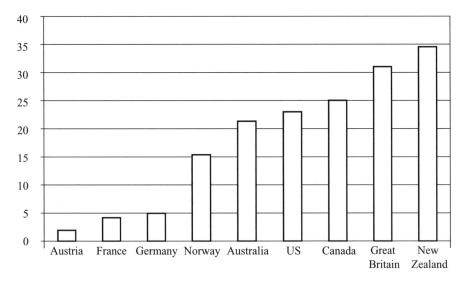

Figure 7.2   Stock of foreign-trained physicians (percentage of total) in selected countries (2000)

Notes:
1   1998 for Australia and Canada; 2000 for France, Germany and New Zealand; 2001 for Austria, Great Britain and the United States; 2002 for Norway.
2   Austria: physicians who have obtained recognition for their qualifications in Austria.
3   France: as a percentage of the medical workforce in France.
4   Germany: as a percentage of the active medical workforce in Germany.
5   Australia: as a percentage of the employed medical workforce in Australia.
6   New Zealand: as a percentage of the active medical practitioners in New Zealand.

Source: OECD (2002: 5).

Is the Rate Increasing?

Historical rates of migration have varied considerably, and it would be mistaken to conclude that recent exchanges are unprecedented. 'In 1970 more Filipino nurses were registered in the USA and Canada than in the Philippines' (Martineau et al., 2002: 2). Historical rates of migration also characterize Jamaica where 'almost two-thirds of nurses trained in Jamaica during the last twenty years ... emigrated, mainly to the United States' (Dumont and Meyer, 2004: 135 citing Thomas-Hope).

Yet migration streams appear to be accelerating, especially in the past decade in absolute terms (Cooper, 2005; Council on Graduate Medical Education, n.d.). Trends are difficult to establish globally because the data are neither uniform nor universally available. However, the migration of nurses in particular displays an increasing trend. For example, the number of non-EU nurses and midwives who have registered in the UK has increased ten- to fifteenfold in one decade. Similarly, in Northern Ireland, the number of non-EU nurses has increased and recently surpassed the number of new nurses from either Ireland or the EU (Buchan et al., 2003: 20). Turning to source countries, we find that even in comparison with the relatively high earlier rates of Filipino migration, recent trends are markedly upward, with a three- to fourfold increase over only five years. Despite shortages of their own, emigration from a number of African source countries to the UK continues to rise. In 2001 in Zimbabwe, of the 737 graduates from nursing programmes, 473 nurses went to the UK alone vs 26 in 1997 (Vijcic et al., 2004). South Africa is an example of a country which is both a source and destination country. But time trend data shows that for various reasons over recent years its emigration has increased while its immigration has decreased. The same general trend is observed for doctors, nurses, and other emigrant health professionals.

What are the Observed Pairings?

The pattern of medical professional migration is complex. Some migration is short-term or reciprocal exchange. Other flows are clearly long term. Most migrants leave open the possibility of return. Also, many source countries may in turn try to replace emigrants with immigrants from other countries, as in the Czech Republic and South Africa. Migration follows what Martineau refers to as a 'carousel' rather than unidirectional flows. The major source regions of migrating medical professionals are Africa, the Caribbean, Southeast Asia, and South Asia. For Africans, the major destination countries are Australia, Belgium, Canada, France, New Zealand, the UK, and USA (WHO, 2004). Caribbean immigrants more often head to North America and South Asians migrate to oil-exporting economies, North America, and occasionally Western Europe (see Ncayiyana, 1999).

Some patterns of migration are empirically well documented. English-speaking countries are a primary destination of emigrating health workers (OECD, 2002: 6). Some countries have developed regional pairings. For example, 20 per cent of migrant physicians in the UK are from Africa; 30 per cent of migrants to the US are from

India and Pakistan. In most cases, including the US and UK, medical migrants come from a relatively small number of source countries. While the greatest *percentage* of foreign-trained relative to nationally trained health professionals is in New Zealand, the greatest *number* of immigrant medical professionals reside in the US or the UK. As is evident, migration from a dozen countries accounts for most of the flows (see Buchan, 2002; Vijcic et al., 2004).

Causes of Medical Migration

The causes of medical migration are complex, and most analyses categorize the forces into 'push' factors in source countries and 'pull' factors in destination countries. Dovlo (2003) identifies six 'gradients' that capture these push-pull forces:

- income (or remuneration): salaries and living conditions;
- job satisfaction: good working environment and utilisation of one's skills to the best technical and professional ability;
- career opportunity: for career advancement and specialisation;
- governance and work environment: political governance and administrative bureaucracy reflected by the efficiency and fairness;
- protection and risk: personal safety, security and risks – especially lack of protective gear from HIV/AIDS in Africa;
- social security: adequate and fair retirement security.

In this chapter we describe clusters of push-pull forces in source and destination countries, as summarized in Table 7.1:

- demography and health;
- remuneration and work environment;
- personal and security.

Demography and Health

The basic pull forces in destination countries operate as magnets to attract medical migrants from source countries. The demand may be attributed to longer-term demographic and epidemiologic transitions. Changing patterns in the burden of disease have implications for care requirements, as does the aging of populations. The demand for health-care workers is further accentuated by shifts towards nuclear family structures, institutionalized elder- and childcare, advances in labour-intensive health technologies, and changing consumer preferences.

For different reasons, source countries' requirements for health workers may also be increasing but their 'pull' is far weaker. The HIV/AIDS pandemic certainly creates a higher demand for medical attention. Along with the growth of population, an increase

Table 7.1   Causes and consequences of medical migration

	Source countries	Destination countries
Causes		
1 Demography and health		
Disease burden	High	Chronic diseases
Demography	Youthful	Aging
2 Remuneration and work environment		
Income	Low	High
Job satisfaction	Low	Variable
Career opportunity	Limited	Prospects
Management	Rigid, unfair	Variable
3 Personal and security		
Personal	Family preferences	Children's future
Security	Safety, HIV risk	Protective practices
Consequences		
4 Migrant and family		
Financial	Remittances	Higher living standard
Social	Higher status	Immigrant - variable
5 National health status		
Health systems	Paralysis, collapse	Public sector, backward regions
Health status	Reduced	Increased
6 Education and public subsidy		
Educational curriculum	Export oriented	–
Public institutions	Loss products	
Private education	Growth for export	–
Public financing	Lost	Captured

in education and public awareness, over time, will enhance the demand for health services. Source countries, however, are unable to translate their increasing need in the labour market into an ability to attract and retain highly skilled medical professionals. They lack the financing to generate an effective demand in the labour market.

Remuneration and Work Environment

The most important factor driving migration is the wage differential between source and destination countries. In source countries wages may be deeply insufficient, and public sector health wages may drop sharply during periods of fiscal austerity. In a

WHO study of five African countries, dissatisfaction with remuneration was the most significant determination of the decision to emigrate (WHO, 2004). While many countries have unfilled vacancies, the wage differential between the main source and destination countries provides a significant incentive for migration. Consider the demand presented by the UK alone which needs to recruit 35,000 new nurses while 50,000 retiring nurses will need replacement by 2008 (Dumont and Meyer, 2004: 127). A South African nurse's salary will double if s/he moves to the UK; a South African physician's salary will increase three- to fivefold if s/he emigrates to the United States. In fact, Vujicic reported that source-destination country wage differentials (adjusted for purchasing power parity) were so large (3–15 times) that marginal increases in source country wages would, alone, not affect migration flows. Non-wage instruments or non-financial incentives are tjis essential.

Migrants also consistently point to the work environment as a critical determinant of migration. Some report heavy work burdens. The environments may not offer job satisfaction due to insufficient supplies or equipment or inadequate facilities. The prospect for continuing education and career advancement may be limited. The social status of medical professionals may be low. Further, the management of health services may be inefficient – or corrupt. Providing an improved work environment needed to retain health professionals in source countries is a significant priority in the short and medium term. It is noteworthy that many destination countries are not able to fill medical positions from their own labour force. Partly this may reflect some of the same relative barriers – suppressed wages in comparison with other professions, for example. Also significantly, the respect and social prestige for health professionals (especially nurses and community health workers) may be lacking. This situation may be exacerbated by practices of physicians and others within the medical community itself.

Personal and Security

A significant if not distinctive cluster of causes relates to personal circumstances. For some, the motivation to emigrate may arise primarily from a desire to join family or to increase the opportunities for children or simply to experience living abroad. Others may remain in the country of origin in order to be near family or to serve a population to which one feels committed. Another cluster of causes has to do with hazards of personal insecurity due to risk of infection, vulnerability to physical violence, and other kinds of hazards. Health workers in sub-Saharan Africa increasingly complain of the risk of HIV/AIDS infection. Indeed, a 1999 ILO study suggested that 18–41 per cent of health workers in sub-Saharan Africa were HIV-positive (ILO, 1999). Similarly, many source countries suffer from criminal violence. Women workers in remote locations are at particular risk to physical insecurity.

Consequences of Medical Migration

The social and economic consequences of medical migration are difficult to validate because of methodological limitations. All sorts of ills or miracles may be attributed to migration but they are not easily proven because of the absence of counterfactuals – what would have happened without migration? Moreover, the consequences of migration would be expected to vary among individuals and source and destination societies. That winners and losers are generated seems likely. At least three areas of consequences should be considered:

- migrants and family;
- national health status;
- education and public subsidy.

Migrants and Family

The biggest 'winners' in medical migration are the migrants and their immediate families, both those who accompany them and those who receive remittances at home. Assuming that they are able to avoid the exploitation of unethical recruitment agents, professional migrants are able to obtain employment with superior compensation, better working environments, opportunities for career advancement, and prospects of personal and family satisfaction.

National Health Status

Country-wise, the winners are destination countries while the losers are source countries. As migrants strengthen the health care workforce in destination countries, the health status of destination societies is presumably enhanced. Equity may also be enhanced because migrants work in rural or otherwise less attractive areas. In contrast, emigration exacerbates the shortage of skilled health workers in source countries, potentially crippling health care systems. Thus, out-migration would be expected to compromise the national health of source countries. Some would argue that it is the very lack of employment opportunities that has generated out-migration. In such circumstances, out-migration is a symptom of deeper malaise.

Vacancy rates among departments of health in many source countries reflect these dire shortages. In 2002, the South African department of health reported more than 4,000 unfilled vacancies for physicians and 32,000 vacancies for nurses, more than a quarter of the total annual vacancies (Dumont and Meyer, 2004: 122). In Ghana in 2002, 47 per cent of doctor posts were unfilled, and 57 per cent of the registered nursing posts were likewise vacant (Dovlo, 2003a; 2003b). Although some attribute these vacancies to out-migration, they may be generated by other factors such as low production and unattractive remuneration. These are the same factors that *cause* out migration, namely high work burdens, poor working conditions and low remuneration.

As argued by Dumont and Meyer (2004: 130), migration may simply be an aggravating factor rather than a root cause: '[f]or example, there are approximately 7,000 South African expatriate nurses in the main OECD destination countries; at the same time there are 32,000 vacancies in the public sector, and 35,000 registered nurses in South Africa are either inactive or unemployed'.

Whatever the primary driver of vacancies, qualitative and case studies confirm that health status in some source countries has descended into crisis proportions. Recently, the BBC reported that an entire cardiovascular unit in a provincial hospital in the Philippines collapsed because of the wholesale migration of all of the nurses in the clinical unit. Repeated and consistent case reports confirm that out-migration whatever its causes has harmful consequences for health among the poor in source countries.

Education and Public Subsidy

The effects of migration on educational institutions can be two-sided. On the one hand, home institutions suffer from the loss of its graduates to national service – in terms of morale, prestige, and national contributions. The prospect of migration may drive the orientation of the curriculum more towards the export market than to the epidemiologic challenges at home. On the other hand, it could be argued that educational institutions that successfully export graduates demonstrate their quality and competitiveness. It improves its attractiveness to potential students seeking international opportunities. Indeed, it has been reported that Ghanaian medical students are required to take equivalency examinations for destination countries before certification examinations for practice at home. Some also argue that the prospect of entering into the international professional market has a positive incentive effect on the numbers of student applicants and the quality of higher professional education.

One definite negative consequence of international migration is financial. Governments invest in medical education to strengthen their national health capacity. As meagre as such training facilities and investments are – 24 Sub-Saharan African countries have one medical school and one has no medical school at all (Hagopian et al., 2004) – the misdirection of resources can be dramatic. In a situation of considerable emigration of medical professionals trained in public institutions, it is clear that emigration drains these investments away from the health needs of the national population. Furthermore, these costs can be considerable. The estimated cost of training a South African doctor approximates $97,000; nurses approximate $42,000 (Dumont and Meyer, 2004: 130). Thus the overall 'loss' from investments in medical education 'may be estimated at around US $1 billion, equivalent to approximately one-third of the public development aid received by South Africa between 1994 and 2000' (ibid: p. 131). At the same time, the prospect of emigration may attract students to medical education who have, from the start, the intention to emigrate, rather than the commitment to serve domestic needs. Thus when medical education is publicly funded, emigration has the effect of shifting the government subsidy from being an investment in health to being either a privatized benefit to one person or an investment in foreign remittances that, it is anticipated, will benefit the country in indirect ways.

Policy Approaches

Understanding social and economic consequences is important because such consequences determine whether public policy intervention is indicated, or not. Only if some aspects of social consequences are considered undesirable would public policies be indicated in source and/or destination countries. No consensus exists with regard to the overall positive and negative consequences of international medical migration. Indeed, while most would accept that the process generates winners and losers, there is no consensus on which parties gain or lose by how much. Consequently, many policy-makers and economists would be reluctant to intervene in global labour markets. The positive externalities of international medical migration are so strong and sustained over time that the benefits may outweigh the costs.

Moreover, far more powerful forces shape the determinants of medical migration, not easily amenable to public policy. These powerful determinants are political stability and economic health. Countries undergoing conflict or political instability are not able to retain their middle-class, including medical professionals. Similarly, societies trapped in a vicious downward spiral of declining economy are unable to provide an inviting environment for a professional workforce. These powerful contextual forces, many claim, are the primary drivers of migration. A major question is whether migration policies can modulate flows in the midst of such political and economic forces.

Others would advocate active policies. There are growing examples where the exodus of skilled health workers is linked to total systems incapacity to grapple with health crises – especially in Sub-Saharan Africa. Even if counterfactual evidence is lacking, there is a strong case that very poor countries experiencing health crises desperately require their skilled human resources. And if compensation and work environment were important determinants of retention, governments and donors should prioritize their investments to ensure the retention of highly skilled workforce. There are, moreover, many arenas of public policy that are amenable to intervention. Policies to be considered among source and destination countries are summarized in Table 7.2. In addition to national policies, one could argue for more effective global migration regimes in medical migration.

Source Countries

There are two distinct, although complementary, strategies that countries facing worker shortages may employ. Protective strategies would attempt to retain workers, slowing down out-migration of highly skilled professionals. Opportunistic strategies would invest in the production of health workers for both domestic and international deployment.

Protective strategies cannot be coercive. Slowing the pace of emigration cannot be done through prohibition of the human right to movement. Ethical issues arise if retention is promoted by restricting travel and punishing emigrants. It is better accomplished by a set of policy actions that reduce push forces as drivers of out-migration. Potential source country policies must address directly the disincentives to health personnel in the form of remuneration, working environments, and security concerns. This will require in many cases the restructuring of the health care system. Donors should prioritize investments in health workers, management experts, and training institutions, to improve remuneration and working conditions and thereby redress some of the causes of emigration while improving the national health system.

Opportunistic strategies recognize that the global demand for health workers is high and growing. Low-income countries could launch longer-term strategies to develop their comparative advantage in producing an abundant supply of highly skilled health workers. They would do so by investing in training institutions, or in encouraging private sector and donor-funded programs. Some countries such as the Philippines, India, and Cuba have deliberately encouraged emigration. For example, the Philippine national development strategy endorses international migration in order to gain remittance income. 'In 2001, 13,536 nurses, about one-quarter of the nurses employed in Filipino hospitals, left the country for foreign jobs' (Philippine Overseas Employment Administration, 2004). The benefit for the source country rests in the remittances that migrants provide, as well as in the extra skills of returnees. While remittances from long-term migrants have been quite satisfactory in the short and medium term, the long-term pattern of remittances merits study, particularly if there is (as would be predicted) a weakening of remittance flows in succeeding generations.

One difficulty of source country strategies that export medical professionals is internal equity. With the exception of Cuba, source countries also suffer from internal maldistribution – insufficient medical professionals in rural, deprived, and backward areas in comparison to more lucrative forms and locations of health care. Exporters such as the Philippines and India suffer simultaneously from deprivation of coverage in backward regions while exporting to overseas markets. Moreover, the immediate challenge of a national and global shortage of health workers must be addressed. The only strategies for the short-term are protection strategies to reduce out-migration and social mobilization to train paraprofessionals rapidly to assume the roles and work of more skilled professionals.

Destination Countries

As destination countries mostly benefit from international migration, there may not be much incentive for these countries to introduce and institutionalize protective policies. After all, importing medical workers enables a country to meet its human resource requirement quickly without the financial, time, and institutional investment in educational institutions. In order to protect its public, destination countries may establish professional norms and standards for foreign-trained medical personnel. On the grounds of human and labour rights, it will also want to protect immigrant labour from unethical and exploitative malpractices.

It should also recognize that it is inherently unfair for rich countries to capture educational subsidies from poorer countries. Proposals for compensatory payments have not been accepted thus far by importing countries. More feasible perhaps is that importing countries should develop self-sufficiency educational policies to produce sufficient numbers of medical personnel to meet their own needs. Alternatively, richer countries should launch a massive re-investment fund to build urgently human resources and capacity in poorer source countries.

Destination countries should also increase temporary (3–5 year) work permits for health professionals from source countries. This form of migration is mutually beneficial: source countries' economies benefit from returnee remittances and savings, and their health system benefits from returnees' improved skills and experience; destination countries benefit from the influx of highly skilled medical professionals who retire elsewhere; migrants themselves benefit from the experience for themselves and their family, the increased remuneration, and prestige. These temporary work permits would address the global economic equity challenges described later. However it might also have practical difficulties, for example, if young professional families with children became rooted in the host society making it difficult to return.

Commonwealth countries have adopted a Code of Ethics for the Recruitment of Health Professionals. The Code requires dialogue between source and destination countries. For example, destination countries should refrain from targeting recruitment (including via the internet) from countries experiencing severe shortages in human resources. Similarly, a quota or cap of visas might be imposed upon professional migrants from distressed countries. If the migrant was trained in a publicly funded educational institution, the migrant and/or the destination country would need to return the public subsidy in medical education. The effect of such a system would be to create a considerable but not unfair disincentive for migration.

Global Regimes

Actions by source and destination countries must be backed by more effective global regimes. The first and most important global function is informational and evidence based. There is an urgent need for more and better information to inform policies, as discussed later under research priorities.

A second arena of global policy relates to the interface of global economic equity and global health equity. Paradoxically, while long term migration clearly undercuts national health in many source countries, temporary labour migration can be positively perceived by both source and destination countries, and would generate widely distributed economic growth. Dani Rodrik has argued that:

> If [WTO] trade negotiators were genuinely interested in devising market-access rules that benefit developing countries, they would focus not on agriculture but on something else entirely: temporary labour mobility. The greatest demonstrable gains to developing nations from relaxing restrictions in the world economy today lie in the liberalization of temporary labour flows. It is hard to identify any other issue in the global economy with comparable potential for raising income levels in poor countries *while* enhancing the efficiency of global resource allocation. Even a relatively small program of temporary [3–5 year] work visas in the rich countries could generate income gains for workers from poor countries that exceed the predictions for all of the Doha proposals put together (Rodrik, 2004: 2; see also Rodrik, 2001).

Rodrik estimates that temporary visas for 3 per cent of rich country labour force 'would easily yield US$200 billion annually for the citizens of developing nations'. The return of temporary labour migrants would also, obviously, contribute to source country health, which is valuable in itself, and also is independently instrumental to economic growth. If Rodrik's estimates have validity, one can easily see the collision course among ministries of health versus ministries of finance in source countries. While the latter seeks global economic equity in exporting skilled human resources, the former wishes to constrain that flow from the health sector. In both source and destination countries, both short- and long-term migration are beneficial – indeed Rodrik argues that the liberalization of immigration restrictions would produce a far bigger 'bang in terms of improved efficiency in the global allocation of resources' than removing agricultural protections, differential tax treatments of investment, intellectual capital protection, or financial market regulations. Political rather than economic arguments constrain migration flows from the global South to the global North. And health rather than economic arguments will have to govern the flow of medical professionals.

Research Agenda

The crisis of human resources in many countries will not disappear, nor will the contentious issues surrounding international medical migration. Policy-oriented research should be launched to provide a stronger evidence-base. In our opinion among priority issues, six stand out.

- *Data and analyses.* We must improve our data, information, and analytical base on international medical migration, probably by building upon current administrative records. Migration statistics are notoriously difficult and expensive to collect and maintain. Even more so for specialized aspects such as medical professionals. Medical migration data, however, are vital in terms of broader health policy demands. Administrative records can provide the broad contours of monitoring trends in medical migration if they are well maintained, and slightly expanded, at little incremental expense. More analytical and specialized studies would be required to delineate causes and consequences of medical migration.

- *Policy effectiveness*. Because it is controversial, the social consequences of medical migration among individuals and source and destination societies deserve high research priority. The positive benefits to individual migrants and to destination societies can be inferred from the voluntary effort to migrate on the part of migrants and recruitment and admission on the part of destination societies. What deserves more rigorous examination are positive and negative consequences, both short and long term, in source countries. The overall impression – which needs to be subjected to further research – is that the emigration of health professionals from countries undergoing health crises to destination countries aggravates global inequality in health. Long term migration is likely to have diminishing economic rewards, whereas short-term migration would have sustained benefits in the source country. Research is also indicated on policy effectiveness of efforts to stem these negative social and economic consequences. We understand very little of how to mitigate the negative consequences of migration.

- *Migration and trade in health services*. Migration of medical personnel is only one of the several transnational flows of health resources. Not only do workers move from country to country, but diseases are transmitted across political boundaries. Moreover, patients may move to new service providers and some services, such as radiology or other diagnostic tests, may be transmitted via new information-communications technologies. Some countries, such as Thailand, have deliberately over-cultivated their domestic specialized health infrastructure in order to attract 'medical tourists' from abroad. In this case, the migrants are patients rather than providers. In Thailand, meeting the needs of 'medical tourism' is estimated to absorb 15 per cent of the highly skilled medical personnel in the country (Wibulpolprasert et al., 2004). Some components of this service industry include remote diagnostic services (from X-ray reading to laboratory tests), or surgeries (laser surgery etc). The World Trade Organization has put services on its agenda with the aim of opening the service sector to global competition. While the economic implications of this model of addressing health worker shortages is uncertain both for the backward areas of the host country as well as for the migrating patients, this and other related flows complicate the pattern of migration yet further. As an emerging health-related international flow, the trade in health services merits priority research attention.

- *Political economy of diaspora*. The economics of health professional migration is complex. On the one hand, the source country's investment in medical education, as well as all of the previous investments in basic education, does not serve the health of its population. These investments are both significant and lost in terms of public purpose. On the other hand, the migrant is likely to contribute economically through remittances – which will certainly benefit the family left behind. While remittances will not support the health sector or the teaching institutions, they do contribute significantly to the national economy. And in some cases, there may be a possibility of encouraging the return of the diaspora (with increased skills at no cost to the source country). Furthermore, the prospect of migration may stimulate private sector investment in medical education, which would improve remittance flows at no marginal cost to the public sector. So the overall economic impact of health professional migration is likely to vary significantly.

- *Ethical analyses.* The migration of medical professionals raises a number of ethical issues related to the migrant as well as to source and destination countries and their populations. These issues relate to the fair distribution of economic and professional advantage. One particular position, adopted in this paper, merits further discussion. A medical professional is him or herself a locus of human rights that are to be protected, such as the freedom of movement, to the right to development, to safe working conditions, or to a living wage. A medical professional is also a crucial instrument of the very health care to which others in a population have a right. It is possible but unlikely to be constructive to frame this as a trade-off that gives the right of a Botswana doctor to migrate greater (or less) weight than the right of hundreds of people of Botswana to have access to a physician. We reject, for example, coercive means of medical professional retention. Instead, we advocate the creation of economic and social incentives to attract and retain doctors in Botswana. However, given the 'exceptional' urgency of the problem, we argue that policies to improve working conditions, increase remuneration, and provide opportunities for career advancement – are ethically imperative as well as functionally necessary. Without them, the MDGs will not be met, the HIV/AIDS programs will not be implemented, and people will suffer. Thus donors, the private sector, and governments of countries in health crisis must work together with an unprecedented urgency to address the push factors of medical professional migration. As crucial instruments of health, doctors and nurses should be treated differently – indeed exceptionally well, exceptionally soon – for ethical reasons that go far beyond their own well-being.

- *Mapping of international institutions.* Medical migration is currently the concern of a plethora of international agencies. It suffers from the problem of 'everybody's business is nobody's business'. Clarity should be achieved with regard to the complementary role of various international agencies and institutions in monitoring medical migration, developing policies and guidelines for regulating such flows, accumulating best practices and lessons learned, and strengthening an overall global medical migration regime. The structure should be imbedded in the evolution of the broader institutional architecture for work in international migration, drawing on specialized medical expertise for this important component of international migration. A host of international agencies addresses various aspects of medical migration. Among them, the WHO as the principal normative UN agency in global health should be supported to play a prominent role in the global regime for medical migration.

Table 7.2   Policy options for source and destination countries

Policies	Source countries	Destination countries
Protective	• Improve working conditions • Improve remuneration • Improve health management systems • Discourage recruiting countries • Bill émigrés for public education • Bond medical graduates • Establish database on migration	• Adopt ethical guidelines or codes • Strengthen code implementation • Monitor compliance with codes • Quotas on immigrant health workers • Attempt self-sufficiency in HR • Transparent recruitment strategies
Opportunistic	• Train excess health professionals • Encourage out-migration • Encourage short term migration • Provide incentives for returnees • Facilitate remittance flows • Increase immigration as needed • Negotiate compensation from destination countries • Encourage private medical schools	• Increase temporary work permits • Facilitate immigrant visa/certification • Provide tax holidays • Compensate for educational costs • Increase debt relief / health aid

Chapter 8

Ghanaian Health Workers on the Causes and Consequences of Migration

Delanyo Dovlo

Introduction

Ghana has high rates of emigration among its health workers especially doctors and nurses but this is also increasingly found among other health workers including pharmacists and laboratory technicians. A study of doctors' migration from Ghana (Dovlo and Nyonator, 1999) estimated that 61 per cent of graduates of the country's main medical school who qualified between 1986 and 1996 had emigrated. The intention of Ghanaian nurses to migrate as measured by requests for verification of their qualifications, showed that the figures for annual requests were nearly twice as high as the replacement training of new nurses (Buchan and Dovlo, 2004).

Intentions of health workers to migrate has remained quite high as a recent WHO-AFRO study shows – 62 per cent of Ghanaian health workers interviewed showed an intention to migrate compared to 26 per cent of Ugandan; 38 per cent of Senegalese, 49 per cent of Cameroonian; 58 per cent of South African and 68 per cent of Zimbabwean health workers (Awases et al., 2003).

The situation in Ghana thus reflects a major dilemma facing Sub-Saharan African countries that are trying to attain development targets such as the *Millennium Development Goals* (MDGs) but are faced with serious losses of health professionals. Wage differentials between these countries and the developed destination countries of their health workers are so marked that they seem impossible to bridge. The paradox is that investments in developing countries put into building a capacity-base for development, merely caters for already developed countries.

Africa's poor face the terror of the near collapse of health services and the inverse relation between an ever increasing burden of disease and a much reduced availability of health workers. This has been caused by continued health professional migration and a lack of international action to mitigate its effects. The severe economic problems of Sub-Saharan Africa have been taken advantage of to encourage utilization of its professionals as a cheap source of labour for health services in destination countries.

Various studies have ascribed the reasons for health worker migration to a number of 'push and pull' factors (Dovlo, 1999; Martineau et al., 2002; Meeus, 2003; Padarath et al., 2003). 'Push' factors originate in the source country, compelling health workers to leave, whilst 'pull' factors arise in receiving countries and tend to attract and encourage immigration. This chapter focuses on a survey of Ghanaian doctors and nurses with the aim of gaining a better understanding of the interests and motivations underlying their intentions to migrate. Focus group discussions held separately with groups of doctors and nurses form the basis of the study. The discussions were structured around five core topics, namely:[1]

- the problems faced by health workers that lead to intentions to migrate;
- expectations/perceptions of working abroad;
- recruitment/the process of getting a job abroad;
- type of migration intended (permanent or temporary);
- awareness of and reactions to government's efforts to provide incentives.

The aim of the focus group discussions was to elicit health workers' opinions on issues influencing their intention to migrate and the factors that enabled or affected their decision-making. I use actual quotes from health workers to illustrate and discuss the factors that influence health worker migration from Ghana. The quotes have been grouped along with other issues expressed during the interviews and analyzed for variations in intentions and experiences between the two professional categories (doctors and nurses) represented in the interviews. The study focused on health worker viewpoints and did not examine other perspectives such as those of health policy-makers and clients of health services which are also very important. The internationalization of the health labour market and its skew towards certain developed countries is also a crucial factor in the migration equation.

The discussions primarily highlight internal 'push factors', though inevitably 'pull factors' are also raised by the respondents. The health workers address the 'push factors' that are perceived by them to be directly affecting their welfare. Also some aspects of 'pull' factors are discussed here as structural motivators (as compared to individual 'push factors') including:

- active recruitment by agents within the country;
- diminished training/production in destination countries (especially in English/ French-speaking developed countries);
- globalization, international trade and economic environments considered unfavourable for the country.

The Ghanaian government has recognized the problem of health worker migration and over the past four years, has instituted incentive measures to stem the outflow of health professionals. The measures have included new allowances such as the *Additional Duty Hours Allowance* (ADHA) that has significantly increased the net income for especially doctors, though increases for other health workers have been less substantial. Subsidized cars have been allocated to health workers and new rural posting allowances have been proposed. In December 2003 a local postgraduate medical college was established to afford speedier access to specialist training for doctors. The quotes of the health workers used in this paper provide some insights into problems with the implementation of these incentives and the value placed on them by health workers. There are also some interesting variations between the reactions of doctors and nurses. It is perhaps intriguing that so many health professionals in Sub-Saharan Africa actually stay on in their countries given the level of frustration expressed.

Results and Discussion

The issues raised by health workers are discussed along five core areas of inquiry. For each discussion area, core quotes that express insights into the perceptions of health workers are highlighted and later analyzed for possible differences expressed between nurses and doctors.

Reasons Underlying the Intention to Migrate

This section deals with some of the immediate causes, frustrations and reasons that may push health workers to the decision to migrate. All persons who participated in the interviews, without exception, expressed a wish to migrate or work abroad and indeed some of the doctors interviewed (three of seven) were preparing to leave within three months. The quotes illustrate frustrations and pessimism about the governance of health services in the country and the poor welfare and benefits systems.

Nurses' quotes

... they are insensitive to our problems. Dialogues with GRNA[2] are never fruitful, never ending.

Working under some doctors is very frustrating, specialized nurses are not allowed to use full potential.

... we have no personal transport, even after 30 years of work I cannot acquire a car.

Retirement benefits are small C20m (US$ 2,500) whilst others working in banks can get up to C500m (US$ 15,000) despite our higher risk and workload.

I have been a nurse for 22 years. I have seen no change in my life.

ADHA[3] has created enmity between the professions ....

... constant improvisation when working in wards, we use a single set of gloves for several patients.

After retirement, nurses are seen in the markets weighing people and taking their blood pressure to survive.

When a nurse is sick it is expensive, for your children you are required to pay for drugs. Pharmacists refuse to give expensive drugs to nurses ... [note: though free treatment is applicable]

Doctors' quotes

We are helpless – professionally. People are dying who can be saved by having some basic inputs.

The system is not incentive based. It does not recognize performance ....

I had to wait 14 months for my first salary. You have to fight to get anything due to you.

The postgraduate training system is very frustrating. You go outside for three years and you can qualify ....

Senior officials are flown out for treatment so they don't care about the health services. The Medical Block[4] has been closed for almost two years!

... it is difficult to find consultants for referrals when needed. They are often absent but receive high ADHA.

Issues and concerns expressed by nurses include a feeling that labour negotiations with governments which had been ongoing for some years have been unproductive. Secondly, career and professional development limits imposed on nurses are also major concerns and allusions are made to the comparatively low incomes of nurses compared to other workers at similar levels in other services. Nurses complain of difficulty in acquiring basic personal needs such as housing and means of transport. Benefits after retirement (including housing and health care) were strongly raised by nurses compared with doctors who barely mentioned it. The recent government incentives were seen by nurses to have been inordinately biased in favour of doctors and the recent spikes in migration among nurses is regarded as a direct result of the introduction of this incentive. Perhaps most demotivating for nurses is having to bear the cost of health care for themselves and their family.

Doctors' issues on the other hand reflected a serious lack of job satisfaction coupled with poor career and professional opportunities. A strong sense of frustration with government's bureaucratic handling of basic administrative functions including the fact that all doctors (whether performing or not) will receive exactly the same pay and overtime compensation. The habit of government-paid expensive health care trips abroad for senior officials was upsetting to young doctors deeply dissatisfied with local health services.

Expectations of Working Abroad

Information on what experiences health workers intending to migrate expected brought out some interesting comments. These revolved around some of the issues expressed in the foregoing section on the reasons for migration. Generally, nurses and doctors' opinions of expectations converged especially in terms of a broad anticipation of better career opportunities abroad.

Nurses' quotes

It is easy to take courses and divert into new careers – some nurses have become pharmacists etc. …

… Ghana's educational system is too rigid – nursing becomes a 'dead-end'.

… outside, you can learn whilst working.

We hear stories of attitude problems, some racism but we shall focus on earning money ….

Some patients do not respect black nurses but we are nurses and we are used to rude patients.

Doctors' quotes

Our preferred country is USA, then the UK, occasionally Australia.

US is expensive but has better professional opportunity. The UK is easy to enter but it is transit to USA.

We hear of racism against black health workers but the benefits by far outweigh the problems.

It is impossible to get promotions in the UK if you are foreign (or get into higher posts).

Nurses' expectations mirrored their frustration with being blocked from further educational and career advancement as their nursing training and experiences was not recognized for entering university degree programmes. Leaving Ghana was expected to create opportunities not only for further training but also to enter new (and presumably better) professions. Nurses enunciated more clearly a focus on earning more money (primarily because salaries compared to other workers in Ghana were considered too low and discriminatory) and though acknowledging perceived disadvantages of working abroad (such as racist or abusive patients), they were prepared to accept these.

Comparatively, professional/career opportunities issues were also strong among doctors though they were more concerned about specialist training opportunities than about entering new and more lucrative professions. Improving career opportunities is also clearly a reason for doctors' preference of the USA over the UK as a destination despite the much higher costs of emigration to the USA. The much higher anticipated remuneration in the USA was a major expectation. Doctors did not face the same educational 'dead-end' that nurses perceived of their profession but their frustration was more with limited specialization opportunities and lengthy training periods required to become a specialist compared to the usual destination countries.

Recruitment Systems for Work Abroad

The process by which health workers get recruited is varied depending on the destination country and differs between nurses and doctors. Recruitment could either be active – where agents of external hospitals or countries actively advertise and recruit staff – or it could be passive where health professionals themselves looked for employment outside. Two countries, the USA and the UK appear to be by far the most favoured destinations which raise the possibility of inter-country agreements that can mitigate the rate of departure of professionals.

Nurses' quotes

It is expensive but we can pay back within 3 months of working in the UK.

There are agents, they come informally. You pay them £2000–3000. They take a percentage from your salary.

We prefer the UK, it is easier to get into.

Canada is also recruiting. From the UK we may continue there. We hear conditions are better.

Doctors' quotes

[We are recruited] through our own individual efforts.

Opportunities are sought for us by our colleagues already working outside.

Frustration starts from when you are a student in Medical School.

Nurses are more targeted with active recruitment whilst doctors utilize a more passive approach of individual efforts to find jobs abroad. This is despite the fact that recruitment of both nurses and doctors involves payment of significant amounts of money upfront for examinations, visas, transport as well as fees to recruitment agents. Despite the expensive cost of entering the external job market, nurses clearly see this as a worthwhile investment. Recruitment of nurses in Ghana is through both formal and informal means, via established recruitment agencies as well as Ghanaian nurses who are already working abroad.

For both nurses and doctors, the choice of destination country is linked to the costs of entering that country as well as the ease of entry requirements such as visas. It also depends on the procedures for verification of qualifications in the destination country's professional accreditation system. Ghanaian doctors interviewed preferred the USA as primary destination whilst the nurses mainly aimed for the UK and at times Canada. For doctors, the USA offered better ease of reaching high professional and career status though the UK was considered relatively easier and less costly to enter. Thus promising career prospects and associated earnings were important factors to doctors.

Intentions of Duration of Stay

Migration intentions of health workers can be either temporary or permanent. Initial decisions may reflect a temporary intention but then this may eventually turn into a permanent stay abroad. However, some professionals do migrate simply for the purpose of raising capital to start a business or to establish their family's financial welfare and a retirement nest.

Nurses' quotes

We want to stay from 3–5 years, maybe more.

We shall come back after acquiring enough money for a house, car and starting a business.

I will stay for longer, can even become a citizen of the UK.

I am old so no further training just to earn money for my retirement.

Doctors' quotes

I will not want to come back – maybe when I retire.

I will come back when older and can have a more relaxed work schedule.

From the discussions, nurses generally expressed migration intentions of a temporary nature whilst doctors tended to have intentions pointing at more permanent settlement. Nurses expressed needs for raising money for basic needs to be able to live in Ghana – generally indicated as housing and a source of good income such as a small business.

Doctors express a strong sense of frustration which already starts whilst they are students in medical school, and is probably transmitted by their lecturers and other senior doctors. This is reflected in the quotes as intentions to migrate for their entire working life. No doctor indicated intentions to only stay temporarily. Nurses' frustrations with the system, however, appeared to start after their initial employment. This difference may be due to the fact that doctors interviewed were generally young whilst the nurses were of mixed ages including some middle aged ones all expressing intentions to emigrate.

Local Retention: Actions and Effects

In response to the migration of health care professionals, the government of Ghana initiated some incentives to help retain health professionals. These measures included allowances based on additional hours calculated to have been spent at work (ADHA) by health workers, the provision of subsidized car and housing loans at subsidized rates etc. The reactions of both professions to the incentives provided have been negative, but are based on different aspects and reasoning.

Nurses' quotes

… slight improvement in salaries compared to two years ago. But, electricity, water and fuel costs are just as higher.

Doctors take maximum ADHA even when away on leave whilst nurses cannot take the maximum no matter what. I take C400,000 when a doctor takes C4 million.

Cars?, we don't know about the cars.[5]

… even if cars are available how can we repay on our salary?

Doctors' quotes

The ADHA has slowed the leaving of doctors but it is picking up again.

We can get our current annual pay within a month in USA.

Instead of a C200 million ($25,000) new car for senior doctors – C40m ($5,000) would give many doctors good second hand cars.

The public are played against the doctors for demanding high pay. That ADHA disrupted the budget.

Many nurses feel strongly that the new allowances have been discriminatory. While the net-income for doctors was raised significantly, nurses only received moderate increases. For both professions, the allowances were not significant enough to influence retention. The nurses blamed the 'free market' policy environment that has doubled the prices of utilities such as fuel, electricity, water, and rents whilst salaries have only been moderately increased. Nurses expressed concern about being unable to benefit from the other incentives offered such as car and housing loans as their current pay levels could not support required repayments. Indeed, the impression is that ADHA had probably fuelled increased migration by nurses because of its unfair nature.

The incentives have clearly made an early impact with doctors, but the income increases simply could not compare with salaries that could be earned abroad. The doctors interviewed perceived the other incentives such as housing and subsidized cars as being hogged by senior doctors and therefore having been of little benefit to them.

Conclusions

The quotes chosen for the concluding section summarize the deep frustrations expressed during the interviews and reflect the core influences of health workers' decisions to migrate. Income and higher living standards as factors hide underlying frustrations of a demoralized work force with poor job satisfaction that see no hopeful future in Ghana. Health worker migration is almost self-fuelling as Ghanaian health workers abroad often assist in recruiting those still at home. The reduced numbers further increases dissatisfaction among the professionals remaining at home. Least developed countries like Ghana make efforts that simply cannot compete with the pull exerted from destination countries.

Concluding quotes

There is no future here. (Young nurse)

I will not want to come back – maybe when I retire. (Young doctor)

We are helpless – people are dying who can be saved by having some basic inputs. (Doctor)

I am old so no further training. Just to earn money for security. (51-year-old nurse)

A major dilemma is facing developing countries' governments and their health workers. Interventions to motivate health workers have to relate to available resources. This has often meant that the incentives provided are too limited to have real impact, while they reduce the available resources to improve health services and enhance job satisfaction. These factors are further confounded by health workers' vision of life after retirement on low pensions and illness when facilities are so limited. There is also a strong sense of frustration with the efficiency of human resource management and with the leadership of the health services. For example one young doctor interviewed had to wait 14 months after he was employed before receiving his first pay-check because of the stiff bureaucracy. The professionals interviewed were unable to anticipate future improvements and the sense of pessimism was very strong and pervasive.

Sub-Saharan African countries face difficulties with retaining health professionals and other skilled persons. Some of these difficulties reflect issues of poor governance and management of health systems. The perception of a discriminatory global trade system, heavy debt burden and other economic problems reinforces a cycle of costly training of skilled human resources which simply results in further migration. In an atmosphere in which many African countries are unable to match the well-resourced destination countries, the continued loss of health workers without compensation can only further worsen the situation.

Positive effects of brain drain may exist in terms of remittances transferred by Ghanaian citizens living abroad as well as from skills transfers that occur when professionals return home. However, it is not clear if these returning resources have an impact on the health of the people. Countries like Ghana could establish the internal dialogue necessary to evolve mitigating strategies and to implement them. Key among these is strategies to show regard for health workers' contributions to national development and to take concrete organizational actions to enhance morale and self respect among professionals. However, industrialized destination countries can also contribute by recognizing a moral responsibility to assist in moderating the sense of despair felt in developing countries when basic health services are jeopardized by health worker losses. Without adequate retention of human resources, it is very unlikely that the United Nation's Millennium Development Goals will be met.

Ghana has instituted some policy changes to manage and utilize the dispersion of its human resources. For example it now recognizes dual citizenship to encourage more economic, social and investment linkages with its diaspora. Secondly, a national Postgraduate Medical College was established in 2003 and is expected to both provide local specialist training opportunities for doctors and shorten the training period considerably. A number of monetary and other incentives have been provided to certain key health personnel.

However, like most Sub-Saharan African countries, even with the actions taken so far, it faces major difficulties in retaining its health professionals. The points raised by the health professionals interviewed reflect strong internal sentiments on poor governance and management of health systems on the part of governments. But governments also have a strong perception of a discriminatory global trade system and an inordinately severe debt burden that reinforces a cycle of costly training of professionals which is simply lost to further migration. With the global situation in which most African countries cannot match the well-resourced destination countries, losses of health workers without recompense further impoverishes countries. In addition to the economic and social dimensions of health professionals' migration, a moral dimension is also important to enable poor and rural Africans receive the health care they have invested for.

Notes

[1] The in-depth discussions involving a smaller number of nurses and doctors took place in July 2003 and were conducted as part of a report for DFID-UK on migration of health workers.

[2] GRNA – Ghana Registered Nurses Association – represents all nurses in negotiations with government.

[3] ADHA – Additional Duty Hours Allowance which mainly favours doctors (about 200 per cent of salary but up to 80 per cent increase for other health workers).

[4] At the teaching hospital which was working out of temporary premises.

[5] Government-procured cars available at subsidized costs which are deducted from staff salaries.

PART 3
PRINCIPLES AND PRACTICES OF MANAGING MIGRATION IN DESTINATION COUNTRIES

Chapter 9

A Philosophical View on States and Immigration[1]

Melissa Lane

Introduction: 'Irresistible Forces Meet Immovable Ideas'[2]

Migration is part of the human condition and is a fundamental fact with which political theory must contend. Where economic or other gradients are sufficiently strong, they create what is essentially an irresistible force for migration. In such cases democratic states tend to find it impossible to stop illegal immigration, if legal immigration is limited. Yet contemporary political theory debates immigration in terms of ideas which prescind from these realities, and which moreover are not always interpreted correctly in their implications for immigration. Three such 'immovable ideas' – sovereignty, democracy, and nationality – are explored in this chapter. I do not pretend here to offer a comprehensive approach to immigration in normative terms, but rather survey grounds for scepticism about the way these three values are commonly invoked in relation to immigration. Before turning to these normative considerations, the remainder of this introduction elaborates on the sense in which migration may count as an 'irresistible force', one which both precedes and in crucial respects supersedes modern states.

A survey in *Scientific American* of 'The Migrations of Human Populations' declared: 'Human beings have always been migratory' (Davis, 1974: 93). Palaeolithic humans had already reached every major part of the globe except for Antarctica; it is only by migration that the globe became fully peopled in all of its habitable parts. The same source suggests that 'migration is generated by significant differences between one area and another' (Davis, 1974: 100).[3] These differences may lie in the environment, in the technological inequality of human groups, or in the demographic composition of those groups (so that groups with excessive young men send them to emigrate, an important factor today driving emigration from the non-EU countries of Mediterranean and Eastern Europe into the EU) (Holzmann and Münz, 2004: 3–7). Global migration is not an optional, adventitious or minor process which may be conveniently ignored in thinking about politics, in the way that John Rawls abstracted from it in assuming that one could make a reasonable (if simplified) model of political society as a closed community entered only by birth and exited only by death (Rawls, 1971). Migration is not marginal or dispensable to politics, even though the terms and drivers of such migration have varied significantly over time.

Today, as in the past, global economic gradients of difference are among the most salient differences motivating migration. Setting aside the cases of refugees and many internally displaced persons, much of current and future global migration is essentially an economic phenomenon. Yet, that fact is too often obscured by the narrowly political terms in which it is debated by political theorists. Modern societies have indeed two animating principles – the political and the economic – which correspond to two different and sometimes conflicting bases for belonging in a society. It has been argued that the conception of full citizenship itself in the last hundred years rests as much on working as on voting (Shklar, 1991), in part because some social rights are conditioned on whether and how much each citizen has worked. Indeed working is widely viewed as more of an imperative than voting. And the discipline of the market driving people to work is relied upon at local, national, and global scales. Yet at the global level individual migrants are often criminalized for responding to the economic incentives which the global economy relies upon for its functioning. In early modern mercantile states, it was skilled would-be emigrants whose movements were typically restricted, while immigrants were largely welcomed to build up population and wealth. In the last half of the twentieth century, the inverse is true: it is immigrants whose entry is typically restricted or barred, because jobs and welfare are now widely (if sometimes wrongly) assumed to be scarce and zero-sum goods. The resulting Catch-22 for would-be immigrants is captured in the defiant statement of the then President of Mexico, Ernesto Lopez Portillo, about illegal Mexican migration to the United States: 'It is not a crime to look for work, and I refuse to consider it as such' (Smith quoted in Teitelbaum, 1980: 46).

It follows that wherever there is a strong economic gradient attracting immigration, states that are integrated into the global economy are unlikely to be able fully to prevent it, though they have the power to force it into illegal channels by restricting the legal ones. In such circumstances, liberal democratic states are expected to lack not only the ability but also the concerted political will to prevent illegal immigration, since some employers and consumers depend on it and can exert political voice in its favour. Some developed economies may even depend on such a black market in cheap labour in order to compete effectively. In such circumstances, it has been remarked that policy-makers may seek to 'finesse social insecurities while concurrently maximizing economic gains ... by shaping policy to address *fears* rather than *flows*' (Rudolph quoted in Tirman, 2004: 8–9). Where that is the case, perceived economic necessity operates in contradiction to proclaimed political principles.

How should we approach such a conflict between self-conceived political and economic imperatives? Two possible analogies may help to clarify this question. One might think that the state's ability to control illegal immigration is like the state's ability to control domestic crime. It is central to the definition of the modern state that it monopolizes the means of legitimate violence and so in principle excludes the possibility of violent crime. Yet no modern state succeeds in preventing violent crime altogether, and this does not impair its legitimacy so long as it maintains some sort of cap on the level of such crime and also succeeds to some degree in punishing its perpetrators. Some governments are able to put up with quite widespread crime waves without losing legitimacy altogether. But the flaw in the analogy is twofold: immigration, unlike ordinary domestic crime, has supranational drivers; and to the extent that it is economically valuable to the receiving country, it benefits the very state that is theoretically committed to suppressing it. So the idea that states are committed, and able, to preventing illegal immigration altogether, must be treated sceptically. It is a claim which states may believe about themselves, and which starry-eyed theorists may also believe, but which is not necessarily a cornerstone of political life or of meaningful political theorizing in democracies today. It is a shibboleth of modernity, one which is not necessarily true of modernity but which is central to the way that moderns view themselves (cf. Latour, 1993).

The second possible analogy is between illegal immigration and prostitution. Enlightened approaches to prostitution, such as those embodied in recent policy in Italy and Sweden, acknowledges that there is at present an irreducible demand to which individual prostitutes are rationally responding. Prostitution is demand-led. If prostitution is viewed as socially undesirable, therefore, it is politically rational to treat the seeking and purchasing of paid sex as the more significant crime than the providing of it. Sweden accordingly now criminalizes the seeking of paid sex and the paying for it but has decriminalized the offering of it.[4]

This analogy usefully suggests that to the extent that politicians seek to prevent or punish illegal immigration, they should do so by putting heavier penalties on the employers of such labour who create the demand for it than on the desperately poor people who merely respond rationally to that economic demand from a relative position of market weakness. Such a redistribution of penalty could be supplemented by a policy of allowing migrants to remain in the country if they are caught while employed and while having been employed for a certain period of time.[5] But the difficulty with this analogy is again that while the economic activity associated with prostitution is not normally seen as a significant public benefit or desideratum, the economic activity associated with illegal immigration is often a major contribution both to the unofficial and the official economy. Whereas in many states public policy would prefer to eliminate prostitution if it could, few states want to eradicate the many parts of the agricultural, food, and service industries which may rely on illegal immigrant labour.

The failure of both crime and prostitution as analogies for illegal immigration reveals the latter as a special kind of problem for modern liberal democratic states in the global commercial economy. It is at once a concomitant of the global economic system and an apparent scandal for domestic political ideas. Yet our ability to discuss this predicament – the irresistibility of migration in certain circumstances, and the factors driving actual state responses to it – is distorted by clinging to an illusion about what the values of sovereignty, democracy and nationality entitle or require us to do.

In the remainder of this chapter, I shall argue that the common assumptions about what each of these values entail for immigration are mistaken, but that a more subtle interpretation of each value exists which does shed helpful light on migration. Our best theories of sovereignty do not rest on state control of immigration, though they do appeal to the principle of individual consent (not state consent) which can help us in understanding naturalization. Our best theories of democracy do not, similarly, rest on a club-like control of admission and exclusion, though they do appeal to a principle of democratic inclusion which likewise gives guidance on the question of naturalization. And our best theories of the value of national culture and identity do not, as many think, automatically outweigh the interests of immigrants in admission.

Scepticism about these claims can open space for policies which are at once more hard-headed about the actual cost of immigration restrictions and more creative about finding ways to handle the inevitable pressures for immigration. Once we are no longer self-blinded about what sovereignty, democracy, and nationality permit or require in this area, we can perhaps avoid some of the self-binding traps which currently bedevil our policies. When 'irresistible forces meet immovable ideas', it is the latter that must give way.

Sovereignty

Consent, Representation and Political Obligation

None of the great theorists of the emerging European state and state order – Grotius, Selden, Hobbes, Locke, Pufendorf, Rousseau and Kant – saw immigration as central to their theories of sovereignty and political obligation. The discussion of political obligation in this tradition seeks to legitimate political authority with reference to each individual and their obligation to obey (see Tuck, 1993). That problem is solved by focusing (in diverse ways according to each individual theory) on the individual's binding himself, or having sufficient reason to consider herself bound, through the notion of consent linked to representation or participation (cf. Hampton, 1995: 89; Bauböck, 1994: 56). Consent is thus classically conceived in terms of whether, and how to know whether, the individual consents to the establishment of sovereignty and to the formation of a political community. It has nothing to do with whether either the sovereign or the community consent to his or her being included in it.

Far from dictating that states must consent to and control immigration, the classic European account of sovereignty focuses attention rather on the acts and choices of individuals themselves. Ironically, this complex of concepts is peculiarly well suited to accommodate immigrants, who according to these theories need only adopt the right self-conception and attitudes, and perform any necessary acts, to acquire the appropriate relationship of membership to a state. The real core of the doctrine of sovereignty is individual consent, not state control, and this means that sovereignty is rightly understood as a guide to naturalization (which on these theories is eminently possible) rather than as a barrier to it. For neither consent nor representation, as operationalized by these thinkers, depends on native birth. Even for Rousseau, who stressed the need of a people to share a common way of life in order to formulate a general will consenting to fundamental legislation, this way of life is a matter of customs, holidays and language rather than a matter of birth or blood.

No more than the philosophers did early modern rulers rest their claims of sovereignty on the control of immigration. Sovereignty was a matter of dynastic or constitutional claim, independent of the actual composition of the nation. Of course we must distinguish between the grounds of sovereignty and its concomitant powers. Sovereign states have long intervened in migration and assumed their entitlement to do so, an entitlement asserted in the United States from 1837 (*City of New York v. Miln*) and crystallized in 1889 (*Chae Chan Ping v. United States*) in the Supreme Court's declaration that the power to exclude foreigners is an incident of sovereignty unrestricted by treaties, previous statute or constitutional limitations (Konvitz, 1953: 1–2). But while sovereign powers may include the right to control immigration, the justification of sovereignty and its relationship to the individual does not rest on the exercise of that right. And indeed the motivation of sovereign states to exclude immigrants has historically been a function of policy and the conception of interest and advantage, rather than a deduction from theories of sovereignty.

Sovereignty is not, of course, the only value invoked to justify limitations on immigration. Democracy and nationality also play key roles here, and indeed were historically crucial in the reconfiguration of the political view of migration. I will consider here arguments of two of the most eminent theorists of each value respectively, Michael Walzer on democracy and David Miller on nationality, in the course of questioning whether these values do imply the strong entitlement of states to control immigration which Walzer and Miller assert.

Democracy

Michael Walzer's (1983) widely quoted contention that '[a]dmission and exclusion are at the core of communal independence' does not exclusively refer to democracy, but it does derive such force as it has from the image of a political community as a self-determining club whose first order of business is to decide who is in and who is out. His dictum nominally applies to ancient Athenian democracy, where the status of citizenship was jealously guarded and claimants suspected of fraud were likely to wind up in court. Here, democratic citizenship was seen as a source of privileges, including the privilege of political participation, which depended and could be accorded only to a bounded realm of participants (cf. Carens, 1987: 252). But it is important to see that this did not mean that Athenians conceived themselves as constantly deliberating about who should be in and who out, on the model of a club to which Walzer's contention is readily linked. For Athenian citizenship was normally limited to those born of two citizens (women for this purpose being accorded a certain status as citizens, though one not possessing rights of speech or voting in the democratic institutions). While a few metics and foreigners were naturalized each year by a complex procedure of the Assembly, the identity of the demos was largely and publicly treated as being fixed by inheritance, as was numerically overwhelmingly true (Hansen, 1991: 88, 90–91).

The idea that democratic communities are constantly exercising such deliberation about admission and exclusion is modern rather than ancient, born of the confluence of new state powers and technologies, economic relationships, and conceptions of naturalization and citizenship. But although we now tend to think of democratic states as clubs able to pick and choose whom to let in, this image is at odds with the economic forcefield which attracts new residents into all but the most authoritarian states, legally or illegally, whenever certain gradients are sufficiently steep. Once illegal immigrants have integrated into the society in terms of work, education, residence, and social belonging, it becomes both impractical and evidently unjust not to grant them at least a path towards full citizenship. Hence the amnesties which have been periodically granted in the United States, southern Europe, and elsewhere.[6]

Whereas the common view of democracy is as implying club-like democratic control, a more realistic understanding of the value of democracy in relation to immigration is as implying the value and practices of what I will call democratic inclusion. Democracy conceived as democratic inclusion values the full recognition of all those who have become incorporated into a society through work and residence. As Rainer Bauböck argues in this volume, those who are so incorporated deserve the chance to become full citizens, though they should not be coerced to do so. But if this path to citizenship is acknowledged, then the idea that the state maintains full plenary powers of deciding upon admission and exclusion as part of the definition of its democratic identity, becomes untenable.

Walzer's conception of admission and exclusion as key to political membership is not, therefore, a universal or timeless truth about the nature of politics or even democratic politics. It attaches only to a relatively active and arduous conception of such membership as conceived in terms of democratic rights and participation, which is grafted onto the somewhat recalcitrant skeleton of the sovereign modern state. And even where such a conception finds support, it remains at odds with the actual economic imperatives driving immigration and then its regularization.

The club-like image which Walzer defends must be further qualified on liberal grounds, given that state 'clubs' monopolize the supply of goods crucial to the whole course of life. Most importantly, Walzer's conception misdirects our attention in the area of democracy, focusing exclusively on collective control and decision-making while obscuring deeper areas of democratic values. The democratic value of inclusion and the older logic of incorporation by sovereign-constituting consent, in which all living under a reasonably benign regime both can and should obligate themselves to it, are better guides to what democracy requires in conditions of economic globalization and inequality than is the old-fashioned image of the democracy as club.

Nationalism

The final value to be examined here as a putative justification for state control of immigration is nationalism. In its mid-nineteenth century heyday, John Stuart Mill already identified its impact in conjunction with democracy in leading to the view that state and national boundaries should coincide, writing in *Considerations on Representative Government* (1861) that '[i]t is in general a necessary condition of free institutions, that the boundaries of governments should coincide in the main with those of nationalities'. Again, this is an idea – child both of the French Revolution and of the resistance to its spread across Europe – which has come to seem natural though scarcely fully realized, since in a world of a limited number of states, some nationalities will inevitably be submerged in the states of others.

Nationality, and its modern re-envisioning as the idea of cultural identity, has come to play an important role in debates over immigration, both practically (as in for example the Latvian immigration and citizenship policies) and ideologically. While conservatives appeal to the need to protect national or cultural identity, a band of 'liberal nationalists'[7] among political philosophers have recently been arguing that liberals too have good reason to value and promote national identities for the sake of individual flourishing and well-being. Such arguments however generally fail to prescribe a metric for how the value of national identity to some individuals – those in an existing state to which immigrants seek entry – should be weighed against the value of freedom and opportunity which immigrants seek to enjoy. In the absence of such a metric, liberal nationalists often speak of 'balancing' these interests, but tend to assume that national identity is sufficiently important as to at least balance against, if not outweigh, the values which immigrants pursue. By examining one such argument, in the work of David Miller, I seek to show that the idea of a balance[8] here is problematic; that historical precedent should make us wary of the claim of 'nationality' in immigration debates; and that the framework of freedom rather than justice is the appropriate one for evaluating the claims of immigrants.

In his first major work defending nationality as a political principle, Miller was relatively sanguine about immigration so long as the immigrants accepted political structures and were willing to enter into dialogue with the existing population in order to mutually fashion an evolving national identity (Miller, 1995: 129; Miller 2000: 30). More recently, however, Miller has identified what he believes to be two good reasons justifying the right of liberal-democratic states to limit immigration. He begins by rejecting the idea that migration is a fundamental human right, an argument which it behoves us to scrutinize before proceeding further. Miller rejects the idea of migration as a human right by suggesting that 'decent states' are able to secure for their citizens both basic rights and also an adequate range of options that makes their autonomy meaningful.[9] According to Miller, citizens of such decent states do not need the opportunity to migrate in order to make adequate use of their autonomy and to enjoy an adequate range of opportunities; citizens of non-decent states may become refugees.

Miller's invented sociological category of 'decent state' is however wildly over-optimistic. Some states may offer basic rights but not adequate options, while many others will provide neither to at least some citizen groups. Further, the judgment by citizens of the rich countries that citizens of much poorer countries enjoy an 'adequate' range of options so that they may be deprived of the freedom to migrate, smacks of hypocrisy and paternalism. As for the fate of those condemned to be born into non-decent states, the category of refugee is wildly inadequate, since many citizens of non-decent states suffer neglect rather than the state persecution which limits the category of refugee in international law.

Indeed, it is symptomatic of Miller's discussion, as of others tending to reject cosmopolitanism in favour of the moral claims of nationalities and states, that the question of the right to migrate is discussed under the rubric of justice rather than freedom. If would-be immigrants can be shown to have no claim of justice upon 'us', then their claim can be legitimately rejected. Even some moral cosmopolitans have rejected the idea of a right to global migration on the grounds that it is not an effective way to conduce to greater global justice, since obligations of justice to the global poor are owed to all the poor rather than a small self-selected group of would-be migrants (see Pogge, 1997).

It may be conceded that global migration will not establish global justice, though its economic impact in reducing poverty is non-negligible (Holzmann and Münz, 2004: 9). But it must be reciprocally conceded by the liberal nationalists that the claims of existing patterns of settlement to justice are themselves extremely dubious. (Why is it fair that I should benefit from American citizenship, but a child born in Argentina in the same year as I should not, simply because my great-grandparents were allowed into the United States from eastern Poland in 1890 and hers were not?) Attempting to establish the baseline justice of the existing dispensation, on the basis of which the claims of migrants may be assessed, will at best result in stalemate.

Freedom, however, provides an alternative argument to that of justice. Just as capitalism need not be defended on the grounds of wealth-production but may rather be defended in terms of the sheer freedom to act and transact, so the right to migrate may be defended in terms of the sheer freedom to pursue better opportunities for oneself, irrespective of the fact that most will not be able to do so (my freedom to apply to Cambridge was not compromised by the fact that most of my peers were not in a position to do so). For those outside the bounds of effective national justice in the 'West', but forced to suffer the claims of a hostile or ineffective state, the freedom to try to better themselves is at least *prima facie* elemental and not hostage to the restrictions of an ever-deferred chimera of global justice.

This brings us to resume consideration of Miller's argument. Rejecting a general right to migrate as noted above, Miller does accept that everyone has the right to emigrate and join at least some other society, but holds that this does not entail a right to join the society of their choice. States are entitled to choose their members, but they do not have the full prerogatives of a club, because the benefits of being citizens of desirable states are substantial and are monopolized by a limited number of states already (so that others cannot just go and start their own clubs). Therefore states may and should strike a 'balance' between their own important interests, and the interests of immigrants who desire access to such states, who have a '*claim* ... – if nothing else ... a strong *desire* to enter' (Miller, 2004: 9–10, italics original). Two state interests in particular may be justifiably used to limit immigration: the interest in 'preserving [their public] culture' (ibid.: 10), and the interest in determining population size in relation to a chosen way of managing its ecological impact. According to Miller, striking a legitimate balance between these competing interests must exclude what he considers to be morally and socially insignificant or insulting features of potential migrants as criteria for admission or rejection. He argues that while the state interest in limiting immigration may override the interest of potential non-refugee migrants in gaining admission, it may not do so in morally irrelevant or insulting ways – such as by deciding on admission on the basis of sex, race, or hair colour (cf. Bauböck, 1997: 23).

Miller nowhere establishes the respective weight of the interests that he would balance. The reader is not told why she should assume that the interest of some people in preserving their public culture is at least as weighty as the interest of others in the freedom and opportunity for a better life through migration. *Prima facie*, one might think that the individual interest in public culture – which may affect the goodness of one's life, by shaping the culture which shapes the options open to one – is outweighed by the individual interest in having a wider range of such options, in enjoying human security for what options that one does have, perhaps even (given the flaw in his argument about 'decent states') in having an adequate range of such options altogether.

There is also a serious flaw in Miller's conception of what it would be to strike a balance between competing individual and aggregate interests at all. In bracketing sex, race, and hair colour as his examples of features which should be ignored in immigration decisions, Miller seems to be relying on the liberal intuition that states should treat their citizens fairly, and that sex, race and hair colour are irrelevant to the moral standing or claims of individual citizens. But, his own argument is that decisions about immigrants are not like decisions about the treatment of existing individual citizens. In considering the claims of immigrants, states, Miller holds, can rightly override the claims of individual immigrants in favour of general state interests and decisions about the welfare and lifestyle of existing citizens. Yet general state interests are precisely considered at the aggregate level at which sex ratios, for example, are far from irrelevant for matters of 'real significance' to the society.

So sex cannot be ruled out of court as a basis for immigration decisions consistently with the overall tenor and basis of Miller's argument. For indeed, the sex of would-be immigrants might be held to be of 'real significance' to a society suffering from badly skewed sex ratios. If societies can decide for themselves how to balance the environment against population increases, why can they not decide to prioritize the improvement of adverse sex ratios by admitting immigrants of a certain sex? (If one is unsympathetic to the idea of a society mitigating its own flawed policies about birth (such as China's one-child policy which resulted due to public attitudes in a surplus of boys), consider a society such as the USSR after World War II which might have wished to mitigate the adverse sex-ratio caused by the war.) If one is going to privilege general interests about the aggregate composition of a society, one cannot then hold that factors which affect that aggregate composition are *a priori* irrelevant to those interests, even if they arise from features of individuals which are morally arbitrary. Sex is a good example of the sort of demographic factor that will in the aggregate have serious implications for the general interest and welfare of a society.

What about race? Race is logically different from sex, since it has implications for general welfare only on views of that welfare and of the moral significance of race which liberals rightly reject as noxious. But national culture has often in the past been invoked as a proxy for views of race and ethnic identity which now strike us as invidious. Consider for example that 'shared culture' was invoked in the United States as grounds for blocking Chinese and Japanese immigration in the 1920s, and again in the 1950s to justify maintaining a system of national quotas which heavily favoured immigration from northwestern Europe (the UK, Germany and Ireland in particular) over southeastern Europe and the rest of the world (Konvitz, 1953: 1–16). And race was blended with an appeal to cultural ideals and to ecological-population considerations in a mixture which might give a liberal nationalist pause, in the US House of Representatives Committee on Immigration and Naturalization report on what became the 1924 permanent quota law:

> With the full recognition of the material progress which we owe to the races from southern and eastern Europe, we are conscious that the continued arrival of great numbers tends to upset our balance of population, to depress our standard of living, and to unduly charge our institutions for the care of the socially inadequate.
>
> If immigration [sic] from southern and eastern Europe may enter the United States on a basis of substantial equality with that admitted from the older sources of supply, it is clear that if any appreciable number of immigrants are to be allowed to land upon our shores the balance of racial preponderance must in time pass to those elements of the population who reproduce more rapidly on a lower standard of living than those possessing other ideals ....[10]

While no liberal nationalist would contemplate racism in their defence of national public culture, the fact remains that culture has in the past served as a potent surrogate for race. If public culture is admitted as a legitimate interest to be weighed in the 'balance' against the interests of immigrants, the danger that invidious and collectivist considerations will sneak into the scales under its wing cannot be discounted.

In sum, Miller's idea of a 'balance' between the interests of nation-states and the interests of immigrants is misleading, in that it facilitates the pitting of aggregate interests against the individual right not to be discriminated against. It becomes fatuous to protect the procedural rights of immigrants not to be turned away on trivial grounds such as hair colour, while allowing their more fundamental interests in liberty, opportunity, and human security to be overridden by state interests that may be far less important. The idea that immigration policy is 'balancing' the interests of states and those of would-be immigrants by refusing to consider hair colour as a criterion, is a curious notion of what it would be to balance an interest, and of the weight of the interests which immigrants have.

This is not to defend the making of immigration decisions on the basis of discriminatory criteria. Such criteria should be excluded, but they should be excluded as a rights-based trump or 'filter' because they offend values of democratic procedure, not as part of an exercise in balancing aggregate interests where their weight is only implausibly absolute. The values of democratic procedure, like the value of inclusion, are elements of democracy which are independent of the claim that the collectivity must control immigration through majority decision or the concern for public culture, concerns which I have shown to be flawed as bases for state limits on immigration. In considering the claims of nationality or culture versus the claims of immigration, we must take care to compare only like with like, true individual values rather than aggregate considerations masquerading as individual interests. A truly liberal nationalism would concern itself exclusively with the interests of individuals, and would not automatically assume that the interests of those already within the scope of the nation outweigh the interests of those outside it. As Friedrich von Hayek tartly asserted, 'It is still loyalty to such particular groups as those of occupation or class as well as those of clan, nation, race or religion which is the greatest obstacle to the universal application of rules of just conduct' (1982 [1976]: 149, 148).

Conclusion

I have argued that we have reason to be sceptical about the claims that either sovereignty, democracy, or nationalism provides fundamental reasons for state concerns to limit immigration. Once we see the state concern with immigration as less noble and fundamental, but rather the creature of circumstance and advantage that it is, we may be freed to consider among other things the real costs of the policies that are currently used to try to limit immigration. In other words, if such policies are not deontologically required by the very nature of our values, we must begin to count their consequential costs.

Those costs include the arbitrariness of the attempt to control flows which remain fundamentally beyond control, arbitrariness which severely damages the human security of migrant workers and inhibits their choices and opportunities. Enforcement and deportation are relatively haphazard and chancy events, and that they are often identified concomitant to other offences. The mass questioning of Arab men in the United States after 11 September 2001, for example, led to a large number of deportations on the grounds of minor immigration violations which would not have been discovered otherwise. Such an arbitrary regime increases the insecurity under which illegal migrants live, making them vulnerable to the politically motivated occasional crackdown, or the vengeful fellow employee. Such 'unwritten rules' of when deportation is actually likely to occur (a term I borrow from Alena Ledeneva's analysis of Russian politics today (Ledeneva, 2001)) are not consonant with the spirit of the rule of law, although they may comply with its letter.

Costs also arise from policies which are counterproductive. For example, if restrictions are tightened, migrants will tend to stay longer on their first trip abroad, or to settle permanently rather than seasonally, contrary to the preferences they would have had had they been more confident of their ability to return.[11] In sum, once the soberness of a consequentialist approach is admitted, one may well find that a remark by Steven Friedman is true beyond its original South African context: 'current forms of control [of migration, in South Africa] are a greater threat to human rights and democracy than the presence of immigrants' (Friedman quoted by Crush, 1998: 3).

There are many other ethical and philosophical issues in the management of global migration, such as the particular vulnerability of women and girls (Bjerén, 1997), or the issue of medical migration and the brain drain of workers in whom sending countries have invested great human and social capital. It is hoped that this chapter, which has sought to remind the reader that migration is an ineradicable part of the human condition and to assess the claims and policies of states in that light (and also in the light of the history of ideas), may be of some indirect use in assessing and responding to these challenges. Global public policy must address a world of states which claim the absolute right to control migration, while acknowledging that migration is ineradicable and that hardly any state will ever be able to control it completely. Policy reforms predicated on and addressing the world of states need to take state perspectives on their rights to control migration seriously, to be sure. But they are also well advised to consider such claims against the backdrop of constant and unceasing human migration both before and since modern states arose to assert such claims. The focus should therefore be on the pragmatic, since the theoretical claims are likely to be inflated. But this in turn puts severe pressure on what can and should be considered to be realistic or practical, since such judgments are themselves a function of economic and political perceptions, ideas, and mobilizations. There is no very secure ethical standpoint from which to survey the world of global migration, yet it is our world and we must endeavour to make all, whether migrants or not, at least reasonably at home in it.

Notes

[1]   I thank Rainer Bauböck, Seyla Benhabib, Martin Baldwin-Edwards, Emile Perreau-Saussine, Jo Shaw, Richard Tuck, and Aristide Zolberg for suggestions relating to this chapter. Special thanks go to David Miller for generously sharing unpublished work, and to Kristof Tamas for detailed comments on earlier versions.

[2]   I borrow this wonderful phrase from the subtitle of Pritchett, 2003, who discusses global migration as an economist; my discussion here aims to complement his by drawing on political theory and the history of ideas.

[3]   For a sophisticated account of the dynamics of migration over time, see Malmberg, 1997.

4   *International Herald Tribune*, 25 April 2004.

5   The principle of time links also to a useful proposal in Hammar, 1994: 195–7, that an international agreement should be reached fixing the maximum period of time after which states ought as a rule to transfer applicants from a lower to a higher immigration status in the sequence of entrant, denizen and citizen status.

6   On the injustice of refusing such a path to inclusion, see Miller, 2004: 16–17; Walzer, 1983; Barbieri, 1998: 4 and *passim*; more subtly, Bauböck, 1991, 1994, and Hammar, 1990.

7   Alan Patten helpfully groups David Miller with Will Kymlicka, Joseph Raz and Yael Tamir under this rubric (Patten, 1999: 4).

8   For a comparable argument about the problems involved in the idea of 'balancing' security and liberty, see Waldron, 2003.

9   Here, Miller is influenced by the Oxford philosopher Joseph Raz's *The Morality of Freedom* (1993).

10   Report to accompany H.R. 7995, 68th Cong., 13–14, as quoted in Konvitz (1953: 11). Compare Max Weber's similar strictures on Polish immigrants to East Prussia, in his Inaugural Lecture in Freiburg in 1895 (Weber, 1994).

11   See the discussion of two studies of migration between Mexico and the United States in the context of NAFTA in Tamas, 2004a: 46–7.

Chapter 10

Citizenship: International, State, Migrant and Democratic Perspectives[1]

Rainer Bauböck

Introduction

Since the last quarter of the twentieth century some traditional elements of state sovereignty have been questioned and, to a certain extent, eroded. Economic globalization, external interventions on humanitarian grounds in domestic conflicts, and supranational political integration in Europe, provide three major illustrations of this trend. In this new world, the state's prerogative to define its own citizenship has remained a bulwark of sovereignty that virtually no state seems willing to abandon. Even in the European Union, where a majority of member states have agreed to abolish internal border controls and national currencies and have put common foreign and security policies on the agenda, member states remain in full control over access to their nationality in spite of formal establishment of a common Union citizenship by the Maastricht Treaty of 1992.

Yet in the same period we have also witnessed the gradual emergence of new citizenship policies that signal a tidal change. These reflect primarily a new attitude towards migration in western receiving countries. Parallel with growing state concerns about controlling immigration, there has been a general shift towards recognizing that those who have settled as legal immigrants need to be offered legal statuses and rights that do not differ fundamentally from those of native citizens. This tendency to blur distinctions between citizens and permanent residents goes together with a second, and somewhat more uneven trend, towards facilitating access to nationality in receiving countries. This can be done through automatic acquisition for children born in the territory, easier naturalization for immigrants, and toleration of dual nationality. In some of the most important source states there has been a parallel policy change towards encouraging emigrants to take up citizenship in the receiving country while retaining that of the source country.

Apart from such convergence in state practices, there are also efforts to establish new norms for citizenship policy at the international level. These are most pronounced in Europe where the Council of Europe adopted the comprehensive European Convention on Nationality (ECN) in 1997 (in force since March 2000). The Council of Europe, the Organisation for Security and Cooperation in Europe (OSCE) and, to a lesser extent, the European Union Commission have also exercised some pressure on certain member states and accession candidates to change their citizenship laws. Estonia and Latvia were specifically asked to integrate their Russian minorities, many of whom were turned stateless after independence, into full citizenship.

This chapter will not discuss extensively these legal and political developments.[2] It will instead build on existing analyses (see for example, Aleinikoff and Klusmeyer, 2000, 2001, 2002; Çınar, 1994; Davy, 2001; Groenendijk et al., 2000; Hansen and Weil, 2001; Martin and Hailbronner, 2003; Nascimbene, 1996; Staples, 1999; Waldrauch, 2001). The chapter will suggest principles for more consistent and inclusive citizenship policies that do not ignore state concerns about self-determination of their own nationals. The need for new principles emerges from two phenomena that are not new in world history but that have been highlighted in dramatic ways in recent decades: moving state borders and moving human populations.

Inclusive citizenship policies could be easily designed for a world with perfectly stable international borders and no international migration. In such a world, everybody could obtain a single citizenship at birth and it would make no difference whether states adopt a *ius sanguinis*[3] or *ius soli*[4] rule for this purpose. There would be no need for regulating the loss of a present citizenship and the acquisition of a new one after birth and there would therefore also be no multiple nationals or stateless persons. In the real world, however, international migration generates massive numbers of citizens living outside and foreign nationals living inside the territorial jurisdiction of states. Multiple nationality emerges from the combination of *ius sanguinis* in countries of origin and *ius soli* in receiving states, from children whose parents have different nationalities, which they both pass on to their offspring, and from the impossibility or unwillingness to enforce the renunciation of a previous nationality in naturalizations. Finally, refugee movements and problems of state succession in the wake of secession or consensual separation generate substantial numbers of stateless persons. This chapter will only deal with migration-related challenges for citizenship policies, although the general principles that it proposes should also apply to state succession.

Why is it important to include principles for citizenship policy in general norms for the regulation of human mobility and international migration? First, because the absence of, or disrespect for, mutually agreed rules on citizenship can generate dangerous conflicts between states. Second, because restrictive and uncoordinated citizenship policies contribute to irregular migration and create major obstacles for legal modes of international migration that benefit both source and destination states. Legal migrants need external protection and return options provided by their countries of origin as well as access to rights and citizenship status in the country of long-term settlement. Where the former element is missing, settlement migration is likely to result in a permanent loss of human capital for the source country (brain drain). Where they are excluded from citizenship in the host state, migrants often form a segregated ethnic underclass whose exclusion contributes to deteriorating standards in employment, housing, health and education. While access to citizenship alone is certainly insufficient, it is a necessary condition for fighting these evils. Third, inclusive citizenship is also an important value from a democratic perspective.

This is most obviously so in immigrant receiving states, where the legitimacy of democratic rule is undermined if a section of the population remains permanently disenfranchised. However, giving emigrants opportunities to participate in political decisions in their countries of origin may also contribute to democratic developments in source countries.

A note on terminology is necessary before starting. Citizenship and nationality are concepts with multiple meanings that overlap in one particular area. Both refer to a legal status that links individuals to states. The term 'nationality' is more often used to describe the international aspects of this linkage, whereas 'citizenship' points towards an internal relation of membership in a polity. In a second, and quite different sense, nationality means membership in a national community of shared history and culture that need not be established as an independent state. The concept of citizenship is broader than nationality and covers also the legal and moral rights and obligations entailed in being a member of a democratic community and the practices and virtues of 'good citizenship' that help to sustain such communities. This chapter will focus on policies regulating the legal status and will therefore use citizenship and nationality as synonyms or two sides of the same coin, but it will also invoke the broader meaning of citizenship as democratic membership when discussing policies that should be adopted in democratic societies.

Interests in Citizenship Policies

Most normative discussions of citizenship policies suffer from a bias of perspective. They fail to consider the full range of relevant interests that ought to be taken into account and balanced against each other. This chapter suggests that there are four interests of this kind: those of the international community, of individual states, of individual migrants and of democratic societies. Of course these interests overlap in many ways, which is why it should be possible to reconcile them with each other. However, they are also distinct in certain regards, which makes it a challenging task to develop consistent and comprehensive principles for citizenship policies.

The International Community

The primary interest of the 'International Community' and the core task of international law is to establish a legal order that helps to sustain peaceful and friendly relations between states. Only since 1945 has the promotion of individual human rights been added as a secondary interest and normative foundation of this order. These two goals are also reflected in legal norms that relate to questions of citizenship.

Since international law is meant to protect the interests of states in such a way that they can peacefully coexist with each other, its constraints on state powers in matters of citizenship have generally been rather weak. The basic norm is stated in the 1930 Hague Convention Governing Certain Questions Relating to the Conflict of Nationalities, whose first two articles state: '1) It is for each State to determine under its own law who are its nationals ... 2) Any question as to whether a person possesses the nationality of a particular State shall be determined in accordance with the law of that State'. The 1948 Universal Declaration of Human Rights (UDHR) contains much stronger language. Its article 15 proclaims: '1) Everyone has the right to a nationality. 2) No one shall be arbitrarily deprived of his nationality nor denied the right to change his nationality'. This article is, however, missing in the 1966 Covenant on Civil and Political Rights (ICCPR) that translated the non-binding Declaration into an international treaty. The ICCPR merely contains a provision that: '[e]very child has the right to acquire a nationality'. Even Article 15 UDHR cannot be interpreted as implying a right of immigrants to naturalization. What it suggests instead is an individual right not to be turned stateless and a right to be released from a given nationality when acquiring a new one.

Concerns of the international community about statelessness have resulted in two special UN Conventions on the Status of Stateless Persons (1954) and on the Reduction of Statelessness (1961). The 1961 Convention establishes a *ius soli* right to nationality for persons born in the territory of a state who would otherwise remain stateless, and a subsidiary *ius sanguinis* right if one parent of a child was a national of a contracting state at the time of birth. It does not, however, regulate the case of mass statelessness resulting from the formation of new nation-states. Problems of state succession, which have created sizeable stateless minorities in Estonia, Latvia and Slovenia, are addressed in chapter VI of the 1997 European Convention on Nationality (ECN).

The other traditional interest of the international community has been the avoidance of multiple nationality. The preamble of The Hague Convention stated 'that it is in the general interest of the international community to secure that all its members should recognise that every person should have a nationality and should have one nationality only'. In 1963 the Council of Europe adopted a Convention on Reduction of Cases of Multiple Nationality. However, the doctrine that multiple nationality is an evil has since lost ground. A 1993 protocol to the Convention considerably undermined state obligations to avoid creating multiple nationals and the 1997 ECN effectively abandoned the basic principle by insisting on a right to retain multiple nationality acquired automatically at birth or through marriage, while leaving signatory states free to require the renunciation of a previous nationality in naturalizations. The objection that multiple nationality would generate conflicts between citizenship obligations towards several states was already undermined by the 1963 Convention, which contained provisions for determining in which state dual nationals would have to perform their obligatory military service.

The ECN, the most comprehensive instrument of international law in matters of nationality so far, reflects recent European experiences of international migration as well as of changing international borders. Although it leaves several issues unresolved that could be addressed by international law it provides a new standard for nationality policies also in other regions of the world. There are, however, limits for the potential of international law to provide sufficiently inclusive and flexible norms in this area. A focus on avoiding conflicts between states and protecting universal human rights cannot fully cover the internal dimensions of citizenship as membership in a particular political community. While, for example, the introduction of *ius soli* and of naturalization entitlements may be convincingly argued in the domestic contexts of immigrant receiving democracies, it would be wrong to expect the backing of international law for these demands.

States

From a realist perspective in international relations, states are assumed to have a primary interest in maximizing their sovereignty and secondary interests in international norms that prevent other states from interfering with their sovereignty. With regard to citizenship policies, this entails three specific concerns: first, control over the acquisition of nationality, second, territorial jurisdiction over foreign nationals, and, third, control over their own external citizens living abroad.

From an economic perspective the general state interest in controlling access to nationality may be explained by conceiving of citizenship as a 'club good' that gives members access to specific benefits provided by public authorities (Jordan and Düvell, 2003; Straubhaar, 2003). All rights of individuals that are guaranteed by states entail public costs – redistributive social welfare benefits as well as negative liberties and rights (Holmes and Sunstein, 1999). One can therefore construe a rational interest of states in controlling access of new members who can claim such rights.

This argument is, however, more plausible for immigration control than for naturalization. The need to control access to nationality depends on the relative benefits attached to full citizenship compared to the legal status of foreign nationals. Very large gaps between these two statuses have become less common than they used to be in the past. In authoritarian or semi-democratic states where the rule of law is weak, neither citizens nor foreign nationals enjoy robust public rights and benefits. In democratic countries these rights have been greatly expanded during the second half of the twentieth century but the gap between foreign residents and citizens has also narrowed considerably. While new immigrants often have restricted access to employment and social welfare benefits, these barriers are generally removed with permanent residence rather than naturalization. And, in contrast with naturalization, permanent resident status is either granted already at the time of immigration or achieved automatically after some period of legal residence.

In liberal democracies there are three core privileges that generally remain attached to citizenship status: the franchise in general elections, the unconditional right of residence (including free entry into the state territory, to return to it and protection against expulsion), and diplomatic protection. These specific benefits explain why even the most liberal citizenship regimes do not permit easy access to citizenship status from abroad or immediately after immigration – except for special categories that are regarded as co-nationals living outside the state territory.[5] Naturalization requires a minimum period of legal residence that varies broadly between two years in Australia and 12 years in Switzerland. State interests in controlling access to specific privileges of citizenship do not, however, explain or justify why many states insist on extensive discretion in naturalization decisions.

The regulation of access to nationality broadly reflects historic experiences as source or receiving countries and self-conceptions as ethnic or civic nations. In traditional countries of immigration that have promoted civic national identities, naturalization is publicly encouraged and made relatively easy; in countries that have produced net emigration over most of their history we find more often that access to nationality is made difficult and depends on discretionary decisions by administrative authorities. Such historic trajectories do not, however, fully determine available policy options. This is best illustrated by the German reform of 1999, which introduced *ius soli* and shorter residence periods for naturalization in a country that had been regarded as the classic example of an ethnic nation based on *ius sanguinis*.

Apart from their desire to control access to nationality immigrant receiving states have a second important interest in unconstrained powers of jurisdiction within their territory. This interest is jeopardized if source states want to exercise jurisdiction over their expatriates. International law recognizes therefore the general primacy of territorial jurisdiction and limits the actions that states of origin may take on behalf of their nationals abroad. The most important right of source states is to provide their nationals with diplomatic protection. International private law also recognizes that in matters of family law such as marriage, divorce or child custody, receiving states may need to take into account legal norms established in the country of origin. One common objection against tolerating multiple nationality is that it would lead to conflicts between states because of overlapping claims to jurisdictions and that it would deprive migrants of diplomatic protection in their countries of origin. These concerns are, however, overstated. A simple rule for resolving most such disputes is that in case of conflict the jurisdiction of the state of habitual residence will predominate.

Yet concerns about external interference by source states on behalf of their nationals in host countries are clearly not limited to conflicts between legal norms. Governments and politicians in receiving countries frequently worry that immigrants can be politically manipulated by their states of origin. If they engage, on the contrary, in political activities directed against this government, there is a corresponding fear that this may imperil friendly foreign policy relations or may import violent conflicts generated by unstable and undemocratic regimes into the receiving country. There is some evidence for both phenomena. However, maintaining control over their nationals living in a democratic state is very difficult for source country governments. Social marginalization may breed a potential for ethnic conflict even among long-term and second generation immigrant populations, but this is an endogenous problem of destination states rather than imported violence from source states. Those immigrants who are relatively well-integrated in economic, legal and political terms are much more likely to export democratic values to their countries of origin than to import undemocratic ones from there.

Much of the literature and research on citizenship and migration has focused on receiving states. However, it is equally important to consider the ties of citizenship between countries of origin and their emigrant communities living abroad. Migrants must be regarded both as immigrants and as emigrants, and the policies of receiving and source states should be mutually acceptable for each other.

Receiving states' interest to full jurisdiction and political control over all residents in their territory conflicts in certain respects with interests of source states in maintaining close ties with expatriates. Yet source states have taken very different attitudes towards those who have left. Strongly nationalistic governments tend towards the opposite extremes of regarding them either as traitors who have abandoned their country or as missionaries whose primary duty is to serve this country and to promote its interests. Both these attitudes are ineffective or counterproductive when applied to large contingents of economically motivated migrants. Source states of larger migration flows have therefore developed more rational policy responses to emigration that try to maximize its benefits for the source economy.

In the initial stages of a labour migration flow, source countries are primarily interested in maximizing the return flow of remittances and also in encouraging return migration of successful migrants who invest their savings and skills acquired abroad in the economy of the source country. When a temporary flow results in family reunification and permanent settlement abroad, source governments must adapt their strategies to shifting orientations among their expatriates. They often encourage emigrant communities to remain connected with their country of origin in the hope that they will be instrumental in forging trade links (for example through import and export businesses) or in influencing bilateral political relations. At the final stage of this development the source country may even promote the acquisition of citizenship in the country of immigrant settlement.

This process can be observed in Mexico and Turkey, the two major source countries for immigration in North America and Western Europe. During earlier stages of the emigration both states had generally discouraged integration in the host society and had withdrawn citizenship from those who had acquired another nationality abroad. In the 1990s they have revised their policies and now encourage their expatriates to naturalize in the receiving state while permitting them to retain their home state's nationality. These policy reversals were partly caused by fears about anti-immigrant mobilizations or legislation. In 1994 California's voters passed Proposition 187 that targeted irregular migrants and the US 1996 Welfare Reform Act deprived legal immigrants of federal welfare benefits; in Germany after unification there was a series of violent racist incidents including arson attacks in 1992 and 1993 that killed several immigrants of Turkish origin in Mölln and Solingen. Such events caused concerns in source countries about unwanted return migration flows and prompted them to campaign for equal rights and full political integration of their expatriates in their new home countries.

Migrants

If individuals are conceived as rational utility maximizers, their interest in citizenship will be to maximize its benefits while minimizing its burdens. Moreover, since states offer different bundles of citizenship rights and duties, rational individuals want to be able to choose a bundle that best satisfies their particular preferences. Economists have suggested a model of local government, in which municipalities compete with each other by offering different bundles of public goods and local taxes. Perfectly mobile individuals would then choose to settle in the municipality that best satisfies their preferences, and competition for immigrants would maximize the efficiency of local government services (Tiebout, 1956).

This model can, however, not easily be applied to international migration. There are today a number of small states that offer their citizenship to wealthy individuals who invest a certain amount of money, sometimes without even requiring that they take up residence there. The main benefits of these citizenships, which are advertised on the internet, are tax evasion and second passports for visa free travel.[6] Even individuals who choose another citizenship for these reasons are, however, rarely willing to give up their original one.

The economic model does not fully capture individual interest in citizenship because this status entails not merely a *specific* bundle of rights and duties provided by a certain political authority, but raises a more fundamental individual claim, directed towards such an authority, for general protection. In the words of US Chief Justice Warren: 'Citizenship *is* man's basic right for it is nothing less than the right to have rights. Remove this priceless possession and there remains a stateless person, disgraced and degraded in the eyes of his countrymen. He has no lawful claim to protection from any nation, and no nation may assert rights on his behalf'.[7]

The primary interest of individuals who migrate across international borders is not to choose the state that offers them the most attractive citizenship, but to avoid losing the protection of some of their most basic interests, such as security of residence, access to employment, living together with family members, retaining property and inheritance rights in their country of origin as well as an option to return there. Apart from these interests in security, family life and economic opportunities, migrants have no less important interests in social respect and symbolic recognition. These include a desire that their origins and ethnic or religious identities be respected rather than merely tolerated and that they be recognized as equal members within a host society where they have settled for good, or a society of origin to which they plan to return. This bundle of interests that can be attributed to migrants has specific implications for citizenship policies.

Firstly, although migrants need not be interested in acquiring the citizenship of countries with which they have not already established important social ties, they do have an interest that their citizenship of origin includes mobility rights that enable them to travel freely and to seek protection or better opportunities in other countries. This desire conflicts with contemporary visa regimes and differential restrictions on residence or access to employment that create a global hierarchy of mobility rights attached to different nationalities (Carens, 1992: 26; Dummett, 1992; Shachar, 2003). Secondly, first generation migrants have an obvious interest in full rights of citizenship in the country where they settle. But they also have an interest in being able to choose whether to acquire this country's nationality through naturalization. Today, this choice is constrained through discretionary decisions by authorities and restrictive conditions for naturalization. Among these are receiving country requirements for renunciation of a previous nationality in naturalizations and source country policies of depriving those who naturalize abroad of their original nationality. A general acceptance of multiple nationality would therefore offer much greater scope for individual choice (Franck, 1999: 63).

Migrants' choices are, however, also constrained by automatic *ius soli* citizenship for their children born in the country of residence. Some countries respect individual choice in this regard by making *ius soli* acquisition dependent on parental registration, or on the child's own declaration at the age of majority. Others make *ius soli* automatic, which can be argued on grounds that children born in the territory are no longer immigrants and must not be distinguished from other native-born citizens.[8] While state practices and reasonable views on the extent of choice for the second generation vary to some extent, virtually all states agree that the country of residence must not impose its nationality on first-generation migrants against their will. Historically, state interests in full jurisdiction over the permanent resident population had led some European states in the nineteenth century to naturalize foreign nationals after several years of residence without asking for their consent.[9] This automatic ius domicili has been abandoned, not so much because it was seen to interfere with individual freedom, but because it infringed upon other states' rights to provide diplomatic protection and to control their nationals abroad.

Ruth Rubio-Marín (2000) suggests that a democratic interest in inclusive citizenship may justify reintroducing automatic ius domicili under the condition that migrants are allowed to retain their nationality of origin. The most obvious objection against this interesting proposal is that satisfying the condition is not within the power of a single receiving country. It requires also compliance by all source countries many of which still automatically withdraw nationality from their emigrants who naturalize abroad. Even if this obstacle could be overcome by establishing an international norm of general acceptance of dual nationality, automatic naturalization might conflict with interests of migrants in being able to determine themselves their formal citizenship status. Imposing the host state's nationality on first-generation migrants may also conflict with their orientation to return to their country of origin and with their own perception of their nationality of origin as an identity that cannot be combined with another citizenship.

Transnational migration creates a broad variety of different identities and affiliations to source and receiving countries. Migrants need rights to access or retain both countries' nationalities but they must also be able to make their own choices about their legal status. Any regime that imposes a uniform citizenship status on all such migrants will violate some legitimate individual interests. A broader scope for individual choice in this area should therefore constrain traditional interpretations of state sovereignty and national self-determination. This need not, however, result in a license to shop for the most attractive citizenships worldwide, which could undermine the integrity of democratic polities.

Democratic Societies

A fourth kind of legitimate interests in citizenship policies, besides those of the international community, of states and of migrants, can be attributed to democratic societies in which citizenship refers not merely to a legal status of formal nationality but also to full and equal membership in a self-governing polity. Democratic interests in citizenship policy reflect the three basic concerns of inclusion, equality and cohesion. These go far beyond international law concerns with human rights and peaceful relations between states, they are not reducible to state interests in sovereign determination of their own nationals, and they conflict with excessive interpretations of migrants' individual self-determination.

Since citizenship in a democratic society is not merely an empty legal status, worries about its devaluation need to be taken seriously. Recent debates about naturalization in the US and several Western European states reveal three different views about the value of citizenship that lead to contrasting policy recommendations. A first view holds that citizenship is devalued through easy access and recommends that naturalization should be made more difficult. The value of citizenship is thus expressed in terms of transaction costs imposed on those who want to acquire this status. The second view sees the value of citizenship in its relative utility, that is in the additional rights and other benefits that citizens enjoy compared to non-citizen residents. From this perspective, citizenship is devalued when rights are extended to foreign nationals. The third view identifies the specific value of citizenship with intrinsic benefits of membership that result from a commitment towards the democratic community. From this perspective, citizenship is devalued if it is chosen for purely instrumental reasons in order to gain additional benefits. In order to decide which of these views is better compatible with democratic principles one must consider how the three norms of inclusion, equality and cohesion ought to be applied to citizenship policies.

Democratic inclusion requires that all those permanently subjected to the laws of a state should be represented in the making of these laws. From this perspective it is illegitimate to exclude long-term immigrants from access to full citizenship by raising high hurdles for naturalization. Inclusion is, however, also diminished when migrants themselves choose not to naturalize. A receiving state that wants to maximize inclusion can respond to such reluctance in three different ways. First, it can naturalize them against their will. Second, it can create incentives for naturalization by depriving long-term foreign residents of important rights. Third, it can promote naturalization through public campaigns while accepting the free choice of those who decline this offer. As discussed above, the first strategy may seem attractive but conflicts with individual liberty. The second strategy must be rejected, too, since in a democratic perspective the value of inclusion must be balanced against the value of equality. Depriving long-term immigrants of secure residence, family reunification, access to employment or social welfare benefits may increase naturalization rates but will at the same time enhance the legitimacy gap of democratic rule by depriving a disenfranchised class of residents of fundamental rights.

The third strategy of promoting naturalization would entail making it relatively easy to meet the requirements but also making it a truly voluntary choice by reducing the gap between the benefits and rights attached to foreign resident and citizen status respectively. This will generally have a negative impact on immigrants' propensity to naturalize, as can be seen in extremely low naturalization rates of European Union citizens residing in other member states (De Voretz and Pivnenko, 2004). While diminishing the transaction costs and the relative benefits of citizenship this strategy maximizes its 'commitment value' since naturalizing immigrants are then seen to choose full membership in their host society voluntarily. In the wider society this promotes a civic republican view of citizenship as entailing commitments towards the common good of the polity. Encouraging naturalization under conditions of easy access and equal protection for long-term residents is therefore the most consistent response that addresses all three democratic concerns about inclusion, equality and cohesion.

When it comes to citizenship policies for the second and subsequent generations born in the country of immigrant parents or ancestry, concerns about inclusion must be much stronger than countervailing freedom of choice. As discussed above, *ius soli* for the second generation may be qualified by respecting parental choice or the children's own choice at the age of majority. This argument is no longer plausible for the third generation whose parents had themselves been born in the country. Maintaining a regime of pure *ius sanguinis* in a country of immigration cannot be justified by pointing to the possibility of ordinary or facilitated naturalization procedures for native-born children of foreign descent. The need to apply for membership is no longer defensible for those who have no other country to whom they are linked by birth and primary socialization. Imposing naturalization requirements on a native-born population supports also an ethnic conception of nationhood among the wider population that stigmatizes persons of immigrant descent as outsiders within the political community. This is incompatible with a democratic conception of cohesion in a diverse society.

Any principle of inclusion also implies exclusion at some point. Making birth and residence in the state territory, rather than descent, the primary criterion of inclusion, suggests that citizens who have left for good or who are born abroad should no longer be able to claim full membership in their country of origin. Some states, among them the USA, make sure that only first generation migrants transmit their original nationality to children born abroad,[10] others require that nationals born abroad who want to retain their citizenship must themselves establish residence in their parents' country of origin until a certain age. Many countries with a strong tradition of *ius sanguinis*, however, allow their foreign nationals abroad to transmit their citizenship to foreign-born children over several generations. In practical terms, the effect of this policy is quite limited if these countries also withdraw nationality from those who naturalize abroad. However, from a democratic perspective it is preferable to adopt a symmetric policy of automatic *ius soli* for the third generation in the country and automatic expiry of *ius sanguinis* for the third generation abroad, with a possibility to reacquire citizenship for those who 'return' to their grandparents' country of origin.

How to interpret equality of citizenship depends on the prior question of inclusion and its limits. In the past, it was quite common to distinguish between citizens by birth and by naturalization. The latter were deprived of access to certain high public offices. A well-known example of such political disabilities is the requirement of the US Constitution that 'no person except a natural born citizen of the United States shall be eligible to the office of President' (Art. II, section I). More far reaching 'political disabilities' of naturalized citizens have been eliminated from the constitutions of several European countries during the final quarter of the twentieth century. Contemporary views of citizenship make it generally illegitimate to have several classes of citizens with distinct individual rights.[11]

At the same time, rights of citizenship are clearly limited by the territorial jurisdiction of states. Nationals living abroad cannot enjoy many of the benefits granted to citizens, and also to foreign residents, in the territory. This applies to all three dimensions of citizenship identified by T.H. Marshall in 1949 (Marshall, 1965). With regard to *civil citizenship*, it is obvious that foreign nationals' basic liberties, such as private property rights as well as freedom of speech and association, must be primarily protected by the state of residence. However, countries of origin do have a right to provide their nationals abroad with diplomatic protection, and international law does not permit governments to expropriate foreign nationals without compensation or to draft them into military service (Goodin, 1988: 668).

Social citizenship rights include provision of public services in education and health care that are obviously tied to residence, but also financial benefits of different kinds that may be transferred to citizens abroad. The general rule adopted by most welfare states is that retirement pensions can be transferred (by citizens as well as by foreign residents returning to their countries of origin), while payments from unemployment insurance and means-tested social assistance are only granted for those living in the country.

The core rights of *political citizenship* are the right to vote and to stand as candidate in democratic elections. Migrants have a dual interest in political participation and representation in their country of origin and the society where they have settled. The extent to which states are willing to accommodate these interests varies widely. From a normative perspective there are also three hard questions to be answered: Should source countries extend active voting rights to expatriates? Should receiving states extend voting rights to foreign nationals who have an opportunity to naturalize? And, finally, should migrants enjoy simultaneously voting rights and representation in two countries?

In most contemporary democracies only citizens who are residents can vote in political elections. There is, however, a growing number of countries that allow their expatriates to participate. The most restrictive rule is that they must travel home to vote on election day. Other countries, among them the US and several Latin American and Caribbean states, have widened the inclusion of emigrants by allowing them to cast absentee ballots from abroad (Itzigsohn, 2000). The most far-reaching representation was introduced by Italy in 1999. Twenty-four seats in the national parliament are set aside for representation of the expatriate constituency.

From a democratic perspective, two objections can be raised against absentee franchise and representation (Bauböck, 2003). Firstly, emigrants are not exposed to election campaigns and may therefore be less well informed about candidates and issues. And, secondly, they seem to be freeriders who neither pay taxes[12] nor have to bear the consequences of political decisions that they influence through their vote. They might therefore also vote in a less responsible way. Both objections are convincing to the extent that emigrants have cut their ties to countries of origin. In this case, however, they are also unlikely to cast a vote.

Since voting from abroad generally takes a special effort (such as applications for registration, certification through witnesses or trips to embassies), those who care to vote signal a special interest in the outcome. Moreover, many first generation migrants do have a stake in the future of their country of origin because of family ties or return intentions. Finally, modern information technologies allow expatriates to be as well informed about election issues as citizens living in source countries. Candidates sometimes even carry their campaigns abroad to mobilize financial support and votes among larger concentrations of emigrant communities. These arguments respond to the general concern that absentee voting undermines the integrity of the democratic process. They apply, however, only to first generation emigrants and not to their children and grandchildren, who often inherit their forebears' citizenship through *ius sanguinis* without maintaining close ties to these countries. Absentee voting should therefore generally be extended only to those who have been born, or have spent some time, in the country of origin.

The second question raised above is about voting rights for foreign nationals. On the one hand, all the objections against involving external citizens in democratic decisions must count as arguments for including immigrants. They pay taxes, they are exposed to elections campaigns and they have a stake in election outcomes since they are deeply affected by the laws of their host states. Yet democratic inclusion of immigrants can be achieved in two ways: by attaching voting rights to residence rather than nationality, or by offering immigrants naturalization. On the one hand, excluding foreign nationals from the general franchise is not obviously discriminatory if and only if naturalization is easy – that is, is an individual entitlement after no more than five years of legal residence, is not costly and does not require renouncing a previous nationality. On the other hand, neither is it obvious that long-term foreign residents must be excluded from elections under conditions where they could choose to naturalize. In New Zealand, they can vote in parliamentary elections but cannot run as candidates. In Britain, Commonwealth and Irish citizens can both vote and be elected to the Westminister Parliament. There is little evidence that this extension of the vote undermines democracy in these countries. In comparative perspective, these are, however, exceptions. There is no trend towards granting general voting rights to foreign residents.

There is a broader trend towards a local franchise for non-citizens. Eight of the fifteen old EU member states currently allow not only EU citizens, but all foreign residents to vote in local elections and some of the new member states are currently reforming their laws in this sense. The European Union Commission has recently proposed a status of 'civic citizenship' for long-term resident foreign nationals in the Union that would entail voting rights in municipal elections (COM (2003) 336 final). Outside the EU such a local franchise exists in Norway and some Swiss cantons. In the US a similar reform has recently been debated in New York city (*New York Times*, 8 April 2004). The Council of Europe has adopted a 1992 Convention on the Participation of Foreigners in Public Life at Local Level, which came into force in May 1997. Article 6 (1) provides for the suffrage and eligibility for all foreign residents after five years.

Why is the case for a non-citizen franchise more powerful at the local level than at the national one (Aleinkoff and Klusmeyer, 2002: 51–4)? A first argument is that immigrants have specific interests in local politics and develop local identities. Most contemporary migrants are attracted to big cities and the economic and cultural opportunities they offer. In receiving countries immigrants tend to develop an urban identity that can be easily combined with an ongoing national affiliation to their countries of origin. Even those who are not ready to fully join their host country's political community, feel that they have a stake in the city. This sense of belonging to the city can be expressed by participating in local elections. As members of low-income groups immigrants are also particularly affected by policy areas, such as public housing, health services and education, where municipal authorities tend to have strong competencies. Granting them the franchise at local level thus provides political representation in decisions that affect some of their most immediate interests and offers a first step of political participation that better prepares immigrants for naturalization.

Second, some reasons for excluding non-citizens from the national elections do not apply at the local level. In contrast with a national polity, local political communities have no immigration control that distinguishes between citizens and non-citizens. The right of free movement within the territory of a democratic state is in general not tied to nationality. Membership in a municipality or federal province shifts automatically with a change of residence. For nationals of the country the local franchise is based on residence and does not require that they apply for 'naturalization' in the local community. Excluding foreign nationals from the same direct access to local citizenship diminishes local autonomy by imposing a distinction that makes sense only from a nation-state perspective but not from a local one.

The third question is about simultaneous voting and representation in two or more countries. Migrants may enjoy an absentee franchise in their country of origin as well as local voting rights in their city of residence. If they naturalize and retain their previous nationality they may also vote in national elections in both countries. This seems like an unjustified privilege compared to native singular citizens. However, multiple nationality and voting rights for migrants may very well reflect the fact that their personal fate is closely linked to two different states. This argument seems to create a conflict between democratic inclusion and equality. Yet the 'one person–one vote' principle merely implies that people can vote only once in each election and that their votes should be counted equally in calculating the election outcome. Votes cast by dual nationals in two different countries have the same weight as those of other citizens in each of the elections. Concerns about democratic equality are thus no reason to diminish inclusion.

Principles for Citizenship Policies

The interests of states, of the international community, of migrants and of democratic societies in citizenship policies are partly internally divergent and partly conflict with each other. The task is to distinguish illegitimate from legitimate interests and to develop policies that adequately balance the latter against each other. Table 10.1 links these particular interests to principles that should be compatible with each other and could thus form guidelines for inclusive citizenship policies.

Principles of this kind can never fully determine specific policies that must be adapted to particular contexts and circumstances. They define either minimum requirements for legitimate policies or goals for desirable ones. In democratic politics, principles will always be open to conflicting interpretations. The following list of principles is also not meant to be fully exhaustive. It is instead oriented towards resolving conflicts between specific interests in citizenship policies discussed above.

Table 10.1   Relevant interests and principles for citizenship policies

Arenas and agents	Relevant interests	Principles
International community	Conflict avoidance	Generalizability of policies
States	Self-determination	Integrity of territorial jurisdiction
Migrants	Freedom of choice	Voluntary acquisition and renunciation of citizenship
Democratic societies	Inclusion, equality, cohesion	Stakeholdership in access and loss

Generalizability

States should refrain from adopting citizenship laws and policies that would inherently conflict with similar laws and policies adopted by other states. Strongly asymmetric policies towards foreign residents in the country and towards a state's own nationals living abroad violate this condition. For example, a state that refuses to release its own nationals when they naturalize abroad, or permits them to retain their nationality when acquiring another one, cannot consistently require that immigrants who obtain its nationality must abandon another one they have previously held. Similarly, states ought to agree on rules for multiple citizenship that can be accepted by all. In the US toleration of dual nationality has emerged from the implicit assumption that anybody who has naturalized and sworn allegiance to the US is deemed to have lost his or her previous nationality. This promotes an attitude that in case of conflict, US citizenship will always take priority, not only within the territory but also abroad. However, conflict is unavoidable if migrants' source and receiving countries both take this stance. The regulation of conflicts in case of multiple nationality must therefore rely on generalizable rules. In some matters (such as personal status law) the choice of jurisdiction may be left to individuals, while in others where there is a conflict between citizen duties (for example tax paying and military service) the nationality of principal residence should prevail.

Not all apparently asymmetric policies fail, however, to satisfy a criterion of generalizability. A *ius soli* regime inside the state's territory can be consistently combined with *ius sanguinis* for children born to citizens abroad if, and only if, the state in question accepts that this combination necessarily generates multiple nationality.

Integrity of Territorial Jurisdiction

The purely formal criterion of generalizability does not explain why territorial jurisdiction over residents should generally predominate over extraterritorial jurisdiction over citizens abroad. The principle that territorial state boundaries must be given greater weight than those of legal nationality emerges from state claims to sovereignty as well as from democratic imperatives of inclusion. It implies that the areas in which foreign nationals are exempted from territorial jurisdiction must be well-defined and the rights of states to intervene on behalf of their nationals abroad must be rather narrowly circumscribed. Included in this predominance of territorial jurisdiction are receiving state decisions to grant a foreign national asylum or citizenship even if these are not recognized by the source country. Such decisions must, however, rest on the consent of the individual concerned. Imposing a new nationality on first generation immigrants against their will could entitle the source state to intervene on their behalf.

In spite of public anxieties and anti-immigrant political rhetoric, legally admitted refugees, economic and family migrants who retain their citizenship do not pose a threat to the territorial integrity of the receiving country. This may be different in the case of some historic national minorities who try to establish links of citizenship with external kin states. Dual citizenship should be seen as entirely adequate for migrants who have multiple social ties and political stakes in source countries and host states. Secondly, it may also be acceptable for historic ethnic minorities that define themselves as diasporas oriented towards an external homeland and do not aim for self-government in the state where they live. Thirdly, dual citizenship may in some cases be a useful instrument for protecting minorities from persecution and oppression and offering them an escape route of emigration. However, it is not generally acceptable for national minorities that have been granted extensive territorial autonomy. Claims of multiple citizenship and territorial autonomy should be seen as mutually incompatible. They would create fears in the host society about irredentist threats to its territorial integrity that cannot be easily dismissed as unreasonable. A general toleration for multiple citizenship in contexts of migration may therefore need to be qualified in contexts where national minorities claim collective self-determination.

Voluntary Acquisition and Renunciation of Citizenship

State interests in control over their nationals must be balanced against individual choice. This chapter has argued that migrants should be offered an option to acquire the citizenship of their country of long-term residence but should not be coerced to do so either by imposition or by depriving them of fundamental rights as long as they retain their foreign nationality.

In the liberal tradition, states have often been regarded as if they were voluntary associations of their citizens. If this view were accepted, it would follow that immigrants have no individual claim of access to citizenship and that states have no right whatsoever to prevent individuals from renouncing their citizenship. In current international law and democratic state practice the latter right is, however, qualified by a requirement of emigration and by the need to avoid statelessness. These are reasonable conditions. Statelessness is not only a problem for international relations but conflicts also with fundamental interests of individuals whom it deprives of basic protection. Refusing to release individuals from nationality into statelessness even when the latter appears to be freely chosen can be justified not only on paternalistic grounds, that is by claiming better insight into the individuals' long-term interests than she herself has, but also as a protection of democratic societies against freeriders. This latter argument applies also to the choice of internal renunciation in case where another citizenship is acquired. The motivations of a migrant who does not want to exchange a present citizenship for that of the host country are different from those of a person who wants to get rid of the citizenship of a country where he or she intends to stay.

With these qualifications, individual freedom of exit from citizenship covers two specific claims: first, the right to be released from citizenship under conditions of residence in the country whose citizenship has been, or will be acquired. Many countries' nationality laws (among them most Arab states) violate this fundamental human right by embracing the ancient doctrine of perpetual allegiance or by deriving their citizenship explicitly from ties of blood that cannot be altered or severed. Second, protection against coercive withdrawal of citizenship. In this respect one can distinguish different degrees of protection. The strongest one must hold for individuals who would thereby become stateless. Reservations against withdrawing citizenship from legal residents in the territory of the state concerned even if these hold, or can acquire, another state's nationality should not be much weaker. These prohibitions correspond with symmetric restrictions on voluntary renunciation. For multiple nationals, exceptions are justified in case of fraudulent naturalization.

However, withdrawal of citizenship should not be used as a punishment in case of criminal convictions, since this would merely imply shifting the burden of dealing with such criminals towards other states to which they have no genuine links. In 1999 Germany introduced a requirement of choosing before the age of 23 one of two nationalities acquired at birth. This is less objectionable than automatic withdrawal of German citizenship would be, but it is still a rule that interferes with legitimate individual interests and that is not justified by any reasonable concerns about the dangers of holding two nationalities. Weaker norms of protection apply to withdrawal of citizenship from those living abroad who possess their host states' nationality or would gain immediate access to it when they lose their external citizenship.

Stakeholder Citizenship

Democratic concerns about inclusion, equality and cohesion suggest that the rights of foreign residents, their access to citizenship as well as protection against its loss should be generally determined by a stakeholder principle. Providing safeguards for the enjoyment of individual rights is the responsibility of those states in whose territory the interests protected by the respective right are anchored and exercised. A more extensive claim to full membership arises when the social conditions and circumstances an individual finds herself in, or has chosen to live in, link her individual interests to the common good of a particular political community. Birth or long-term settlement in a state's territory indicate a relevant social tie of this kind that gives an individual a stake in the polity. Similarly, birth or close family links and life plans that include a return option substantiate a claim to retain the citizenship of a country of emigration.

This principle extends the reasoning of the International Court of Justice in the 1955 Nottebohm case in which the court required proof of a 'genuine link' between an individual and a state that naturalizes this individual (ICJ 4, 1955, WL 1). A stakeholder principle recognizes therefore limits for individual choice and condemns state practices of selling their citizenship to the best bidders. At the same time, it constrains state discretion in naturalizations and withdrawal by defending individuals' rights of access to a new nationality as well as of retaining a nationality of origin as long as they have significant ties to that country. Stakeholder citizenship responds also to democratic concerns about cohesion by defining the boundaries of democratic societies in such a way that they reflect the social reality of international mobility without becoming indeterminate. Migration does not dissolve the boundaries of membership but creates increasingly overlapping citizenship between democratic polities.

The principle also sums up the argument for local voting rights for foreign residents who have acquired a stake in the municipality. It may be invoked negatively when denying national voting rights of foreign nationals who are not prepared to commit themselves fully to the host state by applying for naturalization. One can, furthermore, consider limits to the possibility of holding multiple stakes in more than one political community. Multiple nationals who are elected as members of parliament or accept

Table 10.2 Acquisition of nationality at birth and by naturalization in Western Europe (15 old EU states, Norway and Switzerland)

Country	Regular naturalization		Ius soli		Acquisition after marriage with a citizen	
	Minimum years of residence	Toleration of dual nationality	At birth for 2nd or 3rd generation	Ius soli entitlement after birth for 2nd generation	Minimum residence	Minimum duration of marriage
Austria	10, or 4 for EU/ EEA citizens	No	No	No	1 year marriage and 4 years residence, or 2 years marriage and 3 years residence, or 5 years marriage without residence requirement	
Belgium	3	Yes	3rd generation if registered by a parent	10 years residence of parents, registration until age 12	3 years	6 months
Denmark	7 or 2 for Nordic citizens	No	No	No	6–8 years residence and 1–3 years marriage	
Finland	6	Yes	No	6 years residence: age 18–22	4 years	3 years
France	5	Yes	Automatic for 3rd generation	5 years residence after age 11: until age 18	No minimum residence	1 year
Germany	8	No; with many exemptions	2nd generation if a parent has permanent residence title and 8 years of residence[b]	No	3 years	2 years
Greece	8	Renunciation required in practice	No	No	–	–
Ireland	4	Yes	2nd generation except asylum seekers[c]	Yes	1 year for marriage before 30 November 2002	3 years for marriage before 30 November 2002
Italy	10 or 4 for EU/ EEA citizens	Yes	No	Continuous residence: age 18	6 months residence or 3 years marriage	
Luxembourg	10	No	No	5 years: after age 18	3 years	3 years

Table 10.2 cont'd

Country	Regular naturalization			Ius soli		Acquisition after marriage with a citizen	
	Minimum years of residence	Toleration of dual nationality	At birth for 2nd or 3rd generation	Ius soli entitlement after birth for 2nd generation	Minimum residence	Minimum duration of marriage
Netherlands	5	No, but many exemptions	3rd generation if a parent has main residence in NL and was also born in NL to a parent with main residence there	Continuous residence: age 18–25	No minimum residence	3 years
Norway	7, less for Nordic citizens	No	No	No	7 years minimum residence (may be shortened)	–
Portugal	10, or 6 for Lusophone citizens	Yes	2nd generation if parent resident 10 years, or 6 for Lusophone citizen	No	No minimum residence	3 years
Sweden	5	Yes	No	No	3 years residence and permanent residence title	2 years
Spain	10 , 2 for citizens of Portugal and some Hispanic states	No, except citizens of Portugal and some Hispanic states	No	1 year residence: at age 18–20	1 year	1 year
						No minimum duration
Switzerland[c]	12	Yes	No	No	5 years residence and 3 years marriage, or 6 years residence und close ties to Switzerland	
UK	5	Yes	2nd generation if a parent has been permanent resident for 4 years	If a parent acquires permanent residence and if continuous residency: until age 10	3 years	

Table 10.2 cont'd

Notes:

a) *Ius soli* entitlement refers here only to birth in the territory as a relevant ground for citizenship acquisition after birth. Several states have special provisions for acquisition by minors who have not been born in the territory but have lived there for a certain time. These have not been included in the table.

b) Dual nationals by birth must choose one nationality between age 18 and 23.

c) The present Irish *ius soli* regime will be changed as a result of a referendum in June 2004. The new nationality law has, however, not yet been passed at the time of writing.

Sources: Data collected by Harald Waldrauch, Rainer Münz and Rainer Bauböck; Aleinikoff and Klusmeyer (2000, 2001), Davy (2001), D'Amato and Wanner (2003), Hansen and Weil (2002), Münz and Ulrich (2003), Waldrauch (2001), Weil (2001), Schweizerischer Bundesrat (2001), various websites.

other high public offices may be reasonably expected to renounce their second citizenship. Active voting in separate elections in two different countries need not violate the democratic principle of one person one vote. In contrast, holding a democratic mandate creates a special accountability towards the larger democratic community (and not merely towards a specific electoral constituency, which may be an immigrant community). It is therefore not easily compatible with simultaneous commitments towards another state. If all citizens are stakeholders in a democratic community, then their representatives are trustees who are exclusively accountable towards them.

Conclusion

The discussion of four types of interests in citizenship has shown that these perspectives can be combined with each other in the search for defensible policies. They also need to be combined, since each of these interests taken separately is inadequate or insufficient. On the one hand, state interests in sovereignty and self-determination are the most important obstacle for harmonizing nationality laws in such a way that they do not conflict with each other. On the other hand, international law does not provide a sufficient basis for inclusive citizenship policies that must be argued from a domestic democratic perspective. Democratic citizenship is, however, torn into different directions by conflicts between inclusion, equality, and cohesion. A stakeholder principle can help to find the right balance. Citizens are stakeholders in a democratic community. This idea should not only be applied to current members but also to decisions which outsiders have a right to become citizens and which citizens no longer have a claim to membership. Yet even a democratic perspective is not fully adequate unless it takes into account migrants' interests in choosing between, or combining, alternative memberships. The migrant experience means that stakes derived from birth, childhood, family ties, present residence and future destination are spread over several countries. Taking this into account leads to a more flexible approach to inclusive citizenship in liberal democracies.

Notes

[1] I am grateful to Kristof Tamas for his suggestions for revisions and to Harald Waldrauch for compiling data for Table 10.2.

[2] See Table 10.2 for an overview over current legislation on the acquisition of nationality in Western Europe.

[3] *Ius sanguinis* refers to citizenship acquisition by descent from a citizen parent. Internationally, *ius sanguinis* is the dominant rule for determining citizenship at birth.

[4] *Ius soli* refers to citizenship acquisition derived from birth in the territory. The purest form of *ius soli* is today found in the USA where anybody born in the territory automatically acquires US citizenship.

5 The best-known cases are the Law of Return in Israel and the German Basic Law that provide for automatic access to nationality for co-ethnics upon arrival. Policies of facilitated access to citizenship for immigrants who share a cultural or ethnic identity with the native majority population, are however, relatively widespread.

6 See, for example: http://www.escapeartist.com/passports/passports.htm, http://www.goccp. com/ENG/secondcitizen.HTM, http://www.secondpassports.2itb.com/, all last accessed 20 October 2004.

7 *Perez v. Brownell*, 356 U.S. 44, 64–65.

8 See Table 10.2.

9 For example, between 1811 and 1833 foreign nationals automatically acquired Austrian nationality after ten years of residence.

10 Under current law, US citizenship is acquired by a child abroad only if a parent has resided in the US for five years, two of which after the age of 14.

11 In Great Britain there are several special classes of citizens among populations in overseas territories not all of whom have the right to enter Britain.

12 Only few countries tax their expatriates' income earned abroad in the same way as the US does.

Chapter 11

Legal and Irregular Migration for Employment in Italy and France[1]

Luca Einaudi

The Italian debate on immigration in the last three decades has been dominated by two issues – the management of legal flows for the purpose of employment and the control of irregular flows. This particular focus is typical of a phase of tumultuous development of immigration and Italy indeed was transformed from a legal presence of 148,000 foreigners in 1970 to 2.7 million in 2004. This is very similar to what happened in Spain, Portugal and Greece, all countries which changed from source to destination countries. From this point of view it is possible to present the Italian experience as somehow representative of a new Southern European informal migration regime. The delicate political issue of how to organize some legal and selected economic migration and efficiently curb irregular flows has not been solved. Despite general opinion, however, some substantial improvements have taken place. These issues have played a key role in France as well. The 1974 decision to curtail labour migration to France, never challenged substantially thereafter, has given a more prominent status to the issue of integration without diminishing the emphasis on border control and expulsion policies.

This chapter analyses the parallel developments of the policies of managed labour migration and clandestine migration in Italy and France in the last 30 years. It attempts to assess the relative success of both policies in relation to their initial goals and to their ultimate objectives, coming to some paradoxical conclusions.

General Development of Migration in Italy

Italy became the destination of unskilled workers and later of their families from the second half of the 1960s onwards, with a substantial acceleration in the second half of the 1980s. Their arrival, caused by economic growth and social transformation, was not immediately accompanied by adequate measures of management or control. In 1980 only 200,000 residence permits were issued to foreigners in Italy. To this figure, more than 300,000 illegal workers had to be added, according to the trade unions, and a little less according to the research institute Censis. By 1990 the number of residence permits had reached 548,000. The one million mark was passed in 1997. The last estimate of the number of regular migrants in Italy is 2.7 million in 2004, according to Caritas statistical report.[2]

The development of immigration in Italy has been driven by labour migrants and followed at some distance by family reunification, leading to permanent settlement. This is, of course, a normal pattern for a country changing its status from a source to a destination of migratory flows. In 1990 fewer than 400,000 work-related permits were in place for foreigners compared to almost 1.5 million in 2003.[3] Family-related permits increased more regularly from 98,000 in 1990 to 533,000 in 2003.

The geographical distribution of immigrants within Italy has evolved markedly from 1990 onwards. Migrants have become concentrated in the most dynamic parts of the country. The 'enlarged Northeast', a region covering all the territories east of the line Milan-Ancona, increased its share of the immigrant population of the whole country from 32 to 52 per cent between 1990 and 2002. This result is not surprising, given that it is the most export-driven and economically dynamic part of the country. Unemployment in that area has fallen substantially over the last decade and is now below 4 per cent. Demographic decline is sharp but employment opportunities remain substantial. By 2002 over 11 per cent of new legal employment contracts in Italy concerned foreigners and that rate exceeded 20 per cent in many areas of northeastern Italy.

Foreigners are particularly concentrated in manufacturing, construction, agriculture, cleaning services, hotels and tourism and especially in domestic care. The sectors in which they are employed are also characterized by an individual contact with families or small and very small firms, where tax evasion is high and the proportion of irregular work is higher than average (Anastasia and Sestito, 2003: 11–12). Overall estimates of the Italian underground economy's size are controversial and vary between 14 and 29 per cent of GDP. All types of estimates, however, are higher than those concerning France or Northern Europe. It is therefore quite clear that immigrants working in the informal sector play an important economic role. They also play a social role, given that they sustain the Italian families' and women's employment opportunities, assisting an aging population and taking care of children where otherwise childcare provided by the Italian Welfare State is lacking.

Given the strong impetus of migratory movements towards northern Italy and the overwhelming share of workers, it is not surprising that the regulation of legal flows of workers became a leading issue. I will now explore the parallel evolution of the policies to manage inflows of foreign workers and to control borders and secure expulsions of irregular migrants. It is a process of learning by doing, which started with an almost total lack of legislative instruments and administrative capacity. They were developed slowly but with some level of success. The figures show, as we will see later, an impressive parallel growth of legal economic immigration, of irregular immigration and of the capacity to trace and expel a substantial share of the latter category. The paradox is that the growing efficiency of the policies of control has not brought about any substantial long-term reduction in the number of clandestine immigrants in Italy. The legislative, economic and political path followed by Spain in the same period is almost identical, both in the solutions attempted and the disappointments which have followed.

The Difficult Road to Legal Employment in Italy

Labour migration in Italy was initially regulated by secondary legislation giving the Ministry of Labour power to deny authorizations on the basis of general conditions of the labour market. In 1982, labour inflows were officially suspended pending regularization and the approval of an organic law on the subject. The new law of 1986 (No. 943) introduced a system based on a monthly census of all employment offers left vacant, followed by the programming of foreign workers' demand by regional commissions.

In 1990, after several years of sustained economic growth and a rapid development of immigration, the so-called Martelli law introduced a system of quotas (Magni, 1995). The quotas were meant to facilitate and simplify the arrival of workers. The Deputy Prime Minister Martelli did not expect any form of competition between domestic and foreign workers, given that the latter tended to be confined to positions abandoned by the existing workforce. The quotas were jointly decided by several government departments, in consultation with the employers and the trade unions. Ultimately the implementation of the quota system was delayed by the need to digest the effects of the regularization and by the economic slowdown which started in 1992. The administration continued to follow the 1986 rules, accepting only applications left unfilled by nationals after public advertising.

Only in 1995 a new wave of political discussion on excessive illegal flows and the increase of criminality led to the first implementation of quotas, but at the low level of 25,000 foreign workers a year. Again the real opportunity for immigrants was a new regularization, which was concluded after 244,000 permits were delivered. The quotas declined further to 20,000 in 1997.

In 1998 a major effort to revive the quota system was undertaken by the centre-left government with the Turco-Napolitano law. Following the principle that the availability of an effective legal route to employment in Italy would discourage the use of criminal organizations of smugglers and traffickers, the government decided to expand the quotas and simplify the mechanism. Quotas would be fixed according to estimates of labour market needs, evaluated by the labour ministry and discussed with the social partners and parliament. In order to facilitate job matching and personal contacts between employers and workers prior to the finalization of the contract, the law introduced job search permits.

As usual, the desire to implement the new law starting with a clean sheet and removing the consequences of past mistakes led to a new regularization, as requested by the trade unions to parliament. The quotas were increased very substantially and reached a total of 83,000 in 2001, 50,000 of which were for permanent residence and 33,000 for seasonal work. Demand for foreign workers, however, was booming, thanks to a dramatic recovery of the labour market despite very moderate growth. Quotas never seemed to be sufficient.

While in opposition, the centre-right had criticized the excessive generosity of policies in favour of immigrants, the absence of controls on legal workers in the underground economy and of illegal workers entering Italy unchecked. Once elected to office, the centre-right introduced in 2002 a new law under the name of the leaders of the Northern League and the National Alliance, Bossi and Fini. Its guiding principle was that controls had to be tightened and arrivals could only take place after an employment contract had been concluded. A job market test of 30 days was reintroduced before an authorization could be delivered for the arrival of a new non-EU worker. Job search permits were abolished but otherwise the quota system was not significantly altered.

This time the legalization was introduced only after a protracted discussion in the coalition. The Catholic parties supported it, responding to pressure from the church and the voluntary sector, while the Northern League opposed it. To everybody's surprise it generated over 700,000 applications, almost three times more than any of the previous operations of the same type, revealing that irregular presence in Italy had increased more than experts understood. Given its size, the pressure to obtain more quotas subsided somewhat and total non-EU quotas were fixed at 79,500 units for the following three years, with a growing share for seasonal work. In 2004, however, total quotas were increased substantially because, after the enlargement of the EU, Italy added 36,000 authorizations for the new EU member countries, bringing the year's total to 115,500. In 2005 the authorizations available for new EU members were raised to 79,500 (a large part of which have not been used due to lack of demand) and the total to 179,000. As a consequence non-EU workers could obtain much more stable permits, given that non-seasonal workers reached 54,500 in 2005 against 11,000 in 2003. The limited success of management policies for labour migration has meant a persistent high level of illegal employment both of legal immigrants and of overstayers or purely clandestine immigrants.

The Evolution of Control Policies

The policies of containment of the last 30 years have always oscillated between repression and legalization, most frequently going side by side, but with the legalization becoming the more effective of the two. A total of more than 1.4 million immigrants received a sojourn permit thanks to a regularization between 1986 and 2002. This figure has to be compared with a total of nearly 2.2 million residence permits valid at the end of 2003. There was continuity between different government majorities in favour of a continuing reinforcement of regulations accompanied by regularization, despite the reservations or open dissent of the left wing of each coalition.

Before 1990 the legal system neither provided for adequate legal opportunities to access the Italian labour market or legal residence permits nor did it effectively close the frontiers against those without a legal status. The consequence was a slow but constant increase of irregular foreign residents, followed by periodical micro-crisis and political debate. Until the end of the 1980s such debate was never really heated and the Italian experience as an emigration country weighted against the adoption of repressive policies. Furthermore the administration was poorly equipped to deal

Table 11.1   Quotas for non-EU workers and legal inflows in Italy, 1991–2005

	Total quotas of non-EU workers			Actual legal labour inflows	
	Privileged quotas	Seasonal workers	Total quotas	Dependent workers	of which seasonal workers
1991	None	None	None	6,000	1,659
1992	None	None	None	31,630	2,788
1993	None	None	None	23,088	5,777
1994	None	None	None	22,474	7,587
1995	None	Unspecified	25,000	24,246	8,880
1996	None	Unspecified	23,000	16,619	8,449
1997	None	Unspecified	20,000	26,209	16,560
1998	None	Unspecified	58,000	27,303	20,380
1999	6,000	Unspecified	58,000	35,902	30,900
2000	18,000	Unspecified	83,000	82,115	30,328
2001	15,000	39,400	89,400	91,007	
2002	10,000	60,000	79,500	61,108	
2003	3,600	68,500	79,500	82,461	
2004	20,000	50,000	79,500		
2005	20,800	45,000	99,500		

Sources: for 1990–1997 quotas see Pastore (1998: 1054–5). For 1998–2005, see Documento programmatico triennale 2001–2003 and 2004–2006, various years of DPCM and the Decreti del Ministro del Ministero del lavoro for seasonal workers. See also the statistics of the Ministero dell'Interno. For early 1990 statistics see Bolaffi (1996: 44) and Caritas (various years). See also Baldi and de Azavedo (1999), Censis (2002) and Anastasia and Sestito (2003).

with it. In the 1970s and early 1980s the police were more concerned with terrorism than with a few illegal immigrants. Occasionally, controls would be tightened up after episodes of protest.

In the 1980s the political debate concentrated more on defending immigrants from racism and discrimination and regulating their access to work than on protecting frontiers. At the end of 1989 the Deputy Prime Minister Martelli even announced that Italy would not accede passively to the Schengen Treaty and to its excessively restrictive provisions, but rather remain more open to migratory flows. The beginning of an institutional and political debate coincided with the emergence of dissatisfaction for the lack of control of Italian cities, growing criminality and insecurity, and chaotic development of all sort of autonomous forms of immigrant work, particularly street vendors of fake products avoiding copyright and taxation (Gallino, 1989).

Ultimately the Martelli law was open on refugees, on quotas and on social rights. But the Republican Party managed to introduce some Schengen-type provisions which began to provide some instruments of frontier control. A visa regime was reintroduced and the expulsion regime became more precise and articulate. Foreigners without a legal right to remain or who had been convicted for any of a set of specific reasons were expelled. However, only those expelled for reasons of public safety or security could be escorted forcibly to the frontier by the police. All others received an order to leave the country by their own means within 15 days and could be escorted to the frontier only if they were caught not having respected such an order. In any case the foreigner could appeal in court against the decision of expulsion, during which the expulsion order was suspended.

The removal rate of immigrants ordered to leave (not counting denials of entry) grew from 3 to 23 per cent in the first year of implementation of the Martelli law, but quickly declined to a little more than 10 per cent. The clear inability of the Martelli legislation to keep under check illegal flows rapidly produced a series of attempts of reform, starting in 1991, but all failed until 1998.

In 1995 some disturbances and protests against immigrants in Turin, followed by other episodes in many major Italian cities, indicated a loss of control by the police. Most of the press described again the situation as being explosive, the left-wing review *L'Espresso* described the 'invasion of Italy', mapping it street by street in the main cities. Fears were expressed that a new criminal element was appearing through ethnically-based gangs, who appeared much more violent than their Italian predecessors (see Turani, 1995).

The Northern League, at that time in coalition with the centre-left, took up the issue and asked for tighter expulsion rules, in particular for those who were responsible or were suspected of being responsible for having committed crimes. On the left, the main coalition party, the former communist PDS, tried to soften the League's requests but agreed that some action had to be taken to reassure public opinion, so that a Decree was finally drafted.[4] To balance the expulsion measures, it included also a new regularization. Regardless of that, the Decree was still unacceptable for large sectors of the centre-left, which accused the League of xenophobia after some extreme statements about using rubber bullets against immigrants or taking their fingerprints. The Decree drafted to appease the League was never converted into law, despite being renewed five times until the end of 1996. Only the amnesty was saved by parliament.

The exclusion of Italy in 1995 from the first period of implementation of the Schengen Agreements was perceived as a major challenge. Thereafter the elaboration of a new law on immigration had as one of its key objectives a substantial increase in the efficiency of border controls, expulsion procedures and enforcement capacity, in order to fulfil the conditions for entry into the Schengen area. The centre-left had already started to accept the need for a more restrictive policy in 1995, despite the resistance of its left-wing and pro-immigrant associations.

In 1998 the centre-left government, elected without the support of the Northern League, finally passed a law – the so-called Turco-Napolitano law – in order to achieve several objectives.[5] The Turco-Napolitano law introduced a form of denial of entry exceeding the point of entry itself. Furthermore, expulsion orders could be implemented making more frequent use of police forces and no longer only if the decision was motivated by reasons of public order and public safety or by the violation of a previous order to leave. In a substantial number of circumstances, however, authorities were only given the power to order a voluntary departure within 15 days. That was the case for example with overstayers, whose visa had expired and had not been renewed, or with individuals who had arrived illegally but had valid proof of identity.

The right of appeal was guaranteed, but only in few cases did the appeal suspend the execution of the removal order. Centres for Temporary Permanence and Assistance were created as more dignified alternatives to prisons and with a maximum of 30 days in detention. They served the purpose of preventing the disappearance of immigrants awaiting identification. Judicial control would have to temper the power of the police, as well as the involvement of nongovernmental organizations (NGOs) in terms of legal assistance, health care and services. The Ministry of Interior worked with the NGOs but there were still complaints and appeals to the Constitutional Court against what some considered as an illegal deprivation of liberty. As a result of the Turco-Napolitano law the removal rate of immigrants ordered to leave (not counting denials of entry) increased very substantially, from 17 to 37 per cent between 1998 and 1999, but fell back somewhat the subsequent year. The number of people identified as expellable grew from 64,000 in 1995 to 90,000 in 2000.

The Bossi-Fini law of 2002 hardened the procedures further, making removal with the use of the police the rule and reducing the order to leave voluntarily within five days to a few exceptions. An appeal no longer suspended expulsion and the maximum period of stay in the detention centres was doubled to 60 days in order to give the police more time to ascertain the identity or at least the nationality of the foreigner. The penalty for illegal re-entry was raised from up to six months imprisonment to between six months and one year followed by expulsion. A penalty for a third illegal entry was introduced, carrying between one and four years of prison. The penalty against facilitating illegal entry into Italy was raised from up to three years of prison to between one and four years. Mandatory fingerprinting was introduced for all foreigners applying for residence permits. The number of expulsions increased further after the approval of the Bossi-Fini law, until the effects of the legalization reduced the stock of clandestine immigrants. In 2004 the Constitutional Court ruled against expulsion without a substantial judicial review of each decision.

How Effective were Control Policies in 1984–2004?

The system of privileged quotas for legal workers came off particularly well in containing illegal landings on the Italian coasts. Privileged quotas are determined in favour of a few countries with special agreements for the re-admission of illegal immigrants. Albania, Tunisia and Morocco were the first beneficiaries in 1999, but additional countries were added later. Such agreements include various forms of cooperation and assistance and are part of an integrated package, not an isolated act (Monzini et al., 2004). In most cases the agreements involve some form of technical assistance on the Italian side, for example in drafting legislation against the illegal use of high speed boats in Albania, or training of police forces. Some material assistance, such as the supply of frontier control equipment is also involved. The deal might also include some traditional development cooperation. The main component, however, is a quota of legal migration for employment, without a binding numerical level (Italy decides the level unilaterally every year). The quota is attractive because it secures a possibility of entry for employment purposes even after all other ordinary quotas have been exhausted.

The country benefiting from privileged quotas must fully cooperate in managing irregular flows of immigration and maintain a working readmission agreement, cooperate in controlling illegal departures from its territory, particularly by boat, in identifying illegal migrants held in Italian detention centres and exchange of information. The number of countries involved has increased substantially from three in 1998–1999 to 11 in 2005. The results have been quite spectacular, particularly with Albania (46,000 landings in 1999 in Puglia and only 137 in 2003) and Tunisia (from 9,000 landings in Sicily in 1998 to 2,000 in 1999). Of course the Albanian result is not entirely due to the agreement but also has to do with the economic and political developments of the country and to the shift of third country migration transit routes away from Albania.

Some results are not fully stable or are impossible to show in the data because trafficking organizations are rapidly moving their operation to nearby zones, in a continual game of hide-and-seek. The Italian government then has to negotiate further agreements with other neighbouring countries to restore the equilibrium. This was the case in the last period with Libya and Egypt which had become important transit routes for boats landing in Sicily or Calabria. The number of arrivals in Sicily increased in 2002–2003 because the organizations of human smugglers moved their centre of operation to Libya.

Figures 11.1 and 11.2 concerning expulsions and the number of identified irregular migrants suggest several conclusions. First, there is a strong long-term upwards tendency in the number of immigrants identified and expelled. The absolute numbers increased particularly after the 1990, 1998 and 2002 immigration laws. The only years showing a decline are those following regularizations, when most migrants have become regular and therefore lower absolute numbers do not reflect a lower capacity of apprehension of clandestine immigrants. The overall increase of expulsions concluded, from less than 1,000 in the late 1980s to over 35,000 in 2001–2003 is extremely substantial and demonstrates that Italy has made a major effort in response to domestic and European concerns.

Second, the level of 'efficiency' of expulsions, defined as the percentage of those effectively expelled out of those apprehended away from the frontier, follows very closely the approval of new immigrations laws. It increases dramatically after the approval of each new law. Immediately after, a decline in its effectiveness begins, unless new measures are taken, but the level remains structurally higher than before. It is now over 40 per cent. Two reasons explain that movement. Initially the 'increased efficiency' is statistically amplified by the reduction of the clandestine population induced by the regularization. Afterwards that effect vanishes with the progressive increase of the number of illegal migrants. In addition to that, migrants and pro-immigrant groups and lawyers develop legal tools to achieve more effective appeals' procedures and elusive strategies. This fact points to the need for a continuous maintenance and adaptation of the legislative framework to respond to rapidly changing situations and strategies.

Finally, we can observe fewer illegal landings, more expulsion orders and more effective expulsions: but not everything is as simple in this apparent increase in the effectiveness of control measures. Several costs are hidden and a major flaw is not removed. There is first of all a human cost, particularly important when measured through the increase in the number of migrants dying while attempting to avoid detection. The introduction of visas in 1990 has cancelled the traditional easy transit routes by regular ferry. They were replaced by smugglers, whose rusty boats were more likely to sink during the crossing of the Mediterranean, especially if confronted at sea by police forces. The increase in penalties for traffickers and smugglers meant that they decided to keep more and more distant from the Italian shores, greatly increasing the danger for migrants. In order to escape more quickly, smugglers started throwing their passengers into the sea several hundred metres before they reached coast, causing many to drown. Then they just abandoned the boats a few dozen miles from the Italian coasts without guidance, in order to force the Italian coastguard to rescue immigrants and asylum seekers in peril. Finally, and even more radically, smugglers started loading clandestine immigrants on to boats without a crew, providing only vague directions, with even greater risk of death by hunger and thirst if migrants lost their sense of direction. Overall it is estimated that approximately 1,000 people died in 1996–2002 while trying to reach Italian shores (Manconi and Boraschi quoted by Monzini et al., 2004: 42).

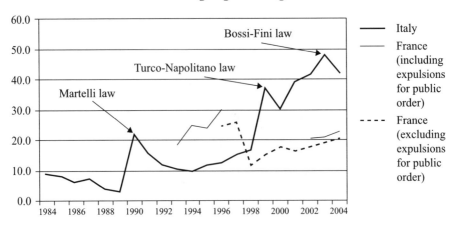

Figure 11.1   Implementation of removal orders in Italy and France, in per cent of removals ordered, 1984–2004

Source: Author's elaboration on statistics obtained from various sources, re-organized to keep homogeneous categories through time. Various sources give slightly different statistics, given that they are recalculated on different dates, so minor differences with other series will appear. See Annual reports of the Interior Ministry (1998–2000 and 2001–2003), Caritas (various years), ISMU (various years), Corte dei Conti (2004). On France see Viet (1998; 2005).

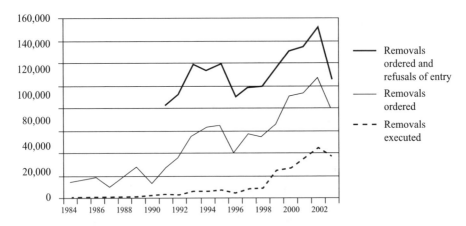

Figure 11.2   Total number of irregular migrants identified and expelled in Italy, 1984–2003

Source: As for Figure 11.1.

Personal costs are not quantifiable but they are significant. They involve migrants themselves as well as their families and their employers whose activity or family life is disrupted. Detention can be quite unpleasant, as illustrated by the recent report by the Italian Mission of the Medecins Sans Frontiers (2004). According to some authors, 'not only forced return is almost always objectively afflictive and sometimes openly breaching human rights, it is also extremely expensive for western countries and in many cases useless in the long term. It is a commonly verified data that expelled migrants tend to return as soon as they have the means to do so and that repatriation unsupported with sustaining actions in favour of the expelled migrants and the context of origin, often only has a delaying effect on the objective "management" of migratory flows, with additional costs and risks' (Coslovi and Piperno, 2004). The hunt for clandestine migrants can become a risk for asylum seekers who less and less frequently receive the status of refugee and appropriate protection.

The financial cost is also extremely high even if it is not fully quantifiable. The Court of Accounts has calculated that, even without including the cost of the personnel employed for controls and expulsion procedures, the cost of combating irregular migration has increased from €65.5 million in 2002 to €164.8 million in 2003 (Corte dei Conti, 2004). All these costs by themselves do not necessarily mean that a firm policy of enforcement should not be pursued, nor that the alternative would be less costly in different ways, but they ought to be taken into consideration and minimized.

Has the efficiency of the policies designed to prevent illegal migration really increased if we define such efficiency in a different manner? It is reasonable not to limit our attention to the number of those expelled but also to the number of individuals irregularly present in the country. The number of applications for regularization has increased very substantially, both in absolute terms (from 5,000 applications in 1982 to 700,000 in 2002) and in terms of annual net irregular flows (from 28,000 in 1983–1986 to 176,000 in 1999–2002).

Let us try to assess the number of those caught, out of those actually present. This exercise is much more difficult to conduct because it is impossible to know how many are really irregular. In exceptional circumstances, however, there is a relatively accurate count immediately after a mass regularization has taken place. If we use that type of information together with figures concerning the legal population, expulsions and so on, we can trace the evolution of the impact of the policies against irregular migration.

Given the data on the last five legalizations, we are clearly facing a paradox: the number of people intercepted has increased in absolute numbers, as has the fraction of those intercepted who have been successfully deported. At the same time, the number of irregular migrants in the country has increased both in absolute numbers and in relation to the existing legal migrant population.

The likelihood that an irregular migrant might be caught and expelled in the year of a regularization increased from 1 per cent in 1986 to 6.3 per cent in 2002. Despite the massive increase in likelihood of an expulsion, even in 2002 an immigrant having waited in hiding the normal four years interval between regularization would have had a 77 per cent chance of not being expelled before the regularization. Had he come midway, two years before the legalization, he would have had an 88 per cent likelihood of escaping expulsion. Despite the reduction in the likelihood to escape expulsion, illegal migration could increase because the balance of risk and opportunities is still in favour of illegal migration.

Table 11.2   Irregular flows and calculated risk of expulsion

	1986	1990	1995	1998	2002	Total
Applications for legalization	113,349	234,841	258,761	250,747	705,400	1,563,098
Successful applications	105,000	222,000	246,000	217,000	634,700	1,424,700
Removals (excluding those denied entry)	1,135	2,776	7,521	8,978	44,706	
Expelled in the year of regularization in per cent of applications for regularization	1.0	1.2	2.9	3.6	6.3	4.2
Average number of years of clandestine residence needed before the likelihood of expulsion becomes higher than 50 per cent	69	58	24	19	11	

Source: Author's calculations from data collected from the sources quoted in Figures 11.1 and 11.2

To understand the balance between risk and opportunities for the migrant it is necessary to evaluate the alternatives available and the rewards offered by the Italian labour market to legal and illegal foreign workers. First of all the imbalance between demand for immigrant labour and opportunities for legal entry has remained high. We can measure the total demand with some imprecise instruments, such as the Excelsior-Unioncamere enquiry on the preferences of the private sector firms. Their inquiries suggest an average request for hiring of foreign workers growing from 100,000 in 1999–2000 to 187,000 in 2003 and declining to 160,000 in 2004. Whatever the credibility of these figures, they show a substantial gap compared to the number of non-seasonal work permits that the government was willing to authorize. The difference between the demand for foreign legal workers and the supply (available quotas) is not exactly identical with the number of irregular migrants having found employment but not a work permit (which is equal to the number of people regularized), given that some employers only want illegal workers, but we can assume it is quite close.

For 1995–1998 we do not have an estimate of total demand for foreign labour, but we know that the government made available an average of 22,400 non-seasonal work permits per year while a build-up of 72,300 illegal workers per year took place. In 1999–2002 the estimate was an average demand of 122,500 foreign workers per year. The government offered 37,300 non-seasonal work permits per year, but the repressed demand for foreign workers reached 158,700 per year, according to regularization proceedings.

Clearly the geographical shift of immigration towards Eastern Europe has facilitated irregular inflows. The 145,000 irregular Romanians who applied for legalization in 2002 were exempted from a visa obligation, given that their country is a candidate for accession to the EU. The 100,000 Ukrainian applicants took the same route and benefited from a safe bus trip, without the risks of a sea crossing. Those inflows have not stopped but rather converted from purely clandestine and maritime to irregular ones by land, less visible and dangerous, using exemption from visas or tourist visas. The Italian trade unions assessed in May 2004 that 600,000 undocumented immigrants were in Italy.

The French Experience

The development of French policies of control and of management of economic migration show some limited similarities with Italy and many more discrepancies. Since closing its borders to mass migration of workers in 1974 there was no serious reversal of policy on that matter. The political focus has been placed on integration, including housing, equal opportunities, non-discrimination, religious issues or the role of institutional Islam. Frontier controls and expulsions were progressively hardened, but they followed a less linear direction and were softened cyclically, whenever the left came to power. Even though the left learned to become tougher on these issues, it is difficult to find the same constant upward trend seen for Italy in the data on irregular migrants and in removals and expulsion orders. Again, this is paradoxically a consequence of an overall result which is more positive, as a limited number of expulsions can be the consequence of a smaller clandestine population.

A Static Management of Legal Labour Flows

Between 1957 and 1974 France had responded to the high demand for labour caused by the economic boom, importing large numbers of workers from Spain, Portugal, Italy, Algeria, Morocco and Tunisia. The Office National de l'Immigration (ONI) registered between 40,000 and 180,000 permanent workers a year and up to 150,000 seasonal workers a year.[6] Many workers arrived in France autonomously, evading the control of the ONI and later registered and were legalized. At its highest point in

1968 regularizations represented 82 per cent of the labour flows (Schor, 1996: 203). In 1974 a decision was taken to stop labour immigration, given that the economic crisis was increasing unemployment. Although family immigration was suspended only very briefly, permanent labour migration suffered a draconian reduction and was kept below 20,000 workers a year from 1976 until the time of writing.

Inflows did not stop entirely because highly qualified economic migrants were still admitted, as were some unskilled workforce needed for construction and other forms of employment requiring the use of physical strength and forms of precarious work. Seasonal migration was reduced more progressively and it still concerned more than 60,000 workers at the beginning of the 1990s, when the introduction of free access to the EU labour market for the Spanish and the Portuguese reduced the number of workers registered by the OMI to fewer than 20,000. Persistent high unemployment and the intense politicization of the subject after the emergence of the anti-immigrant party Front National in the 1980s prevented any serious reconsideration of the policies. In 1993 the Gaullist Interior Minister Pasqua insisted on the need for zero immigration policies, in order to neutralize the political appeal on that subject of the Front National.

After the socialists returned to power, the Weil report in 1997 suggested facilitating the entry of highly qualified foreign workers (professionals) and students but not of unskilled workers (Weil, 1997). It recommended that in evaluating applications for entry of non-EU workers, local labour ministry agencies should consider not only the conditions of the labour market but also the technological and commercial importance of the foreign worker for the development of French companies. These suggestions were adopted by the government.

In 2000 there were some signs that this policy would be modified. A substantial decline in the unemployment rate and some early signs of mismatch in the labour market pointed to some limited sectorial scarcities of workforce. The Confederation of Industries started rethinking its position. The government ordered the administration to evaluate more leniently applications for highly skilled workers, especially for computer-related activities connected to the new economic boom of the period. The return of a strong negative phase of the economic cycle in 2001 increased unemployment again and put an end to the debate on a more open labour migration policy. New permits related to work declined slowly, from 36,000 in 1999 to 31,000 in 2003, and represented only 15 per cent of the total. Only about a third of those were for permanent work.

It is important to recall that France is not really as threatened by demographic decline as Italy is, given that the current birth rate in France is 1.9 children per woman, against 1.2 in Italy. The welfare state provides more services to families and there is not such a large demand for unskilled domestic workers or agricultural workers, as the modest inflow of seasonal workers shows. Irregular work in France is generally less pervasive than in Italy and the share of immigrants in it is declining. In 1992, 13 per cent of the fines for irregular work concerned foreigners, dropping to 7 per cent in 2002 (Gevrey, 2003). For many years an active policy of control of the labour market has contained the underground economy, thanks to a specialized inter-ministerial comnittee to combat irregular work, to several specific laws imposing fines and jail terms to employers and to an active enforcement policy (Weil, 1997).

Nevertheless, the Economic and Social Council recommended in 2003 that France should 'open our frontiers more than in the last period, taking into account the needs identified and forecasted of our economy, in favour of an economic migration managed and organized'.[7] The Economic and Social Council also suggested allowing some foreign job seekers to access the French labour market even before they have received an employment offer, as an alternative to illegal employment. In 2004 and 2005 the issue of introducing quotas to increase 'chosen' labour migration and contain family migration was raised by Sarkozy.

The Cyclical Evolution of French Control Policies

The political debate on immigration in France found in control policies a favourite subject of division. The administration softened the instability of the political decisions a little (Viet, 1998: 470) but changes were much too frequent. After 1997 an attempt to depoliticize the issue was carried out, with some success. Removal policies became more important in France only after mass labour migration had been blocked. The attempt to reduce the number of foreign workers became a favourite rhetorical instrument to fight unemployment. In 1977, the President of the Republic Giscard d'Estaing started a policy of incentives for migrants accepting to return voluntarily to their home country. It was soon transformed in an attempt to force return, but these proposals met a strong opposition in the country and in the institutions and failed (Weil, 1995). In 1980 the Barre-Bonnet law hardened the conditions for entry and extended the possibility of removal under police escort to all those who entered or sojourned irregularly (Blanc-Chaléard, 2001). Previously expulsions were limited to cases of threats to public order. Overstayers or illegal migrants could be fined or jailed, but more often were legalized. The principle of detention in specific centres for foreigners who could not be expelled immediately was also introduced in 1980, 18 years before Italy adopted such a principle.

In 1981 the left arrived in power with a programme favourable to immigrants and human rights. The new government suspended expulsions, except for very serious cases, and decided a regularization in order to compensate the effects of the repressive measures of the Giscard era: 145,000 applications were received, 132,000 of which were accepted. As the legalization programme ended, however, the Interior Minister Deferre decided to return to a policy of expulsions to reassure public opinion and to avoid the alternative of having to jail overstayers (Schor, 1996: 274; Viet, 1998: 412). Particularly after 1983 the socialists restarted controls and the struggle against clandestine immigrants and removed the procedure of appeal against expulsion decisions (Viet, 1998: 472–3). When the centre-right returned to power in 1986, the Pasqua laws hardened removal procedures, and introduced a form of urgent emergency expulsion for those foreigners deemed dangerous to public order. After the terrorist attacks of 1986 a general visa system was introduced for all non-EU countries.

The left returned to the government in 1988 and modified only parts of the Pasqua laws, adding some guarantees against expulsions in particular reintroducing some categories of non expellable immigrants initially defined in 1981. In 1991 a new procedure of regularization was decided in favour of asylum seekers whose case had not been dealt with but who had not left the country. This measure concerned about 20,000 foreigners. The left introduced some additional elements of control, such as special detention centres at airports. These zones targeted foreign air travellers arriving without proper documents and were used to formally deny them entry into French territory for up to 20 days. They could then be deported without the procedures needed for the removal of irregular migrants already in place in France.

The political pendulum moved to the right again in 1993, as Pasqua returned to the Interior Ministry with the objective of zero (illegal) immigration. A specialized department was created at the Interior Ministry to fight against illegal employment as well as illegal entry or residence in France (Viet, 1998: 474). Further restrictive measures were added by Debré in 1997, despite high profile public protests and the emergence of the 'sans papiers' movement in defence of the rights of migrants.

In 1997 the left returned to power and asked for a technical report from the Weil commission on how to change the law. The commission suggested an end to the politicization of immigration, and to the cycle of hardening and softening of control policies (20 changes of the immigration law had taken place between 1974 and 1997) as well as keeping most of the innovations of Pasqua and Debré. The new interior Minister Chevènement accepted the suggestion, eased family reunification and simplified procedures but cancelled only some of the most excessive measures of the past (Blanc-Chaléard, 2001: 88). He did not cancel visas, removal procedures, centres for detention or police controls. Chevènement decided for a legalization procedure as well, which attracted 150,000 applications, 87,000 of which were accepted. In order to avoid a continuous repetition of extraordinary mass legalization procedures, considered disruptive and apt to attract more illegal immigration (Masson and Balarello, 1997–1998), Chevènement introduced a permanent ordinary mechanism for individual legalization. Prefects would take individual decisions according to the specific situation of immigrants already in France since at least five years.

When the centre-right returned to power in 2002 the new Interior Minister Sarkozy designed a new law increasing the maximum period of detention from 12 to 32 days. Sarkozy kept most of the features of the previous laws, including the little used procedure for ordinary regularization on an individual basis, and even called on the police to use it more generously in order to calm down the requests for a new regularization of 'sans papiers' in 2002. There are now about 15,000 of these every year. However, Sarkozy decided to increase the effectiveness of removals setting quantitative objectives to the prefects. The increasingly tough conditions in the detention centres have been questioned by humanitarian organizations in France, as well as in Italy.[8]

It is not easy to compare the effectiveness of the French system in comparison to the Italian one, because of the different legal categories; the difficulty in comparing statistics reflects different situations. It seems possible to say, however, that in the course of the last 15 years, the political instability and very frequent changes have been reflected in the fluctuation of all migrant categories, albeit without a clear upward trend as in Italy. The total number of foreigners either denied entry or subject to a removal or expulsion order declined from 114,000 in 1994 to 85,000 in 1996 and did not increase significantly until 2003. The internal composition instead changed throughout time. The number of irregular migrants stopped at the frontier and denied entry climbed from 44,800 in 1985 to 71,100 in 1987, during Pasqua's first tenure. The numbers then shrunk somewhat but climbed again to 68,600 in 1994, during Pasqua's second tenure, to fall back again to 43,800 in 1996 and to 32.200 in 2003 (Viet, 1998: 475; Wibulpolprasert et al., 2005). Paradoxically the total number of expulsions ordered declined from 47,500 to 41,600, between 1993 and 1996, and then increased massively from 2001 to 2004 to reach 69,600.

The rate of implemented expulsion orders fluctuated significantly without a clear trend, according to the political changes. From 1998 to 2004, however, a continuous slow increase was engineered by both right and left and the main form of implemented expulsions, supervised by prefects, tripled from 4,500 to 13,100, and the rate of implemented expulsion orders increased from 12 per cent to 20.4 per cent. Despite the increase both figures remained significantly lower than the Italian equivalent (37,800 and 48 per cent in 2003). However, the number of applications for regularization and the estimates of the irregular migrant population do not suggest that France has a larger problem of control than Italy does.

Conclusion

Large numbers of expulsion orders, removals or denial of entry are not necessarily proof of success in controlling migration. Control policies are a fact of life and are unavoidable, even if highly unpleasant. Their absence would be dangerous but an exclusive emphasis on them is both ineffective and socially divisive. The issue which should attract more attention is how much migration pressure can and should be accommodated through legal channels in different countries. Several other factors than control policies contribute to contain the pressure of irregular migration towards France and enhance it towards Italy. We are not dealing here with push factors and the reasons motivating departure of migrants but rather with pull factors and why immigrants would choose one country rather than another and which factors attract their arrival.

The first of those factors of attraction is the capacity of the host economy to offer employment and shelter to irregular migrants. This is determined by several components, including level and growth rate of income, the demographic evolution of the local population, the size of the underground economy and the structure of the economy (for example the number of small businesses and of families in need of care and without adequate public social services). If we take into consideration the first two of these factors, France is marginally more attractive for migrants, but there is little difference between Italy and France. If instead we take into consideration the other structural factors, it is much clearer why Italy has a booming foreign population and France does not. If the domestic economy demands high numbers of foreign workers and is willing to employ them informally, then control policies will have little effect, regardless of how many people are stopped at the border or expelled.

Until a few years ago immigrants could be attracted to Italy by weak enforcement of rules, but this is no longer the case as enforcement is now relatively substantial. The persistent issues driving immigration are structural and will not be solved quickly. The frequency of extraordinary regularizations in Italy is both a consequence and a cause by itself of migration pressure, in a self-reinforcing process. Through regularizations the legal system accommodates already existing economic and social developments, but it also facilitates their continuation.

In the last few decades Italy has progressively opened new channels to economic migration in response to these pressures. Historically quotas have been too low, but the optimal level would not have been identical to the average number of legalizations, because there is a structural demand for irregular work that the economy would not absorb through legal quotas anyway. France has kept its doors more closed, but has a different labour market situation, making it much less urgent from a domestic point of view to enlarge labour migration possibilities.

Notes

[1]   The content of this chapter only represents the author's personal views and does not necessarily reflect those of the institutions to which he is associated. The author wishes to thank Gallya Lahav and Kristof Tamas for their useful comments.

[2]   Data has been collected and combined from the various yearly publications of the Caritas (1990–2004), from the ISMU (1995–2004), from various ISTAT, Interior Ministry and other governmental publications. For a new re-evaluation of the evolution of permits see Sciortino and Colombo (forthcoming).

[3]   See www.ismu.org internet site for Interior Ministry statistics until 2002. For 2003 see Corte dei Conti (2004).

[4]   Dini Decree, DL 18 November 1995, No. 489.

[5]   DPR 5 August 1998, and Art. 3 of 6 March 1998, No. 40, p. 9.

[6]   http://www.omi.social.fr.

[7]   Avis adopté par le Conseil économique et social au cours de sa séance du mercredi 29 octobre 2003, sur l'immigration, I, p.25. www.ces.fr/ces_dat2/2-3based/base.htm.

[8]   *Le Monde* (2004) 'L'accès aux droits des étrangers menacé dans le centres de rétention', 11 May.

Chapter 12

Labour Migration and Organized Interests: The Swedish Model

Torbjörn Lundqvist

Introduction

Long-term demographic forecasts point to a major shortage of labour in an aging Europe (see for example Rifkin, 1995). One of a number of proposed solutions is labour immigration. If this type of immigration assumes major proportions we can expect institutional changes in society. A legitimate question in this respect is how welfare systems and labour market arrangements will be affected. In the labour market sector, central government, employers and unions have jointly developed institutions aiming at proper procedure, fair competition and predictability. Corporative arrangements have been a feature of the labour market in several European states. Over the past 20–25 years, liberal market ideas have challenged corporativism and particularly organized union interests. While much has changed during this period, there is reason to ask what the past 50 years have taught us about the relationship between immigration and employment that is worth bearing in mind when discussing future labour immigration or other immigration (see Nelhans, 1973; Lundh and Ohlsson, 1999; Lundqvist, 2002 and 2003).

In what follows, I will examine the arguments presented by unions and employers concerning labour immigration and other immigration in relation to the Swedish labour market, with the aim of identifying coinciding and disparate interests. I will also consider how the country's institutional arrangements in respect of labour immigration have changed over time. I will then seek to apply these historical lessons in a discussion on labour immigration in the future. I will argue that the institutional arrangements must take various organized interests, recruiting costs and social costs into account. Thus the focus will be on the functioning of the labour market rather than on migration policy.

In Sweden, the national union and employer organizations have played a key role since the early twentieth century in developing institutions for the labour market. The original meaning of the term 'Swedish model' related to labour-management cooperation and to the peaceful development of the employment market after the Second World War. The central union body (the Swedish Trade Union Confederation, LO) and its employer counterpart (the Swedish Employers' Confederation, SAF) negotiated pay, working conditions and solutions to many labour market problems. Both organizations were keen to avoid mandatory legislation. Tim Tilton aptly describes the Swedish model as an informal contract between different interests and parties in society: 'It rests on a compromize between the strongest and best-organized capital sector' (Tilton, 1992). Central government, however, came to play an important role in relation to immigrant labour via a national agency, the Labour Market Board (AMS).

During the 1970s, the sensitive balance between the social partners tipped in favour of the LO, which acquired increasing influence over government policies through its links with social democracy. In the 1990s, however, the unions lost ground in terms of both influence and legitimacy. Contributory factors included a general climate of liberalization, a degree of decorporatization, a high rate of unemployment and a liberal-conservative government.

Regardless of how the balance of power has shifted over time, unions and employers have often had mutual interests to defend, but have just as often had different aims and different opportunities for their achievement. Due to the extensive influence that the labour market organizations have had in public life and to the Social Democrats' lengthy term in office, the employment market has held a special position in Swedish politics. It should be recalled that possibly the most forceful political vision of the post-war period was that of a society in full employment. Politics may be defined as power based on interests, and in Sweden's case there is a clear link to the labour market, and also for that matter to large areas of welfare policy.

Where immigration is concerned, the link to the employment market is clearest in the case of immigrant labour. But there is also a connection with other forms of immigration. In Sweden, as in most of Western Europe, labour immigration coincided with the period of labour shortages that in principle extended throughout the post-war period up to the early 1970s (see for example Bade, 2003). When unemployment grew, non-Nordic labour immigration was halted. The 1980s and 1990s saw an increase in other forms of immigration instead (refugees, others in need of sanctuary, family ties). The labour market was unable to absorb these immigrants adequately, leading to unemployment. Thus immigration became a labour market issue.

My object in this chapter is to examine what arguments the social partners have presented regarding labour immigration and other immigration from a labour market perspective. My starting point is that both sides have interests to protect, and the aim is to examine these interests. A further aim, however, is to demonstrate the importance of arriving at a model in which these interests coincide. In this connection, it is vital to consider how labour immigration in Sweden actually developed and what institutional solutions were applied. The study begins with this question and returns to it later when I discuss the lessons of history. The study is based on the assumption that what we have learnt over the past half-century can help us in the years to come, particularly as forecasts concerning the future availability of labour have prompted a debate on labour immigration. Most analysts take the view that labour immigration will be essential in the longer term.

In the public debate, labour immigration and other forms of immigration have generally been discussed as separate issues, which they are to some extent; at the same time, however, their link to the labour market is a common denominator. The issues are also connected in that when the government has rejected labour immigration, critics have drawn on arguments from the immigration debate and accused those supporting the government line of xenophobia, despite the fact that the latter have not opposed regular immigration. The issue is quite simply a sensitive one, and those advocating liberalization have introduced rhetoric from the immigration policy debate. Matters came to a head in connection with efforts to prevent the free movement of labour from the EU's new Eastern European member states by means of transitional rules. The current importance attached to the issue is clear from the Swedish government's decision in 2004 to appoint a parliamentary committee charged with reviewing the regulatory framework for labour immigration from countries outside Europe (the EU/EEA). The aim is to develop a set of rules that can be applied if and when labour shortages arise in the future, without adversely affecting the right of asylum (Ministry of Industry (2004: 21).

Institutional Arrangements in the Twentieth Century

From 1860 to 1910, the principle of free labour immigration applied in Sweden. This period, however, was characterized by mass emigration, primarily to North America. Between 1840 and 1930, some 1.3 million Swedes emigrated, of which 200,000 later returned. The First World War changed much. Passports for entry into Sweden became compulsory again in 1917. From 1919 onwards immigration was subject to the consent of the labour market organizations. Thus the corporative 'Swedish model' in the labour immigration field had arrived, although as yet on a modest scale compared with what was to come.

During the interwar years, a restrictive immigration policy prevailed, due to high unemployment. In the final years of the Second World War, however, citizens of the Nordic countries and the Baltic States were given free access to the Swedish labour market. The 1950s were characterized by a series of institutional changes of a liberalizing nature: the abolition of visa requirements for citizens of a wide range of European countries, the institutionalization of the joint Nordic labour market and the liberal recommendations of the OECD. These changes helped bring about free labour immigration from Europe during 1955–1968.

In the early 1960s, there were a large number of job-seeking foreign citizens in the country, which caused social problems. In particular, a temporary economic decline in 1965 led to criticism of the prevailing set-up. In 1968, this liberal system was abolished and work permits were once again required prior to entry. Efforts were made to match supply to demand. At the same time, collective recruitment of labour was once again given consideration. The Labour Market Board was to consult with the social partners and import labour in consultation with employers. This new policy step was a response to the social problems that had arisen over unemployed 'tourists'.

In 1968, the Riksdag (Swedish parliament) adopted guidelines for immigration policy under which the domestic labour reserve (married women, the occupationally disabled, the elderly) was to be utilized before immigration could come into question. The volume of immigration was to be determined by the current employment situation and by the availability of housing, education, healthcare and other services. From 1972, non-Nordic labour immigration more or less ceased.

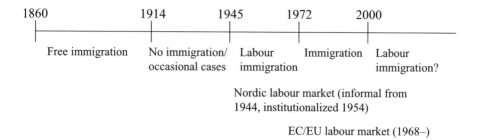

Figure 12.1   Immigration and labour market over time

From 1945 up until the early 1970s, net immigration totalled just over 400,000. During the post-war part of the 1940s and in the 1960s, the immigration surplus was 20,000 per annum, while in the 1950s the figure was only 11,000. Many of the post-war immigrants were refugees and a large number of them remained in the country. Of the total immigrant surplus of just over 200,000 up to 1960, almost 150,000 were citizens of one of the Nordic countries, largely Finnish citizens. A considerable number of the remainder were political or economic refugees from the war or the post-war chaos economies, principally those of Eastern Europe and Germany. Labour immigration during this period, therefore, should primarily be seen as a move to develop a Nordic full employment model. This was one of the main aims of the joint Nordic labour market.

In the 1960s, net immigration was almost twice as large as in the 1950s. Finns continued to dominate, Italians still arrived, but others, especially Yugoslavs, now comprised a substantial group. Greeks, Turks and other nationalities were also attracted to Sweden. From the mid-1970s, immigration almost exclusively involved refugees and later their families. The greatest influx of refugees occurred during the Balkan War of the 1990s, which coincided with Sweden's worst unemployment crisis since the 1930s. Ever since, the integration issue has been linked to unemployment (Ekberg, 2004).

Recruitment Approaches and Labour Immigration Policies

One of the more interesting questions is how labour immigration should be organized in order to be both inexpensive and effective. The institutional arrangements are crucial determinants in recruitment costs, social costs, competitive relations and industrial relations. In the following, I will briefly outline various types of institutional arrangements for recruiting foreign labour. I will seek to analyze the changes that have taken place, applying the concepts of state and market. Both the state (central government) and market mechanisms are present to a greater or lesser degree throughout the period. For the purposes of analysis, however, it is a good idea to try to separate them.

Two types of market solutions were applied during the period: either companies imported labour or job-seekers sought out companies in Sweden. The state laid down rules concerning which countries these two solutions could be applied in. In the case of labour immigration, which was more closely regulated and politically controlled, the government was an active player, recruiting collectively via the Labour Market Board. Meanwhile, employment opportunities in Sweden for individual job-seekers from non-Nordic countries were restricted. Thus recruitment of foreign labour during the period in question took three basic forms: individual job-seeking, recruitment by employers, and government recruitment via the Labour Market Board. There were also variations within these three basic categories. Individual immigration continued throughout the period and was dominated by Nordic citizens entering via the joint Nordic labour market. During the period 1955–1968, large groups also came to Sweden from other European countries as 'tourist immigrants'. Citizens of a number of different countries could freely seek employment in Sweden and then apply for a work permit, which was usually granted.

Company recruitment principally targeted the Nordic countries, especially Finland. In 1950, this sphere of activity came under government regulation via the Labour Market Board. Between 1950 and 1955, companies were required to register their interest in foreign labour with the Board, which in turn worked with the government agencies in the countries concerned. These agencies selected potential recruits, and the Swedish company was then allowed to offer them employment. This elaborate procedure yielded just 15,000 workers.

After 1955, this recruiting approach was little used. The other type of government recruitment was the collective import of labour, which was practised even less. The most significant examples were probably the recruitment of Italians and Hungarians in 1947, followed by that of Yugoslavs in 1966 and Turks in 1967.

Labour migration to Sweden, then, came in different forms. In principle, labour immigration via the joint Nordic labour market was an extension of the Swedish labour market. In the case of European immigration, we can divide the period from the Second World War and up to the early 1970s into three parts: a pre-1955 policy regulating company recruitment or replacing it with collective state recruitment, a period of largely free labour immigration from Europe between 1955 and 1968, and a return in 1968–1972 to government control and regulation of immigration.

The two main types could be described as government action and control on the one hand and a market solution on the other. The latter developed in response to the failure of the former. Government regulation was unable to respond adequately to the demand for labour. In principle, it could be argued that under the government recruitment scheme costs were too high. The classic solution was to let market mechanisms solve the problem. More workers could be recruited at lower cost. When unemployment rose (marginally) in the mid-1960s, social costs ensued. The market solution offered an adequate supply of labour, but the price was deemed too high when foreign job-seekers were unable to find employment and were often left penniless. The authorities were forced to provide them with temporary accommodation in the form of barracks and tents. Policy was reversed, and both regulation and collective recruitment were reintroduced.

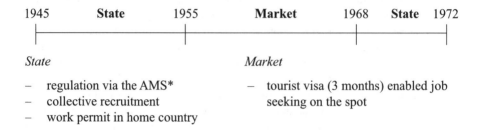

| 1945 | **State** | 1955 | **Market** | 1968 | **State** | 1972 |

State

- regulation via the AMS*
- collective recruitment
- work permit in home country

Market

- tourist visa (3 months) enabled job seeking on the spot

Figure 12.2   State or market: institutional arrangements during the labour immigration period

*   National Labour Market Board.

Union and Employer Interests

Labour Immigration

During the early post-war years, immigration policy in Sweden was informed by economic pessimism. A predicted downturn in the economy bred extreme caution in the view policy-makers took of foreign labour. Imported labour was to be confined to certain 'key industries', which in practice meant export industries. Work permits were to be granted to well-qualified labour, which in practice meant skilled workers. In the early 1950s, the Labour Market Board took steps to curb the influx of unskilled labour to low-paid jobs (Nelhans, 1973: 93). At an abstract level, the immigration of unskilled labour ran counter to the basic tenets of the Rehn/Meidner model according to which labour was to be channelled into more productive companies and industries. The model was intended to soften the inflationary impact of full employment, reduce pay gaps, encourage productivity-boosting restructuring measures and promote industrial peace. The import of labour for low-productivity operations was therefore contrary to the fundamental beliefs of Swedish social democracy (Lundh, 1994).

In the 1950s, both the LO and the SAF began to emphasize the importance of matching immigration to the needs of the Swedish labour market. What appeared on the surface to represent a consensus of opinion between the two bodies, however, disguised the fact that the SAF expected the Labour Market Board to supply Swedish companies with an adequate flow of labour, while the LO expected the Board to restrict the intake so as not to jeopardize full employment.[1]

Early on, a discussion developed about problems involving foreign citizens in the labour market. The Swedish Metalworkers' Union carried out a study in 1946 which concluded that claims of workplace problems with immigrant labour were exaggerated. Some irritation between Swedish and foreign employees had been noted, but incidents were relatively few and small in scale (Nelhans, 1973: 77).

In 1951, the LO conducted a survey in which 750 local union branches were asked for their views on foreign labour. Half of the replies were negative, citing various reasons for their attitude. The most common objection was that immigrant workers were 'reluctant to organize' (Elmdahl, 1951). Initially, the unions demanded that the granting of work permits be conditional upon union membership. In the labour agreements with Italy and Hungary in 1947, for instance, the workers had to pledge union membership before leaving their native countries. The employers applied the same principle so as not to jeopardize industrial peace (Nelhans, 1973: 187).

The LO advocated controls that would enable the unions to deny people work permits. Researchers have shown that union interests were a major factor in the restrictive policies pursued by the government in 1967–1968. Only now was the LO able to gain full political backing for its views. Events in the 1960s could be said to have bolstered the unions' position vis-à-vis the employers. This was clearly demonstrated by the fact that in 1971 the Labour Market Board sided with the union against two major companies, Eriksberg (shipbuilding) and Bofors, and turned down their applications for work permits for 300 and 150 workers respectively (ibid.). In 1972, the LO urged member unions to adopt a generally restrictive attitude, and in principle this put a stop to non-Nordic labour immigration. The crises of the 1970s then ensued, and the matter disappeared from the agenda.

The employers adopted largely the same position throughout the period: as much freedom as possible. For one of the key organizations in Swedish industry at that time, the Engineering Employers' Association, labour supply was a major problem. In fact, only wage drift was considered a greater headache, but this was part of the same complex – labour competition (Lundqvist, 1998).

Still today, labour immigration is not governed by any legal provisions. A corporative model is in place under which the Labour Market Board considers work permits in consultation with the social partners. Ordinarily, work permits are not to be issued to applicants from outside the Nordic area or the EU, but exceptions are made for people in key positions and in shortage occupations (Ministry of Industry, 2004: 21).

Adjusting to Sweden

Immigrants' problems in adjusting to Swedish society and the Swedish labour market became a subject of widespread debate during the 1960s (SOU, 1967: 18). The LO emphasized the importance of immigration *per se* being accepted by the population at large, an essential precondition of immigrant integration. Greater acceptance could be gained, it was felt, by disseminating information about immigration to the general public and by avoiding too heavy a concentration of immigrants in certain areas or companies.

The politicization of the issue and the vision of full employment caused the Social Democrats and the unions to begin questioning the wisdom of labour immigration. It was deemed of secondary importance. The first priority was to ensure full employment for all those already in the country, whether native Swedes or immigrants. The labour reserve of women, the elderly and the occupationally disabled was to be found work before foreign labour was imported. According to the LO, this was both a humanitarian and a social concern. The unions also took the view that immigrants should enjoy the same standard as Swedes in terms of housing, education and social benefits. If this was not available, immigrant labour would have to wait. Companies could not be allowed to pass the costs on to the public sphere, as such a course was thought to adversely affect LO members in particular. For the LO, preventing the emergence of a proletariat paid less than the statutory minimum wage for a blue-collar worker was an important matter of principle. Quite apart from the solidarity principle involved, of course, it was feared that the emergence of such an underclass might lead to deterioration in conditions for the working class in general.

It was here that the question of controlled immigration came into the picture. The LO declared that we should not take in immigrants faster than they could adjust to life in Sweden and have access to the same terms and conditions as native Swedes. This meant that the housing, care and education situation would have to be considered to the same extent as the employment situation. For this reason, effective checks on the flow of immigrants to Sweden were important. Once the immigrants were inside the country, controls could be relaxed.[2] A report from a Nordic committee proposed that aliens denied work permits be granted the right of appeal. This was rejected by the LO. It argued that the general system for considering permit applications might be undermined by judicial review.[3]

At the beginning of the 1970s, refugee policy came under discussion (SOU, 1972: 84). The LO declared that its basic position on immigration policy 'as a whole is that general immigration controls are both one of the pillars of Swedish immigration policy and an instrument for enabling immigrants and other vulnerable groups to assert themselves in the Swedish labour market'. The LO appeared to want refugee immigration, too, to be subject to a work permit review at the general level. Referring to the 1951 Geneva Convention on Refugees, for instance, it emphasized that 'it is left to the national authorities themselves to decide how (the provisions) are to be incorporated into national legislation'. The LO was desperately anxious to avoid the emergence of an immigrant labour reserve living under the threat of unemployment and reducing pay and benefit levels in Swedish working life. This, however, was how the situation in Sweden was already being described by the Nordic committee.[4]

The SAF objected to this description. It claimed there was no such trend in Sweden. Statistics showed that immigrants were no worse paid than native Swedes and were to be found in a wide range of occupations and industries.[5] Without taking a position on whether the SAF actually did not perceive any problems, or simply did not want to perceive any, it is true to say that this standpoint suited those who wished to see a liberalization of the rules on labour immigration, while the reverse is true of those favouring a restrictive policy.

In connection with another government inquiry, the LO proposed that all employment-related immigration be channelled through Sweden's employment offices, and that 'immigrants be given less access to work permits'. Denying them permits was one way of combating the concentration of immigrant labour at workplaces with poor environments or conditions. The LO rejected a proposal to allow refugees and other immigrants temporary work permits pending a decision on their applications (SOU, 1974: 69).

From a union viewpoint, labour immigration was hardly a single, unvarying phenomenon. The relatively controlled situation that existed in the Metalworkers' Union sector differed from the problems that the small union organizations in the service industry had to contend with. The small unions were particularly anxious to see labour immigration controlled.

The SAF, however, was opposed in principle to giving the unions a significant say in work permit cases, arguing that this was a matter for the authorities, and that 'the opinion of a given union organization should not in itself be allowed to decide a case, bearing in mind that the organization must necessarily base its position on the special interests of its own members, and also bearing in mind that the union concerned may have tactical motives for its decision'. The same held true for employer organizations.[6]

Besides their links to the Social Democrats, the unions drew their strength from a high rate of membership and full employment. From a union viewpoint, labour immigration represented a threat to the LO's influence in the community for three reasons: a greater risk of unemployment in the event of a future recession, the risk of lower union membership, and the associated risk of collective union strategies at individual workplaces becoming less effective. Full employment gave the unions a better relative position in the social partnership. Foreign workers did not have the same union traditions and might choose not to join. Local unions were often dependent on being able to display a united front vis-à-vis the employer (Lundqvist, 2000).

Union strength, then, could be eroded by a major wave of labour immigration. Also, large-scale immigration could lead to price dumping, which posed a threat to the LO's function as a cartel. From a union viewpoint, therefore, opposing labour immigration was a rational move. On the other hand, the LO regarded itself as a progressive force that contributed to welfare development by advocating structural improvements, in the spirit of Rehn/Meidner, even if these left members out of work.

Here we have the essence of the union dilemma. Labour immigration could enhance welfare in the country and thus the welfare of LO members as well. At the same time, it might weaken the unions and thereby hamper their members' welfare growth.

Immigrant workers' command of Swedish became a union issue in the 1960s, which can partly be seen as the outcome of a collective union strategy. It was felt that if immigrants acquired a grasp of the language and of how Sweden worked, this would raise their union consciousness. 'Cultural conflicts' had occurred since the post-war years and usually involved accusations that immigrants adopted an excessively individualistic approach to their work, for example, by working harder than prescribed by the collective norm and thereby 'wrecking' piecework agreements. It was sometimes felt that immigrants came to Sweden, worked hard for a couple of years and sent the money home. These 'guest workers' took no collective responsibility for fellow-workers who were older and less robust, or workers who would perhaps remain in the same job throughout their productive lives. The LO, therefore, was opposed to a system of guest workers. Such systems, it argued, tended to upset conditions for those in regular employment and risked endangering union influence at the workplace. Thus there was a logical connection between the LO's immigrant integration policy and its policy on immigration. The object was to integrate immigrants into Swedish society and thereby strengthen the unions.

In sum, the LO stood for a restrictive immigration policy while at the same pursuing an immigrant integration policy emphasizing assimilation and equal rights with the native population. This was a policy founded on union logic and the interests of the working class.

The SAF for its part felt that the 'aliens problem' had been exaggerated in that Nordic citizens were being counted as immigrant labour instead of as migrant workers 'who to a great extent move back and forth' within the Nordic area. Nordic citizens, it felt, should be placed on a par with Swedish citizens. The Employers' Federation also objected to the fact that all aliens were being treated according to what it called a 'standard plan'. Many of them returned home after only a few years in Sweden.

The SAF advocated liberalization. It wanted Sweden to comply with the recommendations of the European Council that member states should introduce the principle of free movement for labour. The SAF was against granting access to the labour market when unemployment prevailed, but the rules were otherwise to be liberal. This represented a fundamentally different approach to that of the LO. The SAF envisaged a European set-up similar to the present EU, where no specific integration policy was required for immigrant labour within Europe. The labour market was to be free and governed by supply and demand. The LO for its part was anxious to protect the standards and rights that the working class had fought for in Sweden.[7]

Immigration and the Labour Market

During the 1980s and 1990s, the immigration focus shifted to refugees. At the same time, Swedish migration policy was internationalized (Tamas, 2004b). In 1995, the LO was given the opportunity to comment on asylum matters and on refugee policy in a global perspective (SOU, 1995: 46). Unemployment was the main topic of the day, and the LO argued that Sweden should pursue an integration policy that enabled immigrants to be assimilated into Swedish working life and into the community. As two-thirds of all non-Nordic immigrants were now unemployed, the LO wanted to either reduce immigration to a minimum to facilitate integration – by adjusting the flexible part of immigration policy downwards – or to upgrade the goals of integration policy. In other words, Sweden should either take in fewer immigrants or improve integration. The LO wanted a clearer budgetary link between immigration and integration policy. Probably as a result of the high unemployment rate, it also wanted the government to invest in return migration.[8]

In 1995, a government report proposed a range of measures for reducing unemployment among immigrants: loans for immigrant entrepreneurs, immigrant recruitment programmes for employers, wage subsidies for immigrants, and government-financed local employment projects for immigrants (SOU, 1995: 76).

The SAF (and the Federation of Swedish Industries) wanted to analyse more closely the reasons why immigrants had been unable to gain a 'permanent foothold' in the labour market in the 1980s, despite the favourable business climate. In the late 1980s, even labour immigration was discussed. Among the reasons cited for the high rate of immigrant unemployment were: cultural background, employer uncertainty about the immigrants' qualifications and demand in the growing service sector for 'specifically Swedish skills'. The latter was described as a cardinal reason: 'one of the problems is that new immigrants in particular lack the specifically Swedish skills that are becoming essential in an increasing number of occupations'. The employer organizations saw deregulation of the labour market as a solution to the problems: 'Large-scale immigration is a powerful reason for deregulating, and for not just amending labour law but also reviewing opportunities for company growth'.[9]

The LO came out strongly against what it called an 'Americanization' of the Swedish labour market: 'Deregulation of the labour market, greater pay differentials and tax relief for domestic services are all [SAF-]proposals that would have a profound impact not only on the Swedish labour market but also on the drive for equality that has distinguished Swedish society.' Such policies would create 'wider social and economic gaps between different sections of the community'. The LO, therefore, opposed the idea of 'some type of sheltered employment' for immigrants, as it felt this reflected the same approach as the proposals to deregulate and split up the labour market. Instead, it called for a policy advocating full employment and an 'upgrading of skills throughout the workforce'. It was also opposed to the use of quotas and wage subsidies for immigrants.

Like the SAF, the LO discussed the importance of culture and language, arguing that 'better Swedish tuition for all who require it is one of the most important instruments of future immigrant integration policy'. The LO wanted the social partners to engage in 'attitude-changing processes', to prepare workplaces to receive people who had been jobless, and to take part in various types of training. It also favoured employers drawing up special recruiting programmes.[10] In 1996, a government report discussed segregation (SOU, 1996: 55). The LO focused on the problem of housing segregation and ethnic discrimination in working life. It called for the introduction of a rule reversing the burden of proof in certain discrimination cases, that is requiring employers to prove their innocence. Also, it strongly emphasized the importance of employment for the achievement of integration. It blamed the failure of the government's integration policies in the 1990s on unemployment.[11]

The LO asserted that in the wake of mass unemployment, 'intolerance, ethnic discrimination and racist violence have become increasingly commonplace in Swedish daily life'. It could be said, therefore, that a policy of full employment was at the root of the LO's stance on integration. Another classic line of approach was a proposal to join the employer organizations in 'helping to bring about a trial programme to develop models for general workplace introductions of good quality'.[12]

While full employment and other lines of approach drawn from the 'Swedish model' made up the LO's strategy, the SAF had a very different course to suggest: 'The problem in our view is rather that the regulatory framework and the institutions which took shape in a homogenous society enjoying full employment seem increasingly abstract in the new society and the new employment situation that is currently emerging in Sweden.' The employer organizations had been pursuing this line since the early 1980s. It was initially applied to wage negotiations and the Swedish model as a whole by the Engineering Employers' Association. In the same spirit, the SAF now urged that top priority be given to 'adapting the labour market rules and reshaping employment policy so as to facilitate recruitment, contract work and self-employment'.[13]

Here, both the SAF and the LO display an ideological continuity with respect to the problem of integration. Also, both organizations are convinced that political control will not solve all the problems. While the LO believes in a combination of partner initiatives and political solutions, the SAF wants flexible solutions, changes of attitude and immigrant enterprises willing to join existing networks in the local business community. The SAF is also suspicious of general political solutions.

Diversity

During the era of labour immigration, the LO pursued an integration policy that more or less espoused the 'Swedification' of immigrants. This policy disappeared when refugee immigration came to dominate the scene. Instead of just helping immigrants to adjust to Swedish society, the idea now was also to help Swedes adjust to immigrants. It was a case of persuading the labour market to accept heterogeneity as a positive factor. Policy-makers began talking about the advantages of diversity. This was largely in line with official government policy. Nor was the SAF's position very different, although it showed less inclination to involve itself in social affairs.

As for the reasons behind the adjustment problems, and the extent of these problems, interpretations differ. The LO has constantly viewed social conflicts and problems relating to immigrants as a serious matter, while the SAF has not. While the LO has sought to explain these adjustment problems in terms of the job shortage, the SAF has argued that unemployment among immigrants is due to labour market regulation. LO members are viewed by the SAF as 'insiders' protected by regulation, while unemployed immigrants are 'outsiders' denied entry to the labour market.

Deregulation is seen as the antidote. During this debate, the LO has been anxious to offer an alternative to deregulation. It's campaigning on behalf of greater diversity in working life and greater employability for immigrants has, quite apart from the solidarity aspects, a strategic dimension. If immigrants find work, and full employment is achieved, this shows that deregulation is unnecessary.

Today, the LO champions diversity, describing it as an asset both to employers and in the labour market. But employers, too, are now beginning to talk about diversity. There are differences of emphasis, however. For employers, diversity means applying the principle of flexibility, that is, tearing down the regulatory barriers in the labour market that impede integration (SAF, 2000). For the unions, diversity represents a political means of achieving full employment. For the employers, diversity provides a motive for deregulating or liberalizing the labour market. As they see it, union interests are an impediment to diversity in working life.

What, then, is the reasoning behind the unions' diversity strategy? Large groups of immigrants from the 1980s and 1990s are either unemployed or outside the workforce. To permit labour immigration in such a situation would be to risk creating a permanent group of unemployed and precipitating the emergence of a proletariat stuck in an insecure, low-paid sector. Such a development runs counter to the goal that has motivated the LO ever since the early twentieth century: to strengthen the working class by collectively raising its standard of living via a wage policy based on solidarity with the low-paid. The high rate of membership among its affiliated unions is attributable to its historical emphasis on low-paid groups.

Sweden is no longer a relatively homogenous society, and the Swedification of immigrants is no longer a realistic strategy. The unions' collective strategies at the workplace, meanwhile, have altered in response to developments in society and changes in the nature of work. The high rate of unemployment that was a feature of the 1990s weakened labour's position in relation to management. Full employment strengthens the union's position. As a union strategy, therefore, to advocate diversity is to promote a policy of full employment. To oppose labour immigration until unemployment has been eliminated is to pursue the same logic.

Consequently, I would maintain that the LO's view of immigrant labour bespeaks continuity. The same apprehension that labour immigration may pose a threat to full employment is evident throughout the period, from 1945 up to the present day, and will probably persist in the future. However, I would also argue that there has been a shift in strategy from emphasizing influence at the local workplace to placing greater emphasis on the logic of full employment by promoting immigrant employability via the diversity approach. This is also a result of the high rate of unemployment that prevailed in the 1990s and the debate on racism and discrimination, in which the LO adopted a leftist stance in opposition to xenophobic 'right-wing extremists'.

Economic historian Christer Lundh argues that the LO's immigration and immigrant integration policies should be viewed in the light of the Swedish model. Immigration was not to be allowed 'to jeopardize full employment, structural reform or the policy of wage solidarity' (Lundh, 1994: 34). At the same time, it was necessary to integrate the immigrants into Swedish society and working life, both for their own sakes and in order to preserve union solidarity. This interpretation appears logical and offers a better explanation of the LO's restrictive position on labour immigration than accusations of xenophobia, which were sometimes levelled in the debate of the 1960s and which are still heard today.

The differing approaches that the LO and the SAF have adopted, the 'Swedish model' versus deregulation, could be said to represent the two main lines of argument in the Swedish debate on the relationship between immigration policy and immigrant integration policy on the one hand and the labour market on the other.

The Future and the Lessons of the Past

There is certain rationality in the way both the unions and the employers view labour immigration and other immigration. While the unions prioritize employment and job security, the employers give precedence to efficiency and growth. Central government for its part needs to embrace both sets of interests, but at the same time the political parties hold disparate views. The Social Democrats are intimately linked to the unions while the views of the political right tend to coincide with those of the employers. A logical approach in this matter might be to ensure that institutional arrangements take the interests of both partners into consideration. Such an approach must not, however, be at the expense of the public interest in general. I have no definitive answer to the question of how such institutional arrangements might look, and researchers are silent on this issue in Sweden. Based on historical experience, however, I intend to make a few points.

Why did the principles of labour immigration undergo change during the period? One of the chief reasons is union influence. But I also contend that on the basis of past experience, it could fairly be argued that the market solution, 'tourist immigration', came about in response to the failure of market regulation. The system of government control could not respond adequately to the strong demand for labour that characterized the 1950s. In principle, it could be argued that the costs for each individual immigrant were too high under the recruiting system permitted or applied by the state during that time.

The classic solution was to let market mechanisms solve the problem. Recruitment costs (job seeking and transportation) were transferred to the immigrant. This gave employers access to a far greater supply at a much lower cost. When unemployment rose (marginally) in the mid-1960s, social costs developed. The market was able to solve the supply problem but the social cost was deemed exorbitant when unemployment set in and posed a threat to full employment. This prompted a return to greater regulation and collective state recruitment.

In historical terms, free immigration has been a prerequisite for the recruitment of large numbers of people. The immigration levels that pertained in 1945–1970 would not have been possible had free labour immigration not been permitted from a number of countries with a labour surplus. Should large-scale immigration prove necessary, some type of free immigration will probably be required. A form of 'tourist immigration' may develop in the EU. Another possibility is market solutions via recruiting agencies, which would probably be very costly. Nor should we forget that refugee resettlement is an alternative to labour immigration.

The arrival of labour immigration coincided with the growth of union influence, the Swedish model and a strong nation-state. The union can hardly expect the same degree of influence in the event of a new wave of labour immigration in the future. Should one develop, the most rational course would probably be for unions and employers to work together to avert disloyal competition and the emergence of an extensive black labour market. Past experience of cooperation in accordance with the Swedish model could guide them in this respect. Disloyal and unlawful behaviour damaged the collective interests of both. In the future, it will continue to be in the interests of both sides to avert such behaviour.

In a government report on EU enlargement and the free movement of labour, past experience of organized recruitment is briefly discussed (SOU, 2002:116). The report describes the recruitment of doctors, primarily from Poland, and concludes that the Swedish county councils' recruitment drive should 'serve as an example for other kinds of organized labour immigration'. This recommendation is based on the recruitment of an occupational category in which unusually high qualifications and language skills are required. Medical training is both lengthy and expensive, given which a relatively costly recruitment process may be motivated. It is clear from the analysis undertaken for the purposes of the report that further research is needed in such an important area for the Swedish economy.

What makes this matter so important? In principle, we could argue that the greater labour immigration is in magnitude, the more important it is to have arrangements in place that help us recruit the right individuals at as low a cost as possible. The problem is that recruiting costs rise with one's level of ambition. In Sweden, we have a range of institutions that help reduce recruitment costs inside the country: a common language, education, culture, employment offices, vocational specification and so forth. When these institutions are not shared by the recruit, the recruiter incurs high transaction costs. In such cases, operations must be organized in such a way as to keep down these costs. When we introduce social costs into the analysis, it becomes clear that the question of how we should organize labour immigration cannot be dealt with in economic terms alone. Labour immigration affects the employment market in different ways, which is one of the reasons why employers and unions have been brought into the work of developing institutional arrangements.

Labour immigration, like other forms of immigration, affects institutional relations in the labour market. Various organized interests seek to influence the design of institutions that have either developed in response to the disruption of the established order or whose purpose is to solve problems that have arisen as a result of immigration. Institutional arrangements are affected by the way in which immigration is organized and by which groups gain support for their positions. In this chapter, I have argued that there is a conflict between recruiting costs and the unions' interest in maintaining good order in the labour market. Quite simply, if there is great demand for immigrant labour, institutional arrangements would have to be introduced to cut down recruiting costs, which in turn is likely to benefit employers at the unions' expense. The challenge facing us is to find solutions that strike a balance between the interests of the state, the employers and the unions.

Notes

1　Submitting a proposal by a governmental committee for consideration by a broad range of interest groups and authorities is an old institution and part of Swedish politics, hereafter 'comment on government report'. The Swedish Trade Union Confederation (LO), 28/1 1952, and the Swedish Employers' Confederation (SAF), 31/1 1952, comments on government report SOU 1951:42, Ministry of Justice, National Archives, 28/1 and 31/1 1952 respectively.

2　LO's comment on government report SOU 1967:18, Ministry of the Interior, National Archives, 11/10 1967.

3　LO's comment on government report SOU 1972:84–85, and Nordisk utredningsserie 16/70, Ds In 1972:20, Ministry of the Interior, National Archives, 7/5 1973.

4　Ibid.

5　SAF's comment on government report SOU 1972:84–85, and Nordisk utredningsserie 16/70, Ds In 1972:20, Ministry of the Interior, National Archives, 10/5 1973.

6　SAF's comment on government report SOU 1974:69. Ministry of Labour, National Archives, 8/11 1974.

7　SAF's comment on government report SOU 1967:18, Ministry of the Interior, National Archives, 20/9 1967.

8　LO's comment on government report SOU 1995:46, Ministry of Labour, Government Offices Archives, 3/11 1995. No comment from the SAF.

9　SAF's (and the Federation of Swedish Industries) comment on government report SOU 1995:76, Ministry of Labour, Government Offices Archives, 13/10 1995.

10　LO's comment on government report SOU 1995:76, Ministry of Labour, Government Offices Archives, 9/10 1995.

11　LO's comment on government report SOU 1996:55, Ministry of Labour, Government Offices Archives, 28/10 1996.

12　Ibid.

13　SAF's comment on government report SOU 1996:55, Ministry of Labour, Government Offices Archives, 24/9 1996.

PART 4
TRANSNATIONAL
COOPERATION AND REGIONAL
MIGRATION PROCESSES

Chapter 13

Asian Labour Migration and Regional Arrangements

Patcharawalai Wongboonsin

Introduction

Labour migration is not a new phenomenon in Asia. Yet it is a challenging issue characterized by three main dimensions. First, Asian labour migration has lately increased in density and complexity. Second, there are adverse effects on migrants' human security as well as national socioeconomic and political security in both source, transit, and destination countries. Third, there are major management drawbacks to aggravate those problems. This chapter focuses on the role of regional arrangements to deal with these challenges of labour migration in Asia. It highlights the importance of the Bangkok Declaration on Irregular Migration and other regional processes for the possibility to arrive at win-win solutions in Asia. While mainly emphasizing the so called APC consultations, the Manila Process and the Bali Process, an analysis of also other regional and subregional initiatives is provided. The aim is to evaluate the robustness and effectiveness of the regional arrangements in terms of outcomes, impacts, and shortcomings. A number of recommendations for further proactive arrangements are also provided.

Challenges of Asian Labour Migration

An Increasingly Complex Phenomenon

Recently, Asia has experienced a changing pattern, magnitude and structure of labour migration. One may notice four growing trends in the regional migration of labour in Asia: 1) asianization of labour migration; 2) feminization of labour migration; 3) unauthorization of labour migration; and 4) perpetuation of transnational crime and migrant trafficking and the lack of an established system for repatriation (Institute of Population Studies and Institute of Asian Studies, 1997; United Nations, 1998; OECD, 2000; Wongboonsin, 2001a).

Many Asian countries have assumed the status of source, destination and/or transit countries of labour migration. Compared to earlier more limited migration for long-term residence or permanent settlement in the West (Pongsapich, 1995), the recent phenomenon dominated by mass contract labour on a temporary basis to Asian countries represents a major shift. Such a shift took place particularly after the decline in oil revenues in the Gulf region and the Persian Gulf War. From the late 1970s to the early 1980s, annual labour migration from eight major source countries in Asia (Bangladesh, India, Pakistan, Sri Lanka, Indonesia, the Philippines, Thailand and the Republic of Korea) was estimated to have increased sevenfold, from about 150,000 to over one million (Abella, 1984). The late 1980s saw another major shift in terms of migration destination from the Middle East to East and Southeast Asia. In the early 1990s, Asian migrants were 36 per cent of world total migrant stock (United Nations, 1996). This trend is likely to grow more rapidly in response to economic change, disparities in demographic structure and social development, as well as increasing intensity in inter- and intra-regional economic relations.

All East Asian and certain Southeast Asian countries have become hosts of an increasing number of female labour migrants from other Asian countries with low income and poor human development. In 1993, women accounted for about 55 per cent of all overseas land-based contract workers from the Philippines (United Nations, 1997), and more than 60 per cent of those from Indonesia in 1994–1999 (Tirtosudarmo, 1997; 1998). Meanwhile, unauthorized or irregular labour migration has increased over the years. Informal and private estimates of irregular migrant labour in Taiwan reflect an increase from 10,000 in the late 1980s to 40,000 in 1990 (Ching-lung, 2000). Similarly in Thailand, the inflow of irregular migrant labour is expected to outnumber legal flows and to continue to grow as it has done since a decade. The widely-cited estimate in 2002 was about 1.2 million irregular migrants. This can be compared to an Immigration Bureau estimate of some 525,500 irregular migrants in 1994, and a Ministry of Labour survey of 944,000 in 1997 (Wongboonsin, 2003). Irregular labour migrants are mostly unskilled. Many of them can be victims of migrant trafficking, perpetuated by transnational crime rings (Hasan, 2001; ADB, 2002). Such trends occur against the backdrop of the lack of an established system for repatriation.

One may expect those trends to outweigh the rising flow of skilled and professional migrant guest workers to facilitate the increasing intensity in inter-and intra-regional economic relations. In Indonesia, skilled and high-end foreign workers increased from about 20,800 in 1990 to 37,200 in 1997 (Tjiptoherjanto, 1998). Those in Thailand increased from 10,000 in 1990 to over 80,000 in 2003 (Wongboonsin, 2003). This can be compared to irregular migration of unskilled labour, caused by the lack of human security, as well as a complex set of socioeconomic and political factors in the source countries. Meanwhile, mismanagement of migration at the national level further explains the increase in unauthorized or irregular migrant workers in Asia at both skilled (Sussangkarn, 1995) and unskilled levels. Some even argue that the single most significant cause of trafficking within South Asia is that countries have failed to negotiate any bilateral agreements for the movement of a limited number of economic migrants (Hasan, 2001).

Adverse Effects of Asian Labour Migration

Besides being induced by the general problem of human security in the source countries, transnational irregular migration of unskilled labour results both directly and indirectly, in widening and deepening human insecurity experienced by individual migrants. In a short-term perspective, unauthorized migrants can be at risk of poor and abusive working conditions with insecure income. They may also be the victims of traffickers, at risk of poor living conditions and vulnerable to violence and sexual abuse. In the long-term, migrant workers may end up in an unsustained working life without appropriate human development to run a dignified life. Moreover, they also risk great financial costs incurred by their transnational migration if they resort to the assistance of smugglers (Wongboonsin and Chantavanich, 2003).

Asia is attempting to position itself to meet the challenges of a globalizing economy. The aims include the strengthening of Asia's global competitiveness and a sustained dynamic growth in the twenty-first century. Fortunately during recent years, most Asian countries have been provided with a potential demographic dividend. The demographic dividend can be defined simply as the economic benefits deriving from demographic transition. It is a one-time window of opportunity, occurring only once during the demographic transition, and is available for only a short period. An increase in the dependency ratio signals the fading away of the opportunity to capitalize on the demographic conditions for a demographic dividend (Bloom et al., 2003; Wongboonsin et al., 2003).

Typically, the transition commences with a decline in mortality due to health improvements. This helps shifting the perception of the population from the desire to have many children to replace those who die or to ensure a sufficiently large family size, towards a new wish for a small family. The combination of falling mortality and fertility contributes to a decline in the dependency ratio. Thereafter, low fertility and stable mortality will result in an increasing share of the population who are elderly.

The dividend can result in a more productive workforce leading to higher economic growth. One third of the economic growth in East Asia and Singapore during the 1960s until the 1990s was attributed to demographic shifts with a 2.7 per cent growth in labour force per year (Mason, 2001). Other Southeast Asian countries are following the trend with more rapid growth of the economically active population than the economically dependent population. Their demographic dividend is currently around 0.7 per cent of per capita annual income growth (ADB, 1997; Bloom et al., 2003). However, the degree of economic benefits to be attained in most Southeast Asian countries is less pronounced than that in East Asia due to the relatively poor productivity of the workforce. The demographic dividend in Singapore, Thailand and Vietnam will fade away in a decade to come. This can be seen from the decline in the labour force – after reaching its peak of almost 69 per cent – to 66 per cent of the total population in 2010. Indonesia and Malaysia will experience a fading demographic dividend from 2025 onward, followed by Myanmar and Brunei Darussalam in 2030 (Wongboonsin and Kinnas, 2004).

Asian countries are expected to formulate appropriate policies and supporting institutions to make their bulging workforce productive enough to achieve sufficient growth before an increase in the old-age dependency ratio starts hampering economic growth. Nonetheless, the dominating strategies in managing the flows of labour migration have not been able to allow Asian countries to fully optimize or to maximize the demographic dividend. The management strategies towards the migration flows have mainly been self-defeating. A side effect of policies has been that migrants, the employers, and the national economies now have to face traps of insecure and unsustained socioeconomic development. This is not only visible in terms of the failure to control the invisible flows of labour migration, but also in terms of the relative slow pace of upgrading the international competitiveness of Asian countries. Meanwhile, foreign migrant workers are considered as a threat to socioeconomic and political security in transit and destination countries. The problem can be expected to aggravate in a few decades to come when the demographic dividend in Asia is fading away.

Migration Management Challenges

Migration control is largely perceived as a sovereign prerogative of states, but migration management is, in itself, a huge challenge in Asia. Migration management has not yet achieved the expected outcomes, including the goals to optimize the benefits of Asian labour migration; to minimize the adverse effects of the flows; and to guarantee an orderly, humane, and safe migration of labour. Many of the shortcomings can be referred to the areas of planning, regulating, and monitoring of labour migration flows.

The complex nature of labour migration and the shortcomings and knowledge gaps in policy-making contribute to the difficulties to adequately manage labour migration in Asia. Shortcomings are evident particularly in terms of matching the demand and supply of migrant workers, and dealing with the real costs and benefits of labour migration, as well as with the strengths and weaknesses of existing mechanisms. All migration statistics face a number of uncertainties as they do not reflect the whole picture (Institute of Population Studies and Institute of Asian Studies, 1997). Such knowledge-deficits lead to problems regarding the management process as well as the tools of management.

During the past decades, the inter-linkage of the following features characterized the approach to the management of transnational migration of labour in Asia: unilateral management approaches, national security and capitalism, unclear positions and different perspectives among authorities concerned, unfair treatment towards irregular migrants, and an emphasis on crack-downs and border control (ibid.; Archavanitkul and Guest, 1999; Wongboonsin, 2001b). These notions have mainly been based on the aim to safeguard local employment and national security. Meanwhile, a side-door is pried up to respond temporarily to the structural demand for migrant workers (Alburo, 1994; Pang, 1992; Skeldon, 1992; World Bank, 1995). This has partly perpetuated the tragedy of human trafficking.

Up to the turn of the century, a number of Asian countries were in need of national migration policy development that could provide the basis for effective responses at both the local, national and regional levels. Thailand, for instance, represented a typical Asian country in need of administrative structures that could provide for a division of authority and enhanced capacity of departments and officials in response to the migration challenges (ADB, 2002).

Some Asian countries have developed complicating legislative and regulatory regimes governing the entry and stay of foreign nationals. Others suffer from weak enforcement of legislative and regulatory measures to control migrant workers and employers. In most South and Southeast Asian countries, it is necessary to carry out a comprehensive legislative review with the aim of amending legislation and/or enacting new legislation to deal with the complex problem of migration. This includes, for instance immigration laws and the enactment of new laws to prosecute traffickers on the basis of international instruments.

Regional Arrangements in Asia

The Bangkok Declaration on Irregular Migration

Asia is characterized by huge differences in culture, religion, language and historical past. Yet, it is characterized by a tremendous potential for constructive cooperation. Asian countries have worked to establish regional cooperation as an approach for the solution to common problems and the consolidation of common interests of the region as a whole. The 1999 Bangkok Declaration on Irregular Migration marks a breakthrough in the quest for Asian collective efforts in migration arrangements. The basic motivation leading to the Bangkok Declaration was the mutual recognition among Asian source, transit and destination countries of migration that migration is a common problem, and that cooperation is necessary for migration management. The Bangkok Declaration signifies a political will of Asian governments to deal with the dilemmas of *common interests* and *common aversions* in labour migration. In the former case the aim is to foster an orderly, humane and safe migration through a win-win approach, i.e. to benefit the migrants as well as the countries concerned. The latter refers to potentially adverse effects of irregular migration and trafficking.

The Declaration mirrors a shared perception of the link between development and migration, migration trafficking, return of migrants, human rights and technical cooperation. More importantly, the win-win vision of the Bangkok Declaration aims to serve as the basic framework for cooperation and action on migration concerns in the region, with particularly a new anti-trafficking legislation as one long-term aim. Such cooperation, it is hoped for, could pave the way for the overall end goal – orderly, humane and safe flows of migration. The Bangkok Declaration highlights three key foundations for better and coherent management of migration flows: the perception and understanding of the problem; an improved migration management process at the national level; and cooperation in migration management beyond national boundaries.

More specifically, the Declaration underscores the strategic elements leading towards the long-term end goals. Among key guidelines, the Bangkok Declaration emphasizes that migration, particularly irregular migration, should be addressed in a comprehensive and balanced manner. It also emphasizes the need for information sharing for a better understanding of the social, economic, political and security causes and effects. Public information campaigns are being encouraged. Their purpose is to raise awareness at all levels about the adverse effects of migrant trafficking and related abuse, as well as of available assistance to victims. The Bangkok Declaration also recognizes the need for technical and financial assistance in order to upgrade the capacities of countries and authorities concerned with migration management.

The aforementioned inputs are expected to facilitate appropriate migration management at the national level with viable and effective policies and legislative measures that balance the rights and obligations of migrants with social and economic interests of the countries concerned. In this regard, the Bangkok Declaration encourages the participating countries to strengthen their channels of dialogue, to reinforce their efforts to prevent and combat irregular migration by improving their domestic laws and measures, and to pass legislation to criminalize smuggling of and trafficking in human beings.

Nevertheless, the Bangkok Declaration is not legally binding, nor provided with an institutional mechanism to monitor and to ensure that its guiding principles are upheld and shape behaviour at the national level and beyond. Given such weaknesses, the following section analyzes how other regional consultative processes and initiatives in Asia provide a political context favourable to the solution of the problems addressed in the Bangkok Declaration.

Other Regional Consultative Processes and Initiatives

Regional consultative processes in Asia can be divided into pre- and post-Bangkok Declaration processes. The former category includes the Intergovernmental Asia-Pacific Consultations on Refugees, Displaced Persons and Migrants (APC), initiated at a Conference on Regional Approaches to Refugees and Displaced Persons in Canberra in November 1996; and the Manila Process, a series of IOM Regional Seminars on Irregular Migration and Migrant Trafficking in East and Southeast Asia, which started in Manila in December 1996.

Pre-Bangkok Declaration regional consultative processes opened channels for source, transit and destination countries of labour migration to exchange their views on migration issues. They paved the way for deepening regional arrangements, of which the turning point is symbolized by the Bangkok Declaration. While the 'older' regional consultative processes continue to perform their function, more regional processes and initiatives have been launched since the Bangkok Declaration. The Bali Process and the Labour Migration Ministerial Consultations for Countries of Origins in Asia are key processes of this sort. Post-Bangkok Declaration regional collaborative processes tend to focus more on operational aspects along the guidelines provided in the Bangkok Declaration.

Substantial progress in migration management is limited to cooperation in certain subregions. This is particularly the case for the South Asian Association for Regional Cooperation (SAARC) and in the Greater Mekong subregion, whereby the SAARC Convention on Trafficking and bilateral memorandums of understanding, respectively, serve as subregional initiatives for better management of migration flows. All regional consultative processes in Asia share the principles of informality, non-binding decisions, flexibility and active dialogue. Yet, they are different in terms of size, mode of operation, and focus. As shown in Table 13.1, most regional consultative processes are under government ownership, that is driven and run by participating countries. This can be compared with the Manila Process, a small-sized regional non-ministerial consultative forum coordinated by the International Organization for Migration (IOM).

The APC Process A part of the strength of the APC-process is that it has continuously widened the scope of issues on the agenda. The focus of the first APC meeting in 1996 was the issue of illegal immigration to which was added the issues of refugees and displaced persons. Since then the APC has started to focus on comprehensive approaches to migration management, regular and irregular labour migration, people smuggling and trafficking, as well as return migration and reintegration. The APC-process also acknowledges the Bangkok Declaration. An APC work program has recently been launched and it is focusing both on current migration trends and comprehensive approaches to durable solutions.

The APC can be regarded as relatively advanced among the government-owned regional consultative processes. The APC is served by only a minor secretariat and changes its member state Chair and Coordinator on an annual basis. The Chair provides advice and guidance to participants while the APC Coordinator facilitates governmental consultations. Participating countries are invited to present and share their respective experiences and perspectives under an agreed theme. Besides financial support from various donors among its members, the APC has received financial and technical support from IOM and UNHCR, both of which have secured the status as participants in various APC meetings.

The APC has held a number of regular meetings each year. Besides an annual plenary meeting, there are expert groups, open-ended working groups, and subregional meetings for the Mekong, South Asia, Southeast Asia, and Pacific subregions. The subregional meetings are considered useful to address the specific needs and concerns relating to regional migration issues in a more systematic manner. For example, the Mekong subregional meeting of the APC in Cambodia in December 1999 considered the themes of reintegration and capacity building specific to the interest of the subregion. On the other hand, the South Asian subregional meeting of the APC in Bangladesh in August 2000 paid attention mostly to a comprehensive national policy,

Table 13.1   Regional labour-migration consultative processes in Asia

Regional process	Participants	Modus operandi	Labour-migration focus	Expected future development
APC Consultations (1996)	*Pre-Bangkok Declaration:* 23 countries in Asia-Pacific; UNHCR; IOM *Post-Bangkok Declaration:* 32 countries in Asia-Pacific; UNHCR; IOM	*Pre-Bangkok Declaration:* government ownership; run by participating countries; ministerial informal, non-binding decisions, flexible and active dialogue *Post-Bangkok Declaration:* as above as well as ministerial annual plenary meetings; expert group meetings when required; working group meetings; 4 ad hoc subregional meetings; website	*Pre-Bangkok Declaration:* regular and irregular migration; trafficking *Post-Bangkok Declaration:* as above	Consultative capacity-building operational forum to promote cooperation in law enforcement, entry and exit management techniques, comprehensive policies for foreign employment, capacity building for temporary employment, sound remittance management system; comprehensive approaches to durable solutions
Manila Process (1996)	*Pre-Bangkok Declaration:* 17 countries in East and Southeast Asia; IOM *Post-Bangkok Declaration:* as above	*Pre-Bangkok Declaration:* non-ministerial, informal, non-binding decisions, flexible and active dialogue; run by IOM *Post-Bangkok Declaration:* as above	*Pre-Bangkok Declaration:* irregular migration; trafficking *Post-Bangkok Declaration:* as above	Consultative and capacity-building operational forum
International Symposium on Migration (1999)	*Pre-Bangkok Declaration:* 18 countries in Asia-Pacific; Hong Kong SAR; UNHCR; UNFPA, IOM, ESCAP, APC, IGC	*Pre-Bangkok Declaration:* International Symposium on Migration, government ownership; consultations at ministerial and official levels under the auspices of Thai government, relevant NGOs, scholars and other stakeholders being invited to voice concerns	*Pre-Bangkok Declaration:* regular and irregular migration; trafficking	On-going operational forum with a plan of action to promote harmonization of policy in a long term

Table 13.1 cont'd

Regional process	Participants	*Modus operandi*	Labour-migration focus	Expected future development
International Symposium on Migration (1999) (cont'd)	*Post-Bangkok Declaration:* same as Pre-Bangkok Declaration, specialists from academic, NGOs	*Post-Bangkok Declaration:* government ownership; senior official and expert levels; informal, non-binding decisions, flexible and active dialogue; under the auspices of Thai government	*Post-Bangkok Declaration:* migration policy and law	
Bali Process (2002)	36 countries in Asia Pacific; international organizations as observers	Ministerial or equivalent level; informal, non-binding decisions, flexible and active dialogue; run by participating countries; under overall coordination of IOM Regional Office in Bangkok; website	Trafficking law enforcement, legislative development	On-going consultative and operational forum; trafficking law enforcement, legislative development
LMMC	10 Asian countries of origin	Ministerial and senior levels; informal, non-binding decisions, flexible and active dialogue; government ownership, sponsored by IOM	Consultative forum to identify steps for follow up in the form of recommendations in three areas: protection of migrant workers and services to migrant workers; optimization of the benefits of organized labour migration; capacity building	On-going consultative forum to identify steps for follow up in the form of recommendations

Note: Pre-Bangkok Declaration refers to a process before the signing of The Bangkok Declaration on Irregular Migration in April 1999; Post-Bangkok Declaration refers to a process thereafter.

Source: Author.

as a first step towards a regional framework for orderly and humane movement of labour across border.

The APC process may so far have had less impact than expected. This may be due to the fact that the working group meetings have not become fully institutionalized. Rather, they are organized only on an *ad hoc* basis with inconsistent and incoherent member state participation. Such inadequate participation may negatively affect the strength of the APC. It is often caused by limited available expertise and resources, or by unclear positions and mandates due to the lack of focal authority or appropriate coordination among the various government agencies concerned.

The Manila Process Unlike the APC, the Manila Process was originally intended as a one-off seminar. Yet, recurrent annual seminars have so far been held in Manila, Bangkok, and Jakarta in 1997, 1998, and 2000 respectively, drawing 17 source, transit, and destination countries in East and Southeast Asia, as well as in the Pacific. The main aim has been to informally discuss and exchange information on irregular migration and trafficking. The recent themes of concern have included cooperation to prevent and better manage irregular migration; labour migration during the economic crisis; and migration and trafficking. The first seminar recognized that it had become impossible for one country to address irregular migration and trafficking on its own, and that regular and irregular migration should not be considered in isolation from each other. Such outcomes and the growing problem of irregular migration and trafficking, particularly during the economic crisis, provided an incentive for further attempts to deepen discussion on the role of information sharing, the root causes of, as well as the prevention and control of the problem. The issues of discussion under the Manila Process were mirrored in the 1999 Bangkok, upon which the Manila Process itself draws as a guide for action in the 2000s (IOM, 2001). The Manila Process is expected to shift from a regional dialogue to a more operational process. So far, however, operational progress remains to be seen.

The Bali Process The Bali Process refers to the Regional Ministerial Conference on People Smuggling, Trafficking in Persons, and Related Transnational Crime, held in Bali in February 2002 and in April 2003. The Bali Process is expected to have a great potential of contributing to better management of migrant smuggling and related transnational crime in the region. First, unlike the Manila Process, the Bali Process was set up and driven by the needs and expectations of states in the region. The process has been ably assisted by the IOM Regional Office in Bangkok, which has been endowed with secretarial, technical and logistical functions (IOM, 2003a). Second, the Bali Process has added political impetus to the discussion at both ministerial and working levels of governments in the region. Compared to the Manila Process and the APC, the Bali Process has been attended by a larger and more diverse range of ministers and senior officials covering source, transit and destination countries. Third, the Bali Process has fostered regional cooperation beyond information sharing. The formation of expert groups and workshops has created a network of officials in the field of law enforcement, legislative development, fraudulent document detection, as well as border and visa systems. Besides attaining concrete results, the Bali Process has also renewed political impetus to work on return migration (as raised in the 1999 Bangkok Declaration).

The LMMC Process Compared to the above-mentioned regional consultative processes, the Labour Migration Ministerial Consultations for Countries of Origins in Asia (LMMC) serves as a consultative forum at both ministerial and senior official levels for a more narrowly defined issue. As the first of its kind, the consultative forum is mainly for ten purely Asian labour-source countries – Bangladesh, China, India, Indonesia, Nepal, Pakistan, the Philippines, Sri Lanka, Thailand and Vietnam. The forum aims to optimize the benefits of an orderly and organized labour migration and to forge greater cooperation to develop a common stance in addressing issues affecting migrant workers.

If functioning efficiently, the forum can be expected to contribute to better regularization of both high and low-end labour migration in Asia. At the least, the forum can provide a good opportunity for labour source countries in the region to learn from others in terms of best practices and policy flaws. At the most, one may expect the work of the forum to lead to subregional agreements and institutional mechanisms for transparent recruitment, better protection and services to migrant workers, larger benefits and lesser costs of migration. For the time being, these ten labour-source countries suffer the problem of financial, personnel, and technical resources.

The potential benefits are not limited to remittances, but also include the use of remittances for sustained development at the individual and societal levels, as well as better use of the skills migrant workers acquire while working abroad. Meanwhile, the costs of migration are not only visible in terms of investment and return, but also as a human tragedy, substantiated by socio-psychological costs and opportunity costs incurred at the individual as well as societal levels. The potential risk of failure is that the forum may face a dilemma of loose cooperation among key competing source countries and free riding, which may aggravate migrants' vulnerability, migration costs, oversupply and unemployment of migrant workers, and an increase in irregular migration.

In practice, the forum has gone beyond being just a talk shop. Steps have been taken to arrive at recommendations concerning fundamental labour migration needs in the region (IOM, 2003); the protection of migrant workers and services to migrant workers; optimization of the benefits of organized labour migration; and institutional capacity-building and inter-state cooperation. Based on the discussions at both the ministerial and senior levels in 2003 and 2004, the forum has provided an opportunity to raise the level of awareness among labour source countries regarding existing and potential employer abuses as well as the discriminatory practices of destination countries. It has also provided them with an opportunity to address these issues, not only through bilateral negotiations, but also more effectively through strong alliances among Asian labour source countries.

A consensus was reached during the 2003 forum to explore possible dialogues between Asian source countries and destination countries in the Middle East. For the 2004 consultations, the focus is the promotion of safe working conditions and protection of migrant workers by source governments and recruitment agencies (Department of Labour and Employment, 2003). Those activities are considered important. Yet, a more fundamental concerted action is required as well as domestic measures to efficiently regulate irregular procedures within the migration process. Participating countries are expected to explore the feasibility of amending their own labour laws and regulations to extensively protect their migrant workers overseas. This has been an area of negligence in the labour laws of most labour-source countries. In this regard, actions within the forum need to go beyond cooperation to attain collaboration with a surveillance system and a clear national focal point.

ASEAN and SAARC arrangements An even further deepening and more focused collaboration along the guidelines provided in the Bangkok Declaration is found in the South Asian and Southeast Asian subregions. At this early stage, despite differences in activity paces and outcomes, there are commonalities in the adoption of a 'victim-first principle' and law enforcement against trafficking. In Southeast Asia, regional anti-trafficking law-enforcement networks are a primary outcome of the Association of Southeast Asian Nations (ASEAN) to establish various fora to fight against trafficking along an ASEAN Plan of Action to Combat Transnational Crime, as an intermediate plan to achieve the ASEAN Vision 2020. Such ASEAN concerted efforts are considered steps behind that of the South Asian Association for Regional Cooperation (SAARC) to catalyze changes in the national legislative and regulatory regimes as well as judiciary institutions along the victim-protection and trafficking-criminalization principles.

As the key output, the long-awaited SAARC Convention on Preventing and Combating Trafficking in Women and Children for Prostitution, signed in January 2002, provides a unique opportunity to combat trafficking in women and children for prostitution, and to move forward on repatriation issues in South Asia. Compared with activities in other parts of the region, the supporting measures provided in the Convention are relatively advanced in meeting the 1999 Bangkok Declaration guidelines: regional capacity-building cooperation for law enforcement mechanism, mutual legal assistance with respect to investigation, inquiries, trials, proceedings, repatriation, care, treatment, rehabilitation, a regional monitoring task force and the encouragement of bilateral agreements to interdict trafficking (FWLD, n.d.). This is the case despite a slow pace in implementation due to traditional socioeconomic and political intertia.

The SAARC Convention attempts to present a set of recommendations which emerged from initiatives in a series of preparatory meetings (UBINIG, 1997). Above all, there has been recognition at the level of the Heads of State of the need for partnership between the official SAARC actors and independent actors, such as scholars, professionals, NGOs, and the media to bring about the potential for a South

Asian economic community with sustainable human development (Wignaraja, 2003). It remains to be seen if the SAARC initiative would explicitly extend its coverage beyond trafficking, and whether it can be ensured that traffickers are charged for all crimes committed. Most of all, it needs to ensure with adequate monitoring mechanisms that victims are immune from criminal liability, deprivation of rights, freedom and dignity. These notions are part of the concerns at the grassroots level of South Asian societies (FWLD, n.d; SAARC People's Forum, 1998).

Compared with other subregions, the Greater Mekong is moving ahead in terms of forging increased intergovernmental agency collaboration in nurturing good governance in the process of repatriation. As noted in the 1999 Bangkok Declaration, the key elements of Memorandums of Understanding (MOUs) within Thailand and between Thai and other governments in the Greater Mekong subregion since 2002, are based upon the 'victim's-needs-come-first' principle. This represents an important shift in authorities' concern, away from a state-centred security focus as the primary goal in migration management. As in the SAARC Convention, the MOUs in this part of the region need to push for viable institutional mechanisms to monitor and to ensure that the needs of the victims are really being met (ADB, 2002).

The Greater Mekong initiative is also driven by the realization among Thai stakeholders – government and non-government – as well as other actors in the subregion of the need to improve the structures and mechanisms for collaboration among themselves before reaching outward across borders. More recently, there are also efforts to seek cooperation between subregions. At the initial phase of this new phenomenon, the efforts are still limited to discussions and exchange of information, lessons learned and good practices between stakeholders in SAARC and the counterparts in the Greater Mekong subregion (ADB, 2002). If such exchanges of information and experiences function on an on-going process, one may expect greater understanding across the region of shared concerns and potential areas for future collaboration between both subregions of Asia to successfully meet the guiding principles stipulated in the 1999 Bangkok Declaration.

Evaluation and Recommendations

Several regional arrangements in the realm of migration are being developed in parallel. Starting with three loose and informal consultative processes at the governmental level with active collaboration from multilateral specialized agencies, Asia has reached its first stage of securing verbal commitments in regional cooperation. The Bangkok Declaration as the key output has provided guidelines for both on-going and new concerted efforts and regional processes on migration in Asia.

Each regional process comes with both strengths and weaknesses in relation to the long-term goals of the Bangkok Declaration. The most fundamental and benign results are firstly, the pan-regional recognition of the need to address the complex problems of migration in a comprehensive and balanced manner; and secondly, region-wide cooperation in migration-related information exchange as an important input to shape interests for viable and effective migration policies among source, transit and destination countries in the region. The surge in the number of fora and participating countries reflects an on-going interest of Asian countries in participation, and the general recognition of the contribution of the regional approach to migration management.

Nevertheless, interests vary across the region and issues of concerns. As a result, proactive and more concrete actions beyond those mentioned above are merely marginal. This is the case when a regional consultative process is moving towards an operational process, starting with capacity building of those countries and their authorities concerned to deal with the complex problem of migration. So far, success on these terms has been limited in both scope and substance. Labour migration is not limited to political and institutional contexts. It is also an individual choice, based on perceived costs and benefits. However, most regional processes and initiatives have paid little attention directly to the individual migrant's interests and reasons for cross-border mobility.

The SAARC Convention on Trafficking and the MOUs in the Greater Mekong subregion represent the key substantive outcomes of regional arrangements to deal with the dilemma of common aversion. Emphasizing the victim's needs, they touch on two areas of practical challenges identified in the Bangkok Declaration: appropriate national legislation and domestic interdepartmental cooperation. Yet, they cannot provide an overall solution to the complex problem of pernicious trafficking. Cooperation between both subregions in terms of information exchange and lessons learned is expected as an on-going process to render regime effectiveness.

It remains to be seen if the limited contribution of existing regional processes in terms of changes in perception and understanding of the migration problem above the level of experts and senior officials, will result in changes of behaviour at a lower level of implementation in most parts of the region. Even in the SAARC and the Greater Mekong subregions, such effects are still to be monitored closely. In general, more concrete and concerted actions require a more active role of the existing regional processes as well as the interplay among them.

Recommended future actions on the part of the regional processes and initiatives in Asia include:

• Participation of non-governmental stakeholders in regional and subregional cooperation. This is particularly important in the capacity-building processes and public information campaigns against irregular migration and trafficking.
• Promotion of synergies and linkages among the existing processes in the region, with strategic plans of action. This includes coordination and cooperation among the various regional initiatives for lessons learned and good practice. Besides, the idea of avoiding a duplication of efforts in regard to the same issues should be recognized among the regional processes.
• Designation of national focal points endowed with an appropriate level of authority to establish measures of cooperation involving the various national entities involved in migration and related concerns. This is a key mechanism to

encourage commitments and dedication of governments to act upon and to devote resources to effectively implement the Bangkok Declaration.

- Greater attention to neglected issue-areas. These include existing concerns such as return and reintegration, improvement in domestic laws and measures, good governance in migration-related institutional mechanisms and processes. Among the renewed concerns are human-development and human-security aspects of optimizing the contribution of migration to sustained socioeconomic development of the countries concerned and their people. It aims at mobilizing the full potential of the regional workforce at all skills-levels in response to the new challenge of a fading demographic dividend in Asia. To do so, human development should be part of the management strategies at the national levels and beyond. Regional arrangements should be equipped with regional surveillance systems and standards. And finally, cooperation between source and destination countries should provide impetus and channels for migrant workers to enjoy the rights to human development with dignity, while facilitating integration and re-integration of migrant workers to better contribute to both the host country and the country of origin.

Concluding Remarks

Asia is facing the challenges of increasingly complex labour migration patterns, with adverse effects at the individual and national levels. Unilateral migration management has not been able to optimize the benefits or to minimize the adverse effects of labour migration. The Bangkok Declaration on Irregular Migration signifies the first concrete step towards widening and deepening regional cooperation in appropriate migration management. Orderly, humane and safe flows of migration are both the key words and the end goal of all regional migration arrangements taking place in Asia. The regional consultative processes have facilitated both the genesis and the implementation of the Bangkok Declaration. Yet, the Bangkok Declaration is not legally binding, and it is neither a matter of regional policy or plan of action, nor the solution to the migration problems in Asia.

The implementation of the Bangkok Declaration in an even more concrete and practical way, requires deepening regional cooperation to better manage migration. More subregional initiatives to catalyze national legislative enactment of policy and the necessary inter-departmental cooperation are needed. An improved robustness and efficiency of the regional arrangements requires a strengthened role of and interplay among existing regional consultative and operational processes, with participation of non-governmental stakeholders, if possible. More than anything else, the solution lies in strengthened efforts with commitments and dedication of governments concerned to act upon and to devote resources to effectively strike a balance between the migrants' human security and human rights with the socioeconomic, and political security of source, transit, and destination countries.

Chapter 14

Cooperation and Barriers to People and Goods: Examples from Africa

John O. Oucho

Introduction

The relationship between Africa and the developed North has consistently been an imbalanced African dependency on the North. The African continent continues to be exploited. It all started with the European and Arab exploits that ushered in the inhuman slave trade. More than 20 million Africans were trafficked to the New World and Europe as well as the Arab world. At the infamous Berlin Conference of 1884–1885, Africa was parcelled into power possessions which Great Britain, France, Belgium, Spain and Portugal ruled for several decades before the possessions became independent. Still, important links are being maintained with these powers.

These historical episodes of the South-North interdependence are crucial in considering current cooperation and barriers to emigration and goods from Africa to the North. In one of the early works on international migration and international trade, Russell and Teitelbaum (1992: 33) noted that the tendency of European countries to use economic transfers (aid, investment and trade) as a tool of stemming immigration from Africa, the Middle East and the then socialist Central-Eastern Europe was overly simplistic. The debate still rages about the outcomes of cooperation and barriers to migration and trade on a sustainable basis in a world currently full of contradictions stemming from globalization. In the concluding chapter of his book, Skeldon (1997: 202) cautions that:

> The idea of a South-North migration of unprecedented magnitude is not only geographically incorrect, but it also obscures the most significant flows ... Much of the reaction against migration is engendered by fear: a fear that the familiar homogeneous nation-state of the last 250 years of Western history is giving way to something different and more complex.

Invoking McNeil's (1986) 'reassertion of the polyethnic norm', Skeldon sees reassertion at the upper levels of the development hierarchy whereas, at the lower end, the idea of the homogeneous state is creating migration. At the bottom end, economic and political forces favour expulsion, while at the top they favour attraction. These contrasts complicate migration policies of most countries.

Although relations between Africa and Europe remain strong, they fail the test when it comes to migration and commodity flows. The policy debates regarding migration and development are continent-centric as both continents focus on their own real or perceived problems and experiences without caring about what affects the other (Adepoju and Hammar, 1996: 8). Invariably the interests of Europe take precedence over those of Africa which clings to its dependency syndrome. As opposed to the period before 1973 when Europe encouraged immigration from North Africa, the period since the mid-1970s has witnessed the opposite as Europe depends increasingly on migration from Eastern and Central Europe. Europe harbours the notion that opening markets to goods from the South inevitably reduces the pressure to migrate (Nassar and Ghoneim, 1998). This is not a situation limited to North Africa-Europe relations, it essentially epitomizes Africa-North migration and trade relations.

This chapter seeks to examine instances of cooperation between particular African countries and countries in the North and cases of barriers to people and goods originating from the region. It should be clear from the outset that, broadly speaking, Africa consists of two distinct blocs: North Africa which has had longstanding connections with Europe and the Middle East, and Sub-Saharan Africa (SSA) which has connections with the two as well as the New World (in particular the Americas). Current South-North migration can be located more or less within the set of dynamics and structures that gave rise to the world system, the incorporation of different parts and regions through colonization and other forms of relationships, and the current processes of global restructuring and globalization (Akin-Aina, 1996: 39). Thus, there are historical, colonial, cultural and migration ties that bind the two poles together (ibid., pp. 41–8). Against the hackneyed conclusion in the literature that the relationship between migration and trade is ambiguous, the chapter calls for core research to be undertaken on the extent to which the two phenomena sustain South-North relations and the consequences of such interdependence.

Cooperation in International Migration and Trade

Europe has received successive generations of African immigrants and virtually all of Africa's exportable goods. The colonization of Africa by European powers gave Europe a stranglehold not only on the labour force they needed but also on acquisition and conversion of African goods into manufactured products that in turn have subsequently been sold to Africa as the most dependable market.

Emigration from Africa to the North

Cooperation has been undertaken mainly in stemming, albeit at times encouraging, emigration from Africa. This is consistent with what the International Conference on Population and Development (ICPD) Plan of Action in Cairo proposed, namely: collaboration between countries of origin and destination in managing migration; developing an approach to the origins of migration in order to stem it and to reduce immigration to the destinations; and fostering productive use of remittances in the countries of origin (UNFPA, 1994: 83–4).

Within this context, increasing attention is being drawn to migration policies. Marmora (1999: 109–227) has for example classified migration policies into five categories: the trinity of international trade, Foreign Direct Investment (FDI) and Overseas Development Assistance (ODA) as well as national development programmes to retain potential emigrant populations; policies promoting or regulating immigration and emigration; policies oriented to migrant recovery: return programmes and reintegration programmes; and policies meant to incorporate immigrants, such as insertion, integration and assimilation, as well as regularization of illegal immigrants. Although useful as categories, these are merely the various policies targeting immigration. Also in the countries of origin there are policies that either permit or restrict emigration in general, or to particular countries.

Aid, Trade and Investment to Stem Emigration

The preferred combination is a triumvirate of policies focusing on aid, trade and investment and governments in the North that are bent on reducing immigration pressures, therefore, tend to promote such transfers. Yet while aid is a government-to-government undertaking, trade and investment are the prerogative of private actors, including Trans-National Corporations (TNCs). In many instances the countries of immigration in the North make it easier for goods to enter than people. The choice between 'aid and trade' should be both, rather than one of the two (Martin and Straubhaar, 2002: 13–17).

Aid in general does not necessarily stem emigration; rather, it is meant to produce the kind of goods (agricultural products, for instance) which industrialized countries manufacture for sale in the emigration countries. Although empirical evidence reveals a positive correlation between ODA from developed countries and migration from developing countries, the relationship may in fact be spurious on two grounds. First, there are strong ties between the United Kingdom, France and Portugal on the one hand and their former colonies on the other which necessitate ODA even when migration is controlled. Second, ODA to some countries may have been for other reasons. For instance, ODA to Turkey (a major emigration country) during the Cold War was provided because the country had strategic importance for Europe, and that to Tanzania, with relatively few emigrants, may have been for reasons other than to stem international migration (Stalker, 2002: 172).

FDI has become the most important transfer from the developed North to the developing South, followed by migrant remittances and ODA in descending order. About 65 per cent of the total FDI inflows to Africa in 1996–1997 concentrated in South Africa, Nigeria and Cote d'Ivoire (Morisset, 2000), the first two now spearheading the African development agenda. Surprisingly, the business climate in 1995–1997 was most favourable in Namibia, followed by Mali, Mozambique, Zambia, Chad and Senegal (Morisset, 2000).

In contrast, countries with either bigger local markets (such as Kenya, Cameroon and DR Congo) or substantial natural resources (DR Congo and Zimbabwe) did not attract as much investment from the North as the former group of countries. One reason may be that these countries have a more risky investment environment. Factors contributing to a viable investment environment in other parts of the region include the GDP growth rate and the openness of the national economies following trade liberalization, which has led to a more general reduction in administrative barriers (Morisset, 2000).

Only a few African countries were among the top 20 recipients of migrant remittances, FDI flows and portfolio and other flows in the world by the late 1990s. Regarding remittances they were Egypt (3rd), Morocco (6th), Algeria (14th), Nigeria (16th) and Tunisia (20th). No African country featured among the top 20 FDI recipients. Only South Africa (18th) ranked among the top 20 recipients of portfolio and other flows (UNDP, 1999: 27). The picture portrayed suggests that even the much-touted North-to-Africa flows benefit only a few African countries, namely those having well-established connections with the sources of the flows. North Africa dominates in migrant remittances and only Nigeria and South Africa, the two African economic powerhouses in the region and chaperoning western and southern sub-regions respectively, received sizeable volumes of remittances and portfolio and other flows respectively.

Migrant Remittances

Migrant remittances from the North to developing countries currently rank second to FDI and exceed ODA. In Africa, Morocco and Egypt lead the pack of recipients (Martin, 2004). In 1975, the bulk of remittances to Africa were received in North African countries – Egypt, Morocco and Tunisia. Recipients in Western Africa included Senegal, Nigeria and Mali and to a smaller extent Ghana, Togo and Niger; and those in Southern Africa were Madagascar and Lesotho (World Bank, 2001, quoted in Oucho, 2003: 226).

Sander and Maimbo (2003) argue that the flow of remittances reflects the patterns of migration to Europe and the Middle East. The authors estimated that in the past decade, North Africa received 72 per cent of the total remittances to Africa, followed by East Africa (13 per cent), Southern Africa (7 per cent), West Africa (5 per cent) and Central Africa (less than 1 per cent). In the regional economic communities (RECs) in Sub-Saharan Africa, workers in SADC generated the highest volume of remittances, followed by ECOWAS, ECCAS and EAC (Sander and Maimbo, 2003).[1] The point to be stressed is that migrant remittances are highly volatile as well as difficult to estimate.

The analysis of remittances by Sander and Maimbo acknowledges the fact that throughout Africa, financial and monetary policies and regulations have created barriers to the flow of remittances and their effective investment. For instance, there has been restrictive licensing of money transfer services and the environment for investment is unattractive thus distracting potential remittances. Apparently, the liberalization of many national economies in the era of structural adjustment has given impetus to the inflow of remittances and eased their utilization by the recipients. Nonetheless, the bulk of remittances end up in domestic consumption and to some extent in community projects. The role of 'home improvement unions' in Nigeria (Dike, 1982) and social welfare associations in Kenya (Oucho, 1996) and similar initiatives in virtually all countries of emigration, complement government efforts in the development of social services in particular.

The Euro-Mediterranean Partnership

The Euro-Mediterranean Partnership (EMP) was launched in late 1994 and formally inaugurated a year later in Barcelona, hence it became known as the Barcelona Process. The Barcelona Declaration urged the partners to:

- establish a common area of peace and stability based on fundamental principles including respect for human rights and democracy (political and security partnership);
- create an area of shared prosperity through the progressive establishment of a free-trade area accompanied by substantial EU support (economic and financial partnership); and
- develop human resources as well as promote understanding between cultures and rapprochement of the peoples in the region (social, cultural and human partnership).

EMP was a European initiative involving ten Mediterranean Non-Member Countries in the Maghreb and Mashrek region ostensibly attempting to contain sudden and violent developments, notably political upheavals in Algeria and the unexpected arrival of 'boat people' from Morocco to Spain (Tovlas, n.d.).[2] Thus, the EMP is an economic partnership with migration, security, trade and development on the agenda. So far, the MEDA programme (*Mesures d'Accompagnement*) has funded structural adjustment, business training and rural development programmes. The social partnership emphasizes civil society exchanges, education, social planning and fighting destructive ideologies, such as racism (CEIP, 2004: 4).

Cooperation and Co-development

The concept of *co-development* has been initiated by France to collaborate with the countries of emigration in establishing programmes and projects that would benefit migrants and stem the flow of potential migrants. A good example is the Mali-France Consultation on Migration. This is an annual bilateral discussion at the ministerial level that was launched in December 2000 for three purposes: 1) the integration of Malians who want to remain in France; 2) co-management of migration flows; and 3) cooperative development in emigration areas of Mali. A significant development since its inception has been the issuance of 25,000 visas to Malians in 2001 compared with 7,000 in 1997, which reduced fraudulence in the acquisition of visas. Furthermore, despite their ethnic diversity, Malians in France have pooled their resources and remitted them back home to support the construction of health clinics, schools and to repair roads as well as to invest in small business enterprises (Martin and Weil, 2002).

From a fund managed by a French-Malian committee, the French allocated €2.6 million in 2002–2004 for the mobilization of Malians abroad for the service of the Malian education system, economy and small business enterprise development. In addition, a contract was to be signed with a Malian bank to guarantee loans to small businesses that needed additional funding to expand. This seemingly benevolent gesture by France has lured about 500 unauthorized Malians in France to return voluntarily in exchange for the equivalent of US $3,600 on arrival back home opening businesses relating to agriculture and providing a variety of services (Martin and Weil, 2002).

The French co-development approach seeks to target ODA at emigration areas in all Francophone Africa, with government support supplementing the migrants' contributions already referred to. Thus, it is radically distinct from the more recent EU strategy to *inter alia* review development cooperation with countries that are insufficiently cooperating with destination countries on especially the return of unauthorized migrants (Martin and Weil, 2002). The recent overture from Prime Minister Tony Blair to strengthen African development emulates the French approach, which the EU should find suitable in fathoming the EU-Africa relations.

In Senegal, there is a Union of Local Initiatives for Co-development (UNILCO) founded by Senegalese representatives and expatriates. It is dedicated to the economic development of the country, with the main goal to help the Senegalese diaspora to participate in developing their homeland and to raise the standards of living of their relatives. It also assists individuals or groups of people willing to start businesses or social services in Senegal by helping them to clarify, formulate and disseminate their projects.[3] Thus, UNILCO both touches the heart of African socialism in which communalism rather than individualism is encouraged, and provides a window of opportunity for those with business acumen or humanitarian disposition to institutionalize development.

The Cotonou Agreement

In June 2000, the EU and the 77-member ACP (Asian, Caribbean and Pacific countries) signed the *Cotonou Agreement* (CA) to reduce and eventually eradicate poverty by promoting sustainable development, capacity building and integration into the world economy. Given the scale of migration from the ACP countries to Europe, the CA drew attention to labour migration, pledging to:

- accord respect for human rights to migrants who reside legally in the countries covered by the CA;
- initiate strategies to tackle the root causes of massive migration flows through 'supporting the economic and social development of the origins from which migrants originate', training of ACP nationals and improving access to their students in the EU; and
- make regulations to counter irregular migration through bilateral and return agreements that facilitate returning and re-admitting all nationals found in an irregular situation.

As a form of migration management, the CA has far-reaching ramifications for the African members of the ACP that have their nationals residing in the EU, although implementation has just recently begun. It draws attention to international migration and international trade, and is probably geographically the most extensive South-North agreement that touches on these issues.

Return Migration Schemes

Return migration is the finale of the three 'Rs', preceded by recruitment and remittances. Unfortunately, return migration has been largely disregarded in the migration literature, receiving systematic attention only since 1973 when economic crisis set the stage for it (Ammassari and Black, 2001: 17). It should be noted, however, that there are different types of return migration. For instance, Cerase (1974, quoted in Ammassari and Black, 2001: 22) identifies four categories as the *return of failure* after a 'traumatic shock' upon arrival and inability to adapt to the new environment in the destination; the *return of conservatism*, involving migrants who maintained links with their origins and who return after residing in a destination for some time; *return of motivation*, involving those who return with some treasured values, ideas and skills which they wish to apply on returning to their home countries (potential 'agents of change' in the latter); and the *return of retirement* of those who have terminated their working careers and who return to their home countries as a matter of cause.

This classification of return migrants implies that institutions engaged in returning migrants often deal with only a small proportion or a particular type of eligible returnees. For example, the IOM and UNDP have been limiting themselves to returning skilled migrants. NEPAD envisions doing the same thing, as it desires to return the African brain drain and convert it into brain gain. Clearly, Cerase's (1974) classification omits refugees – Africa's greatest liability (Oucho, 2003) – returned as a result of *refoulement* or returning voluntarily after conditions improve in their countries of origin. As return programmes have become commonplace in Africa, the hand of the North can easily be discerned, especially in institutions such as the UNDP and IOM which are driven by the North. Returned migrants, whether voluntary migrants or refugees and asylum seekers, are potentially a great asset to their countries of origin, but only if they are deployed or empowered to invest in particular areas of need.

They provide the energy, ideas and entrepreneurial vigour needed to start or expand businesses at home, and workers abroad return with the skills and discipline needed to raise productivity at home (Martin, 2004).

From TOKTEN to RQAN and MIDA Following the outcry of countries of the South that brain drain was crippling their development efforts, UNDP and the IOM embarked on a return migration scheme known as the Transfer of Knowledge Through Expatriate Nationals (TOKTEN). Although the United Nations Economic Commission for Africa (ECA) and the IOM entered into a TOKTEN pact in the 1970s, the results were far from impressive. Richard Black (cited in Martin, 2004) has characterized return programmes as 'expensive failures', that are temporary and without the capacity for investment. Even when the IOM later came up with the Return of Qualified African Nationals (RQAN) to replace TOKTEN, it did not make an impact on African countries.

Lately, the IOM, viewing migration through a positive lens, has initiated the Migration for Development in Africa (MIDA), which aims to build relationships between host countries and countries of origin to foster positive effects of migration for their mutual benefit and limit the negative effects of brain drain. Although the IOM has been providing financial incentives to return migrants in all the return schemes, it has failed to reach the target, let alone to convince the large number of Africans abroad to embrace the opportunity. Worse still, the IOM has received little support from its African member states that are supposed to collaborate with it in the MIDA programme.

Return schemes have failed because of several reasons. First, the conditions that sparked emigration of professionals and the highly trained have deteriorated rather than improved in their countries of origin. Returning doctors and nurses find dilapidated health programmes with obsolete or irreparable equipment; teachers return to find schools with poor learning-environments and grossly lacking basic facilities; university lecturers are confronted with unbearably large classes, lack of equipment and poor research facilities, including lack of research funds; and returning migrants with capital and entrepreneurial skills cannot afford to invest in a risky economic environment ravaged by crime, corruption and bad governance. Their immediate reaction is pretty predictable: take off to yet another emigration episode never to look back until retirement. Second, the public service (represented by national governments), which is supposed to benefit from return migrants, merely sign (and hardly adhere to the provisions of their) agreements with the IOM or other parties. Thirdly, even those returning to retire find a most shocking homecoming where relatives await gifts from them rather than collaborate with them in whatever initiatives they offer.

The NEPAD vision The New Partnership for Africa's Development (NEPAD), the latest institution of hope in the Africa-North relations, wishes to develop the region's human resources by: 1) reversing the brain drain and turning it into a brain gain; 2) building and retaining the region's human capacities; and 3) developing strategies for utilising the skills of Africans in the diaspora for the development of the region. NEPAD intends to achieve the three respective objectives by creating viable political, social and economic conditions that could attract the return of brain drain; establishing a reliable data base on the brain drain and the African diaspora; and ensuring the utilization of the African experts abroad in NEPAD-designed projects. Sadly, the NEPAD vision is grossly presumptuous and raises some questions: If in the first place African countries do not even have records of their brain drain, how does NEPAD expect to ascertain the volume, destinations and characteristics of the region's brain drain? What is NEPAD's depth of knowledge of the size, diversity, successive generations and the geography of the African diaspora?

This is an area that requires immediate and carefully designed research before NEPAD proposes any meaningful programmes. Analysis of the African diaspora (not taking into account that in the United States) suggests that it is sizeable in France, Italy, the United Kingdom, Germany, Spain and Canada; and the leading sources of the African diaspora are Morocco, Senegal, Ghana and Nigeria (Oucho, 2004). In these countries, and indeed many more countries (Somalia, Mali, Burkina Faso, Uganda, Eritrea and Ethiopia), strong networks between the diaspora and non-migrants exist and point to the utility of engaging the diaspora in development.

NEPAD is considered an 'African rescue plan'. Apart from the human resources initiative already described, NEPAD has ambitious programmes in the fields of international trade, ODA, FDI and portfolio flows to Africa. Canada has removed virtually all trade restrictions to developing countries (including African ones). The United States is providing $15 billion to fight HIV/AIDS and for other development undertakings in Africa. The European Union, the U.S. and Canada have pledged large percentage increases in ODA to unblock US $1 billion for previously approved debt relief (Herbert, 2004). At face value, NEPAD provides hope for Africa, but it remains to be seen how it unfolds in a continent which has been preoccupied with experimenting with framework after framework.

Barriers to African Immigration and Goods in the North

This section examines barriers to immigration in terms of controls or restrictions and to African goods from the perspective of trade policies and the rampant imbalance of trade between the North and Africa. Schiff (1996) contends that the South would gain from trade liberalization in either the North or the South, and the North would gain from imposing an immigration tax. Analysis by Schiff (1996) suggests that optimal immigration tax and full internalization could result in four main pairs of alternative scenarios. First, the national welfare in the South is higher than that in the ambiguous North; second, both the South and the North gain from a decrease in migration costs; third, the South loses and the North gains from a tariff in the South; and finally, the North loses and the South gains in the case of illegal migration which increases with the migration tax.

In the early 1990s researchers claimed that migration and trade may be complements in the short run and substitutes in the long run; they held the view that there is a migration 'hump' as trade is first liberalized, and substitution will follow liberalization continues (Russell and Teitelbaum, 1992; Martin, 1993; US Commission for the Study of International Migration, 1990, quoted in Schiff, 1996). To this end, complementarity is likely to dominate in the case of Africa-North migration while trade liberalization between the North and Sub-Saharan African countries is likely to result in increased migration and/or in a worsening of the migrants' skill composition (Schiff, 1996). However, the situation is highly unstable because migration and international trade are dynamic phenomena that elude successful tracking. This also sets the context for assessing the impact of globalization on the South-North migration and trade relations.

Countries of the North, including the United States that favour corporate driven globalization adopted 'trade, not aid' in the 1960s and 1970s to open up markets in the South. Under the Generalized System Programme (GSP), the United States government supported US companies investing in Africa and the creation of free-trade areas in Africa. Lately, the United States has been extremely aggressive in entering the African market, taking advantage of the changing political situation which has ushered in improvements in democracy and governance; it has even supplanted the old colonial powers that for long have had economic hold of Africa (Barry, 1997). By the close of the last century, the United States approved the African Growth Opportunity Act (AGOA) to permit African goods in the American market, and several African countries have exploited this opportunity, thus formalising trade links where they did not exist before.

Constraints to African Immigration in the North

Empirical research has revealed that the notion that immigrants come from poor groups is flawed. In many instances, migrants are those who can either fund or be assisted to fund the cost of migration, and even the cost of initial settlement at the destination. For Africa, any discussion of international migration cannot be complete without drawing attention to refugees and asylum seekers; yet a discussion of the latter falls outside the scope of this chapter.

At the turn of the 1990s, a notable African scholar addressed South-North migration from an African perspective (Adepoju, 1991). The issues raised drew the interest of the IOM to identify him to coordinate the African component of the UNFPA-funded research project, 'Emigration Dynamics in Developing Countries' in 1994–1998. Subregional research conducted under the auspices of this project reveal that a variety of demographic, economic, political, sociocultural and environmental factors push Africans out of their countries to other countries within and outside of the region (Adepoju and Appleyard, 1996).

Several events in Europe at the turn of the 1990s dealt a serious blow to immigration from Africa. The events included the fall of the Berlin Wall, the collapse of the Soviet Union, and a new wave of democratization and governance unknown before in Central and Eastern Europe. These events created a new order and subsequently a new migration regime in which Europe could afford to dispense with immigration from Africa due to several factors: Central-Eastern Europeans are the same stock, 'brethren' who are obviously more easily accepted than Africans even if racial sentiments do not surface; immigrants in the East-West European migration system are better trained and skilled, and would be less costly to recruit, being in the same geographical region; they would be less selective in employment opportunities given their emergence from centrally controlled economies, politically repressive experience to market-driven economies with, as it were, limitless democratic space.

The General Agreement on Trade in Services (GATS) Mode 4 providing for temporary presence of 'natural persons' is constrained by a number of barriers in order to distinguish it from regular labour immigration. It has two categories of measures: those affecting 'service suppliers' of a member state of the GATS and those affecting the natural persons of a member state who are employed by such service suppliers. The barriers include visa formalities that regulate immigration legislation and labour market policy; quotas imposed on foreign providers of services due to preference of national service providers; observance of wage-parity conditions for foreigners and nationals that often disadvantages the former; discriminatory treatment (e.g. residency or citizenship, social security and other requirements) of foreigners that also disadvantages them; and non-recognition of foreigners' professional qualifications as well as burdensome licensing requirements (Chaudhuri et al., 2004).

Members' commitments tend to be limited to higher skilled categories such as managers, specialists and professionals (Nielson, 2002), which makes them rather restrictive. That the barriers noted stand in the way of African countries, implies an inability of these countries to benefit from GATS Mode 4, especially as the countries lag behind Asian and Latin American countries. Indeed, the differences between developed and developing countries came to the fore recently in the Uruguay Round, provoking polarized defensive positions of the two groups (Self and Zutshi, 2003, quoted in Chaudhuri, et al., 2004).

Constraints to International Trade and their Effects

As the current strand of globalization (since 1980) gets a firmer grip of the world economy, the gap between the South and the North keeps widening from a variety of fronts, such as trade imbalance or the digital divide. The question that keeps propping up is who are the winners vis-à-vis losers in the balance sheet of economic globalization in particular? With the expansion of trade and foreign investment, developing countries have seen the gaps among themselves widen (UNDP, 1997: 82), not to mention the gap between them and the North. And given that Africa lags behind in trade with, as well as receipt of FDI, ODA and remittances from the North, the existing gaps are expected to widen even more.

There have also been bad rules governing international trade. Take the Uruguay Round, for instance, which left intact the protection of industries and agriculture in industrialized countries, and ignored the plight of the poor countries, in particular the problem of debt and the management of primary commodities. It enables the industrialized countries to enjoy much greater tariff reductions – 45 per cent compared to 20–25 per cent for developing countries (UNDP, 1997: 85). In April 1994, the Marrakech Agreement ended the Uruguay Round of General Agreement on Tariffs and Trade (GATT), reducing virtually all tariffs and other barriers and introducing a 'rules based' global regulation in trade (UNDP, 1999: 29). Thus, the doors were widely opened for the North to create and dictate rules to countries of the South in a 'carrot and stick' game relationship.

Globalization has become the concept most frequently invoked in both authoritative discourse and in general conversation. Viewed differently by different analysts representing various disciplines, globalization (according to the World Bank) has had four waves: 1870–1914, the inter-war years (1914–1945), 1945–1980; and the fourth wave began in the 1980s. Treating globalization as the interdependence of economies, Kotilainen and Kaitila (2002) identify seven forms: 1) foreign trade of goods and services; 2) FDI; 3) cooperation of firms relating to foreign equity, technology supply or franchising contracts; 4) international migration; 5) foreign borrowing and lending; 6) ODA; and 7) integration of macro-economic policies. The third wave has been characterized by a large group of developing countries breaking into the global market as other developing countries (notably those in Africa) become increasingly marginalized and bear the brunt of declining incomes and increasing poverty, international capital movements and migration. Kotilainen and Kaitila note that by 1980, trade of manufactured goods was generally freed of barriers, agricultural products were restricted (even in the South-North trade) and imports of developing countries were liberalized as long as they did not compete with those of the developed world.

For Sub-Saharan Africa, economic globalization or market integration has been closely linked to structural adjustment programmes (SAPs). Opportunities created by SAP for rapid growth have however not been as significant as the risks of low or negative growth in the face of weak governments; non-inclusive governance; rampant corruption in public offices; general economic mismanagement; and risky investment in many SSA countries. This raises the question whether Africa is integrating with the global economy according to the dictates of globalization. Africa's integration into the world economy entails adopting the standard package of trade liberalization and creation of a foreign exchange market, deregulation of domestic markets (including the financial sector and privatization), reduced budget imbalances, tax reforms and public sector reforms. Some statistics summarized by Bigsten and Durevall (2002) tell a depressing story: Africa's share in world exports fell from 3.5 per cent in 1970 to 1.5 per cent in 1997, and its share of imports fell from 4.5 per cent to 1.5 per cent during the same period. In this scenario, one can see the hand of trade barriers to African goods and international trade policies propelled by international organizations in which the G8 and other powerful nations hold sway.

In this time of free trade, Africa, a region endowed with abundant natural resources, continues to export its natural resources and agro-forestry products to the North even when commodity prices plummet to the detriment of the countries craving for development and for a better deal for their products. As Barry (1997) puts it, the region is 'falling out' of the global economy as the formerly war-torn countries such as Rwanda, Somalia, Ethiopia, Chad and Liberia are grappling with post-conflict rehabilitation; and SAPs have in fact de-industrialized and undermined the capacity of African countries to develop their own local and regional markets.

Evaluating development theory in historical perspective, Tandon observes that there is a tentative return to Keynesian economics that legitimates state intervention in the economic system; that development theories propound the integration of the developing economies into the global economy dominated by the TNCs and a few major players; that the South's need of capital compensates the North's greater hold through power as well as fresh sources of cheap labour; and that the wars declared by the North (such as the 'beef battle' or the 'banana war') are waged between powerful nations themselves and between the TNCs (backed by the Big Powers) and the South.[4] In his view, therefore, it is an illusion to think that 'development-oriented' capital can be 'attracted to Africa by some 'policy initiatives'.

What Needs to be Done?

The centralization of capital in the hands of the North is one thing that needs to be reviewed carefully. Tandon (n.d.) offers different categories of solutions to the controlling role of TNCs. Of paramount importance is the suggestion that African governments should maintain national control over economic and social policies, ensure that domestic savings contribute effectively to the local capital accumulation and target FDIs that are deemed necessary in the national interest.

If the position of NEPAD is that return migration is inevitable and brain drain should be avoided at all cost, then it has to renegotiate its human resource and trade relations with the North. Instead of treating trade, FDI, ODA and migration as unrelated issues, it should ascertain their individual and combined impacts in not only the national development process but also in regional development.

Africa remains a continent of many crises. In the economic sphere, African countries must of necessity formulate the right economic policies implemented by the right institutions, eliminate excessive corruption and engage both skilled migrants, well-trained stayers and trainable nationals in the development process. For African countries to continue decrying trade imbalances and brain drain, relying exclusively on ODA and FDI and ignoring the potential roles of migrant remittances, is to postpone its development potential and miss the path toward integration in the world economy. Furthermore, African countries should embark on systematic rehabilitation programmes for returned refugees and asylum seekers in their countries of origin or the chosen countries of resettlement. The wanton wastage of human resources that has occurred in the region should provide the incentive for well-planned redress.

Tandon suggests what African governments should do within broad political-economic parameters. First, they should close all the channels by which domestic savings are spirited out of the country. Countries such as Botswana and Nigeria are keener to increase their foreign reserves overseas than to utilize them in national development at home while poverty keeps biting hard at their nationals. Second, Africa must resist the WTO pressure to conform to inequities brought about by the latter. Third, after protecting their domestic savings, African countries need to audit carefully the kind of technologies they need and try to procure them from non-patented sources, Finally, there should be no 'open door' policy towards FDIs in general; whenever allowed, FDI should be by national consensus involving the Government, the local private sector, the workers and small farmers and other organs of the civil society.[5]

The future of ACP-EU trade relations is uncertain and therefore calls for a critical review. The total EC imports from the ACP has been decreasing, as has FDI on the reverse; the imports decreased from 6.7 per cent in 1976 to 2.8 per cent in 1999 and the decrease of FDI was from 2.8 per cent in 1996 to 1.7 per cent in 1999. The lessons to be learned are that ACP-EU cooperation has been limited in its ambition; tariffs are progressively losing their importance in international trade whereas non-tariff measures (standards, veterinary, sanitary and phytosanitary rules or measures) for environmental protection are of growing importance; and ACP-EU trade cooperation has not reduced the high dependency of the ACP on a few commodities and a few markets (Feustel, n.d.).

For the South to benefit from returning migrants from the North, presumed to have capital and viable skills, they should emulate the work being undertaken by the Sussex Centre for Migration Research (SCMR) in collaboration with some African countries. For, instance, under the auspices of the 'Globalization and Poverty' project, SCMR has undertaken studies on linking migration return with small enterprise development as a route to poverty alleviation in Ghana (Black et al., 2003).

Conclusion

This chapter has demonstrated that whatever migration, trade, aid and investment takes place between the North and the South, such flows usually are intended to benefit the North. In any case, the North operates through groupings and the institutions it controls to exploit the South ostensibly through cooperation and agreements that have scarcely benefited the South. Africa, the most exploited and apparently callous developing region, suffers the most. Its emigrants are subjected to ever changing immigration policies, and its goods are condemned to consistently lowering tariffs in world trade. The region receives the least ODA, FDI and portfolio flows from countries in the North and relies on migrant remittances that are yet to be factored in productive development programmes in African countries. It is now time Africa considered emigration of its human resources, whether unskilled or skilled, as part of the whole package of its trade and other relations with the North.

According to GATS Mode 4, temporary mobility is permissible for people moving to deliver services. For Africa, this is absurd because before services are delivered, the trading partners must have developed adequate trust between themselves. Yet that necessary condition has been lacking in the present migration regimes, which invalidates GATS Mode 4 from the outset. Such agreements, which African countries enter into without a critical study of their implications, tend to perpetuate barriers to African emigration and outflow of goods.

Given the lopsided relationship between the South and the North, countries of the South should establish strong South-South structures to foster migration and trade among them. There is a lot that could happen between Africa on the one hand and Asia, Latin America and the Caribbean on the other to sustain such relations for the benefit of the countries and peoples of these regions.

Notes

1 The acronyms stand for Economic Community of West African States (ECOWAS); Economic Community of Central African States (ECCAS) and East African Community (EAC).
2 http://europa.eu.int/comm/external_relations/euromed/htm; downloaded on 3 June 2004.
3 http://perso.club-internet.fr/unilco/summary.htm; downloaded on 6 June 2004.
4 http://rorg.no/rorg/dok/arkiv/ytfdi2.htm; downloaded on 24 May 2004.
5 http://rorg.no/rorg/dok/arkiv/ytfdi2.htm; downloaded on 24 May 2004.

Chapter 15

Challenges and Opportunities of International Migration for Europe and its Neighbourhood[1]

Robert Holzmann and Rainer Münz

Background and Options

The Challenges of Demographic, Economic, and Political Gaps

Western and Central Europe[2] is home or host to some 40 million international migrants (Table 15.1), about 8 per cent of its population. In absolute terms, Europe's immigrant population is about the same size as the number of immigrants in the United States.[3] Europe has become one of the main destinations on the world map of international migration.

After having been primarily countries of emigration for more than two centuries, during the last 50 years, all countries of Western Europe gradually became destinations for international migrants. In Central Europe the Czech Republic, Hungary, Slovakia, and Slovenia already have a positive migration balance (Table 15.2). Many Europeans, however, still do not see their homelands as destinations for immigration. Today, this contrafactual perception of demographic realities has become an obstacle to the development and implementation of proactive migration regimes.

Europe's demographic situation is characterized by low fertility, an increasing life expectancy, and a projected shrinking of populations in the decades to come. This contrasts with the neighbouring south and southeastern regions, where fertility is much higher, albeit declining, life expectancy is also increasing, and overall population is projected to grow at a high pace. Low fertility and increasing life expectancy in Europe both reverse the age pyramid, leading to a shrinking number of younger people, an aging work force, and an increasing number and share of older people.

According to projections by the United Nations, Western and Central Europe's[4] total population size will remain stable during the next 20 years (2005: 472 million, 2025: 479 million) and start to decrease only during the following decades (by 2050, 462 million). But in the absence of massive recruitment of economically active migrants, the number of people between ages 15 and 64 will decrease from 317 million (2005) to 302 million (or −5 per cent) until 2025 and to 261 million (−18 per cent) by 2050 (Table 15.3).

Table 15.1 **Foreign-born populations in Western and Central Europe (EU 25+)**[*]

Country	Size of foreign-born population thousands	Foreign-born as % of total population	% of foreign-born with citizenship of country of residence
EU 25			
Austria	1.002	12.5	40.7
Belgium	1.099	10.7	40.8
Cyprus	46	6.3	
Czech Rep.	448	4.4	79.8
Denmark	361	6.7	40.3
Estonia	252	18.6	
Finland	145	2.8	41.6
France	5.868	10.0	53.1
Germany	10.256	12.4	46.0
Greece	1.123	11.0	41.5
Hungary	293	2.9	71.1
Ireland	300	7.8	45.2
Italy	2.500	4.3	
Latvia	435	18.8	
Lithuania	334	9.7	
Luxembourg	143	32.5	13.0
Malta	9	2.2	65.0
Netherlands	1.615	10.1	
Poland	775	2.0	96.1
Portugal	651	6.3	66.3
Slovakia	119	2.2	84.2
Slovenia	52	2.6	
Spain	2.664	6.3	30.9
Sweden	1.078	12.0	62.5
UK	4.866	8.3	
Subtotal	**36.420**	**8.0**	
Other Western Europe			
Iceland	16	5.5	
Liechtenstein	12	25.3	
Norway	334	7.3	47.6
Switzerland	1.571	21.6	29.3
Total	**38.353**	**8.2**	

[*]   Latest available year (2000–2004).

Source: OECD Data Base, UN (2002).

During the same period, the number of people older than 65 in Western and Central Europe will increase from 79 million (2005) to 107 million by 2025 (+35 per cent) and to 133 million in 2050 (+68 per cent). As a result, the old age dependency ratio (population 65+ divided by population 15-65) is likely to increase from 25 per cent (2000) to 35 per cent (2025) and 51 per cent (2050; Table 15.3).

The situation in Eastern Europe, the Balkans, Turkey, and Central Asia (EECA-20)[5] is similar to the one in the EU-25. Continuing population growth is expected for Azerbaijan, Turkey, and most parts of Central Asia, but most Balkan countries, Russia, and Ukraine face considerable demographic decline (Table 15.4).

In contrast, the situation in Europe's southern and southeastern neighbours, that is, the Middle East and North Africa (MENA-15[6] without the Gulf states) is characterized by higher – but declining – fertility, rising life expectancy, and sustained demographic growth. Total population in the MENA-15 grow steadily from 313 million in 2005 to 438 million by 2025 (+40 per cent) and to 557 million by 2050 (+78 per cent). During this period, the number of people between ages 15 and 64 will almost double: from 195 million in 2000 to 289 million by 2025 (+48 per cent) and to 365 million by 2050 (+78 per cent). At the same time, this region also faces an aging problem and its population over age 65 will grow almost fivefold over the next 45 years (Table 15.5).

The change in the economically active population, however, will be smaller than the projected changes for the 15–64 age group, because only 60–80 per cent of this age group are currently employed or self-employed. Today the size of Western and Central Europe's labour force is 227 million. After 2010, this region (the EU-25, EEA, Switzerland) can expect a decrease in the active population. Until 2025, the decrease will be –16 million. During the same period (2000–2025), the active or job-seeking population will still increase by 7 million people in the EECA-20 and by 66 million in the MENA-15. In the EECA-20, this increase will mainly take place in Turkey and Central Asia. In countries such as Bulgaria, Serbia and Montenegro,[7] Moldavia, and Romania the active or job-seeking population is already shrinking.

Throughout the twenty-first century, Europe will be confronted with a rapidly shrinking (native) work force (–44 million until 2050) while the potentially active population will continue to grow in Europe's southern and southeastern neighbors (+118 million until 2050 for the MENA-15) and in Turkey (+16 million until 2050).

For Europe, the main challenge is the changing ratio between economically active and retired persons. With a projected employment rate of 70 per cent, the number of employed persons per persons aged 65 and over will decline from 2.7 in 2010, to some 2.2 in 2020, to only 1.5 in 2040. If, after reaching the so-called Lisbon target, the employment rate were to rise further to 75 per cent between 2010 and 2020, the decline in this ratio would be attenuated, reaching 2.4 in 2020.

In North Africa and the Middle East the main challenge is to absorb those currently unemployed and those entering the labour market during the next two decades. In order to fully cope with this challenge the MENA-15 countries would have to create 45 million new jobs until 2010 and more than 100 million until 2025 while Europe is confronted with choices concerning higher pensionable age, higher labour force

Table 15.2   Demographic indicators for Europe, 2003

	Population January 2003 in 1,000	Births	Deaths	National population decrease/increase per 1,000 population	Net migration	Total population change in 1,000	Poulation January 2004
EU 25	**454,560**	**10.4**	**10.0**	**0.4**	**3.7**	**4.1**	**456,449**
Germany	82,537	8.6	10.4	-1.8	1.8	0.0	82,539
France	59,635	12.7	9.2	3.5	0.9	4.4	59,901
UK	59,329	11.6	10.2	1.4	1.7	3.1	59,516
Italy	57,321	9.5	10.0	-0.5	8.9	8.4	57,804
Spain	41,551	10.4	9.1	1.3	14.2	15.5	42,198
Poland	38,219	9.2	9.5	-0.3	-0.4	-0.7	38,191
Netherlands	16,193	12.4	8.7	3.7	0.2	3.8	16,255
Greece	11,006	9.3	9.4	-0.1	3.2	3.1	11,255
Portugal	10,408	10.9	10.5	0.4	6.1	6.5	10,475
Belgium	10,356	10.7	10.2	0.5	3.4	3.9	10,396
Czech Republic	10,203	9.2	10.9	-1.7	2.5	0.8	10,212
Hungary	10,142	9.4	13.5	-4.1	1.5	-2.5	10,117
Sweden	8,941	11.0	10.4	0.6	3.2	3.8	8,976
Austria	8,082	9.5	9.5	-0.0	4.0	4.0	8,114
Denmark	5,384	12.0	10.7	1.3	1.3	2.6	5,398
Slovakia	5,379	9.6	9.7	-0.1	0.3	0.2	5,380
Finland	5,206	10.9	9.4	1.5	1.1	2.6	5,220
Ireland	3,964	15.5	7.3	8.2	7.1	15.3	4,025
Lithuania	3,463	8.8	11.8	-3.0	-1.8	-4.8	3,446
Latvia	2,332	9.0	13.9	-4.9	-0.4	-5.3	2,319
Slovenia	1,995	8.6	9.6	-1.0	1.7	0.7	1,996

Table 15.2 cont'd

	Population January 2003 in 1,000	Births	Deaths	National population decrease/increase per 1,000 population	Net migration	Total population change in 1,000	Poulation January 2004
Estonia	1,356	9.6	13.3	-3.7	-0.2	-4.0	1,351
Cyprus[a]	715	11.3	7.7	3.6	17.9	21.5	731
Luxembourg	448	11.8	9.1	2.7	4.6	7.3	452
Malta	397	10.1	8.0	2.2	4.3	6.5	400
Other EEA							
Iceland	289	14.2	6.2	8.0	-0.8	7.2	291
Liechtenstein	34	8.8	5.0	3.8	10.0	13.8	34
Norway	4,552	12.0	9.4	3.1	2.4	5.5	4,578
EEA	**459,435**	**10.4**	**10.0**	**0.4**	**3.7**	**4.1**	**461,352**
Other Europe							
Switzerland	7,318	9.7	8.5	1.2	5.6	6.8	7,368
Croatia	4,442	9.0	11.4	-2.4	2.0	-0.4	4,440
Bulgaria[b]	7,846	8.4	14.3	-5.7	n.a.	-5.7	7,799
Romania	21,773	9.6	12.2	-2.5	-0.3	-2.8	21,716
Turkey	70,173	21.0	7.1	13.9	1.4	15.3	71,254

Notes

[a]   Population on the territory under control of the government in Nicosia only (Greek part of Cyprus).
[b]   No data on migration available for 2003; population size for January 2004 is an estimate without migration.

Source: EUROSTAT, Chronos Database.

Table 15.3   **Demographic and labour force development in the EU-25 and other West European countries[a] by age group, 2005–2050 (millions)**

	2005	2015	2025	2050
Age group 0–14	75.6	71.4	69.6	68.6
Index	100	94	92	91
Age group 15–64	317.1	315.3	302.1	261.1
Index	100	99	95	82
Age group 65+	78.9	91.0	106.8	132.6
Index	100	115	135	168
Total	**471.7**	**477.7**	**478.6**	**462.2**
Index	100	101	101	98
Labour force[b]	226.7	223.4	210.5	183.3
Index	100	99	93	81
Old-age dependency ratio				
Age group 65+/age group 15–64	0.25	0.29	0.35	0.51
Age group 65+/labour force	0.35	0.41	0.51	0.72

Notes

a   Channel Islands, Iceland, Liechtenstein, Norway, and Switzerland.

b   Population projection based on Medium Variant of UN (2005) assuming a net inflow of some 30 million migrants into this region. Numbers for labour force calculated by aggregating country data, based on national participation rate projections for 2005 and 2010 over age group and sex by the ILO, and population projections for 2005, 2015, 2025, and 2050 over age group and sex by the UN, multiplying population projections for 2015–2050 with participation rate projections of 2010.

Sources: ILO, 1997–2002, UN, 2005, Koettl, 2005 and authors' calculations.

participation of women, and the recruitment of immigrants. The current labour market conditions in many MENA-15 countries raise doubts whether these economies will be able to absorb the significant expansion of the labour force. As a consequence of persistent, large-scale unemployment in many MENA-15 countries, migration pressures on the contracting labour markets in Europe will increase.

Economic indicators clearly show two things: the large gap between Europe and neighbouring world regions, but also considerable heterogeneity within these regions. The maximum ratio of per capita income between the richest European and poorest MENA-15 country is 82:1; for the regional per capita averages, the ratio still amounts to almost 7:1.[8]

In 2000, Western and Central Europe (the EU-25, the EEA and Switzerland) had 465 million inhabitants, with an average per capita gross domestic product (GDP)

Table 15.4   **Demographic and labour force development in the Balkans,[a] Eastern Europe,[b] Turkey and Central Asia[c] by age group, 2005–2050 (millions)**

	2005	2015	2025	2050
Age group 0–14	83	80	75	64
Index	100	96	91	77
Age group 15–64	276	283	274	240
Index	100	103	99	87
Age group 65+	46	45	57	79
Index	100	98	124	173
Total	**404**	**407**	**406**	**384**
Index	100	101	100	95
Labour force[d]	207	212	206	177
Index	100	102	99	85
Old-age dependency ratio				
Age group 65+/age group 1–64	0,17	0,16	0,21	0,33
Age group 65+/labour force	0,22	0,21	0,28	0,45

Notes

[a]   Albania, Bosnia-Hercegovina, Bulgaria, Croatia, Macedonia, Romania, Serbia-Montenegro (including Kosovo).

[b]   Armenia, Azerbaijan, Belarus, Georgia, Republic of Moldova, Russian Federation, Ukraine.

[c]   Kazakhstan, Kygyzstan, Tadjikistan, Turkmenistan, Uzbekistan.

[d]   Population projection based on Zero Migration Variant of UN (2005). Numbers for labour force calculated by aggregating country data, based on national participation rate projections for 2005 and 2010 over age group and sex by the ILO, and population projections for 2005, 2015, 2025, and 2050 over age group and sex by the UN, multiplying population projections for 2015–2050 with participation rate projections of 2010.

Sources: ILO 1997–2002, UN 2005, Koettl 2005 and authors' calculations.

of US\$ 19,000, ranging in Western Europe from US\$ 42,000 (Luxembourg) to US\$ 11,000 (Portugal) and in the new EU member states from US\$ 9,400 (Slovenia) to US\$ 3,200 (Latvia). The EECA-20 region had 402 million inhabitants, with an average per capita GDP of US\$ 1,600, ranging from US\$ 4,600 (Croatia) and US\$ 2,100–2,200 (Russian Federation, Turkey) to a mere US\$ 170 (Tajikistan). The Middle East and North Africa in 2000 were home to 313 million people, with an average per capita GDP of US\$ 2,600 per year (UN Common Database).

Political, ethnic, or religious conflicts exist in all world regions compared in this chapter. But as asylum and displacement figures show, only some of these conflicts

Table 15.5 Demographic and labour force development in other countries of the Middle East and North Africa[a] by age group, 2005–2050 (millions)

	2005	2015	2025	2050
Age group 0–14	104.3	115.0	120.1	116.2
Index	100	110	115	111
Age group 15–64	195.2	243.7	289.2	364.8
Index	100	125	148	187
Age group 65+	13.7	18.1	28.5	75.6
Index	100	132	208	551
Total	**313.2**	**376.8**	**437.8**	**556.6**
Index	100	120	140	178
Labour force[b]	118.3	154.7	183.6	236.2
Index	100	131	155	200
Old-age dependency ratio				
Age group 65+/age group 15–64	0.07	0.07	0.10	0.21
Age group 65+/labour force	0.12	0.12	0.16	0.32

Notes

[a] Algeria, Djibouti, Egypt, Iran, Iraq, Israel, Jordan, Lebanon, Libya, Morocco, Syria, Tunisia, West Bank and Gaza, and Yemen.

[b] Population projection based on Zero Migration Variant of UN (2005). Numbers for labour force calculated by aggregating country data, based on national participation rate projections for 2005 and 2010 over age group and sex by the ILO, and population projections for 2005, 2015, 2025, and 2050 over age group and sex by the UN, multiplying population projections for 2015–2050 with participation rate projections of 2010.

Sources: ILO, 1997–2002, UN, 2005, Koettl, 2005 and authors' calculations.

create migration pressure, which explains, at least in part, the annual inflow of some 400,000–450,000 people seeking asylum in Europe. Migration is partly spurred by differences in political stability, the human rights situation, and the general rule of law between Europe and neighbouring regions, with the EU countries at the top of the score, most Eastern European and Balkan countries in the medium range, and many of the MENA countries in the lower segments. Conditions in the last category, may significantly reduce individual security and hence impact the decision to remain in the country of origin or to emigrate.

Such imbalances explain why Europe is and will continue to be a major destination for migrants, even in times of slow economic growth, high domestic unemployment in many EU countries, and growing efforts to control and eventually reduce the inflow of asylum seekers and regular and irregular labour migrants. In 2003, the annual net gain from migration of the EU-25 was just over 1.7 million people (about 3.7 per 1,000), which explains 90 per cent of Europe's population growth (Table 15.2).

Even if economic conditions in the source countries were to improve, one should not expect the economic push factors to disappear quickly. The current levels of economic growth and job creation in source countries in the wider Europe (in particular, MENA and Central Asia) and other parts of the world with migratory links to Europe (for example, Sub-Saharan Africa, South Asia) are not sufficient to absorb the projected demographic growth and, in particular, growth of the labour force in these countries. Large cohorts will try to enter the labour market during the coming years, while unemployment and underemployment are already high.

One also has to bear in mind that the majority of migrants either do not come from the lowest-income countries, but rather from the middle-income countries, or they come from low-income countries but have a middle-class background. It seems that emigration only occurs once a certain level of development has been reached, which allows a first generation of potential emigrants to acquire the necessary means for leaving their home country.[9]

Migration: An Important Issue for the EU, its Member States and Neighbouring Countries

Intensified trade relations, as in EU partnerships with neighbouring and developing countries, have been put forward as a substitute for interregional migration and indeed as a means of containing mass migration from poorer to richer countries. Increased trade is expected to lead to higher growth – in particular in poorer countries – and the ensuing economic convergence should reduce the incentives for migration. Yet research on trade and migration suggests that trade liberalization and migration control are not substitute policies, at least not in the short term. On the contrary, there are strong indications that both are complements, particularly if trade liberalization happens between richer and significantly poorer countries (Faini and Zimmermann, 1999). At least initially, migration pressure may surge or not be reduced substantially, as has been shown by the aftermath of the North American Free Trade Agreement (NAFTA) Papademetriou (2004). Furthermore, there are convincing claims that overall welfare gains from liberalization of labour flows are expected to be far higher than any effects from full liberalization of trade.

Data from the Organisation for Economic Co-operation and Development (OECD) suggests that 20–30 per cent of all physicians in the United States, Canada, and the United Kingdom earned their degrees abroad – in the majority of cases, in developing countries (OECD, 2002). Analysis carried out by the World Bank also shows that by 2000, some 60 per cent of East Asian adults living in the United States had attended college or graduate school in their home country (Lucas, 2001). This could be seen as a substantial subsidy by source countries' publicly funded education systems for more developed receiving countries.

However, it has been argued that the anticipation of such opportunities could increase the number of people interested in higher education. Because many of them ultimately do not emigrate, human capital formation could be stimulated (see Stark et al., 1998).

It is as yet undecided whether and under what conditions international migration causes brain drain that is detrimental to the economic and social development of particular source countries or under what conditions it leads to circulation of skills, their improvement, and eventual later return while high unemployment at home would lead to a considerable under-utilization of these skills and therefore eventually to 'brain waste'. Whatever the actual results are, certain source countries and nongovernmental organizations have accused receiving countries of 'skimming off' skills while severely damaging certain sectors of source countries – in particular, the health care sector.

For a certain number of countries, it could be argued that the emigration of skilled people ultimately leads to higher remittances that more than compensate for the net loss. Recent estimates for India suggest that in 2001, fiscal loss due to emigration amounted to a maximum of 0.6 per cent of Indian GDP, and the total value of remittances equaled 2.1 per cent of GDP (see Desai et al., 2001).

Remittances are a core topic related to international migration, and the World Bank is actively engaging in research to document both the magnitude and the direction of flows and to determine the impact of remittances on development. An assessment of documented flows indicates that their total volume has become substantially larger than the combined total of public and private official development assistance (ODA) (Ratha, 2003).

Empirical evidence suggests that remittances have a positive impact on poverty reduction (Adams, 2003). Some of the EU's main foreign labour sources (countries such as Turkey, Tunisia, Morocco, and Albania), as well as India, are major receiving countries of remittances (Ratha, 2003). Among the EU countries, France and Germany are the main sources of official remittances, which are mainly channelled by money transfer providers. It has to be stressed, though, that official numbers can be assumed to be substantially underreported, because there are no data available on the extent of unofficial remittances. As a result of the high costs of official money transfers, migrant communities quickly develop parallel and alternative ways of transferring money back home, usually based on informal personal and ethnic networks. It is often conjectured that such networks can eventually be abused for money laundering and other illegal activities, including financing terrorism.

The recruitment of qualified migrants can be seen as a possible answer to shortages of skills and labour. But Europe would have to compete with traditional and, perhaps, new receiving countries (such as Japan and the Gulf States) for qualified and motivated potential migrants. Europe would therefore have to adapt its migration regime to such competition. Certain industries and sectors of Europe's economy already rely heavily on foreign labour – for example, health care, agriculture, the tourism industry, and, to a certain extent, construction. Seasonal workers play an important role in many of these sectors. In many parts of Europe, regular and irregular employment of migrants in households (to do housework, childcare, gardening, small-scale construction and repair) is now a common phenomenon. Such recruitment is not directly related to demographic trends or shortages of skills but rather reflects unstable, unattractive, or low-paid segments of formal and informal labour markets where either vacancies cannot be filled 'from within' or domestic labour is substituted by regular and irregular migrant workers.

In most countries of Europe today, public concern has brought about a political emphasis on immigration restriction, if not prevention, on the assumption that the social and fiscal costs (and therefore also political costs) of immigration may outweigh its benefits. Recent terrorist activities in Europe and the United States have intensified security concerns. The opposite is true for most source countries. There, emigration is seen as an opportunity for the mobile segment of society, a relief for domestic labour markets, and a major source of national as well as individual income through remittances from successful migrants. This creates considerable disincentives for source countries to effectively police their borders, insist on orderly departure and transit, and repatriate their citizens from abroad. At the same time, EU member states allocate more resources for the control of their external EU/Schengen borders, processing of asylum seekers, and repatriation of third-country nationals without entitlement to residency.

These efforts of EU member states to control (and through this control, to reduce) access to their territory have led to higher 'costs of entry' for irregular migrants and asylum seekers. As a result, smuggling and human trafficking have increased dramatically during the last decade. This also implies that several hundred irregular migrants die each year as a result of unsafe attempts to enter or cross EU countries.

The European Commission recognizes the potential benefits of immigration, but nevertheless is concerned about the consequences of a continued or even accelerated flow of migrants to the EU member states, including the consequences for the developing world. The European Commission therefore sees the necessity to shape its external relations to focus on the root causes of international migration (with the aim of reducing migration pressure) while considerably increasing the migration management capabilities of the EU and its neighbouring countries (see European Commission, 2002). As a consequence, the EU tries to make migration and readmission an issue in newly negotiated trade and cooperation agreements.

The EU enlargement of May 2004 has probably caused some increase in regular migration from new to old EU member states. Citizens of new EU member states (with the exception of Cyprus and Malta) have no immediate and general access to Western Europe's labour markets, but they have the right to immigrate for educational purposes, family reunion or establishing a business. A few old EU member states, however, are less restrictive than others.[10] As a result, between Spring 2004 and Spring 2005, some 250,000 citizens of new EU member states have become part of Western Europe's legal work force.

In countries that have implemented the transitory regime granting EU citizens from East Central Europe the right to reside in Western Europe while restricting their access to national labour markets could be interpreted as an invitation to engage temporally in irregular economic activities. At the same time restrictions during the transitional period could eventually lead to an increased migration of mobile and ambitious people from Central Europe to traditional immigration countries overseas, which could be seen as a potential loss for Europe.

In the medium and long run, however, the new EU member states of the accession rounds 2004 and 2007 do not have the demographic potential for large-scale emigration to Western Europe, because most of them have more rapidly aging and eventually shrinking populations. Economic growth after EU accession and the effects of EU regional funds will not only reduce emigration pressure but will sooner or later turn Central Europe into an area of immigration.

Main Options

In light of the trends described so far, it is worth considering how to manage economically motivated migration, as well as that induced by catastrophes or persecution, and assess some of the social and economic consequences for both receiving and source countries and for the migrants themselves. Europe has several options including the continuation of the status quo, tighter controls and/or proactive recruitment.

Today, most of the long-term inflow to the EU-25 is linked to three 'gates of entry': family unification, asylum, and co-ethnic return migration. These three components explain up to 85 per cent of recent long-term inflows into Northern and North-western Europe, while Southern Europe still attracts a larger share of regular and, in particular, irregular labour migrants. But in most of the old 15 EU member states, admission for humanitarian reasons is more important than admission for economic reasons.[11]

This structure of inflows is similar to the situation in the US where family migration also prevails over economically motivated admission, with one important difference: Unlike in the US, which gives all legal immigrants immediate access to its labour market, many of the long-term immigrants settling in Europe have either no legal access to the labour market or do not manage to enter the labour market, which leads to below-average labour force participation and higher unemployment of foreign immigrants on the one hand and, on the other hand, to above-average involvement of immigrants in activities related to irregular labour and service markets (Münz and Fassmann, 2004; EU Commission, 2003). The latter clearly indicates that there is and continues to be a gap – apparently a widening gap – between reality and the immigration and residency laws, and it hints at a suboptimal selection of immigrants. At the same time, an apparently growing number of migrants enter Europe as tourists or illegally and become part of the irregular work force. Their actual size is unknown. But recent amnesties and regularization programmes (1995–2003) have allowed some 2.5 million irregular migrants to adjust their status (Apap et al., 2000; Papademetriou et al., 2004).

One way of reducing the disparities among existing immigration, residency and asylum laws, and the reality created by migration could be an attempt to further enforce controls both at the external EU/Schengen borders and internally, particularly at work sites. This would probably lead to reduced legal inflows, but there may be a shift from regular to irregular migration. Such a conclusion could be drawn, with some caution, from the example of the United States during the 1990s and early twenty-first century (INS, 2000; Cornelius, 2001). This raises the question to what extent tightening border controls has a real effect on the quantity and composition of immigration flows, and to what extent it can be considered a symbolic measure trying to address public concern and win support from domestic audiences.

From the viewpoint of a potential migrant, tighter border control measures implemented by otherwise attractive and liberal industrial democracies raise the costs of entry. They force potential migrants to switch to alternative (usually more costly and dangerous) entry routes provided by the growing human smuggling business. Once irregular migrants reach the target countries, they are less likely to return to their home country because of the high re-entry costs. Growing fees for smugglers increase the potential for exploitation of migrant workers.

The economic, demographic, and political imbalances described above make it less likely that immigration to Europe will be significantly reduced. The reverse might be true. Increasing globalization and interdependence could further enhance international labour mobility. In this situation, the EU and the economies and societies of its member states could try to gain more from migration by opening new possibilities for a systematic and proactive recruitment of skilled migrants and opening their economies to lawfully admitted migrants.

Becoming Proactive

Proactive Recruitment – a Problem for the EU in Need of Reframing?

In the twenty-first century, most countries of Europe will have to recruit highly skilled and maybe also semi-skilled immigrants. In this field, the EU and its member states will have to compete with both traditional and new countries of immigration. This is a new phenomenon: For most of its modern history, Europe was the world region with the highest number of overseas emigrants, whereas mass immigration to most countries of Western Europe set in only after World War II or, in Central Europe, is only about to start. Opening economically motivated 'gates of entry' might in part reduce pressure in the asylum and family reunion 'gates'. But it would primarily change the composition of migrants and may well lead to both more and better qualified migrants.

To attract qualified potential migrants, select them according to Europe's needs, and integrate them economically and socially, the EU member states will have to embrace cultural and institutional changes. First, future immigration would have to be understood as a permanent process and no longer as a short-term reaction to shortages on domestic labour markets or humanitarian crises abroad. Second, future immigration should possibly be seen as a managed process. This requires the introduction of efficient and transparent selection criteria and admission systems. Third, the implemented criteria and systems should be flexible enough to be adapted if empirical evidence shows adverse selection effects. Finally, proactive recruitment from third countries should be coupled with measures to increase intra-EU mobility. This requires not only a higher compatibility of social security systems but also freedom of movement for third-country nationals lawfully residing in one EU member state but so far not entitled to settle and work in any other EU member state.[12]

Impact on Destination Countries

The potential impact of a proactive migration policy on the EU and its member states is manifold and not fully predictable. Under optimal conditions, the EU and its member states could first and foremost expect a positive impact on economic output in both absolute and in per capita terms. It is obvious that an increase in the population should have positive effects on supply capacity and demand, which will result in output gains. What is more important, though, is that one may also expect additional momentum for productivity growth – and therefore per capita income – from increased migration of qualified people and from a certain degree of heterogeneity. It is clear that this requires access to the labour market.

Longitudinal data on recent permanent immigrants in Australia clearly show that 18 months after arrival, those admitted for their skills (employer-sponsored or through the points system) displayed much lower unemployment rates and earned on average much more than those admitted under the family reunion program or for humanitarian reasons.[13] Macroeconomic forecasts project additional fiscal gains from taxes and social security contributions of migrants in the order of \$A30 billion by 2014, generated to a large extent by the skilled immigrants (Econtech, 2004).

It is in the interests of the EU and its member states to reap some of the skills that are available worldwide and benefit from the 'brain circulation' induced by international migration. The intention of a proactive migration policy is to compete for the skilled labour potentially ready to migrate, thus ensuring that the EU economy catches up with other economies like the United States in terms of innovation and competitiveness. A dynamic economy requires not only innovation and the accumulation of human capital, but also competitive wages in the low-skilled labour segment. Such wages allow migrants – particularly unskilled migrants – to enter formal labour markets, and they should also make it easier to fight irregular and illegal labour markets.

Different types of labour competition in the low-skilled sector can be distinguished. First, there are sectors in which migrants do not compete with domestic labour. Without migrants accepting a particular (lower) wage or without them having access to formal and informal labour markets, no additional economic activity would unfold in these sectors. As a result, employment is created that would not exist otherwise. Both the domestic employer and the migrants are better off, and domestic labour is not affected. Examples of sectors in this category are services provided in households (care for children and the elderly, cooking, cleaning, gardening) and the agricultural sector (fruit picking and other methods of harvesting).

Second, there are numerous sectors in which foreign labour does compete with domestic labour and where this competition has a potentially negative effect on wages paid to the domestic work force, occupational welfare, and general work conditions. For this reason, receiving countries have to take measures that protect both the domestic work force and new immigrants from unfair competition as a result of unequal labour costs due to informal work arrangements, the potential lack of respect for existing labour codes, and the lack of social security coverage for migrants.

Furthermore, if migrant workers lack the skills to rapidly adapt to employer demands or adjust to changing labour market conditions, immigration can potentially increase welfare program costs. Preferably, the host country would not only admit migrants for a particular sector that suffers from labour shortages, but also migrants with a high educational level and the necessary language skills and cultural background. Once labour market conditions change, better-educated migrants are able to move to work in other sectors faster than migrants with lower or very specific skills.

Finally, there is also evidence that an economy benefits from a certain level of heterogeneity within its population. A diverse population can comprise entrepreneurs and employees capable of bridging cultural barriers and dealing with particular markets abroad, in command of a large spectrum of languages, and able to add innovations and ideas from various cultural backgrounds. Although recent studies from the United States hint at possible drawbacks from diversity in terms of financing public goods, the importance of ethnic and cultural heterogeneity for innovation and creativity should not be underestimated (Alesina and Glaeser, 2004).

More attention has to be given to policies dealing with cultural diversity and cultural integration in receiving countries. At this time, most EU member countries do not have coherent policies dealing with this dimension of international migration. The lively and sometimes bitter debate on the ban against Muslim girls' and/or teacher's headscarves in German and French schools highlights how controversial such policies can be. Better cultural integration and better handling of cultural identity and diversity issues related to migration could have a strong impact on changing the cost-benefit balance of migration for both the receiving society and the migrants. This would require a closer look at best practices promoting cultural integration, mutual tolerance, and the formulation of non-negotiable principles (Ray, 2004).

Impact on Source Countries

Source countries face both favourable and adverse consequences from migration. Most source countries suffer from substantial unemployment or underemployment, thus their governments usually are in favour of out-migration as a means of reducing the aggregate labour force. A reduced labour force would also improve the usage of the domestic labour stock as employers intensify their search for scarce labour, promising higher wages and overall increasing the base of the economically active population.

On average, migrants typically are better educated, younger, and more mobile than the majority in their country of origin. Hence, source countries may not only lose a substantial number of their well-educated domestic work force, but also some of their innovative and motivated youth. Significant out-migration could lead to both a brain drain and a youth drain from poorer countries. However, there are potential benefits, particularly in the form of remittances from successful migrants and skill transfers through returning migrants.

The World Bank is conducting substantial research in the fields of migration and remittances. The evidence so far suggests that migration and remittances have a significant positive effect on poverty reduction (Adams and Page, 2003). In addition to remittances, migrants can also have a positive impact on developing countries by starting up small-scale businesses or engaging in other types of investments upon their return to their home country, which could result in a transfer of skills they acquired while living and working abroad. The issue of skill transfers has not yet been explored intensively.

Nevertheless, skill transfers also fall under the broader concept of brain circulation, which is of great concern to the developing world because of the often cited brain drain. The fear is that a proactive migration policy of labour-importing countries will lead to the recruitment of the intellectual elite of the developing world by the developed world. The return on education is low in the developing world, thus more highly educated individuals face considerable incentives to migrate.

The problem of the labour-exporting countries is that they finance the education of their intellectual elite only to see these people leave when they have finished their education. The developing economies cannot reap the benefits and potential spill-over effects from the human capital formation they finance, and the governments cannot benefit in terms of public finance because these people leave without paying taxes in their home country.

The World Bank conducted a study on 24 labour-exporting countries and found that small countries close to large labour-importing regions are most likely to suffer from brain drain. Of the MENA-15 countries, Tunisia and Morocco stand out with a share 33.3 and 43.5 per cent, respectively, of their tertiary-educated people living in OECD countries (Table 15.6) (see Adams, 2003). Large countries like Egypt suffer less from brain drain because they have a much larger base of tertiary-educated people. The outflow of tertiary-educated migrants seems to be fairly independent of the size of the country, mainly as a result of visa quotas in labour-importing countries, which usually do not reflect the population size of source countries. In the case of Europe, one therefore would have to look at effects for such countries as Moldova, Morocco, and Tunisia.

Table 15.6   **Migrants living in OECD countries, compared with domestic population of selected countries of origin, by education level**

Country	Total	Educational level* Primary or less	Secondary	Tertiary
East Asia				
China, PR	0.1	0.1	0.1	1.9
Indonesia	0.1	0.1	0.2	2.0
Philippines	1.1	0.2	0.7	3.6
EECA				
Turkey	5.7	1.0	11.5	39.1
LAC				
Brazil	0.2	0.1	0.6	1.3
Jamaica	8.7	1.2	10.6	95.8
MENA				
Morocco	4.0	0.3	6.9	43.5
Tunisia	3.1	0.3	5.2	33.3
Egypt	0.1	0.1	0.1	0.5
South Asia				
Bangladesh	0.1	0.1	0.2	1.5
India	0.1	0.1	0.1	1.3
Pakistan	0.1	0.1	0.3	3.3
Sri Lanka	0.7	0.1	0.4	16.5

Note: * Numbers are to be interpreted as follows: for Morocco, the number of Moroccans with tertiary education living in OECD countries equals 43.5 per cent of the tertiary educated living in Morocco.

Source: Adams (2003).

Institutional Requirements and Changes to Move Towards Win-Win Solutions

To move towards a win-win situation, policy adjustments and changes in the receiving countries and source countries – and, perhaps most important, cooperation between them – in a number of key areas are required.

Areas for Review in Destination Countries

In pursuit of a proactive migration approach, the EU and its member states will need new recruitment strategies to manage economically motivated migration. To this end, several gates of entry need to be reviewed, which may combine the advantages of existing selection and admission mechanisms already implemented by some of the traditional countries of immigration:

- admissions sponsored by domestic employers, based on labour market testing, or both may be used to make the selection of immigrants sensitive to immediate economic needs;
- temporary work programmes and student visas will not automatically lead to permanent status but may be used to preselect some of those who later may qualify for permanent status. This makes immigration programs for temporary labour easier to manage and provides better information on potential permanent immigrants, allowing greater selectivity;
- admissions based on individual applications and selection via a points system may be considered to bring in young, talented, and highly motivated immigrants with the skills that benefit the economy of the receiving country most;
- long-term and permanent immigrants may be allowed (and perhaps even encouraged) to bring family members along, a strategy that may help newcomers integrate more easily. These family members may be given access to the labour markets to maximize potential gains from migration and avoid any unnecessary welfare dependency of newcomers.

Both temporary migrants and permanent immigrants, as well as their children, should benefit from social protection and should have access to services provided by educational and health care institutions in the receiving society on the basis of similar rights and equal treatment. The EU and its member states has done some work already, but should more clearly define guiding principles for the social and political integration of long-term or permanent immigrants, offering them some sort of 'civic citizenship'. When fulfilling basic residency requirements, they should not only be eligible for naturalization, but also have the right to become citizens of their new country of residence. Wherever acquisition of citizenship via *ius sanguinis* prevails, the children of immigrants should have a legal claim to 'fast-track' naturalization, particularly if they attended a school in the new country. Integration policies would have to include not only laws facilitating that goal but also targeted measures against discrimination against immigrants and their children (Bauböck, 2004).

The selection and admission of migrants based on a proactive migration policy as well as the subsequent integration of long-term immigrants can and will work only if supported by a majority of people in the receiving society. This is not just a matter of legal and institutional change or political declaration. The necessity of such changes has to be communicated along with potential benefits and challenges deriving from a proactive migration regime. Alternatives such as a rise in pensionable age, lower public pensions, or decreasing quality of services provided by the health care sector should be openly discussed (Holzmann, forthcoming).

In most of the old EU member states (EU 15), immigrants from middle and low income countries – in particular from the Maghreb and Turkey – have lower labour force participation rates and higher unemployment rates than natives (see Münz and Fassmann, 2004; European Commission/Directorate General Employment and Social Affairs, 2003, ch. 6). This clearly indicates a mismatch between the skills of people migrating to Europe and the requirements of Europe's formal labour markets. Such gaps are partly related to the predominant gates of entry, that is, asylum and family unification instead of proactive selection and admission. But they are also the result of regulations excluding legal foreign residents from certain sectors of formal labour markets. They also hint at hidden barriers and eventual discrimination. Any successful migration policy must therefore be followed by an active integration policy, otherwise receiving societies can fully profit from neither the complementary labour and skills acquired through migration nor additional tax and social security contributions – and migrants cannot make full use of their talent and skills.

Areas for Review in Source Countries

Source countries with low per capita income and high unemployment usually are not opposed to the emigration of parts of their population. So far, however, several of them are not putting much emphasis on orderly departure and safe travel arrangements for people leaving their territory. Many source countries are also reluctant to readmit nationals who have entered another country without a necessary visa, whose residence permits have expired, or whose claims for asylum have been rejected. Some countries even seem unwilling to help in identifying their nationals abroad and issuing travel documents. Most receiving countries see these as problems that have a negative impact on bilateral relations.

Source countries should also lobby, wherever necessary, to help their citizens get access to social security (in particular, pension and unemployment insurance) and to such services as health care and education. By the same token, governments of source countries should give returning migrants access to social services and social protection at home. These governments should also help returning migrants to keep their claims towards social welfare systems in the countries where they worked as migrants.

Source countries should also develop an interest in strengthening ties with their emigrant diasporas. This may include preferential treatment for descendants of emigrants and certain political and other rights for emigrants and citizens abroad, including the right to vote; to sell, buy, or inherit property; and to remain citizens of the source country when naturalizing in the receiving country. In some European countries, the last point is a politically sensitive issue.

Areas of Cooperation between Source and Destination Countries for Win-Win Solutions

The cooperation of the EU and its member states with the source countries is crucial to move towards a regime of orderly departure and arrival and effective entry and exit controls. This also implies action against human trafficking and human smuggling, as well as attempts to decrease the death toll – particularly in the Mediterranean area. Such measures, however, must not force source countries to impose travel and mobility restrictions on their citizens.

Such measures (in particular, tighter border controls), which effectively increase the entry costs for irregular migrants, are foremost in the interest of the receiving countries. They should therefore be accompanied by a review of visa types, visa allocations, and labour permits to simultaneously decrease the entry costs for legally admitted migrants. In exchange for improved border cooperation, the EU and its member states might offer an attractive number of visa and labour permits for citizens of source countries. Such a package could contain a combination of temporary and permanent visas and link recruitment of migrants with skill levels, knowledge of language, and other required features.

If the EU and its member states wish to reduce irregular migration, they should recruit most of the unskilled labour needed to remedy labour shortages in certain sectors from countries with a common border or in the vicinity of the EU. Countries with a small population that are close to labour-importing regions are most likely to suffer considerable brain drain (for example, Albania, Moldova, Morocco, and Tunisia with respect to the EU). It may be in the interest of such countries to try to reduce the outflow of highly skilled and well-educated citizens while negotiating for more generous quotas for their unskilled labour. From their point of view, highly skilled migrants should be recruited from larger countries with an extensive tertiary-educated population, such as Egypt; and from more distant countries, such as India and China.

Remittances are an important area of potential cooperation between source and receiving countries. First, governments should aim at securing the flows of remittances by improving the reach of money sent home by migrant workers. Second, in doing so, governments should also try to enhance remittance flows by reducing the fees associated with such transfers. Currently, these fees are relatively high, especially for irregular migrants and migrants without access to a bank account. Lower fees would almost certainly lead to more (official) remittances.

There are already various examples of how viable and cheaper alternatives to money transfer organizations and informal channels can be developed. These efforts revolve around banks and credit unions. In countries where alternatives exist because the local banking sector is sufficiently developed, fees are considerably lower (Orozco, 2003). A good example is the establishment of a clearinghouse between the US and Mexican banking systems, which greatly improved money transfer procedures between these two countries.

The driving factors to accomplish fee reductions are cost cuts stemming from network sharing and technological innovation. The upfront costs of establishing money transfer systems with a sufficiently large number of outlets at both the source and the receiving sides, as well as associated network externalities, result in the money transfer industry tending to display features of imperfect competition, which leads to higher pricing. Regulations to increase competition, subsidies for the establishment of new networks, or the encouragement of cooperation between different providers are a few of the available policy options. Countries might also encourage migrants and their family members to make productive use of remittances beyond consumption, for example, by investing part of the transferred money in housing, health, and education.

There is a general need to give migrants access to checking accounts and financial services – in particular, bank loans. This would help them to set up new businesses and expand existing ones. It would also enhance both economic integration and economic performance of migrants because, on average, they engage more often in entrepreneurial activities than the native-born population. Such activities based on ethnic entrepreneurship and ethnic networks can promote foreign direct investment (FDI), tourism, and trade beneficial to both source and receiving countries.

Governments of source countries have (or should have) an interest in their citizens being protected against exploitation or unfavourable working conditions and having sufficient access to such social services as health care, education, unemployment insurance, and pension systems while living and working abroad. At the same time, destination countries are not always willing or prepared to offer full social protection to migrant workers and their families and give them access to social services. Reduced access to welfare provisions is even seen as a policy tool that can make a receiving country less attractive to certain categories of migrants. Also, migrants may not have spent enough time in a particular country to be entitled to claim certain welfare provisions. In addition, they may have no claim when they return to their country of origin.

In this context, source and destination countries should develop mechanisms guaranteeing transferability of social welfare benefits such as pensions and health insurance. Such mechanisms could encourage return migration. An increase in the return rate should also have positive effects on the cost of the health care system. It can be assumed that both return migration of older migrants and some retirement migration among native-born citizens of EU member states will increase in the future. Mediterranean regions with a favourable climate (for example, southern Turkey) could become prime destinations. Again, the EU and its member states have an interest in their citizens being able to claim pensions and health care (eventually at lower costs) in these countries, which adds to the incentives to engage in political dialogue and negotiate bilateral agreements.

In its communication on migration and relations with third countries, the European Commission (2002) mentions the strengthening of transnational communities. Enabling migrants to keep ties with their country of origin might have several effects: In any case, it increases economic, social, and cultural ties between Europe and a larger number of countries, thus enhancing economic and other opportunities.

Maintaining loyalty to the former home country, a particular community in that country, or the extended family network may increase the willingness to provide economic support through remittances, as well as invest in the old home country, start business initiatives, engage in political activities, and encourage other engagements of migrants from the country of origin.

Migrant diasporas living in Europe or Australia, Canada, New Zealand, or the United States often support democratization for countries with no democratic rule 'back home,' and they also serve as pools for alternative elites that may become relevant after political changes. However, diaspora politics might lead to the importation of emerging or existing conflicts among or within former home countries of migrants. Such importation of violent or potentially violent conflicts can become a threat to internal security and public order of declared and undeclared immigration countries, and it could lead to a radicalization within established migrant populations.

One way of dealing with skills shortages in Europe is the formation of additional skills in neighbouring and other world regions. The EU could sponsor training of specifically needed skills in schools and universities in the source countries. Co-financing of training centres and higher education helps the receiving countries to adjust required skills and respond to labour market changes. The source country benefits from financial resources that are used for the education of future emigrants as well as additional human capital formation. Improvement of higher education and training may have spill-over effects and could also lead to the mutual recognition of tertiary degrees.

Support of educational facilities in neighbouring regions would counterbalance potentially negative effects of brain drain for source countries. It would also make it clear that the recruitment of educated and talented migrants by Europe is not taken as a de facto subsidy from the developing to the industrial world. Another proposal relating to the brain drain problem is to tax expatriates who received their education in the country of origin but left once they finished their education to work and live abroad. However, long-term immigrants should not have to pay higher taxes for comparable income than the native-born population, thus such taxation seems viable only if the receiving countries share a small amount of their tax revenues from migrants with the countries of origin of their immigrant work force.

It is often stressed that according to economic theory, mainly the Heckscher-Ohlin model, trade and migration are substitutes (Flam and Flander, 1991). In that sense, increased trade and the transfer of production facilities to low-income countries could serve as tools to reduce migration flows. But empirical studies are inconclusive as to whether trade and migration actually act as complements or substitutes (Razin and Sadka, 1997). In principle, reduction in trade barriers should increase trade, lower the wage differential, and ultimately reduce migration flows. By the same token, reduction of surplus labour through emigration should lead to higher wages in the source country while lowering the wage level in certain low-skill labour market segments of receiving countries. This would increase the wage inequality within receiving countries. Yet the literature also concludes that under certain assumptions – for example, imperfect competition, differing technologies across countries, and external economies of scale – trade and migration can act as complements. In these cases, migration could eventually lead to a widening in the wage gap between source and destination countries and therefore worsen the situation in the source country, reinforcing migration incentives.

The effects predicted by the Heckscher-Ohlin model probably hold true for migration from Eastern to Western Europe, where migration costs are relatively low and increased trade and FDI already seem to have reduced migration flows considerably (Fassmann and Münz, 2000). Where migration costs are important and credit constraints are binding for poorer migrants, trade and migration may be complements for low-skilled migrants and substitutes for high-skilled ones – in which case, trade liberalization and higher FDI can affect the skill composition of migrants. Also, complementarity is more likely when migration is driven by networks between migrant populations and communities in source countries. Such networks can substantially lower trade costs and therefore enhance trade along with migration.

One option to address migration pressures is to encourage certain sectors that suffer from labour shortages to outsource parts of their production to countries with lower wages and a large supply of labour, which usually are also emigration countries. This is obviously a politically highly charged issue, but nevertheless the European Commission mentions it as a viable strategy in its communication on migration and relations with third countries (European Commission, 2002). Sectors with a potential for outsourcing to labour-exporting countries are Europe's and North America's agricultural sector (shielded from competing products by import restrictions and tariff barriers), labour incentive segments of the manufacturing sector, and certain service sectors (for example, call centres, software development, back office work of banks and insurance companies). In practice, such strategies also depend upon Europe's readiness to open EU and EEA markets to agricultural and other products (for example, textiles) that are processed or manufactured in third countries with surplus labour and lower wage costs.

Negotiations on future bilateral and multilateral trade and cooperation agreements between the EU and neighbouring or developing countries might well include and regulate both import-export and migration-related issues. Among the latter are migration related to the export of services, mutual recognition of tertiary degrees and other certificates of educational attainment, visa regimes and labour permits, orderly departure and safe travel arrangements, living and working conditions of migrant workers and permanent immigrants, brain drain and skill formation, and transferability of claims towards social security.

Conclusions and Implications

International migration is caused by major economic, demographic, political, and security gaps between source and destination countries. But international migration is also a process with the potential to reduce such gaps. Therefore, source and destination countries should explore win-win solutions that allow the countries and economies involved as well as the migrants to gain from geographic mobility of labour and skills.

From a European point of view, immigration should be seen as a partial answer to aging and eventually shrinking domestic societies. Migration can play such a role only if Europe is able to attract migrants with needed skill levels and these migrants have access to formal labour markets and the possibility to establish their own businesses. Europe will have to develop a comprehensive migration policy that balances economic and humanitarian aspects and incorporates selection and admission procedures for people who qualify for economic reasons as temporary migrants or as permanent immigrants. Experiences of traditional countries of immigration – in particular, Australia, Canada, and New Zealand – should be analyzed and adapted. In this context, the EU and its member states also have to review and improve integration policies and arrangements regulating claims of migrants to social security benefits (including the portability of such claims in case of remigration) and services such as education and health care.

A permanent dialogue between the EU and source countries could explore the possibility of cooperation in various migration-related fields. Among them are joint border management, visa regimes and labour permits, orderly departure and safe travel arrangements, living and working conditions of migrant workers and permanent immigrants, brain drain and skill formation, co-financing of educational systems, transferability and portability of claims towards social security, dual citizenship, channels, average costs, and productive use of remittances. Such migration-related issues might also become elements of future trade, cooperation, and association agreements between the EU and third countries.

All attempts to develop and implement coherent migration regimes, as well as integration and citizenship policies, need public support among domestic populations and polities of source and receiving societies. It is therefore necessary to explain why and how shaping – not preventing – future migration to Europe, influencing the characteristics of the migrants, and incorporating those who will (and should) stay for an extended period can be managed in the best interests of both migrants and Europeans themselves.

Such an implementation and management strategy has short-term and long-term horizons. For example, lowering costs of remittances and securing such flows has an immediate positive impact on migrants and remittance-receiving countries and should be undertaken without delay. On the other side of the timeline, shrinking native populations and work forces in many EU member states will be an issue for the next 15 to 20 years and beyond. But even here, it makes sense to analyse the implications of demographic trends well before they could negatively influence Europe's economic performance and the welfare of its citizens. Sound migration policies responding to such trends will have to be implemented gradually, and some degree of trial and error will be inevitable. Furthermore, if the EU envisages recruitment of skilled migrants in the wider Europe and other world regions, the build-up of such skills would be enhanced if people in source countries can anticipate the possibility of later emigration to Europe. In this context, a long-term migration strategy formulated by the EU and its member states may have a crucial signalling function that could influence both expectations and future investment of individuals in secondary and higher education.

The EU also has to consider to what extent future enlargement (or some form of association) will lead to the integration of countries with growing populations and work forces (for example, Turkey). This would shift some of the challenge from the management of international migration to that of intra-EU mobility. In the medium and long term, however, even an enlarged EU may face the need to attract more migrants from more distant world regions with comparable education systems.

Notes

1   A longer version of this chapter was published as Holzmann and Münz (2004).
2   Defined as the EU-25; Iceland, Liechtenstein, and Norway (European Economic Area [EEA]); and Switzerland, with 467 million inhabitants.
3   The comparison has to take into account that some of Western and Central Europe's 40 million foreign born have come from another country of this region.
4   The 28 EU+EEA countries and Switzerland.
5   The EECA-20 countries are Albania, Armenia, Azerbaijan, Belarus, Bosnia-Hercegovina, Bulgaria, Croatia, Georgia, Kazakhstan, Kyrgyz Republic, Macedonia, Moldova, Romania, Russian Federation, Serbia-Montenegro, Tajikistan, Turkey, Turkmenistan, Ukraine, Uzbekistan.
6   MENA-15 countries are Algeria, Djibouti, Egypt, Iran, Iraq, Israel, Jordan, Lebanon, Libya, Morocco, Syria, Tunisia, West Bank and Gaza, and Yemen.
7   Without Kosovo.
8   At current exchange rates.
9   For an overview of current research and activities of relevant stakeholders on issues, causes and effects of international migration and international cooperation on migration issues, see Tamas (2003).
10   From 2004 to 2006, citizens of new EU member states have access to the labour markets of Ireland, the Netherlands (contingent), Sweden, and the United Kingdom.
11   For the composition of recent immigration to Europe see European Commission/ Directorate General Employment and Social Affairs (2003) and OECD (2004). For an economic analysis of the root causes of asylum seeking in Europe and the effectiveness of stricter policies during the 1990s, see Hatton (2004).
12   These recommendations are in line with findings of the Independent High-Level Study Group (2003). For a proposal of a more coordinated pensions system in Europe, see Holzmann (2004).
13   See Australian Department of Immigration and Multicultural and Indigenous Affairs (2003).

Chapter 16

Western Hemispheric Integration and Migration in an Age of Terrorism

Robert L. Bach

Introduction

If current wisdom about terrorism is true, states that curtail immigration, soften support for asylum seekers, or discourage settlement and adaptation are surrendering to their enemy's primary objectives. Terrorists, we are told, seek to undermine the global economic infrastructure, disrupt the ability of markets to function, and destroy the legitimacy of democratic institutions that support them. In today's world, however, security is not imposed by erecting barriers that impede mobility; it is won by strengthening the institutions that protect transborder commercial and migration flows.

The Western hemisphere did not need the tragic events of 11 September 2001, in the United States to learn that lesson. Insecurity, lawlessness, lack of legitimacy and even terror has been embedded in the hemispheric political-economy for decades. Dictatorships produced thousands of 'missing persons', civil wars covertly undermined democracy and market economies, and narco-states produced outright terror. The consequences have been evident among the numerous refugees, mass asylum seekers, and internally displaced.

Even the apparent, entrenched labour flows in the hemisphere rest upon foundations of denied democracy, human insecurities, and unchallenged inequality. The familiar Mexican labour flow to the United States, for instance, commenced only one election beyond a century-long period of authoritarian political rule. Nicaraguan labour migration to Costa Rica remains driven by the impoverishment of a region only years from civil war.

Unfortunately, many observers have taken the wrong lessons from the terrorist events of 9/11 in the United States. Rather than reinforcing their attention to the ramifications of this foundation of regional instability, many officials and researchers have emphasized the stability and orderliness of migration, and blamed US reaction to terrorism for a retreat from regional economic integration involving cross-border mobility of goods and people. Strong border enforcement, to which the US rushed following the terrorist attacks, interrupted what many believed was an uncontested movement toward integration of transnational labour markets and regional economic integration. Such views, however, dramatically misrepresent the character of migration flows in the Western hemisphere and the challenges of regional integration.

The purpose of this chapter is to highlight a different lesson from 9/11 for hemispheric integration and migration. The lesson is more fundamental than the need for improvements at border crossings or the quest for new visa or contract labour regimes. National security, human security, and economic integration depend on institutional foundations of democracy and good governance that are weak and faltering throughout the Western hemisphere. Improving the conditions for migration flows throughout the region depends not as much on balancing security and facilitation at borders as it does on dramatically improving democratic institutions throughout the hemisphere.

A Shaky Bedrock

Perhaps more so than other regions of the world, Latin America's experiences challenge the economic and political benefits that international financial institutions (IFIs) – such as the World Bank and the International Monetary Fund, as well as those in many developed countries – predicted from the spread of neoliberal, macroeconomic growth policies. After decades of inward-looking, protectionist economics, enforced by strong authoritarian governments, neoliberal strategies offered promise. By opening countries to the world market through liberalized trade, relaxed rules on private, foreign investment, and improved management of financial accounts and monetary flows, the strategy aimed to stimulate growth and raise standards of living. For a while, the decades of economic stagnation, political repression, and terror that had plagued much of the Americas finally gave way to the market-led reforms that appeared to foster growth. Most welcome of all, the hemisphere struggled towards democracy. By the late 1990s nearly every country in the hemisphere had celebrated successful democratic elections.

The same international financial institutions and governments that crafted and supported these neoliberal strategies also believed that increased migration – like expanded trade – would significantly raise the region's wealth. States were encouraged to align their policies to promote emigration as a form of labour market adjustments. In liberalized, transnational labour markets, workers would respond quickly to the shifting opportunities that would follow from new investment and export-led job growth. Once initiated, the flow of information and financial support from employers, relatives and family would create a self-reproducing, integrated labour market that matched the needs of the modern engines of economic growth. Through the late 1980s and into the 1990s, transnational labour markets emerged and expanded. Mexican and Caribbean migrants accelerated their move into the United States, Central Americans circulated in and out of Mexico, and Bolivians, Paraguayans and others settled in Buenos Aires and Sao Paolo.

The storyline appeared so clear that some Latin American scholars turned to an odd industrial metaphor to explain how these migration flows developed (Massey et al., 2002). Like other goods that are produced *en masse* and distributed onto the market, migration resulted from a development 'machine' that routinely produced workers from existing, inadequate job opportunities, alerted them to opportunities in regional and transnational labour markets, and distributed them to employers who purchased and consumed their talents. A World Bank study argued that, if this machinery worked well and produced a dramatic increase in cross-border migrations, the positive impacts on economic growth could offset many of the difficulties that the struggling economies in the region were experiencing.

The industrial metaphor, and neoliberal expectations underlying it, however, ignored the turmoil and downside risks that threatened many migrants and the communities which they had left or to which they relocated. Such views also lagged behind the IFIs' increasing recognition that earlier predictions of growth were falling short. They began to acknowledge that a broad set of institutional conditions had to be achieved before a country could reach sustainable growth and increases in well-being (World Bank, 2001). Unlike the neoliberal model, some embraced a human development and human security agenda that placed priority on investments in reducing hunger, poverty, and disease. The new agenda required development of human and social capital through broad-based strategies of social inclusion, including involvement of women and minorities, into productive enterprise. It also required consolidation of democratic gains beyond formal adherence to electoral mechanics (Lederman et al., 2003).

For Latin America, the new approach highlighted the realities of poverty and inequality in the region, features of the Western hemisphere that had been pushed deep into the background of policy discussion and analytical debate. Until recently, IFI analysts even argued that income inequality 'should not be seen as negative,' provided the incomes of the poorest did not fall (Wade, 2001). Yet, for the Western hemisphere, inequality and poverty had proven remarkably intractable and, increasingly, a direct impediment to the region's growth plans.

The level of inequality in Latin America is higher than the world's average. In at least 15 countries of the region, more than 25 per cent of the population lives below the poverty line. In seven of these Latin American countries, more than half of the people are poor. During the 1990s, although progress was made in health and education, unemployment and underemployment rose. According to UN projections, only seven of the 18 Latin American countries studied were likely to meet their poverty reduction targets by 2015. Even for those expected to improve, the situation worsened soon after these projections became public. For instance, the projected gains included optimistic growth in Argentina, which soon collapsed into economic crisis. The Dominican Republic, Honduras, Panama and Uruguay also suffered recent declines in their growth rates. Chile's strong economy slowed to a modest growth rate in 2003 and its unemployment rate (9.5 per cent) returned to levels that existed two decades before. Caribbean economies continued to stagnate and job growth stumbled along without clear improvement.

Privatization, a key to neoliberal growth strategies, helped to slash government expenditures. Yet, it also cut existing safety nets and eliminated job alternatives. With shrinking alternatives, aggressive growth plans accelerated the pace of economic and social disruptions without generating the jobs to which displaced peoples could relocate. Exposure to transnational labour markets did not overcome these vulnerabilities for the migrants or their households. Few of the benefits and protections that a domestic labour market had previously offered its citizen workers were made available to transnational workers.

The prevailing patterns of hemispheric migration reflect these highly uneven episodes of economic stagnation, dispossession from land and community, collapsed support systems, and declining realistic alternatives at home. They also reveal the equally uneven and highly selective 'growth poles' that formed around the concentration of production facilities and jobs, and the geographical centralization of workers.

The primary feature of the pattern of Western hemispheric migration is the geographical evidence of the centrality of the North American economy. Migrants are drawn more and more towards the United States and Canada, with the number of newcomers growing fast. According to the UN Population Division, the number of migrants in North America increased during the 1990s by 48 per cent. In North America, one in every ten residents is a migrant, many having arrived in the last two decades (United Nations, 2002).

This lopsided geographical unevenness has historical roots in the 1970s. Earlier, most developed countries, including the United States and Canada, received migrants from other developed countries. Decolonization and shifting patterns of the world economy in the 1970s and 1980s altered these flows. Around 70 per cent of migrants to the United States and Canada now originate from less developed countries. Simultaneously, the Caribbean and most of Latin America experienced net outmigration, which has steadily increased over the last two decades. The number of migrants residing in Latin America and the Caribbean declined by one million during the 1990s, lowering the share of the foreign-born resident in their own countries to only one out of every 70 people.

Migrant flows also shifted increasingly toward dominant growth poles, including the larger cities in the emerging subregional economies. In Central America, for instance, the movement of Nicaraguans since the end of the civil war increasingly shifted toward San Jose, Costa Rica. More recently, Colombians and other South Americans have begun settling there in significant numbers. In South America, an estimated 2.5 million people from neighbouring countries moved to Buenos Aires, Sao Paolo, and Montevideo. Many settled as illegal immigrants, working in low wage industries and earning far below the minimum wage. In the United States, the economic boom in the second half of the 1990s accelerated the flow of Mexican immigrant into US cities and, increasingly, into mid-sized towns.

The hemispheric pattern also consists of a patchwork of select migratory flows attached to particular economic sectors. Agriculture, in particular, remains a source of strong transnational labour market organization. It also has the dubious distinction of demonstrating some of the worst human conditions throughout the hemisphere. Agricultural workers move from Haiti to the Dominican Republic, Central America into Southern Mexico, Mexico into the United States, and Brazil to Paraguay. Each of these flows involves hundreds of thousands of people and typically involves minority populations that face serious difficulties integrating into either the migrant source or migrant destination communities.

Underlying these diverse and uneven geographical and social patterns of migration is a persistent form of political instability. At the beginning of the twenty-first century, Latin America's market reforms and democratic transitions faltered, suffering one crisis after another. Argentina's economic collapse widened to affect Uruguay and Brazil. Growth rates throughout the entire Southern Cone slowed. Democracy itself, the most cherished outcome of years of struggle throughout the hemisphere, also faced risks. An attempted coup in Venezuela, continuing armed conflict in Colombia, political uncertainty in Guatemala, Bolivia and Ecuador, stalled reforms in Mexico, and collapse in Haiti shook the foundations of the hemisphere's confidence in its concerted move toward democratic reforms.

The centrality of the US economy in the hemisphere had long been matched by the nation's political leadership in the region. However, even before the 9/11 events, the United States took a hard right-turn from its established framework for working with the region. In Argentina, the US decided not to intervene with financial assistance. In Venezuela, the US came far too close to becoming entangled in perceptions that it supported the coup attempt. And in Haiti, the United States has been accused, even by its own former Ambassador, as hastening a 'regime-change' that did not have the support of the majority of the Haitian people.

US leadership in advocating a hemispheric free trade agreement, in which it put much of its energy, also began to fuel opposition to an excessive focus on trade and investment as the underpinnings of regional integration. The election of President Lula in Brazil, long considered a relatively marginalized left-wing, populist candidate, symbolized and underscored the region's growing concerns with a US-led model of hemispheric integration. The US position was perceived in the region as heavy-handed, unfair to developing countries, and inconsistent with its own principles and practices. In particular, the US position continued to advocate for reduced tariffs and protections while increasing subsidies to its own domestic agriculture and export industries.

The political shift has had grave consequences for migration policies. In particular, the new US strategy turned migration into primarily a matter of labour market integration – an economic issue – rather than one of institutional capacities, human development and human security. Its trade priorities reinforced the errors of the neoliberal strategy that had produced the region's migration problems. It especially limited attention to the complex issues related to human rights and democracy and to alternative approaches to reducing poverty and inequality (Shifter, 2003).

US policy toward Haiti also deeply affected the legitimacy of its immigration policies. As human rights organizations and journalists reported rising levels of civil disorder, politically-motivated violence and persecution, US authorities failed to follow established refugee and asylum procedures when responding to Haitians attempting to flee the country. In their place, US authorities substituted an automatic detention policy that applied to only one national group – Haitians (Bach and Maguire, 2002).

Elsewhere in the region, the fragility of the democratic transitions accounts as much for the diversity of migration patterns as does the convergence of labour market supply and demand. Mexico, for example, has not consolidated its new electoral gains and the continued development of its migration trends may influence how it moves beyond its authoritarian legacy. Governments in Central America now agree that the region has become dependent on continued migration to the United States to support its struggles to maintain progress toward democracy. Their dependence on outmigration, however, makes them vulnerable to US immigration policy. The United States currently grants and updates special immigration statuses for Central Americans – so-called temporary protected status – because of the belief that large scale returns of their citizens would undermine progress toward political reconciliation. The migrations that now encompass Colombia, Ecuador and Venezuela, which were born of civil war and political strife, may also now be so extensive that, independent of their origins, their scale and consequences may have become politically destabilizing.

The diversity of migration in the hemisphere is a reminder of the region's shaky foundations. When states falter, as they have in Haiti, Colombia, and Central America, migration pressures rise significantly. It reveals the region's institutional shortcomings. It also demonstrates that the challenging conditions facing migrants and their families throughout the hemisphere are clear reminders of the downside risks of a strategy that ignores the human and institutional preconditions for sustainable development (Bach, 2003).

Institutional Prerequisites

The Western hemisphere has had some success historically in responding to the migration consequences of political and economic instability. During the height of the Central American civil wars, for instance, Costa Rica, Mexico, and the other governments in the region forged an innovative framework, based on the Cartagena Declaration, to provide protections for displaced persons and refugees dispersed throughout the region. The Declaration drew on existing United Nation's conventions, but it also changed definitions and institutional responsibilities to meet the conditions at hand.

In contrast, for the last decade or so, most institutional attention in the hemisphere has been aligned with trade negotiation objectives. The analyses and negotiations over migration have often appeared more like extensions of customs agreements and debates over tariffs than a focus on the social and human dimensions of mobility. Their primary goals have been border regulations, including visa policies, international standards of documentation and inspection, and smuggling. As a result, efforts to manage migration in the hemisphere have been limited to border controls and cross-border facilitation, and have largely neglected efforts to build institutions that could implement the numerous international agreements that call for protecting the rights and standards of labour migrants and their families.

The focus on visas and border inspection regimes developed during the 1990s as international organizations combined efforts with states to build bilateral and multilateral mechanisms for dialogue on migration issues. The initiatives followed international recognition of the growing difficulties that both source and destination countries were having with migration throughout the world. For example, in 1994, the United Nations convened the International Conference on Migration and Development (ICPD) in Cairo, which formulated broad principles and objectives for responding to migration policy cooperation. The Conference laid out a global blueprint to address the causes, consequences, and long-term implications of international migration and displacement.

Governments in the Western hemisphere launched a complementary series of regional consultative processes aimed at fostering similar principles and objectives. In 1996, for instance, the governments of Belize, Canada, Costa Rica, El Salvador, Guatemala, Honduras, Mexico, Nicaragua, Panama, and the United States agreed to participate in a regional forum, labelled the Puebla Process, which would seek to improve the understanding of migration and strengthen diplomatic relations among the participating states (Government of Costa Rica, 2001). A widely-acclaimed feature of these consultations was the rare inclusion of non-governmental organizations in the direct discussion among the states and international organizations.

Regional consultations proliferated, involving states in the Southern Cone of South America, the Andean region, and the Caribbean. Migration issues were also taken up in the Summits of the Americas. In 1998, the Summit held in Santiago, Chile, incorporated a migrant worker initiative into its Plan of Action. In each case, these consultations produced an annual re-affirmation of the principles and objectives enshrined in international conventions and treaties.

These consultative mechanisms have certainly energized discussion of migration issues throughout the region. They have also been widely complimented by the United Nations General Assembly and other international organizations. Yet, the value of these regional and sub-regional dialogues to support reforms that could change the conditions of migrant labour flows is much less certain. The consultations have been non-binding regional discussions frequently dominated by the agenda of the larger and economically more powerful participants. Although each meeting produces a long list of desirable objectives, discussions of shared responsibilities for migrants' conditions have rarely produced concrete actions with the required resources needed for implementation.

As the consultative meetings have grown in number and frequency, they may even have undermined the very objectives they pursued. The processes became parallel, multilateral institutions that absorbed the diplomatic attention of states and non-governmental organizations. In a sense, they provided an escape from the difficult tradeoffs and reforms that are needed to change the current conditions of migration throughout the region. Surprisingly, despite the difficult circumstances for many migrants and their families left behind throughout the hemisphere, states became in the 1990s more satisfied with existing migration trends. The change in attitudes had little consequence for improvements in migration policies or the underlying conditions facing migrants.

The Puebla Process is a case in point. While it has received fairly wide acclaim from its participants and has helped to educate governments on migration issues, there are few concrete actions that have followed from its routine meetings. The process, which was formally launched by the Government of Mexico, was inspired by the US and Canadian governments' interests in generating regional counterparts to take responsibility for the conditions in migrant source countries. Against those goals, the Process has largely failed. The regional dialogue has focused more on the conditions of migrants in the destination countries, and has provided a platform to push agendas for more emigration. Mexico's 'open border' proposals, for instance, which persistently resemble trade negotiations, focus on greater access to foreign markets, and a reduction in any barriers that may impede the increased flow.

An exception to these limited achievements involves the recent Mercosur agreement among Argentina, Brazil, Uruguay and Paraguay to allow some 250 million people throughout the South American region to live and work in each country with the same rights of the citizens of each state. The agreement is of particular interest for several reasons. First, rather than a trade-like framework, the agreement fulfils a vision of South American integration that, from the outset, was understood as pursuing internal political and economic reforms in each country (Rohter, 2002).

The agreement also resulted from a commitment to a broad process of regional integration, not from efforts to improve the management of border regulations, contract labour schemes or visa regimes. It showed that effective action required significant reform of the policies, rights, and conditions that are preconditions for sustainable migration.

Second, the agreement occurred after the collapse of the Argentine economy, when insecurities among migrants and governments were at their peak. Rather than seeking to expel migrants, the governments sought to reinforce the process of regional integration. The timing stands out because most migration policy reforms in the hemisphere have sought to align them to moments of economic expansion – like that in the late 1990s. The goal often appeared to be a timing of reforms to cycles of growth in hopes of disguising the hardships that many migrants face and the opposition of source and destination communities to the terms and conditions of the reforms.

Overall, beyond specific dialogues and agreements, the Western hemisphere faces a complex agenda of institutional reform if it is to meet the preconditions for effective, sustainable regional integration involving large-scale migration. The following three areas are critical elements of that agenda. As neoliberal strategies are abandoned or modified, concrete action in each of these areas could significantly strengthen the foundations of migration throughout the hemisphere.

Democratic Governance

Despite laudable progress toward formal electoral systems, the region remains in the throes of a transition to democracy whose outcome is still uncertain (UNDP, n.d.). Twenty-five years ago, only three out of 18 Latin American states studied by the United Nations Development Program met the requirements of a democratic regime. Only a handful does not satisfy the requirements today. Yet, all of them have fragile and incomplete democratic institutions under extreme pressure from high levels of poverty and the highest levels of inequality in the world (UNDP, 2002).

The connections between democracy and migration are fundamental. According to one Mexican scholar, for example, Mexico embarked on a new migration initiative in 2000 aimed at addressing conditions in the source regions only after overturning the one-party monopoly that gripped the nation's political power (Durand, 2004). These connections, however, have been largely ignored. Part of the reason, as highlighted above, is the predominance of neoliberal models of economic development and their neglect of institutional capacities. Institutions were, for the most part, viewed as barriers to economic growth strategies. Democracy, however, is tied to human development, which in turn is a precondition for economic growth (UNDP, 2002).

Democratic institutions affect migration in at least three ways. First, they create possibilities to connect the problems that potential emigrants face to the capacity of states to reach political solutions for them. In many migrant source countries, increasing frustration at the lack of opportunities and high levels of inequality, poverty and social exclusion is expressed in a loss of confidence in the political system and a crisis of governance. People migrate because they lose an ability to seek and find solutions at home. The denial of democracy in these migrant source societies has reached a point in which many governments and even some analysts believe there are no choices left. Some argue that migration, or at least the migration that currently exists, has become 'inevitable'. For example, in a 2001 report, Mexico's National Population Council argued that '[m]igration between Mexico and the United States is a permanent, structural phenomenon. It is built on real factors, ranging from geography, economic inequality, and integration, and the intense relationship between the two countries, that make it inevitable' (CONAPO, 2001).

These real factors, however, do not necessarily close off alternatives. The shortfall of job growth compared to population growth, and the omnipresent reality of higher wages abroad, do not relieve source countries of a responsibility to protect and prevent the conditions that give rise to the move. Within a democratic regime, states cannot neglect their obligation to ensure that their citizens have the capability to find or create options to survival or a decent standard of living.

By expanding possibilities, however, democratic institutions also require increased accountability. States must take responsibility for the choices made, and those denied. Democratically-induced responsibility for migration has not been the subject of the regional consultations that have taken the first steps toward institution-building in the hemisphere. Yet, it is the precondition for building an economy that can sustain growth and productive mobility.

Mexico's largely peaceful and orderly transition to democracy offers other, more promising lessons. For example, since leaving his post in government, former Mexican Foreign Minister, Jorge Castenada, has argued that the 'democracy challenge' still confronting his nation requires the success of two primary internal reforms (Castenada, 2004). First, Mexico has not been able to consolidate its democratic gains beyond an initial free election and remains under the 'rule of order' rather than the rule of law. Institutional reforms are needed, he argues, to strengthen the judicial system, create a national police force, and change laws related to basic property and personal rights. Castenada also calls for fundamental reform of Mexico's education system – a core pillar of human development. Institutional reforms in both areas, he notes, are so fundamental to the Mexican political economy that they will require extensive legislative action and even constitutional change.

Until these institutional reforms are undertaken, however, Mexican citizens will continue to be 'compelled' to leave Mexico, as Mexican President Vicente Fox has phrased it. The persistent pressure on Mexican outmigration is not a simple result of inevitable job shortages, but the failure to consolidate a democracy with institutions and policies that could offer alternatives. Without a focus on these internal reforms, Mexico's policy priorities of seeking 'open borders' with the United States remain as much a recognition of its own democratic failures as it does a tactic to promote economic growth.

Secondly, the democracy deficit in the Western hemisphere affects migration because the prolonged transition has severely weakened the strength of states to meet the needs of their citizens and to be effective partners in a regional context. Throughout the hemisphere, serious deficiencies remain in terms of the control that citizens are able to exercise over the actions of the state. Latin American leaders report that political parties are deeply distrusted as representatives of the people and need strengthening to effectively channel and meet popular demands (UNDP, 2002).

One result of this weakness is that states have been able to improve legislation and enter into international agreements without having the capacity to implement the plans of action and guarantees of rights and protection. Most countries in the region have ratified the main international treaties and enacted domestic laws that uphold the highest principles of individual rights and social protections. These include the annual reaffirmations of commitments to migrants' rights. Still, the democratic institutions that could respond to the serious consequences of sustained poverty and inequality, discrimination, and abuse are largely missing or underdeveloped.

A source of this weakness involves the exclusion of many groups from participation in civic activities. Ironically, efforts to increase civic participation in migrant source areas are systematically undermined by the practices that promote or compel outmigration. Not surprisingly in many transnational communities, for instance those formed by Dominicans, Mexicans, or Central Americans in the United States, migrants have often increased their civic participation at home only after they have settled abroad. They reach back to come to the aid of those remaining behind under authoritarian legacies.

Third, the challenge of democracy also affects migrant destination countries that are traditionally considered more stable. Even before 9/11, the United States withdrew from a vigorous effort to support institutional reforms in migrant source countries. It also took a step back from efforts in the 1990s to strengthen the protection of the rights and conditions of immigrants. In effect, the United States reduced its support for institution-building, which had long been an essential ingredient in its relations with other countries in the hemisphere.

The result was that US leadership on migration issues in the region began to suffer from a loss of legitimacy. Political legitimacy depends in part on the exercise of rightful authority and the adherence to high standards of legal and moral norms when that authority is exercised. US legitimacy has been shaken by its persistent and even open disregard for its own laws governing immigration. US acceptance of sustained illegal immigration, for instance, especially when it condones substandard conditions and denial of migrants' rights, undermines the authority and practical ability of the United States to push for a new migration regime in the region.

Transparency and Corruption

Corruption is a second source of institutional weakness affecting governance of migration in the Western hemisphere. Corruption corrodes the legitimacy of existing institutions and forestalls efforts to build public support during the region's transition to democracy (UNDP, 1997). It specifically limits the effectiveness of migration policies in developing countries, and delegitimizes policies in the migrant destination countries.

Although corruption is difficult to measure, Transparency International has developed a Corruption Perception Index for 69 countries that includes many of the migrant source and destination countries in the Western hemisphere. The Index compares the impact of corruption on the ability to conduct business with other issues such as taxes, infrastructure shortages, terrorism, price controls, policy instability, regulations, crime, and financing. In Latin America, corruption ranked first as the most important barrier (Transparency International, 2004).

The Index values for many of the Western hemispheric countries provide evidence of the pervasive and deep concern about corruption. Yet, corruption has not received much attention from international financial institutions, governments, or migration analysts. According to one source, the World Bank did not even allow references to corruption in its official publications until 1996. It was only recently that World Bank President Wolfensohn highlighted anti-corruption programs as essential to development. Such programmes help to prevent the undermining of legitimate institutions, market rules and governance.

Corruption, of course, can be defined in a variety of ways, ranging from a narrow violation of law by an individual to expansive neglect of laws and regulations by authorities for special gain. The familiar definition involves the abuse of public office for private gain – including promises and payments, immediate or deferred, to a civil servant in exchange for special treatment. Other forms of corruption are more difficult to identify and evaluate, though they may be more frequent. These include nepotism, giving contracts to supporters, and using privileged information to win contracts and grants.

Petty forms of corruption routinely and pervasively affect migration throughout the hemisphere. They include the use of false documents, outright smuggling, bribes, and payoffs. Corruption pervades the special arrangements that are contained in contracts between employers and job contractors in certain industries, such as agriculture or construction, between smugglers and family members, and within the exercise of discretionary authority among public officials. The most obvious form, which occurs in migrant source and migrant destination countries alike, involves the actions of some lower level public officials engaged in passport and visa issuance and inspections in general (UNDP, 1997). The extent of this type of corruption is often revealed only when governments attempt to take action against it. For example, Mexico has recently attempted to reform the agencies that work on its northern border with the United States. It found that corruption had been forestalling many of its innovative efforts to protect migrants from the dangers of border crossing (Frontera NorteSur, 2004).

The most corrosive character of corruption, though, is the systematic incorporation and acceptance of illegality into labour market activities and policies. At the core of labour market corruption is the active recruitment of migrant workers under abusive conditions and without social and legal protections (Sullivan, 2000). This may involve clear criminality. Yet, it more frequently involves seemingly casual and informal practices that are difficult to discover and to document for criminal enforcement. Much of the activity appears 'voluntary' and works just on the edge of legality. For instance, employers may conspire to smuggle illegal workers into their region, but do not take the individual actions themselves to recruit and hire migrants. As a result, employers knowingly avoid exposure to a smuggling charge, while using contractor intermediaries and even the migrants' relatives and friends to transport the workers to the jobsite. Migrants are coerced, lied to, seduced, and simply induced by higher wages or a friendly recruiter to violate laws related to crossing borders, obtaining official documents or securing employment (Marizco and Steller, 2004). These are the greatest threats to the protection of migrants and to the positive developmental contributions of regional mobility.

Corruption is further rooted in the complex and frequently changing laws and regulations governing migration. The discretionary power of government officials to interpret these laws and regulations, for instance, often provides the opportunity for individual employers to benefit from hiring illegal workers. Corruption also thrives in markets where legal systems are ambiguous or deeply contested, especially when apparently open public policy debates and decisions persistently yield unfair advantages to particular private employers and organizations. This systemic corruption is hidden within the ambivalence of governments to patrol borders effectively while simultaneously cooperating with employers who use illegal workers to help them avoid the costs of disturbing their workforce.

For decades, US policy toward illegal, undocumented immigration has implicitly recognized the pervasiveness of selective compliance and enforcement. The acceptance is so widespread that it has become almost a national charade. The presence of large numbers of illegal workers, labouring under substandard conditions and terms of employment, is widely known in the hotel, restaurant and other service sector industries. Yet, very little action is taken to either enforce the laws or to change them in a way that would be effective.

A similar policy of so-called 'benign neglect' has riddled the agricultural labour system between the United States and Mexico for decades. In the 1990s, however, when federal authorities in the United States attempted to implement laws against smuggling and trafficking in sectors heavily reliant on illegality and corruption, employer associations, some public officials, and even immigrant advocacy groups openly opposed the regulatory action. Opposition persisted in the face of evidence gained from criminal investigations using wiretap methods that employers were personally and directly conspiring to bring workers illegally from Mexico and Central America, subjecting them to hazardous transport, and using them to displace local workers.

Corrupted labour markets, even those that appear on the surface to be benign, often turn desperate and dehumanizing. In the late 1990s, governments and civil society organizations awoke to the extent to which illegal, informal, and inhuman practices were routinely used to support the migration of hundreds of thousands of people throughout the hemisphere. In the United States, trafficking has reached substantial levels. The Department of State estimates an annual flow of approximately 20,000 persons, and some observers put the total number of trafficking victims residing in the United States at 150,000. These practices surpass beyond simple crimes and often work in ways that make it difficult to separate legal from illegal. In Central America, for instance, assisting people to migrate abroad is legal also when the 'travel agent' knowingly aids illegal entry into a neighbouring country.

In recent years, one of the primary reasons for a growing concern about systemic forms of corruption is that it disproportionately harms the poor and low wage workers whether at home or abroad. Illegality and corruption are not structural necessities for successful economic development, as some analysts have argued. Corruption is a waste of resources. Businesses resist investments in unpredictable environments, the poor lose jobs and income directly, and the benefits of public resources that could go into infrastructure, education, and other pillars of human development are misdirected to give advantage to special groups.

Corrupt institutional arrangements also mean that most impoverished and powerless workers, including migrants in particular, have none of the judicial protection or political clout to hold employers, their advocates, civil society organizations, or government officials accountable for the collusion that occurs in public policymaking that compromises their security and protections (UNDP, 2000). As a result, corruption embedded in migrants' labour markets has one fundamental consequence for the hemisphere. Over the long run, it delegitimizes the rule of law and, with it, democracy. The forms of corruption that are part of illegal migration increase inequality, benefit some over others without transparent, fair competition, and place a much heavier burden on the migrants themselves. In the end, labour markets that have become 'embedded niches' for illegal workers, or depend on the 'inevitable' use of unprotected workers, are not stable or sustainable over time.

Labour Standards and Protections

A third area of institutional weakness that puts migrants and the migration system at risk involves the failure of governments to deal with difficult labour conditions at home. The problem exists in both migrant source and destination countries and is a recurring, core dilemma of transnational labour markets throughout the region.

Migration can be a powerful development asset and, for decades, governments and international financial institutions have searched for its benefits by increasing its volume (UNFPA, 2004). The goal has been, like trade, to increase income through selling more products on the external market. In the last ten years, migrants' remittances have begun to fit this model well, returning billions of dollars to the governments of sending countries. For example, migrants from Mexico send home on average US$ 378 per month; Nicaraguans remit US$ 146 per month (Orozco, 2004). Returning immigrants also represent tourist-like dollars that have an especially large impact on smaller economies, such as Jamaica and El Salvador. In short, if the export of goods has been limited, the export of people can usefully augment the return on a growth-oriented strategy.

Like the low-wage production of goods for the world market, however, this 'people export' strategy has had less than expected and undesirable consequences on labour at home. Whether the work occurred at home as a consequence of direct foreign investment or abroad through migration of citizens, there has been an irregular and uneven expansion of employment and income for some, and increased inequality and vulnerability for others.

Transnational labour markets, for instance, have done little to mitigate the problem of poverty in migrant source countries, and social conditions at home have not changed dramatically. This remittance-lead strategy, or 'integration from below' (Portes, 1999), is also inherently unstable. First, it often reinforces the authoritarian tendencies of transitional regimes to protect the highly uneven concentration of wealth, land and power in the migrant source areas. Second, while the increase in work and wages is an unquestioned benefit, the need to move thousands of miles away and to maintain separate households increases social tensions among family members and expands their vulnerabilities. The social and geographical distance also introduces substantial costs to workers from transportation and redundant subsistence expenses that cut into the real value of their wages. Third, large-scale outmigration may substitute for effective development strategies at home. In Central America, for instance, migration may encourage acceleration of trade-based reforms that undermine poor farmers' ability to generate survival income. Fourth, excessive dependence on long distance, transnational labour markets subjects employment, household subsistence, and community stability at home to the vagaries of politics and economic cycles in another country (Bach, 2000). In a sense, it detaches participation in the economy (which is abroad) from participation in political and social activities (which are at home).

Long-distance migration and dependence on remittances, in many ways fail to take into account the fragility of political economies that are sources of emigration. As Polaski (2003) has argued extensively for free-trade in general, the current course of the dominant growth strategy for Mexico and Central America could be a development disaster for migrant source regions. The current model of hemispheric integration provides little attention to these connections between employment protections and migration. The lure of remittances has enticed international financial institutions and governments to focus their attention simply on expanding the pool, increasing rates of return (for example reducing the cost of remitting income), or gaining market share by trying to negotiate temporary, contract labour programmes with neighbouring governments.

The question for the hemisphere is whether and to what extent this employment can be organized in a way that sustains its growth and protects those who can not gain access to it. The answer requires the provision of some institutional support and alternatives to allow migrants to benefit more fully from their earned income abroad, protect low-wage export workers at home from abusive practices, and sustain impoverished households that are excluded from these highly selective advantages.

Weak institutional conditions for the region's workers make it virtually impossible to generate alternative job opportunities for would-be migrants, and renders it even more difficult to turn the potential development benefits of work abroad into a reality. The weakening of institutional structures for those 'left behind' also undercuts the value of wages earned outside the country and sent home. People in migrant source regions need more work, and higher wages, whether they need to remit them because their work is outside the country of origin, or they are simply sharing within an intact household. But they also require better work. Labour law reform is a critical prerequisite for supporting and building a regional migration system.

Conclusion: Putting First Things First

The Western hemispheric experience demonstrates a critical lesson about migration in an age of terrorism. Terrorism has not created new problems related to migration, but it has recalibrated the urgency and necessity to respond to those that were already evident. If the institutional framework that supports migration depends widely and pervasively on free trade models and strategies for development, all the pressure and necessary vigilance to keep terrorists at bay will continuously intervene and interfere. If movement and exchange are the priorities for regional integration, then security concerns will almost necessarily become a barrier to integration rather than a promoter. Yet, if the priorities are to enhance and enlarge cross-border institutional capacities, migration can foster integration, promote political and economic development, and reduce insecurities involved in moving back and forth across borders.

Unfortunately, the institutional challenge is not now present in the dominant strategies to integrate the hemisphere or in the various efforts to turn migration into a development asset. Some regional leaders, however, have recognized the challenge. The US Under Secretary for International Trade, Grant Aldonas, has warned that 'the full potential of the FTAA [Free Trade of the Americas] will require negotiators to work on areas that have often been inadequately addressed, including the need for strong rule of law, democratic institutions, independent judiciaries, reliable regulatory agencies, dependable law enforcement, and efficient banking and social services' (Aldonas, 2002).

Turning to that challenge will require attention to three features of a strong foundation for the Americas. First, a strategy must respond to inequality in the region. That can not be done by adjusting the volume of migration or managing more effectively the ease or difficulty of crossing borders in a heightened security environment. Inequality is persistent and pervasive and affects each aspect of cross-border integration. Migration itself is rooted in inequality, and great care needs to be taken to understand how various mobility strategies affect its uneven origins.

Second, the region's transition to democracy is a compelling precondition for successful reforms to support economic development and social stability. It is also essential for building the capacity of states in the region to negotiate effective and sustainable migration agreements. That capacity will require democratic, participatory institutions that take concerted efforts to combat the corruption that is presently so engrained in migration throughout the hemisphere.

Finally, a regional strategy needs to strengthen the shared values of a hemispheric community. The battle against terrorism can be the catalyst for that mobilization. For if what we are told about terrorism is true, their goal is to destroy the legitimacy and value of democratic institutions around the world. That legitimacy does not result from the amount of wealth that can be generated from trade or by enlarging or reducing the volume of migration. It also should not depend on the daunting task of successfully screening the personal backgrounds of everyone who crosses borders. The fight against terrorism, as the Western hemisphere moves to integrate its economies and societies, is to build upon the shared commitment to democracy's principles and objectives, which will also demand equal commitment to democracy's responsibilities.

Chapter 17

Towards an International Regime for Mobility and Security?[1]

Rey Koslowski

Introduction

Advances in transportation and communications technology increase the potential for international migration around the world. As international migration becomes less inhibited by physical or economic constraints and more of a function of legal constraints imposed by states, it turns into an increasingly important issue in politics among states. As such, international migration is an issue area for possible international cooperation within international organizations or through less formal international regimes.[2]

The number of international regimes has increased greatly over the past few decades in an expanding breadth of areas, including global trade and finance (Keohane, 1984; Findlayson and Zacher, 1988), international security (Jervis, 1983; Van Ham, 1993), human rights (Sikkink, 1993), the environment (Young, 1989; Haas, 1989); transportation and communications (Cowhey, 1990; Zacher, 1996), and the Internet (Franda, 2001). Nevertheless, international cooperation among states to regulate international migration has been very limited. Putting the international refugee regime aside, there is little in the way of international cooperation on international migration at the global level – no international migration regime. There are longstanding, but undersubscribed, conventions of the International Labour Organization (ILO), limited cooperation on high-skilled migration under the General Agreement on Trade in Services (GATS) and increasing cooperation on illegal migration, human smuggling and trafficking within the context of the United Nations Convention on Transnational Organized Crime. The limitations of international cooperation on migration and its potential have been well surveyed in the project on the New International Regime for Orderly Movements of People (NIROMP) directed by Bimal Ghosh (2000b) and the report of the Migration Working Group chaired by Michael Doyle submitted to UN Secretary General, Kofi Annan (United Nations, 2003a).

As policy-makers recognize that economic development in many source countries depends upon migrant remittances and that destination countries increasingly depend upon immigration to support aging populations, there have been more discussions of establishing a regime facilitating the international movement of labour similar to the international trade regime based on the General Agreement on Tariffs and Trade and subsequently the World Trade Organization (see for example Ghosh, 2000b;

Straubhaar, 2000). The fundamental obstacle to international cooperation on labour migration, as Ari Zolberg (1991; 1992) and James Hollifield (1992) have pointed out, is that migrant destination countries have little incentive to join such a regime because foreign labour, especially low-skilled labour, is in abundant supply. If labour shortages develop during periods of economic growth, states can get as much labour from abroad as they like with bilateral agreements or simply by opening labour markets to migrants while at the same time avoiding any commitment to keep labour markets open during economic downturns. A global migration regime may make sense in terms of increasing economic efficiency worldwide (Staubhaar, 2000) and insuring poorer migrant source countries' access to richer migrant destination country markets for the sake of international development and reducing global inequalities (UNDP, 1992). However, the additional economic gains to individual destination countries of joining such an international regime, as opposed to maintaining the unilateral status quo, are negligible in comparison to the non-economic costs of large-scale immigration on a destination country's security, society and culture. Such non-economic costs, whether real or just perceived, have domestic political consequences and make a policy of multilateral engagement on migration even more difficult for destination country policy-makers to sell to sceptical publics than international free trade agreements. Hence, there appears to be little interest among UN member states to expand the international legal and normative framework for migration policies as reflected in answers to a questionnaire posed to them in which only 47 favoured convening a global conference on the issue while 26 opposed and 111 did not reply (United Nations, 2003).

Although international cooperation on migration for the sake of economic considerations has languished, security concerns in the wake of the 11 September 2001 attacks have motivated international cooperation on international mobility that encompasses migration and travel. In addition to the 175 million international migrants, which the UN defines as the number of people who have lived outside of their country of nationality for at least one year, there are the millions of tourists, students and business people who travel internationally for shorter stays. Contrary to much of the early discussions in the media that all of the hijackers entered legally and that border controls were irrelevant to their entry, the *National Commission on Terrorist Attacks Upon the United States* (also known as the 9/11 Commission) concluded that '15 of the 19 hijackers were potentially vulnerable to interception by border authorities' (9/11 Commission, 2004a: 384). The hijackers entered the US on tourist and student visas under false pretences and used the same modalities of travel document fraud and visa abuse characteristic of illegal migration to the US. Al-Qaeda operated a 'passport office' at the Kandahar airport to alter travel documents and train operatives, including Mohamad Atta (9/11 Commission, 2004a: 169) and at least two, and perhaps as many as 11, of the 11 September hijackers used fraudulently altered passports. One of the hijackers entered with a student visa but never showed up for class, three had stayed in the US after their visas expired and several purchased fraudulent identity documents on the black market that primarily services illegal migrants (9/11 Commission, 2004b: 138–9).

In response to the 11 September attacks, the US changed its visa policies and border control processes in ways that have reverberated around the world. US authorities are demanding passenger manifests and passenger name records of US-bound travellers. They are also requiring all non-immigrant visa applicants to be interviewed at US consulates and to submit biometric data. Other nations are adopting similar visa and border control policies. In order to facilitate travel, while at the same time increasing security, the member states of the International Civil Aviation Organization (ICAO) have agreed to issue machine readable travel documents with biometrics on Radio Frequency Identification (RFID) chips. ICAO member states have also recently put forward proposals for international cooperation on electronic submission of advanced passenger information and the sharing of passenger name record data.

Given that contemporary migration often begins as tourism, study or temporary work abroad, *international mobility* is a more all-inclusive category for understanding the dynamics of international migration and the potential for its regulation by states. By shaping the processes of international travel and migration, increasing international cooperation on human smuggling, travel document security and passenger data sharing are the first steps toward an international regime for mobility and security. These first steps have been recognized by the 9/11 Commission when it argued that '[t]he US government cannot meet its own obligations to the American people to prevent the entry of terrorists without a major effort to collaborate with other governments. We should do more to exchange terrorist information with trusted allies, and raise US and global border security standards for travel and border crossing over the medium and long term through extensive international cooperation' (9/11 Commission, 2004a: 390).

An international regime for orderly migration has greater security value in the post-11 September world. Previously, the security threats posed by illegal migration and human smuggling were that of 'disruptive movements of people' (Ghosh, 2000b: 221) that could provoke immediate border security problems because of the scale of such movements or adverse domestic political reactions to perceived governmental 'loss of control' of borders. Now the threat may come from small groups or even individuals within larger illegal flows. By increasing the share of migration that is orderly, properly-documented, pre-screened and comes through ports of entry rather than around them, an international migration regime can help border authorities focus their limited resources on travellers and visitors that potentially pose the greatest security risks. Since the legislatures and publics of many major migration destination countries are very interested in maintaining international mobility while at the same time increasing security, international cooperation on mobility and security as advocated by the 9/11 Commission may also serve as a stepping stone toward broader cooperation on migration as a whole.

I will elaborate on these arguments in the following six sections. First, I review the relationship among international migration, mobility and security and describe the first steps taken after 11 September 2001 to increase security while maintaining international mobility. Second, I examine the development of European cooperation on migration and consider its implications for the development of global regimes.

Thirdly, I examine international cooperation to combat human smuggling. Fourthly, I describe the development of international cooperation on travel documents and passenger data exchange on a transatlantic basis as well as on a global basis within the ICAO. Fifthly, I assess the prospects for the formation of a global regime for mobility and security by focusing on leadership. Finally, I will explore the possibility of linking cooperation on security to global cooperation on labour migration under the rubric of a General Agreement on Migration, Mobility and Security.

Migration, Mobility and Security

From the standpoint of most international relations scholars, migration has been understood to have its primary impact on domestic politics, with only marginal consequences for international relations in general (see Koslowski, 2000: 1–29). Some point to the fact that the vast majority of people do not cross borders and the international migrants actually constitute only a small fraction (only some 3 per cent) of the world's population. Thus they have a relatively small effect on international politics in general. From a realist standpoint, the migration of unarmed refugees and guest workers across international borders should not enter into security considerations because such migrations only affect the balance of power at the margin, if at all. For the most part, therefore, international migration has usually been relegated to the analysis of the 'low politics' of international economics rather than the 'high politics' of international security concerns.

International migration has however always been a security issue for several reasons. First, the phenomenon of migration can be understood not only in economic terms but also as a matter of people moving across borders from parts of the world that are not secure (due to international and civil war, political or religious persecution or pervasive street crime) to areas of the world that are more secure (Schmitter Heisler and Heisler, 1989), and particularly to 'security communities,' areas of the world where states no longer resort to war among themselves to resolve disputes, most notably North America and Western Europe (Deutsch et al., 1957). Second, many international relations theories routinely assume state sovereignty and territorial integrity but not all of the world's states have the capability, and their policy-makers the political will, to stop the citizens of other countries from entering without authorization (Cornelius et al., 1994; Sassen, 1996). Third, the policy impact of migration is often out of proportion with the actual size of migratory flows because of public perceptions in the host country that migrants increase employment competition, challenge religious, cultural or ethnic homogeneity or pose threats to national security (Weiner, 1995: 45–74). Whether or not these perceptions are well-founded, they often influence domestic political contests and thereby influence policy-making. When the perception of migration as a threat leads to more general changes in host state policies toward source countries, migration can have a significant impact on foreign policy and national security (Tucker et al., 1990; Weiner, 1993; Teitelbaum and Weiner, 1995).

Contrary to realist assumptions that states with sufficient military capabilities are the only actors of significance in world politics, a handful of people crossing unarmed into another country can have tremendous consequences for international security, as the attacks of 11 September 2001 amply demonstrated. The world's most powerful states are now threatened by the possibility of asymmetric warfare by non-state actors armed with weapons of mass destruction (Betts, 1998; Allison, 2004). Homeland security officials are preparing for distributed simultaneous attacks of suicidal terrorists arriving in airports posing as tourists who then infect themselves with smallpox and spread it to unsuspecting crowds at major tourist attractions. Strategies of nuclear deterrence that dominated international security policy and theories in the second half of the twentieth century no longer apply when the opponent is not a state that can be threatened with retaliation but rather a suicidal individual.

It is crucial to understand that it is not international migration that is the new security threat but rather international mobility in general. The number of international migrants is a small fraction of the number of people who cross international borders every year. For example, in the year before 11 September 2001 there were approximately 500 million people who came into the United States through its ports of entry. Approximately 1.3 million people were apprehended by the US Border Patrol while attempting to enter clandestinely (DHS, 2004, Table 37) and the number that evaded apprehension may be several times that. Although a compilation of records of all entries of individuals into all the UN member states is not available, one can surmise that this number would be in the billions. It is this larger number of people who cross international borders for any length of time, migrants included, that may prose a security threat to any given state.

In response to 11 September attacks, the Bush Administration announced a set of initiatives to create a 'Smart Border' of the future that leverages new technologies 'to screen goods and people prior to their arrival in sovereign US territory ... Agreements with our neighbours, major trading partners, and private industry will allow extensive pre-screening of low-risk traffic, thereby allowing limited assets to focus attention on high-risk traffic' (White House, 2002). Indeed, as expanding e-government and private sector submission of electronic data enables the pre-clearance of passengers and cargo, thereby removing the necessity of inspection at territorial boundaries, borders may increasingly become 'virtual borders'.[3]

The Enhanced Border Security and Visa Entry Reform Act[4] passed in the US Senate by a vote of 97 to 0 and in the House by 411 to 0. The Act includes a requirement that commercial airlines and ships electronically submit passenger and crew manifests before arrival to the US, and sets out fines for non-compliance and loss of landing rights for those airlines that have not paid their fines. The act mandates an automated entry-exit tracking system that has now been dubbed the United States Visitor and Immigrant Status Indicator Technology (US-VISIT) programme. The Act further requires the use of biometrics to verify the identities of foreigners. US-VISIT currently collects digital photograph and fingerprint scan biometrics from those individuals arriving by air or sea and travelling on a non-immigrant visa to the United States.

In February 2004, Bureau of Customs and Border Protection (CBP) Commissioner Bonner (2004) proposed the Immigration Security Initiative (ISI). Modelled after existing programs of Australia, Canada, the UK and the Netherlands, this initiative will station teams of CBP officers in the key foreign hub airports from which the majority of US-bound passengers depart. The officers will use advanced manifest data to identify high-risk passengers before they board planes (CBP, 2004).

These transportation and border initiatives will require extensive international cooperation and the US has taken steps to engage the international community. So far international cooperation on passenger security has been primarily pursued bilaterally or in transatlantic US-EU negotiations. The positive G-8 and EU responses to US border security initiatives constitute first steps toward a transatlantic-centred mobility and security regime that leverages regional cooperation on each side of the Atlantic.

European Migration Regimes and Global Cooperation

A regime governing intra-EU migration was first articulated in the Treaty of Rome, reaffirmed in the Single European Act (SEA) and formally codified in the European Citizenship provisions of the Treaty on European Union (TEU) signed at Maastricht. A regime governing migration into the EU from non-member states began to emerge with the 1990 Dublin Convention on jurisdiction for asylum applications, the 1990 Schengen Convention on border controls and Title VI of the 1992 Maastricht Treaty dedicated to Cooperation in Justice and Home Affairs (JHA) and then became more fully articulated with the 1997 Amsterdam Treaty.

Title VI of the 1992 Maastricht Treaty formalized longstanding cooperation among the member states regarding border controls, migration and asylum. Cooperation in the fields of Justice and Home Affairs (JHA) formed one of three 'pillars' of the EU along with the First Pillar of the original European Community and the Second Pillar of Common Foreign and Security Policy (CFSP). The pillar structure effectively kept this cooperation on an 'intergovernmental basis' outside of the original Treaty on European Community (TEC). The 1997 Amsterdam Treaty incorporated the Schengen Convention into the EU treaties and set out a plan to put policies on visas, asylum, immigration and external border controls under Community procedures and into the Community legal framework by May 2004 (European Commission, 2004).

In the immediate aftermath of the attacks on the World Trade Center and the Pentagon, the European Council (2001) asked member states to strengthen controls at external borders and strengthen surveillance measures. A new 'European Agency for the Management of Operational Co-Operation at the External Borders of the European Union' agency will co-ordinate the implementation of common policies by member state border police but it lacks policy-making or implementing powers of its own (European Commission, 2003a). The 11 March 2004 Madrid bombing then prompted the European Council to establish the position of an EU counter-terrorism coordinator and take even more measures to strengthen border security.

Like the US, the EU has focused on using information technology to strengthen border controls. The Schengen Information System (SIS) is designed to enforce the common external border and build confidence in this common border so as to enable member states to remove all internal border controls. Integration into the system is necessary for the Schengen Convention to become effective for any signatory. Scheduled to become operational in 2007, SIS II will increase data capacity and be able to store digital images and biometric data (European Report, 2003). With rising concerns about illegal migration into Europe and the possibility of terrorists being smuggled into the EU or entering by visa fraud, the European Commission proposed a common online database that would complement secure identity documents (European Commission, 2001) and then put forward a legislative proposal to create and fund a visa information system (European Report, 2003).

EU member state cooperation on migration greatly exceeds that of other regional organizations of comparable advanced industrialized states. The decades of economic and political integration that has laid the groundwork for the lifting of border controls among EU member states may prove extremely difficult, if not impossible, to replicate in other regions.[5] The EU may provide the best example of an international migration regime, but it is perhaps inappropriate to use it as a point of comparison for other regions, let alone a global migration regime.

In fact, European cooperation on migration, asylum policy and border control may even be at cross-purposes with global cooperation in these areas. Much like the dilemma posed to global free trade by the formation of regional economic blocs with discriminatory policies that favour members over non-members, if cooperation aimed at free movement within the EU prompts polices that are less open to the rest of the world, EU migration regimes may limit rather than further global cooperation on migration as a whole (European Insight, 1995).

To hear it from Secretary General Kofi Annan, European cooperation on asylum policies may very well be responsible for the demise of what little global cooperation on migration that does exist – the refugee regime. Speaking to the European Parliament Annan said that 'when refugees cannot seek asylum because of offshore barriers, or are detained for excessive periods in unsatisfactory conditions, or are refused entry because of restrictive interpretations of the [1951 Refugee] Convention, the asylum system is broken and the promise of the Convention is broken, too' (Annan, 2004).

Simply put, increasing European cooperation on migration need not lead to liberal outcomes that benefit asylum seekers and would-be migrants seeking to enter the EU. International cooperation is by and for states and if states collectively opt for more restrictive policies, international cooperation may reduce migration rather than lift barriers to it. European cooperation on border control and migration presents a dilemma to advocates for global cooperation on migration in that it may serve as a step forward toward a global regime for mobility and security while at the same time eroding the international refugee regime and erecting obstacles to the formation of a more comprehensive global migration regime.

International Cooperation to Combat Human Smuggling and Trafficking

During the 1990s, policy-makers from the major migration destination countries such as United States, Germany, Canada, Australia, the UK, France, Italy and Austria became increasingly concerned with the smuggling of migrants across their borders. Trafficking in persons, particularly, women and children into forced prostitution presented a growing human rights problem and human smuggling was increasingly viewed as a security issue of uncontrollable borders (see Koslowski, 2001). The prospect of terrorists being smuggled into target states was considered as a potential threat in some law enforcement circles but it was not until the attacks of 11 September and 11 March that human smuggling was viewed as a security threat in a qualitatively different way. It became clear that terrorists could take clandestine routes that transnational criminal organizations use to smuggle illegal migrants into the US (9/11 Commission, 2004b: 61; Simpson et al., 2004).

During the 1990s, Austria took the lead in encouraging fellow UN member states to pass laws that specifically criminalize human smuggling and draft an international convention on the smuggling of illegal aliens (Schuessel, 1997). In December 1998, the UN General Assembly initiated an Ad Hoc Committee that was charged with drawing up a comprehensive international convention against transnational organized crime and in November 2000, the 'UN Convention against Transnational Organized Crime,' and its 'Protocol to Prevent, Suppress and Punish Trafficking in Persons, Especially Women and Children,' and the 'Protocol against the Smuggling of Migrants by Land, Sea and Air' were adopted by the UN General Assembly. The Convention went into effect 29 September 2003, the anti-trafficking protocol on 25 December 2003 and the anti-smuggling protocol on 28 January 2004.

The objectives of the human smuggling protocol are twofold – establishing the smuggling of migrants as a criminal offence and facilitating cooperation in the prevention, investigation and prosecution of the crime of smuggling migrants. To this effect, the draft protocol provides rules for interdicting and boarding ships suspected of carrying illegal migrants, approves of state use of carrier sanctions and encourages information exchanges between states. The protocol also calls for strengthening border controls and intensifying cooperation among border control agencies by establishing and maintaining direct lines of communication.

Although the International Organization for Migration (IOM) has a smaller membership[6] than the UN and is much more specialized and limited as a forum for migration policy-making than regional organizations such as the EU, the IOM is a major actor when it comes to international cooperation in the area of human smuggling and trafficking in persons (IOM, 1994). The IOM has been sponsoring regional processes dealing with irregular migration and migrant trafficking in Europe, the Americas, East and Southeast Asia. While the IOM has emerged as a leading international organization in the area of research and policy dialogues devoted to human smuggling in general (see Ghosh, 1998), operational programs have primarily focused on trafficking in women and children for forced prostitution, whether in terms of publicity campaigns to discourage women from turning to traffickers or return programs with which the IOM is very experienced. By specifically targeting human smuggling organizations this international cooperation addresses an increasingly important component of terrorist travel.

From Transatlantic to Global Cooperation on Travel Documents and Passenger Data Exchange

As US and EU border control officials took steps to tighten border controls through deploying new technologies in the effort to screen out threats from legitimate travel flows, border control officials on both sides of the Atlantic realized that transnational threats posed by terrorist networks required stepped-up international cooperation. While the split between the US and individual EU member states, such as France and Germany, over the Iraq war led some commentators to declare US-European relations as being in crisis, France and Germany, among other EU member states, were busily signing agreements and exchanging information with US border control authorities. The European Commission and the US Department of Homeland Security (DHS) have been taking international cooperation into sensitive areas of state sovereignty dealing with border controls, government surveillance, data collection and exchange that before 11 September 2001 would have been unthinkable. As Mark Miller has pointed out, to the extent that there is an embryonic international migration regime, 'it is centered in the transatlantic area' (Miller, 2000). Similarly, an emerging regime for mobility and security is also centered in the transatlantic area and it is developing rather quickly. Nevertheless, there still are many legal and political obstacles to further transatlantic cooperation in this area that have yet to be overcome.

Transatlantic cooperation emerged through US security initiatives and negotiations with the EU that have set up a variety of arrangements and more formal agreements. The 2001 US aviation and transportation security legislation requires that airlines with US-bound international flights 'shall make passenger name record information available to the Customs Service upon request'.[7] Passenger name record (PNR) data is created each time a passenger books a flight and it is stored in the airlines' reservation systems. The US Customs Service requested PNR data from European-based airlines but several resisted, contending that it would be a violation of EU data protection rules.

The US Congress required that all passports of Visa Waiver Program countries issued after 26 October 2004 contain biometrics. Many countries signalled that they could not meet this deadline and Secretaries Tom Ridge and Colin Powell asked Congress for a postponement to December 2006 (Powell and Ridge, 2004). Congress responded with legislation, however, that it only allows a one year extension to 26 October 2005. The US Congress deferred to ICAO on setting the biometric standard and it was not until 28 May 2003 that the ICAO announced an agreement – facial recognition plus optional fingerprints and/or retina scans stored on a contactless integrated circuit

(IC) chip (ICAO, 2003). Central to the vision of the 'revolution in border security,' the contactless IC chip is part of a Radio Frequency Identification (RFID) system in which data on a chip or tag is transmitted via radio waves to a reader. Although State Department officials expressed confidence that European countries could meet an October 2006 deadline, it is not clear that the one year deadline extension will be enough. Transatlantic cooperation on PNR data collection and exchange as well as the setting of biometric standards requires acceptance of mutual constraints on the range of state action in the area of border control – one of the defining aspects of territorial sovereignty. Further cooperation, however, may be interrupted by differing legal regimes governing privacy and personal data protection. Given the increasing concern over the privacy of PNR data raised in the US Congress (for example Collins, 2004) and by the European Parliament, there may be major limitations to further transatlantic PNR data transfer without global multilateral agreements and implementing legislation on the national level. Similarly, visions of a 'virtual border,' with secure documents with biometrics on RFID chips, require international cooperation on data-sharing and technical standards.

Global Regime Formation: A Question of Leadership?

Regional cooperation on border control and migration, global cooperation on human smuggling and transatlantic cooperation on transportation and border security do not, in and of themselves, add up to a global regime for mobility and security. These are only possible steps toward such a regime. Hence, the remaining discussion in the rest of this paper is highly speculative and is not intended to be prescriptive. I will describe various scenarios and possible strategies based on international regime formation in other issue areas and suggest ways in which they may be relevant in this case. Moreover, there may be other routes toward the realization of a global regime for mobility and security that may prove to be more successful than the suggestions found in the following ruminations.

Today's international trade and monetary regimes were put in motion with US leadership after the devastation of Europe in the two World Wars and these regimes have persisted despite the US's economic decline in the 1970s relative to an economically rebounding Europe and rising East Asia. Establishment of the post-war international monetary regime required the 'hegemonic stability' of a 'lender of last resort' and post-war expansions of free trade depended upon a US tolerance of 'free-riding' by states in Europe and East Asia that took advantage of US market openings to imports but retained measures to protect their own markets (Kindleberger, 1973; Keohane, 1984).

Formation of a regime for mobility and security will most likely also require similar hegemonic stability with a leader that will facilitate standardization of secure travel documents and biometrics, pay the initial development costs of new border control technologies, initiate deployments of new documents and systems, underwrite the institutionalization of international law enforcement cooperation and be willing to extend foreign assistance to states that may wish to participate in the regime but do not have the requisite border control capacities. At the same time, the hegemonic leader must maintain international mobility by keeping its own ports of entry open to legitimate travellers and migrants and spending additional resources to ensure that new security requirements and technologies do not significantly slow legitimate travel flows.

Given all of the post-11 September border security initiatives and transatlantic cooperation described above, it appears that the US government is committed to international leadership on border security, however, it is not clear that the US is properly equipped to do so, or that the Bush administration and the US Congress is politically willing to change that. The US has taken a leadership role in standardizing requirements for travel documents and biometrics in ICAO but it has been slow to implement systems that impose new biometric requirements on its own citizens. The 9/11 Commission has now recommended a biometric entry-exit system that enrols all US, Canadian and Mexican nationals (9/11 Commission, 2004a: 387–9). This provides an opportunity to adopt these recommendations in passing new laws that would enable the US to take a leadership position in the formation of a global regime for mobility and security.

The Bush administration has been reluctant to fund the implementation of border security measures at US ports of entry, let alone underwrite a major expansion of international law enforcement institutions. The DHS Budget has increased from $31.2 billion in 2003, to $37.6 billion in 2005 (DHS, 2004: 3, 12). However, as Stephen Flynn points out, additional spending on homeland security in the two years since 11 September 2001 is a minuscule 4 per cent of the annual Defence Department budget (Flynn, 2004a).

If domestic politics and budgetary priorities constrain the US government from providing leadership necessary to form a global regime for mobility and security, the EU could potentially fill the role, especially given that the EU has extensive experience in the institutionalization of international law enforcement, cooperation on border controls and building border security capacity in the new EU member states. While US lawmakers are skittish of proposing the establishment of a national ID card, let alone one with embedded biometrics, many European societies are very accustomed to ID cards, some of which have included fingerprints for some time now. Denmark and Sweden are pioneering ICAO compliant biometric passports and the French Interior Ministry has decided on new IDs with both facial and fingerprint biometrics on RFID chips (eGovernment News, 2004).

Another alternative would be transatlantic hegemonic leadership. That is, if the US, Canada and the EU could each agree to lead on issues where they are best able and the others follow that lead in turn, one could imagine a core group of states that push the agenda of global mobility and security as well as support it through exemplary implementations, financial contributions and political muscle. This scenario may offer the greatest possibility for regime formation but it is also the most diplomatically complex and would require that the domestic constituencies of a relatively large number of states do not resist either of the two steps of such international cooperation. Moreover, such transatlantic agenda setting offers little to those states outside the core group and could prompt significant diplomatic resistance from the rest of the world should transatlantic hegemonic leadership actually take shape. This brings us to the question of what stake, if any, migrant source countries may have in a global regime for mobility and security.

A General Agreement on Migration, Mobility and Security (GAMMS)?

Given that international regime theory largely developed to help explain international cooperation outside of formal international organizations, as was the case with the GATT, analogies to the GATT for thinking about an international migration regime can be useful, as several authors have demonstrated (Harris, 1995; Ghosh, 2000b; Straubhaar, 2000). Most have envisioned rounds of negotiations toward an overarching agreement that links the well-established refugee regime and cooperation in trade in services, or even international trade in general (Hollifield, 2000: 101), to areas of international migration that have not been subject to international regulation. Given that migration destination countries have not been particularly responsive to economic and human rights arguments for the initiation of such rounds of negotiations, perhaps the security implications of accelerating international mobility may provide increased impetus toward broader cooperation that links source countries to destination countries.

Discussions of a global migration regime based on an agreement similar to the GATT have focused on a principle of 'regulated openness' that is in contradiction to labour market protectionism through the exclusion of migrants as well as the liberal doctrine of unfettered free movement of labour across the boundaries of sovereign states (Ghosh, 2000b: 25). A global regime for the orderly movement of people would involve a bargain in which destination countries would permit legal migration of labour while source countries would agree to do what they could to suppress illegal migration as well as accept orderly repatriation of their nationals who migrated illegally. From the destination countries' perspective there is little incentive for international commitments to keep labour markets open to immigrants. There is no compelling reason to change the status quo when legal labour migration can be permitted (and illegal migration tolerated) on a unilateral basis in periods of economic growth and shut down in time of recession. From the source countries' perspective this bargain is inherently problematic. Not only do their economies increasingly depend upon remittances from legal and illegal migrants alike but there is little that a state can do to prevent its nationals from leaving without at the same time transgressing international human rights law and possibly also infringing on citizens' constitutional rights.

In the wake of 11 September 2001, the stakes in establishing a global regime for mobility and security are much higher for the US, EU member states and other migration destination countries than past incentives for establishing a global labour migration regime. For source countries, participation in a global regime for mobility and security involves the practical implementation of international norms on document security and biometrics, information exchange and international cooperation among border control authorities and law enforcement agencies that may be prohibitively expensive and administratively very difficult. As currently pursued by the US and EU, the envisioned global border security cooperation makes heroic assumptions regarding the identity documentation of much of the world's population. If identity and travel documentation systems of the US and other advanced post-industrial states are so susceptible to fraud and counterfeit, what are we to expect of less developed countries?

Similarly, international information exchanges have been enabled by the internet, however, they rely on a state's capacity to collect, store and retrieve required data. Finally, the international cooperation on border control and law enforcement required for a global mobility regime may involve source and transit countries' acceptance of US and/or EU border control officers in their airports and seaports and that may be considered by many domestic political actors as an intolerable infringement of state sovereignty. Hence, it may be politically difficult for many migrant source countries in the developing world to agree to a global regime for mobility and security. Even if such agreement is reached, implementation may be just as, if not even more, difficult to achieve.

If US and EU vital security interests are at stake in a global regime for mobility and security, and if cooperation on document security and law enforcement is linked to orderly international labour migration, perhaps a more all-encompassing General Agreement on Migration, Mobility and Security (GAMMS) could be negotiated. Incorporation of orderly labour migration into the global regime for mobility and security would require leadership of the US in expanding legal immigration of migrant labour while at the same time enforcing employer sanctions to dry up demand for illegal migrant labour. It would require that those EU member states that have resisted opening their labour markets to immigrants do so and agree to an EU framework for labour migration. In return, source countries in the developing world would agree to rapid implementation of ICAO travel document standards, automated information exchanges and increasing international border control and law enforcement cooperation.

Trading labour market access for cooperation in combating terrorist travel, however, may very well prove unworkable. Destination countries advocates for border security may argue that reducing terrorist mobility increases the security of all states and should not need to be tied to agreements on labour migration. In many developing countries, the threats of malnutrition and disease overshadow concerns over border security, terrorist travel and the prospect of truck bombs detonated in front of hotels that cater to foreigners. Sending state advocates for increasing opportunities for international labour migration may reject any linkage that 'securitizes' migration and prefer to focus instead on convincing destination countries of the benefits of legal labour migration.

International cooperation on border security that remains limited to the transatlantic area and does not embrace the whole world will not be as effective as a global regime for mobility and security. Source countries in the developing world may resist imposition of biometrics in their documents and foreign law enforcement officers in their airports, however, some states will cut bilateral deals that facilitate travel of their nationals and trade through their ports. With increasingly globalized economies, those states that resist cooperating with the US and EU on border security may suffer significant economic costs from decreasing mobility of their nationals and exports.

International cooperation on migration whether on a global or regional basis need not necessarily lead to liberal outcomes that make it easier for prospective migrants and asylum seekers to cross borders. A global regime for mobility and security would facilitate travel of tourists, businesspeople and migrants deemed legitimate and 'wanted' by the states receiving them. At the same time, it would strengthen state capabilities to not only intercept suspected terrorists but also to decrease the 'unwanted' migration of illegal workers and asylum seekers.

Given the requirements for leadership necessary to establish such a global regime and the domestic political barriers to governments seeking to assume that leadership, the steps toward a global regime for migration and security described above may not go much further. If they do, however, source countries in the developing world will have choices forced upon them. There may be opportunities for collective actions that translate into additional broader cooperation on international labour migration in the form of a General Agreement on Migration, Mobility and Security. The prospects for such cooperation, however, may only be slightly better than the past efforts toward global cooperation on migration that have yet to produce very much.

Notes

[1] The research for this chapter was supported by a fellowship from the Woodrow Wilson International Center for Scholars.

[2] International regimes were initially defined as 'mutual expectations, rules and regulations, plans, organizational energies and financial commitments, which have been accepted by a group of states (Ruggie, 1975: 570). Later, a 'consensus definition' by a group of leading international relations scholars emerged: 'Regimes can be defined as sets of implicit or explicit principles, norms, rules and decision-making procedures around which actors expectations converge in a given area of international relations. Principles are beliefs of fact, causation and rectitude. Norms are standards of behavior defined in terms of rights and obligations. Rules are specific prescriptions or proscriptions for action. Decision-making procedures are prevailing practices for making and implementing collective choice' (Krasner, 1983b: 2).

[3] The term 'virtual borders' was used by Customs and Border Protection Commissioner Robert Bonner in remarks at a reception preceding the 2003 Customs and Border Protection Trade Symposium, 19 November 2003 and in the 28 November 2003 'Request for Proposals for US-VISIT Program Prime Contractor' (DHS, 2003).

[4] Section 402 of the 'Enhanced Border Security and Visa Entry Reform Act of 2002', Public Law 107–173, 14 May 2002.

5   For a discussion on the limitations of implementing a Schengen-'North American Perimeter', see Koslowski (2004).
6   102 states as of November 2003.
7   Section 115 of the 'Aviation and Transportation Security Act,' Public Law 107–71, 19 November 2001.

Bibliography

Abella, M., 'Labour migration from South and South-East Asia: Some Policy Issues', *International Labour Review*, 123/4 (1984): 491–2.

Acemoglu, D. and J. Angrist, *How Large are the Social Returns to Education: Evidence from Compulsory Schooling Laws*, Working Paper 7444 (Cambridge, MA: NBER, 1999).

Adams, R., 'International Migration, Remittances, and the Brain Drain: A Study of 24 Labor-Exporting Countries', Policy Research Working Paper 3069, World Bank (Washington, DC, 2003).

Adams, R. and J. Page, *International Migration, Remittances, and Poverty in Developing Countries*, Policy Research Working Paper 3179 (Washington, DC: World Bank, 2003).

ADB, *Regional Technical Assistance Combating Trafficking of Women and Children in South Asia: Exposure Visit to Thailand*, RETA:5948 (Agriteam Canada Consulting Ltd, 2002).

——, *Emerging Asia* (Manila: 1997).

Adepoju, A., 'The Links Between Intra-Continental and Inter-Continental Migration in and from Africa', in A. Adepoju and T. Hammar (eds), *International Migration In and From Africa* (Dakar: PHRDA and CEIFO, 1996).

——, 'South-North Migration: The African Experience', *International Migration*, 29/2 (1991): 205–22.

Adepoju, A. and R. Appleyard, 'The Relevance of Research on Emigration Dynamics for Policymakers in Sub-Saharan Africa', *International Migration*, 34/2 (1996): 321–33.

Ahmed, I., 'Remittances and their Economic Impact in Post-War Somaliland', *Disasters*, 24/4 (2000): 380–89.

Akin-Aina, T., 'Ties between Emigration and Destination Countries: Historical, Colonial and Cultural', in A. Adepoju and T. Hammar (eds), *International Migration In and From Africa* (Dakar: PHRDA and CEIFO, 1996).

Alburo, F.A., 'Trade and Turning Points in Labor Migration', *Asian and Pacific Migration Journal*, 3/1 (1994): 49–80.

Alburo, F. and M. Abella, *Skilled Labour Migration from Developing Countries: Study on the Philippines*, International Migration Papers 51 (Geneva: ILO, 2002).

Aldonas, G.D., 'The FTAA: Mapping the Road to Economic Growth and Development', *Economic Perspectives*, October (2002): 324–45.

Aleinikoff, T.A. and D. Klusmeyer (eds), *Citizenship Policies for an Age of Migration* (Washington, DC: Carnegie Endowment for International Peace and Migration Policy Institute, 2002).

—— (eds), *Citizenship Today: Global Perspectives and Practices* (Washington, DC: Carnegie Endowment for International Peace, 2001).

—— (eds), *From Migrants to Citizens: Membership in a Changing World* (Washington, DC: Carnegie Endowment for International Peace, 2000).

Alesina, A. and E. Glaeser, *Fighting Poverty in the US and Europe: A World of Difference* (Oxford: Oxford University Press, 2004).

al-Ghul, A., *Mulahathat an al-Higrat al-Kharagiyya [Observation on External Migration]* (Khartoum: Council on Economic and Social Research, 1982).

Allison, G., *Nuclear Terrorism: The Ultimate Preventable Catastrophe* (New York: New York Times Books, 2004).

Alvarez-Plata, P., H. Brücker, B. Silverstovs, *Potential Migration from Central and Eastern Europe into the EU-15. An Update* (Brussels: EC/DG Employment and Social Affairs, 2003).

Ambroso, G., *Pastoral Society and Transnational Refugees: Population Movements in Somaliland and Eastern Ethiopia 1988–2000*, Working Paper No. 65, UNHCR (Geneva, 2002).

Amjad, R. (ed.), *To the Gulf and Back: Studies on the Economic Impact of Asian Labour Migration* (New Delhi: ILO-ARTEP, 1989).

Ammassari, S. and R. Black, *Harnessing the Potential of Migration and Return to Promote Development: Applying Concepts to West Africa*, IOM Migration Research Series, No. 5 (Geneva: IOM, 2001).

Anand, S. and T. Bärnighausen, 'Human Resources and Health Outcomes: Cross-country Econometric Study', *The Lancet*, 364/9445 (30 October 2004).

Anastasia, B. and P. Sestito, 'Il lavoro degli immigrati e l'economia sommersa', paper presented at the conference *L'incidenza economica dell'immigrazione* (Florence, 2003).

Andrade-Eekhoff, K. and C. Marina Silva-Avalos, *Globalization of the Periphery: The Challenges of Transnational Migration for Local Development in Central America*, Working Document, FLACSO (2003).

Annan, K., 'Address to the European Parliament upon receipt of the Andrei Sakharov Prize for Freedom of Thought', 29 January 2004, United Nations Press Release SG/SM/9134 (Brussels: 2004).

Apap, Joanna, Philippe de Bruycker and Catherine Schmitter, 'Regularization of Illegal Aliens in the European Union: Summary Report of a Comparative Study', *European Journal of Migration and Law*, 2/3 (2000).

APWLD Labour and Migration Task Force, 'Seminar on Trafficking', *Forum News*, 12/2 (1999).

Archavanitkul, K. and P. Guest, 'Managing the Flow of Migration: Regional Approaches', paper presented at the *International Symposium on Migration: Towards Regional Cooperation on Irregular/Undocumented Migration*, the Ministry of Foreign Affiars of the Kingdom of Thailand and the International Organization for Migration (IOM) (Bangkok, 21–23 April 1999).

Australian Department of Immigration and Multicultural and Indigenous Affairs (DIMIA), *Fact Sheet: Labor Market Results* (2003). Accessed 29 April 2004 at http://www.migrationexpert.com/ applications/dimia_labour_market_outcomes.pdf.

Awases, M., A. Gbary, J. Nyoni and R. Chatora, *Migration of Health Professionals in Six Countries: A Synthesis Report* (Brazzaville: WHO-AFRO DHS, 2003).

Bach, R.L. 'Global Mobility, Inequality and Security', *Journal of Human Development*, 4/2 (2003): 65–85.

——, 'From State-Centered to People-Centered Data Needs', background note for the *Consultation on International Migration* (Berlin, October 2002).

——, 'Combating the Transnational Underground in the Western Hemisphere', paper presented at the Conference on Transnational Gangs, organized by the Organization of American States, Florida International University (December 2000).

—— and R. Maguire, *Next Steps for US Policy Toward Haiti* (Washington, DC: International Affairs Program, Trinity University, November 2002).

Bade, K.J., *Migration in European History* (Oxford: Blackwell, 2003).

Baldi, S. and C. de Azavedo, *La popolazione italiana verso il 2000* (Bologna: Il Mulino, 1999).

Barbieri, W.A., *Ethics of Citizenship: Immigration and Group Rights in Germany* (London: Duke University Press, 1998).

Barclay G.W., A.J. Coale, M.O. Stoto and T.J. Trussell, 'A Reassessment of the Demography of Traditional Rural China', *Population Index*, 42/4 (1976): 606–35.

Barry, T., 'Africa in the Time of Free Trade', *IRC Bulletin*, No. 49 (December, 1997).

Basch, L., N. Glick Schiller and C. Szanton Blanc, *Nations Unbound: Transnational Projects, Postcolonial Predicaments, and Deterritorialized Nation States* (Amsterdam: Gordon and Breach Publishers, 1994).

Bauböck, R. 'Civic Citizenship – A New Concept for the New Europe', in R. Süssmuth and W. Weidenfeld (eds), *Managing Integration: European Union Responsibilities Towards Immigrants* (Brussels: Bertelsmann Foundation, 2004).

——, 'Towards a Political Theory of Migrant Transnationalism', *International Migration Review*, 37/3 (2003): 700–23.

—— (ed.), *From Aliens to Citizens: Redefining the Status of Immigrants in Europe* (Aldershot, Avebury, 1994).

——, 'Migration and Citizenship', *New Community*, 18/1 (1991): 27–48.

Becker, E., 'Adding Value to Immigrants' Cash', *New York Times* (6 June 2004).

Berry, B.J.L., 'Transnational Urbanward Migration, 1830–1980', *Annals of the Association of American Geographers*, 83/3 (1993): 389–405.

Besley, T., *From Micro to Macro: Public Policies and Aggregate Economic Performance*, mimeo, London School of Economics (2000).

Besteman, C., *Unraveling Somalia: Race, Violence, and the Legacy of Slavery* (Pennsylvania: University of Pennsylvania Press, 1999).

Betts, R., 'The New Threat of Mass Destruction', *Foreign Affairs*, 77/1 (1998): 26–41.

Bigsten, A. and D. Durevall, *Is Globalisation Good for Africa?*, Working Papers in Economics, No. 67, Department of Economics (Göteborg: Göteborg University, 2002).

Bjerén, G. 'Gender and Reproduction', in T. Hammar, G. Brochmann, K. Tamas and T. Faist (eds), *International Migration, Immobility and Development: Multidisciplinary Perspectives* (Oxford: Berg Publishers, 1997).

Black, R., R. King and R. Tiemoko, 'Migration, Return and Small Enterprises Development: A Route out of Poverty?', paper prepared for the *International Workshop on Migration and Poverty in West Africa*, University of Sussex (13–14 March 2003).

Blanc-Chaléard, M.C., *Histoire de l'immigration* (Paris: La Découverte, 2001).

Bloom, D. and J.P. Sevilla, 'Should There be a General Subsidy for Higher Education in Developing Countries?', *Journal of Higher Education in Africa*, 2/1 (2004).

Bloom, D.E., D. Canning and J. Sevilla, *The Demographic Dividend: A New Perspective on the Economic Consequences of Population Change* (Santa Monica: Rand, 2003).

Bolaffi, G., *Una politica per gli immigrati* (Bologna: Il Mulino, 1996).

Boly, R.C., *Money Transmitters, Remittances, Exchange Rates, and Mechanisms for Money Laundering in the Dominican Republic*, paper prepared for the US Embassy (Santo Domingo, 1996).

Bongaarts, J. and R.A. Bulatao, *Beyond Six Billion: Forecasting the World's Population* (Washington, DC: National Academy Press, 2000).

Bonner, R.C., 'Remarks to Center for Strategic and International Studies (CSIS), Transnational Threats Audit Conference' (11 February 2004). Accessed 5 April 2004 at <http://www.cbp.gov/xp/cgov/newsroom/commissioner/speeches_statements/mar032004.xml>.

Boserup, E., *Population and Technological Change: A Study of Long Term Trends* (Chicago: University of Chicago Press, 1981).

——, *The Conditions of Agricultural Progress* (London: Allen and Unwin, 1965).

Bourgignon, F. and C. Morrison, 'Inequality Among World Citizens: 1820–1992', *American Economic Review*, 92 (2002): 727–44.

Brown, R.P.C. and J. Connell, 'The Global Flea Market: Migration, Remittances and the Informal Economy in Tonga', *Development and Change*, 24/4 (1993): 611–47.

Brown, R.P.C., J. Foster and J. Connell, 'Remittances, Savings, and Policy Formation in Pacific Island States', *Asian Pacific Migration Journal*, 4/1 (1995): 169–85.

Buchan, J., *International Recruitment of Nurses: United Kingdom Case Study*, report for WHO and International Council of Nurses and the Royal College of Nursing (Geneva, 2002).

Buchan, J., T. Parkin and J. Sochalski, *International Nurse Mobility: Trends and Policy Implications*, report for WHO, International Council of Nurses and the Royal College of Nursing (Geneva, 2003).

Buchan, J. and D. Dovlo, *International Recruitment of Health Workers to the UK: A Report for DFID* (February 2004). Available at: <http://www.dfidhealthrc. org/Shared/publications/reports/int_rec/int-rec-main.pdf>.

Bundred, P. and C. Levitt, 'Medical Migration: Who are the Real Losers?', *The Lancet*, 356/9225 (2000): 245–6.

Burki, S., 'Migration from Pakistan to the Middle East', in G. Papademetriou and P. Martin (eds), *The Unsettled Relationship: Labor Migration and Economic Development* (Westport: Greenwood Press, 1991).

Burney, N.A., 'A Macro-Economic Analysis of the Impact of Workers' Remittances on Pakistan's Economy', in R. Amjad (ed.), *To the Gulf and Back: Studies on the Economic Impact of Asian Labour Migration* (New Delhi: ILO-ARTEP, 1989).

Buzan, B., *From International to World Society? English School Theory and the Social Structure of Globalisation* (Cambridge: Cambridge University Press, 2004).

Carens, J., 'Migration and Morality: A Liberal Egalitarian Perspective', in B. Barry and R. Goodin (eds), *Free Movement* (London: Harvester, 1992).

——, 'Aliens and Citizens: The Case for Open Borders', *Review of Politics*, 49/2 (1987): 251–73.

Caritas, *Dossier statistico immigrazione*, Edizioni Nuova Anterem (Rome, 1990–2004).

Carnegie Endowment for International Peace (CEIP), *The Barcelona Process*, Policy Brief, No. 29 (Washington, DC, 2004).

Casanelli, L., *The Shaping of Somali Society: Restructuring the History of a Pastoral People 1600–1900* (Pennsylvania: University of Pennsylvania Press, 1982).

Castenada, J., *The New Agenda for Change in Mexico* (Washington, DC: Woodrow Wilson Center, July 2004).

Customs and Border Protection (CBP), *US and Poland Sign Agreement to Begin Screening Program at Warsaw Airport*, Press Release (8 September 2004). Accessed 10 September 2004 at <http://www.cbp.gov/xp/cgov/newsroom/press_releases/09082004.xml>.

Censis, 'I lavoratori stagionali immigrati in Italia', *Note e commenti*, No. 4 (2002).

Chantavanich, S., 'Thai Migrant Workers in East and South-East Asia', paper prepared for the *International Workshop on Migration and Socio-economic Change in Southeast and East Asia* (Lund: 14–16 May 2001).

Chaudhuri, S., A. Mattoo and R. Self, *Moving People to Deliver Services: How Can the GATS Help?*, World Bank Policy Research Working Paper (Washington, DC, 2004).

Chen, L.C., 'Health and Migration in a Global Era', research notes for the *1st Workshop on Global Migration Regimes*, organized by the Institute for Future Studies (Stockholm: June, 2003).

Chesnais, J.C., *The Demographic Transition: Stages, Patterns, and Economic Implications: A Longitudinal Study of Sixty-Seven Countries Covering the Period 1720–1984* (Oxford: Clarendon Press, 1992).

——, 'Demographic-Transition Patterns and Their Impact On the Age Structure', *Population and Development Review*, 16/2 (1990): 327–36.

Ching-lung T., 'Labour Flows from Southeast Asia to Taiwan', in S. Chantavanich, A. Germershausen and A. Beesey (eds), *Thai Migrant Workers in East and Southeast Asia 1996–97*, ARCM No. 19 (Bangkok: Chulalongkorn University Printing House, 2000).

Choucri, N., *A Study of Sudanese Nationals Working Abroad*, unpublished (MIT: Cambridge MA, 1985).

Çınar, D., 'From Aliens to Citizens: A Comparative Analysis of Rules of Transition', in R. Bauböck (ed.), *From Aliens to Citizens: Redefining the Status of Immigrants in Europe* (Aldershot: Avebury, 1994).

Cohen, R. and Z. Layton-Henry (eds), *The Politics of Migration* (Northampton, MA: Edward Elgar, 1997).

Collins, S., *Senators Call on TSA to Explain its Role in Obtaining Sensitive Airline Passenger Information*, Press Release from the Office of Senator Susan Collins, Chair of Senate Committee on Government Affairs (13 February 2004).

9/11 Commission, *The 9/11 Commission Report: Final Report of the National Commission on Terrorist Attacks Upon the United States* (New York: W.W. Norton, 2004a).

——, *9/11 and Terrorist Travel: Staff Report of the National Commission on Terrorist Attacks Upon the United States* (2004b). Accessed 19 August 2004 at <http://www.9-11commission.gov/staff_statements/index.htm>.

Commission on Human Security, *Human Security Now* (New York: 2003).

Commonwealth Secretariat, *Commonwealth Code of Practice for the International Recruitment of Health Workers and Companion Document*, Commonwealth Secretariat (London: 2003).

CONAPO, Mexican National Population Council, cited in 'Political Support for Immigration Pact May Have Evaporated, but in Mexico, Migration Pressures are on the Rise', Americas Program Feature (Silver City, NM: Interhemispheric Resource Center, February 2001).

Condé, J., P. Diagne and N.G. Ouaidou, *South-North International Migrations, A Case Study: Malian, Mauritanian and Senegalese Migrants from Senegal River Valley to France*, Development Centre of the OECD (1986).

Connell, J. and R. Brown, 'Migration and Remittances in the South Pacific: Towards New Perspectives', *Asian and Pacific Migration Journal*, 4/1 (1995): 1–33.

Cooper, R.A., 'Physician Migration: A Challenge for America, a Challenge for the World', *Journal of Continuing Education in the Health Professions*, 0894–1912, 25/1 (1 January 2005).

Cornelius, W.A., 'Evaluating Enhanced US Border Enforcement', *Migration Information Source* (2004).

——, 'Death at the Border: Efficacy and Unintended Consequences of US Immigration Policy'. UCSD Working Paper 27, University of California (San Diego, 2001).

Accessed 29 April 2004 at <http://www.ccis-ucsd.org/PUBLICATIONS/wrkg27. pdf>.

——, *Labor Migration to the United States: Development, Outcomes and Alternatives in Mexican Sending Communities*, Report of the Commission for the Study of International Migration and Cooperative Economic Development (Washington, DC, 1990).

Cornelius, W.A., P.L. Martin, and J.F. Hollifield, *Controlling Immigration: A Global Perspective* (Stanford: Stanford University Press, 1994).

Corte dei Conti, *Programma di controllo 2003. Gestione delle risorse previste in connessione al fenomeno dell'immigrazione* (Rome: 2004).

Coslovi, L. and F. Piperno, *Espulsione, e poi? Alcune riflessioni sui percorsi di rimpatrio forzato in Marocco e Albania, a partire da una prima ricognizione empirica*, Cespi Working Paper (2004).

Council on Graduate Medical Education, 'Sixteenth Report: Physician Workforce Policy Guidelines for the United States, 2000–2020' (Rockville, MD: Council on Graduate Medical Education, 2005).

Cowhey, P.F., 'The International Telecommunications Regime: The Political Roots of Regimes for High Technology', *International Organization*, 44/2 (1990): 169–99.

Crisp, J., 'Poverty, Migration and Asylum', statement to the *Wider Conference on Poverty, International Migration and Asylum* (Helsinki: 27–28 September 2002).

——, *Policy Challenges of the New Diasporas: Migrant Networks and Their Impact on Asylum Flows and Regimes*, Working Paper No. 7, UNHCR (Geneva, 1999).

Crush, J., 'Introduction: Immigration, Human Rights and the Constitution', in J. Crush (ed.), *Beyond Control: Immigration and Human Rights in a Democratic South Africa* (Cape Town: IDASA and Queens University Canada, 1998).

Dairiam, S., 'Effective Legal Strategies to Combat Trafficking in Women and Children', paper prepared for the *Seminar on Promoting Gender Equality to Combat Trafficking in Women and Children* (Bangkok: 7–9 October 2002).

Davis, K., 'The Migrations of Human Populations', *Scientific American*, 231/3 (1974): 93–9.

Davis, K., 'The Amazing Decline of Mortality in Underdeveloped Areas', *The American Economic Review*, 46/2 (1956): 305–18.

Davy, U., *Die Integration von Einwanderern: Rechtliche Regelungen im europäischen Vergleich* (Frankfurt: Campus, 2001).

Department for International Development (DfID), *Report and Conclusions from the International Conference on Migrant Remittances* (London, 9–10 October 2003).

Department of Homeland Security (DHS), *Homeland Security Budget in Brief: Fiscal Year 2005* (2004). Accessed 7 March at <http://www.dhs.gov/dhspublic/ display?content=3131>.

Department of Labour Employment, 'Ten Countries Agree to Develop Common Stance on Issues Affecting Migrant Workers', *DOLE News* (Manila, 20 April 2003). Accessed at: <http://www.dole.gov.ph/news/pressreleases2003/April/125.htm>.

Desai, M., D. Kapur and J. McHale, *Sharing the Spoils: Taxing International Human Capital Flows*, Paper No. 02–06, Weatherhead Center for International Affairs, Harvard University (Cambridge, MA, 2002).

Desai, M., D. Kapur and J. McHale, *The Fiscal Impact of the Brain Drain: Indian Emigration to the US*, Weekly Political Economy Discussion Paper, Harvard University (Cambridge, MA, 2001).

Despradel, C., 'Importancia de las Remesas Para La Economia Dominicana', paper prepared for the *Seminar on La Comunidad Domincana en los Estados Unidos y Su Impacto en la Economia Nacional Santo Domingo* (August, 1997).

Deutsch, K.W., S.A. Burrell, R.A. Kann, M. Lee Jr, M. Lichterman, R.E. Lindgren, F.L. Loewenheim and R.W. van Wagenen, *Political Community in the North Atlantic Area* (Princeton: Princeton University Press, 1957).

DeVoretz, D.J. and S. Pivnenko, 'The Economics of Canadian Citizenship', paper presented at the IZA seminar, 17 February (Bonn, 2004).

Dike, A.A., 'Urban Migrants and Rural Development', *African Studies Review*, 25/4 (1982): 85–94.

Dovlo, D., 'The Brain Drain and Retention of Health Professionals in Africa', case study prepared for *Improving Tertiary Education in Sub-Saharan Africa: Things that Work!* (Accra, Ghana, 2003a).

——, paper prepared for the *Consultative Workshop on HRH in East, Central and Southern Africa* (Arusha: Tanzania, 2003b).

——, *Issues Affecting the Mobility and Retention of Health Workers/Professionals in Commonwealth African States*, Consultancy Report, Commonwealth Secretariat (London: 1999).

Dovlo, D. and F. Nyonator, 'Migration by Graduates of the University of Ghana Medical School: A Preliminary Rapid Appraisal', *Human Resources for Health and Development Journal*, 3/1 (1999): 40–51.

Dugger, C.W., 'An Exodus of African Nurses Put Infants and the Ill in Peril', *New York Times* (12 July 2004): 1, 8–9.

Dummett, A., 'The Transnational Migration of People Seen from Within a Natural Law Tradition', in B. Barry and R. Goodin (eds), *Free Movement* (London: Harvester, 1992).

Dumont, J.C. and J.B. Meyer, 'The International Mobility of Health Professionals: An Evaluation and Analysis Based on the Case of South Africa', in *Trends in International Migration: 2003 SOPEMI Edition*, OECD (Paris, 2004).

Durand, J., *From Traitors to Heroes: 100 Years of Mexican Migration Policies* (University of Guadalajara, March 2004).

——, E.A. Parrado and D.S. Massey, 'Migradollars and Development: A Reconsideration of the Mexican Case', *International Migration Review*, 30/2 (1996): 423–44.

Econtech, *The Economic Impacts of the Current Migration and Humanitarian Programs* (Canberra, 2004).

eGovernment News, 'Future French Electronic ID Card to Include Two Biometrics', *eGovernment News* (3 September 2004).

Ehrlich, P.R., *The Population Bomb* (New York: Ballantine Books, 1968).

Ehrlich, P.R. and A.H. Ehrlich, *Population, Resources, Environment: Issues in Human Ecology* (San Francisco: W.H. Freeman, 1970).

Ekberg, J. (ed.), *Invandrarna, Arbetsmarknaden och Välfärdsstaten*, SOU 2004:21 (Stockholm: Fritzes, 2004).

Elmdahl, J., 'Arbetskraftsbrist Under Högkonjunktur', *Landsorganisationens (LO) skriftserie*, 65 (1951): 35–42.

Escobar, C., 'Dual Citizenship and Political Participation: Migrants in the Interplay of United States and Columbian Politics', *Latino Studies*, 2/1 (2004): 70–90.

European Commission, *First Annual Report on Migration and Integration*, Communication from the Commission, COM (2004) 508 Final (Brussels, 16 July, 2004).

——, *Communication on Immigration, Integration and Employment*, COM (2003) 336 final (Brussels: EC, 3 June 2003).

——, *Establishing a European Agency for the Management of the Operational Co-Operation at External Borders*, RAPID Press Release IP: 03/1519 (Brussels, 11 November, 2003a).

——, *Communication on the Common Asylum Policy and the Agenda for Protection*, COM 152, Final (Brussels, 2003b).

——, *Communication on Integrating Migration Issues in the European Union's Relations with Third Countries*, COM 703, Final (Brussels, 2002).

——, *Communication on A Common Policy on Illegal Immigration*, COM (2001) 672 Final (Brussels, 15 November 2001).

European Commission/Directorate General Employment and Social Affairs, *Employment in Europe 2003 – Recent Trends and Prospects* (Luxembourg: EC, 2003).

European Council, *Declaration on Combating Terrorism* (Brussels, 2004).

——, *Conclusions and Plan of Action of the Extraordinary European Council Meeting on 21 September 2001* (2001).

European Insight, 'EU Makes Protection of Refugees Less Secure', *European Insight, European Information Service* (1 December 1995).

European Report, 'Commission wants New Schengen Data base to Store Biometrics', *European Report*, No. 2828 (13 December 2003).

Faeamani, S., 'The Impact of Remittances on Rural Development in Tongan Villages', *Asian and Pacific Migration Journal*, 4 (1995): 139–55.

Faini, R., J. de Melo and K. Zimmermann (eds), *Migration: The Controversies and the Evidence* (London: Centre for Economic Policy Research and Cambridge University Press, 1999).

Fassmann, H. and R. Münz, 'EU Enlargement and East-West Migration in Europe', in F. Laczko, I. Stacher and A. Klekowski von Koppenfels (eds), *New Challenges for Migration Policy in Central and Eastern Europe* (Geneva: International Organization for Migration, 2002).

—— (eds), *Ost-West Wanderung in Europa* (Vienna-Cologne-Weimar: Boehlau, 2000).

Feustel, I. (n.d.), *The Future of ACP-EU Trade Relations: Economic Partnership Agreements.* Accessed 24 May 2004 at <http://www.dse.de/ef/wto02/feustel. htm>.

Findlayson, J.A. and M.W. Zacher, *Managing International Markets: Developing Countries and the Commodity Trade Regime* (New York: Columbia University Press, 1988).

Fink-Nielsen M., P. Hansen and N. Kleist, 'Repatriering: Afsluttet eller fortsat mobilitet', *Den Ny Verden*, 32/3 (2002): 52–65.

Flam, H. and M.J. Flander (eds), *Heckscher-Ohlin Trade Theory* (Cambridge, MA: MIT Press, 1991).

Flynn, S.E., *America the Vulnerable: How our Government is Failing to Protect US from Terrorism* (New York: HarperCollins, 2004a).

——, *Testimony on the 9/11 Commission Report and Maritime Transportation Security*, Coast Guard and Maritime Transportation Subcommittee of the House Transportation and Infrastructure Committee (25 August 2004b).

FOCAL, *Final Report: Hemispheric Integration and Transnationalism in the Americas* (Guatemala City, 2004).

Foner, N., *From Ellis Island to JFK: New York's Two Great Waves of Immigration* (New Haven: Yale University Press, 2000).

Franck, T., *The Empowered Self: Law and Society in the Age of Individualism* (Oxford: Oxford University Press, 1999).

Franda, M., *Governing the Internet: The Emergence of an International Regime (Ipolitics)* (Boulder: Lynne Rienner Publishers, 2001).

Frontera NorteSur, 'Mexico's Migrant Rescue Groups', 20 April 2004. Available at <http://frontera.nmsu.edu/Matamorosnews.html>.

Frushone, J., *Welcome Home to Nothing: Refugees Repatriate to a Forgotten Somaliland*, Committee for Refugees (USCR) (Washington, DC, 2001).

FWLD (n.d.), *Prevalence of the Problem*, Forum for Women, Law and Development, Kathmandu.

Galaleldin, M., *Migration of Sudanese Abroad* (Khartoum: Council on Economic and Social Research, 1979).

Gallino, L., 'L'ipocrisia delle porte aperte', *La Stampa* (17 December 1989).

Garson, J., 'Emigration and Financial Flows: Issues for Maghrebian Countries', paper prepared for the *Conference on Migration and International Cooperation*, OECD (Paris: 1993).

GCIM, *Migration in an Interconnected World: New Directions for Action*, Report of the Global Commission on International Migration (Geneva: October 2005). Available at < http://www.gcim.org>.

Geddes, A., *The Politics of Migration and Immigration in Europe* (London: Sage Publications, 2003).

Georges, E., *The Making of a Transnational Community: Migration, Development, and Cultural Change in the Dominican Republic* (New York: Columbia University Press, 1990).

Gevrey, M., *Les défis de l'immigration future*, Commission Spéciale du Plan, 2003–22 (2003).

Ghosh, B (ed.), *Return Migration: Journey of Hope or Despair?* (Geneva: International Organization for Migration and the United Nations, 2000a).

— (ed.), *Managing Migration: Time for a New International Regime* (Oxford: Oxford University Press, 2000b).

Glick Schiller, N., 'Transnational Theory and Beyond', in D. Nugent and J. Vincent (eds), *A Companion to the Anthropology of Politics* (Malden: Blackwell, 2004).

—, 'The Centrality of Ethnography in the Study of Transnational Migration: Seeing the Wetland Instead of the Swamp', in N. Foner (ed.), *American Arrivals* (Santa Fe: School of American Research, 2003).

—, 'Transmigrants and Nation-States: Something Old and Something New in the US Immigrant Experience', in C. Hirshman, P. Kasinitz and J. DeWind (eds), *The Handbook of International Migration* (New York: The Russell Sage Foundation, 1999).

Goldring, L., 'Gender Status and the State in Transnational Spaces', in P. Hondagneu-Sotelo (ed.), *Gender and US Immigration* (Berkeley: University of California Press, 2003).

—, 'The Mexican State and Transmigrant Organizations: Negotiating the Boundaries of Membership and Participation', *Latin American Research Review*, 37/3 (2002): 55–99.

—, 'Disaggregating Transnational Social Spaces: Gender, Place and Citizenship in Mexico-US Transnational Spaces', in L. Pries (ed.), *New Transnational Social Spaces: International Migration and Transnational Companies in the Early Twenty-First Century* (London: Routledge, 2001).

Goodin, R., 'What is So Special About Our Fellow Countrymen?' *Ethics* (July, 1988).

Government of Costa Rica, 'Convergence of Regional Processes in the Americas in Addressing Migration Issues', report to the November 2001 meeting of the Regional Consultation Group on Migration, San José, Costa Rica (2001).

Groenendijk, K., E. Guild and R. Barzilay, *The Legal Status of Third Country Nationals Who Are Long-Term Residents in a Member State of the European Union*, study on behalf of the European Commission (Nijmegen: Centre for Migration Law, 2000).

Grover, A., 'Trafficking in Women and Children: Can SAARC Check the Menace?', *Asian Affairs* (2002). Available at: <www.asianaffairs.com.march2002/society_trafficking.html>.

Guarnizo, L.E., 'The Economics of Transnational Living', *International Migration Review*, 37/3 (2003): 666–700.

Guarnizo, L.E., A. Portes and W. Haller, 'Assimilation and Transnationalism: Determinants of Transnational Political Action among Contemporary Migrants', *American Journal of Sociology*, 108/6 (2003): 1211–48.

Gundel, J., 'The Migration-Development Nexus: Somalia Case Study', in N. Van Hear and N.N. Sørensen (eds), *The Migration-Development Nexus* (Geneva: UN and IOM, 2003).

Haas, P.M., 'Do Regimes Matter? Epistemic Communication and Mediterranean Pollution Control', *International Organization*, 43/3 (1989): 377–404.

Hagopian, A., M.J. Thompson, M. Fordyce, K.E. Johnson and L.G. Hart, 'The Migration of Physicians from Sub-Saharan Africa to the United States of America: Measure of the African Brain Drain', *Human Resources for Health*, 2/17 (2004).

Hammar, T., 'Legal Time of Residence and the Status of Immigrants', in R. Bauböck (ed.), *From Aliens to Citizens: Redefining the Status of Immigrants in Europe* (Aldershot: Avebury, 1994).

——, *Democracy and the Nation State: Aliens, Denizens and Citizens in a World of International Migration* (Aldershot: Avebury, 1990).

Hammar, T. and G. Brochmann (eds), *Mechanisms of Immigration Control: A Comparative Analysis of European Regulation Policies* (Oxford: Berg Publishers, 1999).

Hammar, T., G. Brochmann, K. Tamas and T. Faist (eds), *International Migration, Immobility and Development: Multidisciplinary Perspectives* (Oxford: Berg Publishers, 1997).

Hampton, J., 'Immigration, Identity and Justice', in W.F. Schwartz (ed.), *Justice in Immigration* (Cambridge: Cambridge University Press, 1995).

Hancock, G., *Lords of Poverty: The Power, Prestige, and Corruption of the International Aid Business* (New York: Atlantic Monthly Press, 1989).

Hansen, M.H., *The Athenian Democracy in the Age of Demosthenes: Structure, Principles and Ideology* (Oxford: Blackwell, 1991).

Hansen, P., *Migrant Transfers as a Development Tool: The Case of Somaliland* (Danish Institute for International Studies, 2004).

——, 'Revolving Returnees: Return Migration in Somaliland', paper prepared for the *Workshop on Determinants of Transnational Engagement*, organized by the Diaspora Programme, DIIS and FLACSO (Santo Domingo: November, 2003).

Hansen, R., and P. Weil (eds), *Towards a European Nationality: Citizenship, Immigration and Nationality Law in the EU* (Houndmills: Palgrave, 2001).

Harris, N., *The New Untouchables: Immigration and the New World Worker* (London: I.B. Tauris, 1995).

Hasan, M.N., 'Trafficking in Women and Children', *Media Monitors Network* (11 July 2001).

Hatton, T., 'Seeking Asylum in Europe', *Economic Policy* (April) (2004): 5–62.

Hatton, T. and J. Williamson, 'Demographic and Economic Pressure on Emigration Out of Africa', 105/3 (2003): 465–86.

——, *What Fundamentals Drive World Migration?*, Working Paper 9159, National Bureau of Economic Research (Cambridge, MA: NBER, 2002).

——, 'What Drove the Mass Migrations from Europe in the Late-19th-Century', *Population and Development Review*, 20/3 (1994): 533–59.

Hayek, F.A. von, *Law, Legislation and Liberty*, vol. 2: *The Mirage of Social Justice* (London: Routledge and Kegan Paul, [1976] 1982).

Herbert, P., *NEPAD has Changed World Views but More Needs to be Done*, North-South Institute (2004). Accessed 21 May at <http://www.nsi-ins.ca/ensi/news-/oped51.htm>.

Hollifield, J.F., 'Migration and International Relations: Cooperation and Control in the European Community', *International Migration Review*, 26/2 (1992): 568–95.

Holmes, S. and C. Sunstein, *The Cost of Rights: Why Liberty Depends on Taxes* (New York: Norton, 1999).

Holzmann, R., *Migration and the Welfare State: A Social Protection Perspective from Three Angles* (Munich: CESifo, forthcoming).

——, *Toward a Reformed and Coordinated Pension System in Europe: Rationale and Potential Structure*, Social Protection Discussion Paper 0407 (Washington, DC: World Bank, 2004).

Holzmann, R. and R. Münz, *Challenges and Opportunities of International Migration for the EU, Its Member States, Neighboring Countries and Regions: A Policy Note* (Stockholm: Institute for Futures Studies, 2004).

Home Office, *Home Office Departmental Report 2003* (2003). Available at <http://www.homeoffice.gov.uk/docs2/annrep2003.html>.

Huntington, S., *Who are We? The Challenges to America's National Identity* (New York: Simon and Schuster, 2004).

Hyun, O.-S. 'The Impact of Overseas Migration on National Development: The Case of the Republic of Korea', in R. Amjad (ed.), *To the Gulf and Back: Studies on the Economic Impact of Asian Labour Migration* (New Delhi: ILO-ARTEP, 1989).

ICAO, *Biometric Identification to Provide Enhanced Security and Speedier Border Clearance for the Travelling Public*, International Civil Aviation Organization, PIO/2003 (2003). Accessed 20 November at <http://www.icao.int/icao/en/nr/2003/pio200309.htm>.

ILO, *Terms of Employment and Working Conditions in Health Sector Reforms* (Geneva: ILO, 1999).

IMF, *World Economic Outlook* (Washington, DC, 2005).

INS, 'Is Gatekeeper Working?', *Migration News*, 7 (9 September 2000). Accessed 29 April 2004 at http://migration.ucdavis.edu/mn/more.php?id=2183_0_2_0.

Institute of Population Studies and Institute of Asian Studies, *Human Resource Development and Migration Pattern Among ASEAN Member Countries*, Working Paper for Ad-hoc Committee on Human Resource Development, ASEAN Interparliamentary Organization (20–23 August 1997).

Integrated Regional Information Networks, *A Gap in their Hearts: The Experience of Separated Somali Children* (Nairobi: UN Office for the Coordination of Humanitarian Affairs, 2003).

International Labour Organization (1997–2002), *Economically Active Population, 1950–2010*, diskette database (Geneva: ILO).

IOM, *World Migration 2005* (Geneva: IOM, 2005).

——, *World Migration 2003: Managing Migration – Challenges and Responses for People on the Move*, IOM, World Migration Report Series, Vol. 2 (Geneva, 2003a).

——, 'Annex I', *Eighty-Sixth Session: IOM's Role in Enhancing Regional Dialogues on Migration,* MC/INF/266 (10 November 2003b).

——, *The Role of Regional Consultative Processes in Managing International Migration*, IOM Migration Research Series, No. 3 (Geneva, 2001).

——, *Seminar on International Responses to Trafficking in Migrants and the Safeguarding of Migrant Rights* (Geneva: IOM, 26–28 October 1994).

ISMU, *Rapporto sulle migrazioni* (Milan: Franco Angeli, 1995–2004).

Itzigsohn, J., 'Immigration and the Boundaries of Citizenship: The Institutions of Immigrants' Political Transnationalism', *International Migration Review*, 34/4 (2000): 1126–55.

Jervis, R., 'Security Regimes', in S.D. Krasner (ed.), *International Regimes* (Ithaca, NY: Cornell University Press, 1983).

Joint Learning Initiative Report, *Human Resources for Health: Crisis and Sustainability Strategies* (Cambridge, MA: Harvard University Press, 2004).

Jones-Correa, M., 'Under Two Flags: Dual Nationality in Latin America and Its Consequences for the United States', *International Migration Review*, 35/4 (2001): 997–1029.

Jordan, B. and F. Düvell, *Migration: The Boundaries of Equality and Justice* (London: Polity Press, 2003).

Jordão, M., 'The European Migration and Refugee Policy in the Context of Wider Global Refugee Movements', paper prepared for the *Cicero Foundation Great Debate Seminar on European Refugee Policy: New Developments* (Paris: February 2001).

Jurado, G., *Labor Mobility Issues in the Asia Pacific Region*, PASCN Discussion Paper No. 99–01, Philippine APEC Study Network Centre (1997).

Kapp, C., 'HIV Overshadows South African Health Advances', *The Lancet*, 363/9416 (2004): 1202–3.

Kapur, D., 'Remittances: The New Development Mantra?', paper prepared for *G24 Technical Group Meeting* (Geneva: September 2003).

Keohane, R.O., *After Hegemony: Cooperation and Discord in the World Political Economy* (Princeton, NJ: Princeton University Press, 1984).

Khagram, S. and P. Levitt, *Constructing Transnational Studies*, Working Paper No. 24 (Cambridge, MA: Hauser Center for Non-Profit Organizations at Harvard University, 2004).

Kindleberger, C., *World in Depression, 1929–1939* (Berkeley: University of California Press, 1973).

King, A., *Hargeisa Urban Household Assessment*, FEWS Net. FSAU, Save the Children UK, Municipality of Hargeisa, Candlelight (2003). Available at <http://www.releifweb.int/library7documents/2003/few-som-16may.pdf.>.

Koettl, Johannes (2005), *Demographic and Labor Force Projections from 2005 to 2050: New Data from the 2004 Revision – Medium and Zero-Migration Variant*, World Bank HDNSP discussion paper (Washington, DC: World Bank).

Konvitz, M.R., *Civil Rights in Immigration* (Ithaca, NY: Cornell University Press, 1953).

Koslowski, R., 'International Cooperation to Create Smart Borders', paper prepared for the conference on *North American Integration: Migration, Trade, and Security*, Institute for Research on Public Policy (Ottawa: 1–2 April 2004).

——, 'Economic Globalization, Human Smuggling and Global Governance', in D. Kyle and R. Koslowski (eds), *Global Human Smuggling in Comparative Perspective* (Baltimore: Johns Hopkins University Press, 2001).

——, *Migrants and Citizens: Demographic Change in the European States System* (Ithaca, NY: Cornell University Press, 2000).

Kotilainen, M. and V. Kaitila, *Economic Globalisation in Developing Countries: The Case of Nepal and Tanzania* (Finland: The Reseach Insitute of the Finnish Economy/ETLA, 2002).

Krasner, S.D., *International Regimes* (Ithaca, NY: Cornell University Press, 1983a).

——, 'Structural Causes and Regime Consequences: Regimes as Intervening Variables', in S.D. Krasner (ed.) *International Regimes* (Ithaca, NY: Cornell University Press, 1983b).

Krieger, H., *Migration Trends in an Enlarged Europe* (Dublin: European Foundation for the Improvement of Living and Working Conditions, 2004).

Krueger, A. and M. Lindahl, 'Education for Growth: Why and for Whom?', NBER Working Paper 7591 (2000).

Kurowski, C., 'Global Opportunities and Responsibilities', in *Health and Human Resources Report*, draft (Cambridge, MA: Joint Learning Initiative and Global Equity Initiative, 2004).

Lahiri, T., 'A Hometown Away from Home: Mexican Migrants in New York United to Give Back', *New York Times* (30 June 2004).

Landolt, P., 'Salvadoran Economic Transnationalism: Embedded Strategies for Household Maintenance, Immigrant Incorporation, and Entrepreneurial Expansion', *Global Networks*, 1/3 (2001): 217–42.

Latour, B. (trans. C. Porter), *We Have Never Been Modern* (London: Harvester Wheatsheaf, 1993).

Ledeneva, A., *Unwritten Rules: How Russia Really Works*, Essay Series (London: Centre for European Reform, 2001).

Lederman, D., W.F. Maloney and L. Servén, *Lessons from NAFTA for Latin America and the Caribbean Countries: A Summary of Research Findings* (Washington, DC: World Bank, December 2003).

Leenders, M., 'From Inclusion to Exclusion: Refugees and Immigrants in Italy Between 1861 and 1943', *Immigrants and Minorities*, 14/2 (1995): 115–38.

Lewis, I.M., *A Pastoral Democracy: A Study of Pastoralism and Politics Among the Northern Somali of the Horn of Africa* (London: Oxford University Press for the International African Institute, 1961).

Levitt, P., *The Transnational Villagers* (Berkeley: University of California Press, 2001a).

——, 'Transnational Migration: Taking Stock and Future Directions', *Global Networks*, 1/3 (2001): 195–216.

Levitt, P. and R. de la Dehesa, 'Transnational Migration and a Redefinition of the State: Variations and Explanations', *Ethnic and Racial Studies*, 26(4) (2003): 587–611.

Levitt, P. and N. Glick Schiller, 'Transnational Perspectives on Migration: Conceptualizing Simultaneity', *International Migration Review*, 38/145, Fall (2004): 595–629.

Lindh, T. and B. Malmberg, *Forecasting Global Growth by Age Structure Projections,* Arbetsrapport (Stockholm: Institute for Futures Studies, 2004).

LO, *Comment on Government Report SOU 1967:18*, Ministry of the Interior, National Archives (11 October 1967).

——, *Comment on Government Report SOU 1951:42*, Ministry of Justice, National Archives (28 January 1952).

Loewenson, R. and C. Thompson (eds), *Health Personnel in Southern Africa: Confronting Maldistribution and the Brain Drain*, Equinet Discussion Paper No. 3 (Harare, 2003).

Lowell B.L. and A. Findlay, *Migration of Highly Skilled Persons from Developing Countries: Impact and Policy Responses*, International Migration Papers No. 44, ILO (Geneva, 2001).

Lozano-Ascencio, F., *Las Remesas de los Migrantes Mexicanos en Estados Unidos: Estimaciones Para 1995*, background paper for Binational Study on Migration (1996).

Lucas, R.E.B., *Diaspora and Development: Highly Skilled Migrants from East Asia*, Report prepared for the World Bank (Washington, DC, 2001).

Lundh, C., 'Invandrarna i den svenska modellen: hot eller reserv?', *Arbetarhistoria*, 18/2 (1994): 23–36.

Lundh, C. and R. Ohlsson, *Från arbetskraftsimport till flyktinginvandring* (Stockholm: SNS, 1999).

Lundqvist, T., 'Arbetskraftsbristens problem: historiska lärdomar?' in C. Florin and T. Lundqvist (eds), *Historia: en väg till framtiden?: perspektiv på det förflutnas roll i framtidsstudier* (Stockholm: Institute for Futures Studies, 2003).

——, 'Arbetskraftsinvandringen och facket: debatt och historia i framtidsperspektiv', in B. Malmberg and L. Sommestad (eds), *Befolkning och välfärd: perspektiv på framtidens välfärdspolitik* (Stockholm: Institute for Futures Studies, 2002).

——, *Arbetsgivarna efter 1945: arbetskraftsbrist och kartellstrategi: Verkstadsföreningen, samt Bryggeriarbetsgivareförbundet och SAF*, Arbetslivsrapport 1998:38, ALI, Institute for Working Life (1998).

Magni, R., *Gli immigrati in Italia*, Edizioni del lavoro (Rome, 1995).

Mahmud, W., 'The Impact of Overseas Labour Migration on the Bangladesh Economy', in R. Amjad (ed.), *To the Gulf and Back: Studies on the Economic Impact of Asian Labour Migration* (New Delhi: ILO-ARTEP, 1989).

Mahroum, S., C. Eldridge and A.S. Daar, *Diaspora Options: How Developing Countries Could Benefit from their Emigrant Populations*, draft paper prepared for two working groups of the Joint Learning Initiative on Human Resources for Health (Cambridge, MA, 2004).

Malmberg, G., 'Time and Space in International Migration', in T. Hammar, G. Brochmann, K. Tamas and T. Faist (eds), *International Migration, Immobility and Development: Multidisciplinary Perspectives* (Oxford: Berg Publishers, 1997).

Malmberg, B. and L. Sommestad, *Heavy Trends in Global Developments: Idea Platform for MISTRA's Future Strategy*, Institute for Futures Studies Working Paper 28 (Stockholm, 2000a).

——, 'The Hidden Pulse of History: Population and Economic Change in Sweden, 1820–2000', *Scandinavian Journal of History*, 25/1–2 (2000b): 131–46.

Marizco, M. and T. Steller, 'Busline Admits It Smuggled Entrants', *The Arizona Daily Star*, April (2004).

Marmora, L., *International Migration Policies and Programmes* (Geneva: UN and IOM, 1999).

Marshal, R., *Final Report on the Post Civil War Somali Business Class* (Paris: European Commission, Somalia Unit, 1996).

Marshall, T.H., 'Citizenship and Social Class', in T.H. Marshall, *Class, Citizenship, and Social Development* (New York: Anchor Books, 1965).

Martin, D.A. and K. Hailbronner (eds), *Rights and Duties of Dual Nationals: Evolution and Prospects* (The Hague: Kluwer Law International, 2003).

Martin, P., *Migration and Development: Towards Sustainable Solutions*, Discussion Paper No. 153, International Institute for Labour Studies (Geneva, 2004).

——, 'Managing Migration: The Economic Challenges', paper prepared for the 10th Anniversary of the International Center for Migration Policy Development (Vienna, 2003).

Martin, P. and T. Straubhaar, 'Best Practices to Reduce Migration Pressures', *International Migration*, 40/3 (2002): 71–85.

Martin, S., 'Forced Migration and the Evolving Humanitarian Regime', Working Paper 20, *Journal of Humanitarian Assistance* (2001a). Available at <http://jha.ac/articles/u020.htm>.

——, 'Remittance Flows and Impact', paper prepared for the *Regional Conference on Remittances as a Development Tool*, organized by the Multilateral Investment Fund and the Inter-American Development Bank (Washington, DC, 2001b).

Martin, S. and P. Weil, 'Fostering Cooperation between Source and Destination Countries', *Migration Information Source* (Washington, DC: Migration Policy Institute, 2002).

Martineau, T., K. Decker and P. Bundred, 'Briefing Note on International Migration of Health Professionals: Levelling the Playing Field for Developing Country Health Systems (Liverpool: Liverpool School of Tropical Medicine, 2002).

Mason, A. (ed.), *Population Change and Economic Development in East Asia: Challenges Met, Opportunities Seized* (Stanford: Stanford University Press, 2001).

Massey, D., J. Durand and N.J. Malone, *Beyond Smoke and Mirrors: Mexican Immigration in an Era of Economic Integration* (New York: Russell Sage Foundation, 2002).

Massey, D., R. Alarcón, J. Durand and H. González, *Return to Aztlán: The Social Process of International Migration from Western Mexico* (Berkeley: University of California Press, 1990).

Masson, P. and Balarello, J., *Commission d'enquête sur les régularisations d'étrangers en situation irrégulière*, RAPPORT 470 (97–98), Tome I – COMMISSION D'ENQUETE: <http://www.senat.fr/rap/l97-4701/l97-4701.html>.

McGown, R.B., *Muslims in the Diaspora: The Somali Communities of London and Toronto* (Toronto: University of Toronto Press, 1999).

McNeill, W.H., *Polyethnic and National Unity in World History* (Toronto: Toronto University Press, 1986).

Médecins Sans Frontières, Missione Italia, *Rapporto sui Centri di permanenza temporanea e assistenza* (January 2004).

Meeus, W., *'Pull' Factors in International Migration of Health Professionals: An Analysis of Developed Countries' Policies Influencing Migration of Health Professionals*, University of Western Cape School of Public Health, Masters Thesis (Cape Town, 2003).

Meyers, D.W., *Migrant Remittances to Latin America: Reviewing the Literature*, Working Paper, The Inter-American Dialogue and The Tomas Rivera Policy Institute (1998).

Migration News, 'Latin America: Remittances', University of California, Davis, 10/2 (2003). Available at: <http://migration.ucdavis.edu/mn/more_entireissue.php?idate=2003_04andnumber=2.>.

Milazi, D., 'Immobility: Low Inter-Continental Emigration from Sub-Saharan Africa: A Sociological Investigation', in A. Adepoju and T. Hammar (eds), *International Migration in and from Africa* (Dakar: PHRDA and CEIFO, 1996).

Mill, J.S., *Utilitarianism; On Liberty; Considerations on Representative Government; Remarks on Bentham's Philosophy*, ed. G. Williams (London: [1861], 1993).

Miller, D., 'Immigration: the Case for Limits', in C. Wellman (ed.), *Contemporary Debates in Applied Ethics* (Oxford: Blackwell, 2004).

——, *Citizenship and National Identity* (Cambridge, MA: Polity Press, 2000).

——, *On Nationality* (Oxford: Clarendon Press, 1995).

Miller, M.J. 'International Migration in Post-Cold War International Relations', in B. Ghosh (ed.), *Managing Migration: Time for a New International Regime* (Oxford: Oxford University Press, 2000).

Ministerio de Relaciones Exteriores de El Salvador (MREES), 'Unidos por la Solidaridad, algo más que un nombre, algo más que un eslógan', Comunidad En Accion (28 February–3 March 2003). Avaliable at <http://www.comunidades.gob.sv/comunidades/comunidades.nsf/pages/CenANoti4-2802-060303>.

Ministry of Industry, Employment and Communication, *Kommittédirektiv: Översyn av regelverket för arbetskraftsinvandring*, Dir 2004:21 (Stockholm, 2004).

Ministry of Interior, Annual Reports, *Documento di programmazione triennale dell'immigrazione* (Rome, 1998–2000 and 2001–03).

Montclos, M.A. and P.M. Kagwanja, 'Refugee Camps or Cities? The Socio-economic Dynamics of the Dadaab and Kakuma Camps in Northern Kenya', *Journal of Refugee Studies*, 13/2 (2000): 205–22.

Monzini, P., P. Pastore and G. Sciortino, *L'Italia promessa, geopolitica e dinamiche organizzative del traffico di migranti verso l'Italia*, Cespi Working Papers No. 9 (2004).

Morawska, E., 'Immigrant Transnationalism and Assimilation: A Variety of Combinations and the Analytic Strategy it Suggests', in C. Joppke and E. Morawska (eds), *Toward Assimilation and Citizenship: Immigrants in Liberal Nation-States* (Hampshire, UK: Palgrave Macmillan, 2003).

Morgenthau, H., *Politics Among Nations*, 5th edn (New York: Knopf, 1973).

Morisset, J., *Foreign Direct Investment in Africa: Policies Also Matter*, Policy Research Working Paper 2481, World Bank (2000).

Moretti, E., 'Estimating the Social Return to Higher Education: Evidence from Longitudinal and Repeated Cross-sectional Data', *Journal of Econometrics*, 121 (2004): 175–212.

Münz, R., 'The Demography of International Migration: Facts, Assumptions, Gaps', in M. Jandl, and I. Stacher (eds), *Towards a Multilateral Migration Regime* (Vienna: ICMPD, 2004).

Münz, R. and H. Fassmann, 'Migrants in Europe and their Economic Position: Evidence from the European Labour Force Survey and from Other Sources', paper prepared for the European Commission, DG Employment and Social Affairs (Brussels: European Commission; Hamburg: HWWA, 2004).

Nascimbene, B. (ed.), *Nationality Laws in the European Union – Le Droit de la Nationalité dans L'Union Européenne* (London: Giuffrè Editore, 1996).

Naim, M., 'The New Diaspora: New Links between Émigrés and their Home Countries Can Become a Powerful Force for Economic Development', *Foreign Policy*, 131 (2002): 96–9.

Nair, K. and F. Abdullah, *Somalia 1997–98: A Status Report* (Nairobi, 1998).

Nair, P.R.G., 'Incidence, Impact and Implications of Migration to the Middle East from Kerala (India)', in R. Amjad (ed.), *To the Gulf and Back: Studies on the Economic Impact of Asian Labour Migration* (New Delhi: ILO-ARTEP, 1989).

Narasimhan, V. et al, 'Responding to the Global Human Resources Crisis', *The Lancet*, 363/9419 (2004): 1469–72.

Nassar, H. and A. Ghoneim, *Trade and Migration, Are They Complements or Substitutes: A Review of MENA Countries*, ERF Working Paper Series, No. 0207 (Cairo: Economic Research Forum, 1998).

Nayyar, D., 'International Labour Migration from India: A Macro-economic Analysis', in R. Amjad (ed.), *To the Gulf and Back: Studies on the Economic Impact of Asian Labour Migration* (New Delhi: ILO-ARTEP, 1989).

Ncayiyana, D.J., 'Medical Migration is a Universal Phenomenon', *South African Medical Journal*, 89/1107 (1999).

Nelhans, J., *Utlänningen på arbetsmarknaden* (Lund, 1973).

Nicholson, B., 'Economic Migration and Asylum: A Case for Rethinking Immigration Policies', paper prepared for the *Wider Conference* (Helsinki, 2002).

Nielson, J., 'Current Regimes for Temporary Movement of Service Providers: Labour Mobility in Regional Trade Agreements', paper prepared for the *WTO-World Bank Symposium on Movement of Natural Persons (Mode 4) Under the GATS* (11–12 April 2002).

Niessen, J. and Schibel, Y., *Demographic Changes and the Consequences for Europe's Future: is Immigration an Option?* (Brussels: MPG, 2002).

OECD Health Project, *International Migration of Physicians and Nurses: Causes, Consequences and Health Policy Implications*, OECD draft report (Paris, 2002).

OECD, *Trends in International Migration: Sopemi 2003* (Paris, 2004).

Orozco, M., *Migration and Development: Economy and Policy Opportunities for Social Change* (Washington, DC: InterAmerican Dialogue, 2004).

——, *Hometown Associations and their Present and Future Partnerships: New Development Opportunities?*, report commissioned by USAID, InterAmerican Dialogue (Washington, DC, 2003a).

——, 'The Future Trends and Patterns of Remittances to Latin America', paper prepared for the *Remittances as a Development Tool*, conference organized by the InterAmerican Development Bank (Washington, DC, 28 October 2003b).

——, 'Remittances to Latin America: Money, Markets, and Costs', paper prepared for the conference on *Remittances as a Development Tool*, organized by the Inter-American Development Bank (Washington, DC, 26 February 2002).

——, 'Family Remittances to Latin America: the Marketplace and its Changing Dynamics', paper prepared for the conference *Remittances as Development Tool*, organized by the Inter-American Development Bank (Washington, DC, 17–18 May 2001).

Østergaard-Nielsen, E.K., 'Transnational Political Practices and the Receiving State: Turks and Kurds in Germany and the Netherlands', *Global Networks*, 1/3 (2001): 261–82.

Oucho, J.O., *Urban Migrants and Rural Development in Kenya* (Nairobi: Nairobi University Press, 1996).

——, 'Refugees and Internally Displaced: Africa's Liability for the Next Millennium', in D. Jolly (ed.), *Global Changes in Asylum Regimes* (London: Palgrave Macmillan, 2002).

——, 'Linkages between Brain Drain, Labour Migration and Remittances in Africa', in *World Migration 2003*, IOM (Geneva 2003): 215–38.

——, 'The African Migrant Labour Situation in Comparative Perspective', paper prepared for the *ICFTU-AFRO Regional Conference on Migrant Labour in Africa* (Nairobi: March 2004).

Padarath, A., C. Chamberlain, D. McCoy, A. Ntuli, M. Rowson and R. Loewenson, *Health Personnel in Southern Africa: Confronting Maldistribution and Brain Drain*, Discussion Paper No. 3, Regional Network for Equity in Health in Southern Africa (EQUINET) Health Systems Trust, South Africa and MEDACT, UK (2003).

Pang, E.P., 'Structural Changes and Labor Flows in East and Southeast Asia', Asia Club Papers No. 3, Tokyo Club Foundation for Global Studies (Tokyo, 1992).

Pang, T., M. Lansang and A. Haines, 'Brain Drain and Health Professionals', editorial, *British Medical Journal*, 324/2 (2002): 499–500.

Papademetriou, D.G., 'Immigrant Selection and Admission Systems: Lessons from the Traditional Countries of Immigration', paper prepared for the Department of Social Affairs of the Ministry of Labor and Social Policy, Italian Republic, Como (November 2003).

Papademetriou, D., K. O'Neil and M. Jachimowicz, 'Observations on Regularization and the Labor Market Performance of Unauthorized and Regularized Immigrants', paper prepared for the European Commission, DG Employment and Social Affairs (Brussels: European Commission; Hamburg: HWWA, 2004).

Pastore, F., 'Migrazioni internazionali e ordinamento giuridico', in L.Violante (ed.), *Legge Diritto Giustizia, Storia d'Italia*, Annali 14, Giulio Einaudi Editore (Turin, 1998).

——, '"More Development for Less Migration" or "Better Migration for More Development"? Shifting Priorities in the External Dimension of European Migration Policy', paper prepared for the Cicero Foundation International Seminar for Experts on European Migration and Refugee Policy (Rome, November 2003).

Patten, A., 'The Autonomy Argument for Liberal Nationalism', *Nations and Nationalism*, 5 (1999).

PeaceWomen, 'Women, Peace and Security: Somalia' (2003). Available at UNIFEM Women, War and Peace web portal, <http://www.peacewomen.org/WPS/Somalia.html>.

Pécoud, A. and P. de Guchteneire, *Migration, Human Rights and the United Nations: An Investigation of the Obstacles to the UN Convention on Migrant Workers' Rights*, Global Migration Perspectives, No. 3, August, GCIM (2004).

Pessar, P. and S. Grasmuck, *Between Two Islands: Dominican International Migration* (Berkeley: University of California Press, 1991).

Philippine Overseas Employment Administration, 'Deployed New Hire Land Based Workers, 1992–2002' (2004). Available at <http://www.poea.gov.ph/html/statistics.html>.

Physicians for Human Rights, 'An Action Plan to Prevent Brain Drain: Building Equitable Health Systems in Africa', report by Physicians for Human Rights (Cambridge, MA: Physicians for Human Rights, 2004). Available at <http://www.phrusa.org/campaigns/aids/pdf/braindrain.pdf>.

Pogge, T., 'Migration and Poverty', in V. Bader (ed.), *Citizenship and Exclusion* (London: Macmillan, 1997).

Polaski, S., *How to Build a Better Trade Pact with Central America* (Carnegie Endowment for International Peace, July 2003).

Pongsapich, A., 'International Migrant Workers in Asia: The Case of Thailand', in *Proceedings of the International Conference on Transnational Migration in the Asia-Pacific Region*, organized by ARCM, ISIS, and Research Division of the Office of the President of Chulalongkorn University on 1–2 December 1994, Chulalongkorn University, Bangkok (1995).

Popkin, E., 'Transnational Migration and Development in Postwar Peripheral States: An Examination of Guatemalan and Salvadoran State Linkages with their Migrant Populations in Los Angeles', *Current Sociology*, 51/3–4 (May/July) (2003): 347–74.

Popper, K.R., *The Poverty of Historicism* (London: Routledge and Kegan Paul, 1960).

Portes, A., 'Conclusion: Towards a New World – the Origins and Effects of Transnational Activities', *Ethnic and Racial Studies*, 22/2 (1999): 463–77.

——, W. Haller and L. Guarnizo, 'Transnational Entrepreneurs: The Emergence and Determinants of an Alternative Form of Immigrant Economic Adaptation', *American Sociological Review*, 67/2 (2002): 278–98.

Powell, C. and T. Ridge, 'Letter to Jim Sensenbrenner Jr., Chairman, Committee on the Judiciary, House of Representatives' (17 March 2004). Accessed 29 March 2004 at <http://www.house.gov/judiciary/ridge031704.pdf >.

Preker, A.S., J. Ruthkowski, D. Smith, C. Kurowski, M. Vujicic and R. Scheffler, *Impact of Globalization and Macro Economic Policies on Health Care Labour Markets*, background report prepared for Working Group 3, Joint Learning Initiative (2004).

Pritchett, L., 'Divergence: Big Time', *Journal of Economic Perspectives*, 11/3 (1997): 3–17.

——, 'The Future of Migration: Irresistible Forces Meet Immovable Ideas', paper prepared for *The Future of Globalization: Explorations in Light of the Recent Turbulence Conference*, Yale University (October, 2003).

Puri, S. and T. Ritzema, *Migrant Worker Remittances, Micro-finance and the Informal Economy: Prospects and Issues*, Working Paper No. 21, ILO (Geneva, 1994).

Ramamurthy, B., *International Labour Migrants: Unsung Heroes of Globalisation*, Sida Studies No. 8 (Stockholm: SIDA, 2003).

Ratha, D., 'Worker's Remittances: An Important and Stable Source of External Finance', in *Global Development Finance* (Washington, DC: World Bank, 2003).

Ravenstein, E.G., 'The Laws of Migration', *Journal of the Royal Statistical Society*, 52/2 (1889): 241–305.

Rawls, J., *A Theory of Justice* (Cambridge, MA: Harvard University Press, 1971).

Ray, B., *Practices to Promote the Integration of Migrants Into Labour Markets*, paper prepared for the European Commission, DG Employment and Social Affairs (Brussels: European Commission; Hamburg: HWWA, 2004).

Raz, J., *The Morality of Freedom* (Oxford: Clarendon Press, 1993).

Razin, A. and E. Sadka, 'International Migration and International Trade', in M.R. Rosenzweig and O. Stark (eds), *Handbook of Population and Family Economics* (Amsterdam: North-Holland, 1997).

Reinke, J. and Patterson, N. 'Remittances in the Balance of Payments Framework', paper prepared for the *International Technical Meeting on Measuring Remittances*, World Bank, Washington, DC (January, 2005).

Ridge, T., 'Testimony of Tom Ridge, Secretary of the Department of Homeland Security, before the House Committee on the Judiciary' (21 April 2004).

Rifkin, J., *The End of Work: The Decline of the Global Force and the Dawn of the Post-market Era* (New York: G.P. Putnam's Sons, 1995).

Rodrigo, C. and R.A. Jayatissa, 'Maximising Benefits from Labour Migration: Sri Lanka', in R. Amjad (ed.), *To the Gulf and Back: Studies on the Economic Impact of Asian Labour Migration* (New Delhi: ILO-ARTEP, 1989).

Rodrik, D., *How to Make the Trade Regime Work for Development*, mimeo, Harvard University (2004).

Rogers, A., 'Requiem for the Net Migrant', *Geographical Analysis*, 22/4 (1990): 283–300.

Rohter, L., 'South American Trading Bloc Frees Movement of Its People', *The New York Times*, 24 November 2002.

Rubio-Marín, R., *Immigration as a Democratic Challenge: Citizenship and Inclusion in Germany and the United States* (Cambridge: Cambridge University Press, 2000).

Ruggie, J.G., 'International Responses to Technology: Concepts and Trends', *International Organization*, 29/3 (1975): 557–84.

Russell, S.S., 'Remittances from International Migration: A Review in Perspective', *World Development*, 14/6 (1986): 677–96.

Russell, S.S. and M.S. Teitelbaum, *International Migration and International Trade*, World Bank Discussion Papers, No. 160 (Washington, DC, 1992).

Russell, S.S. and K. Jacobsen, *International Migration and Development in Sub-Saharan Africa*, World Bank Discussion Paper No. 160 (Washington, DC, 1988).

Russell, S.S., K. Jacobsen, and W.D. Stanley, *International Migration and Development in Sub-Saharan Africa*, Vol. 1: *Overview*, World Bank Discussion Papers, Africa Technical Department Series (Washington, DC, 1990).

SAARC People's Forum, *Memorandum* to the Honorable Members of the Standing Committee of the 10th SAARC Summit (1998).

SAF, *Mångfald i praktiken: En skrift om företagsverksamhet och mångfald* (Stockholm: 2000).

SAF, *Comment on Government Report SOU 1951:42*, Ministry of Justice, National Archives (31 January 1952).

Sander, C. and S.M. Maimbo, *Migrant Labor Remittances in Africa: Reducing Obstacles to Developmental Contributions*, Africa Region Working Paper Series No. 64 (Washington, DC, The World Bank, 2003).

Sassen, S., *Losing Control? Sovereignty in an Age of Globalization* (New York: Columbia University Press, 1996).

Schiff, M., *South-North Migration and Trade*, Policy Research Working Paper No. 1696, International Economics Department, International Trade Division, World Bank (Washington, DC, 1996).

Schmitter Heisler, B. and M.O. Heisler, 'Comparative Perspectives on Security and Migration: The Intersection of Two Expanding Universes', paper prepared for the *Annual Meeting of the American Sociological Association* (San Francisco: 9–13 August 1989).

Schor, R., *Histoire de l'immigration en France* (Paris: Armand Collin, 1996).

Schuessel, W., 'Statement by Austrian Vice-Chancellor and Federal Minister for Foreign Affairs, Wolfgang Schuessel, to the Fifty-Second Session of the United Nations General Assembly, New York, 25 September 1997', Austrian Information Service (Washington, DC, 1997).

Sciortino, G. and A. Colombo, 'Italy's Many Immigrations', *Journal of Italian Modern Studies* (forthcoming).

Shachar, A., 'Children of a Lesser State: Sustaining Global Inequality through Citizenship Laws', in S. Macedo and I.M. Young (eds), *Child, Family and State*, NOMOS XLIV (New York: New York University Press, 2003).

Sen, A., *Commodities and Capabilities* (Amsterdam: North Holland, 1985).

Shifter, M., *A Policy for the Neighbor* (Washington, DC: InterAmerican Dialogue, July 2003).

Shklar, J.N., *American Citizenship: the Quest for Inclusion* (Cambridge, MA: Harvard University Press, 1991).

Sikkink, K., 'Human Rights, Principled Issue Networks and Sovereignty in Latin America', *International Organization*, 47/3 (1993): 411–41.

Simkin, P., *Somali Diaspora Enterprise Survey* (unpublished, 2002).

Simpson, G.R., D. Crawford and K. Johnson, 'Crime Pays, Terrorists Find: Group in Europe Smuggles Immigrants and Forges Passports', *The Wall Street Journal* (14 April 2004).

Siri, G. and P.A. Delgado, *Uso Productivo de las Remesas Familiares En El Salvador*, study prepared for FUSADES (1995).

Skeldon, R., *Migration and Development: A Global Perspective* (London: Addison Wesley Longman, 1997).

——, 'International Migration within and from the East and Southeast Asian Region: A Review Essay', *Asian and Pacific Migration Journal*, 1/1 (1992): 19–63.

Smith, M.P., 'Transnationalism, the State, and the Extraterritorial Citizen', *Politics and Society*, 31/4 (2003): 467–502.

——, *Transnational Urbanism: Locating Globalization* (Oxford: Blackwell Publishers, 2001).

Smith, R.C., 'Transnational Localities: Community Technology and the Politics of Membership within the Context of Mexico-US Migration', in M.P. Smith and L.E. Guarnizo (eds), *Transnationalism from Below* (New Brunswick: Transaction Publishers, 1998).

Solow, R., 'A Contribution to the Theory of Economic Growth', *Quarterly Journal of Economics*, 70/1 (1956): 65–94.

SOU 2002:116, *EU's utvidgning och arbetskraftens rörlighet* (Stockholm: Fritzes offentliga publikationer, 2002).

SOU 1996:55, *Sverige, framtiden och mångfalden* (Stockholm: Fritzes offentliga publikationer, 1996).

SOU 1995:76, *Arbete till invandrare* (Stockholm: Fritzes offentliga publikationer, 1995).

SOU 1995:75, *Svensk flyktingpolitik i ett globalt perspektiv* (Stockholm: Fritzes offentliga publikationer, 1995).

SOU 1995:55, *Ett samlat verksamhetsansvar för asylärenden* (Stockholm: Fritzes offentliga publikationer, 1995).

SOU 1995:46, *Effektivare styrning och rättssäkerhet i asylprocessen* (Stockholm: Fritzes offentliga publikationer, 1995).

SOU 1974:69, *Invandrarna och minoriteterna* (Stockholm: Fritzes offentliga publikationer, 1974).

SOU 1967:18, *Invandring och problematik* (Stockholm: Fritzes offentliga publikationer, 1967).

Soysal, Y.N., *Limits of Citizenship: Migrants and Postnational Membership in Europe* (Chicago: University of Chicago Press, 1994).

Stalker, P., *The Work of Strangers: A Survey of International Labour Migration* (Geneva: ILO, 1994).

Staples, H., *The Legal Status of Third Country Nationals Resident in the European Union* (The Hague: Kluwer Law International, 1999).

Stark, O., C. Helmenstein and A. Prskawetz, 'Human Capital Depletion, Human Capital Formation, and Migration: A Blessing or a 'Curse'?', *Economic Letters* 60/3 (1998): 363–7.

Stepputat, F., *Refugees, Security and Development: Current Experience and Strategies of Protection and Assistance in the 'Region of Origin'*, Policy Paper, Danish Institute of International Studies (2004).

Stepputat, F. and N.N. Sørensen, 'The Rise and Fall of 'Internally Displaced People', the Central Peruvian Andes', *Development and Change*, 32/4 (2001): 769–91.

Stern, A., *Thailand's Migration Situation and its Relations with APEC Members and Other Countries in Southeast Asia*, Asian Research Center for Migration (ARCM), Institute of Asian Studies, No. 011 (1998).

Stillwell, B., K. Diallo, P. Zurn, M. Dal Poz, O. Adams and J. Buchan, 'Developing Evidence-based Ethical Policies on the Migration of Health Workers: Conceptual and Practical Challenges', *Human Resources for Health*, 1/8 (2003).

Stolnitz, G.J., 'Recent Mortality Trends in Latin America, Asia and Africa: Review and Re-interpretation', *Population Studies*, 19/2 (1965): 117–38.

Straubhaar, T.,'Why do we Need a General Agreement on Movements of People (GAMP)?', in B. Ghosh (ed.), *Managing Migration: Time for a New International Regime* (Oxford: Oxford University Press, 2000).

——,'Wird die Staatsangehörigkeit zu einer Klubmitgliedschaft?', in D. Thränhardt and U. Hunger (eds), *Migration im Spannungsfeld von Globalisierung und Nationalstaat*, Leviathan Sonderheft 22 (Opladen: Westdeutscher Verlag, 2003).

Sullivan, J.D., 'Anti-Corruption Initiatives from a Business View Point', Sixth Annual Harvard International Development Conference, Center for International Private Enterprise, US Chamber of Commerce, April 2000.

Sussangkarn, C., 'Labour Market Adjustments and Migration in Thailand', *ASEAN Economic Bulletin*, 12/2 (1995).

Sørensen, N.N., *Migrant Transfers as a Development Tool*, Policy Paper, Danish Institute for International Studies (2004).

Sørensen, N.N. and N. Van Hear, *Livelihood and Reintegration Dynamics in Somaliland*, Policy Paper Danish Institute for International Studies (2003).

Sørensen, N.N., N. Van Hear and P. Engberg-Pedersen, 'Migration, Development and Conflict: State of the Art Overview', in N. Van Hear and N.N. Sørensen (eds), *The Migration-Development Nexus* (Geneva: UN and IOM, 2003a).

——, 'The Migration-Development Nexus: Evidence and Policy Options', in N. Van Hear and N.N. Sørensen (eds), *The Migration-Development Nexus* (Geneva: United Nations and International Organization for Migration, 2003b).

Taeuber, I.B., 'The Demographic Statistics of Southern and Eastern Asia', *Journal of the American Statistical Association*, 40/229 (1945): 29–37.

Tamas, K., *Mapping Study on International Migration* (Stockholm: Institute for Futures Studies, 2004a).

——, 'Internationalising Migration Control: Swedish Migration Policy from 1985 to 2004', in M. Jandl and I. Stacher (eds), *Towards a Multilateral Migration Regime* (Vienna: ICMPD, 2004b).

Tan, E., *Migrants' Savings, Remittances and Labour Supply Behaviour: A Comparative Experience of Asian Countries*, Asian Regional Program on International Labour Migration (New Delhi: ILO-ARTEP, 1987).

Tandon, Y. (n.d.), 'The Role of FDIs in Africa' (2004). Accessed 24 May 2004 at <http://rorg.no/rorg/dok/arkiv/ytfdi2.htm>.

——, 'Evaluating Aid and Aid Strategies' (2000). Accessed 24 May 2004 at <http://rorg.no/rorg/ISGNeva.htm>.

Teitelbaum, M.S., 'Right versus Right: Immigration and Refugee Policy in the United States', *Foreign Affairs*, 59/1 (1980): 21–59.

Teitelbaum M.S. and M. Weiner (eds), *Theatened Peoples, Threatened Borders: World Migration and US Policy* (New York: W.W. Norton, 1995).

Tiebout, C., 'A Pure Theory of Local Expenditures', *Journal of Political Economy*, 64/5 (1956): 416–24.

Tiglao, R., 'Migrants' Manna', *Far Eastern Economic Review* (8 August 1991).

Tilton, T., 'The Role of Ideology in Social Democratic Politics', in K. Misgeld, K. Molin and K. Åmark (eds), *Creating Social Democracy: A Century of the Social Democratic Labor Party in Sweden* (University Park, PA: State University Press, 1992).

Tingsabadh, C., 'Maximising Development Benefits from Labour Migration: Thailand', in R. Amjad (ed.), *To the Gulf and Back: Studies on the Economic Impact of Asian Labour Migration* (New Delhi: ILO-ARTEP, 1989).

Tirman, J. (ed.), *The Maze of Fear: Security and Migration after 9/11*, Social Science Research Council (New York: The New Press, 2004).

Tirtosudarmo, R., 'The Indonesian State's Response to Migration', paper prepared for the *Workshop on Migration in Contemporary Southeast Asia*, organized by ISEAS, Singapore (22–23 January 1998).

——, *From Emigration to Transmigration: Continuity and Change in Migration Policies in Indonesia*, PSTC Working Paper No. 97–05, Brown University (1997).

Tjiptoherjanto, P., 'International Migration: Process, System and Policy Issue', paper prepared for the *Workshop on International Migration at the Population Studies Center*, Gadjah Mada University at Yogyakarta (10 March 1998).

Toppozada, H.K., 'Progress and Problems of Family Planning in the United Arab Republic, *Demography*, 5/2 (1968): 590–97.

Tovias, A. (n.d.), 'The Political Economy of the Partnership in Comparative Perspective'. Accessed 25 May 2004 at <http://ies.berkely.edu/research/AlfredTovias.pdf>.

Tuck, R., *Philosophy and Government, 1572–1651* (Cambridge: Cambridge University Press, 1993).

Tucker, R.W., C.B. Keely and L. Wrigley, *Immigration and US Foreign Policy* (Boulder, CO: Westview Press, 1990).

Turani, G., 'Questa Milano non è più da bere', *La Repubblica* (5 October, 1995).

UBINIG, *Resistance Against Trafficking in Women and Children in South Asia* (Narigrantha Prabartana, Bangladesh: The Feminist Bookstore, 1997).

United Nations, *United Nations Common Database 2002* (2004). Accessed 29 April 2004 at <http://unstats.un.org/unsd/cdb>.

United Nations, *World Population Prospects. The 2004 Revision* (New York, NY: UN, June, 2005).

——, *Background Report on Migration Prepared for the Senior Management Group*, Migration Working Group, Draft, United Nations (18 March 2003a).

——, *Trends in Total Migrant Stock: The 2003 Revision* (POP/DB/MIG/2003/1 and ESA/P/WP.188), data in digital form (2003b).

——, *World Urbanization Prospects: The 2001 Revision*, POP/DB/WUP (New York: UN Department of International Economic and Social Affairs, 2002a).

——, *International Migration Report*, Population Division, ST/ESA/SER.A/220 (2002b).

——, *World Population Prospects: The 2000 Revision*, Population Division (2001a).

——, *World Population Prospects: The 2000 Revision File 3: Crude Birth Rate by Major Area, Region and Country, 1950–2050 (per 1,000)* (New York: Population Division, Department of Economic and Social Affairs, 2001b).

——, *World Urbanization Prospects* (New York: UN Department of International Economic and Social Affairs, 2000).

——, *International Migration*, Population Division, Department of Economic and Social Affairs, ST/EAS/SER.A/161 (1998).

——, *International Migration and Development: The Concise Report* (New York, 1997).

——, *Trends in Total Migrant Stock, Revision 4*, Population Division, POP/1B/DB/96/1/Rev.4 (1996).

——, *International Migrations Policies* (1995). Available at <http://www.un.org/esa/population/pubsarchive/migpol95/fimp.htm>.

UNAIDS, *Migrants' Right to Health*, UNAIDS Best Practice Collection (Geneva, 2001).

UNDP, *Human Development Report 2002* (New York: Oxford University Press, 2002).

——, *Human Development Report – Somalia*, UNDP Somalia Country Office (Nairobi, 2001).

——, *Human Development Report 2000* (New York: Oxford University Press, 2000).

——, *Human Development Report 1999* (New York: Oxford University Press, 1999).

——, *Human Development Report 1997* (New York: Oxford University Press, 1997).

——, *Human Development Report* (New York: Oxford University Press, 1992).

UNDP, *Report on Democracy in Latin America* (UNDP-RBLAC), internal report (n.d.).

UNDP and ECSU, *Feasilibity Study on Financial Services in Somalia* (Nairobi, 2003). Avalailable at <http://www.so.undp.org/Remittance/Final%20Feasibility%20Study%20April.pdf>.

UNFPA, *State of World Population, 6 Billion A Time for Choices* (New York: 1999).

——, *Programme of Action of the International Conference on Population and Development (ICPD)* (New York: 1995).

UNHCR, *Somalia Country Report* (Nairobi, 2002).

United Nations Population Fund, *Meeting the Challenges of Migration* (New York: 2004).

Van Ham, P., *Managing Non-Proliferation Regimes in the 1990s: Power, Politics and Policies* (London: Pinter Publishers with RIIA, 1993).

Van Hear, N., *From 'Durable Solutions' to 'Transnational Relations': Home and Exile Among Refugee Diasporas*, Working Paper No. 83, UNHCR (Geneva, 2003).

——, *New Diasporas: The Mass Exodus, Dispersal and Regrouping of Migrant Communities* (London: University College London Press, 1998).

Van Kessel, G., 'Global Migration and Asylum', *Forced Migration Review*, 10 (2001): 10–13.

Venier, P., 'Migration of Keralites to the Persian Gulf', paper prepared for the *Conference of the IGU Globality Study Group on Human Mobility in a Borderless World* (Italy: 20–22 April 2001).

Viet, V., *La France immigrée, construction d'une politique 1914–1997* (Paris: Fayard, 1998).

Vujicic, M., P. Zurn, K. Diallo, O. Adams, and M. Dal Poz, 'The Role of Wages in Slowing the Migration of Health Care Professionals from Developing Countries', *Human Resources for Health Journal* (2004).

Wade, R.H., 'The Rising Inequality of World Income Distribution', *Finance and Development*, 38/4 (2001). Available at <http://www.imf.org/external/pubs/ft/fandd/2001/12/wade.htm>.

Waever, O., B. Buzan, M. Kelstrup and P. Lemaitre, *Identity, Migration and the New Security Agenda in Europe* (London: Pinter, 1993).

Waldrauch, H., *Die Integration von Einwanderern: Ein Index der rechtlichen Diskriminierung* (Frankfurt: Campus, 2001).

Waldron, J., 'Security and Liberty: The Image of Balance', *Journal of Political Philosophy*, 11/2 (2003): 191–210.

Walle, E. (v.d.) and H. Page, 'Some New Estimates of Fertility and Mortality in Africa', *Population Index*, 35/1(1969): 3–17.

Walt, G., 'Globalisation of International Health', *The Lancet*, 351/9100 (1998): 434–7.

Walzer, M., *Spheres of Justice: A Defense of Pluralism and Equality* (New York: Basic Books, 1983).

Weber, M., 'The National State and Economic Policy' [Inaugural Lecture, Freiburg, 1895], in M. Weber, P. Lassman and R. Speirs (eds), *Political Writings* (Cambridge: Cambridge University Press, 1994).

Weil, P., 'Access to Citizenship: A Comparison of Twenty-Five Nationality Laws', in T.A. Aleinikoff and D. Klusmeyer (eds), *Citizenship Today: Global Perspectives and Practices* (Washington, DC: Carnegie Endowment for International Peace, 2001).

——, *Mission d'étude des législations de la nationalité et de l'immigration, rapport au Premier Ministre* (Paris: La Documentation Francaise, 1997).

——, *La France et se étrangers, l'aventure d'une politique de l'immigration de 1938 à nos jours* (Paris: Gallimard, 1995).

Weiner, M., *The Global Migration Crisis: Challenge to States and to Human Rights* (New York: HarperCollins College Publishers, 1995).

—— (ed.), *International Migration and Security* (Boulder, CO: Westview Press, 1993).

White House, *Fact Sheet: Border Security* (White House, 5 January 2002). Accessed 27 January 2002 at <http://www.whitehouse.gov/news/releases/2002/01/20020125.html>.

WHO, *Recruitment of Health Workers from the Developing World*, WHO Executive Board Document (Geneva, 2004a).

——, *Estimates of Health Personnel: Physicians, Nurses, Midwives, Dentists, Pharmacists* (most recent data provided by regions and countries) (Geneva: WHO, 2004b).

Wibulpolprasert, S., S. Pitayarangsarit and P. Hempisu, 'International Service Trade and Its Implication on Human resources for Health: A Case Study of Thailand', draft paper for Human Resources for Health and Development JLI Working Group 3 (2004).

——, *Les orientations de la politique de l'immigration* (2005).

Willetts, A. and T. Martineau, *Ethical International Recruitment of Health Professionals: Will Codes of Practice Protect Developing Country Health Systems?* Report for Liverpool, Liverpool School of Tropical Medicine (January 2004).

Wimmer, A. and N. Glick Schiller, 'Methodological Nationalism, the Social Sciences and the Study of Migration: An Essay in Historical Epistemology', *International Migration Review*, 37/3 (2003): 576–610.

Wolf, M., 'Economics Alone Will Not Settle the Immigration Debate', *Financial Times* (14 April 2004): 17.

Wongboonsin, K., P. Guest and V. Prachuabmoh, 'Demographic Change and the Demographic Dividend in Thailand', paper prepared for the *International Conference on the Demographic Window and Healthy Aging: Socioeconomic Challenges and Opportunities*, Beijing (27 October 2003).

Wongboonsin, P., 'Migrant Labour in Thailand', paper prepared for the *International Conference on Migrant Labour in Southeast Asia: Needed, Not Wanted*, organized by UNE Asia Centre and School of Economics, University of New England (1–3 December 2003).

——, 'Transnational Migration', in P. Wongboonsin et al., *Research Report on the Impact of Migration on Transnational Labor Migrants: The Case of Thailand*, College of Population Studies in cooperation with Institute of Asian Studies, Chulalongkorn University (Bangkok: Chulalongkorn University Printing House, 2001a).

——, 'Comparative Migration Policies in the ESCAP Region', paper prepared for the *Ad Hoc Expert Group Meeting on Migration and Development: Opportunities and Challenges for Poverty Reduction in the ESCAP Region*, organized by the Economic and Social Commission for Asia and the Pacific, United Nations (28–30 November 2001b).

—— and S. Chantavanich, 'Insecurity in Population Displacement in APEC Economies and Possible Indicators for A Security Surveillance System', in *Promoting Human Security*, presented to APEC Study Center Consortium Conference, Chulalongkorn University (June 2003).

—— and J. Kinnas, 'Maximizing Demographic Dividend via Regional Cooperation in Human Resource Development', paper prepared for the *Concurrent Session on Demographic Changes and Demograhic Dividend in Asia* at the 6th ADRF General Meeting (Bangkok: 2004). Forthcoming in K. Wongboonsin and P. Guest (eds), *Demographic Changes and Demograhic Dividend in Asia*.

World Bank, 'Development Cooperation and Conflict', Operational Policy 2.30, January 2001.

——, *World Development Report 1995: Workers in an Integrating World* (Washington, DC, 1995).

Young, O.R., 'The Politics of International Regime Formation', *International Organization*, 43/3 (1989): 349–55.

Young, W.C., 'The Effect of Labor Migration on Relations of Exchange and Subordination among the Rashaayda Bedouin of Sudan', *Research in Economic Anthropology*, 9 (1987): 191–220.

Zacher, M.W., *Governing Global Networks: International Regimes for Transportation and Communications* (Cambridge: Cambridge University Press, 1996).

Zolberg, A.R., 'Labour Migration and International Economic Regimes: Bretton Woods and After', in M.M. Kritz, L. Lean Lim and H. Zlotnik (eds), *International Migration Systems: A Global Approach* (Oxford: Clarendon Press, 1992).

——, 'Bounded States in a Global Market: The Uses of International Migration Regimes', in P. Bourdieu and J.S. Coleman (eds), *Social Theory for a Changing Society* (Boulder, CO: Westview Press, 1991).

Index